THE CRACK IN THE TEACUP

The Life of an Old Woman Steeped in Stories

JOAN BODGER

M&S

Cloth edition published in 2000
First paperback edition published in Canada in 2001

Paperback edition published in the United States of America
in 2002 by McClelland & Stewart Ltd.,
P.O. Box 1030, Plattsburgh, New York 12901

Library of Congress Control Number: 2002102186

National Library of Canada Cataloguing in Publication Data

Bodger, Joan
The crack in the teacup : the life of an old woman steeped in stories

ISBN 0-7710-1119-9 (bound).—ISBN 0-7710-1120-2 (pbk.)

1. Bodger, Joan.   2. Storytellers – Canada – Biography.   3. Authors, Canadian
(English) – 20th century – Biography.   I. Title.

PS8553.O44Z53 2000   C813'.54   C00-931778-3
PR9199.3.B62Z463 2000

We acknowledge the financial support of the Government of Canada through the Book Publishing Industry Development Program for our publishing activities. We further acknowledge the support of the Canada Council for the Arts and the Ontario Arts Council for our publishing program.

An earlier version of "The Desert Sighs in the Bed" appeared in *Saturday Night* magazine; "The Glacier Knocks in the Cupboard" and "Among the Alien Corn" appeared in slightly different form in *Common Boundary* magazine.

Typeset in Times by M&S, Toronto
Printed and bound in Canada

McClelland & Stewart Ltd.
The Canadian Publishers
481 University Avenue
Toronto, Ontario
M5G 2E9
www.mcclelland.com

2   3   4   5   6   06   05   04   03   02

Page vi constitutes a continuation of the copyright page.

In memory of my parents

CONTENTS

Preface

"YOU SHOULD WRITE a book about storytelling," some people said. I soon discovered that I can't write about storytelling without writing about my life. "You should write the story of your life," some people said. I can't write about my life without telling the stories – not only stories lived, but stories told: from myth, legend, folklore; from children's tales, both traditional and literary.

I have spent a lifetime reading and listening to fairy tales, learning to *tell* them, by heart, from mind and memory. I have read extensively in the fields of folklore, psychology, anthropology, archaeology, and I have traveled to mythic and symbolic places. I have had years of psychotherapy. (I would not be the splendid creature you see before you, except for all those fruitful clinical hours.) Perhaps because I trained as a Gestalt therapist, and have developed a method of using story in group sessions, as a communal dream, I developed some notion of using my experience, erudition, and knowledge to explain the meaning and symbolism of the stories.

Knowledge comes, but wisdom lingers, wrote Alfred, Lord Tennyson. I had not counted on the *wisdom* of the stories. As, over years, I wrote this book, I became more humble. I came to perceive that it was not so much my place to explain what the ancient stories mean, but to accept what they are telling me about the life I have lived.

Because our family moved so often, I was constantly being jolted into sharp awareness of new surroundings. Always a newcomer, poised on the edge, I learned not only to look, but to see. Our family did not take many photographs; we skewered life with push-pins of carefully chosen words. The aim was to present an account of the day's doings that would grab attention at the dinner table. What I found difficult to discuss was the abstract, constantly shifting, idea of who I was. Class, caste, sex, attitudes toward race, toward gender, position in the family, position in the pecking order at school, on the playground, in the dating game, in the nation, and in the world, were made more complicated because I had not grown up in one place. I had no benchmarks. The payoff may have been a sharpening of perception, a widening of perspective, and permission to be who I would be, when I chose to be.

My life (so far) spans three-quarters of the twentieth century, and slops over into the new millennium. I was born in 1923, in Oakland, California. My British mother's life, especially, had been forever changed by the War of 1914-1918, the shadow of which lay across my childhood. Although my father held a steady, salaried job, I was old enough to be aware of the ravages of the Great Depression, and the burgeoning of the New Deal under the Roosevelts. Always, in the background, was the stuff of nightmares: ancestral voices prophesying war. A mere twenty years lay between my parents' Great War, and my generation's World War II.

Six weeks after the Japanese bombed Pearl Harbor, I graduated from high school. A few months later I went off to Pomona College, in Claremont, California, to study the humanities. After two years, I enlisted in the Women's Army Corps, U.S. Army. I returned to college, met and married a man with whom I seemed eminently well-suited. We had two children. When a succession of disasters fractured our cozy domesticity, my life fell apart – not once, but several times. My ability to survive, and more than survive, I ascribe to my sense of story.

I want to acknowledge the financial support I have received from the Canada Arts Council, the Ontario Arts Council, and the Arts Council of Toronto. I also thank the Bromberg family: my friend, Evelyn Bromberg, remembered me in her will. I have looked upon her bequest as a grant, and have used it to buy time to write.

I want to thank Pat Kennedy, my editor at McClelland & Stewart, for her faith in my writing and for her steadfast encouragement to finish this book. I also thank professional archivist Daniel Ladell, who cleared the decks so I could write. He straightened my files, and took in stride my love-hate relationship with computers.

For more than twenty years, the storytelling community of Toronto has listened patiently to this work in progress, sometimes on the occasion of One Thousand and One Friday Nights of Storytelling in Toronto, sometimes at their annual festival, and several times in formal concert. They enabled me to test my personal stories on an audience, trained to be listeners as well as tellers by the Storytellers School of Toronto. I also thank Jan Andrews and Jennifer Cayley who, in 1990, arranged for me to tell an evening of *The Crack in the Teacup* stories in Ottawa, at the National Library of Canada. In 1996, Liz Gilmore, director of the Langham Cultural Centre in Kaslo, British Columbia, arranged for me to be writer-in-residence there, and to read chapters from *Teacup* to audiences in Kaslo, and at the nearby towns of Denver and Nelson. Expenses were paid by a Canada Council arts grant.

I wish I could thank my friend, Bette Diver, for being so intellectually challenging, and for keeping me in touch with news and memories of Shanks Village, but she died in 1998. I thank the Rockland County Historical Society for arranging a 1999 reunion of (approximately) fifty Shanks Village residents, who reminisced and corroborated some of the stories, especially details about the Paul Robeson incident. Wanda Hiestand, one of the founders of the Shanks Village Health Committee, has been helpful in chasing down details, not only about Shanks, but about Professor Jean Betz, of Columbia Teachers College, and about the catalogue descriptions of courses she taught in the late 1940s.

I thank my friends Jan and Mark Robinson of Hay-on-Wye, owners of The Haven, a guest house on the Welsh border. Every year for ten years they offered a quiet place to write, the run of their library, help with Ordnance maps and timetables, and shared junkets in their car to rediscover places connected to my mother's family, most notably to Saint Lawrence, in Chepstow. Through them, a local historian, Robert Davis, was able to contact me and open up a lode of research about my grandfather. Bob Davis discovered that a prize-winning book had been privately published in Australia: *The Corfields: A History of the Corfields from 1180 to the Present Day*, by Justin Corfield (1993). Amazingly, the book not so much afforded new material as it affirmed the tales told by my mother. I also owe thanks to Jan Shivel of Hay, who drove me down to Cardiff so I could spend time with the Glamorgan Archive Services, and thus determine the addresses of my grandfather's office and town house, and the whereabouts of the beautiful old Coal Exchange (now being restored). His office building, across the road, was bombed out during World War II, but the Ship and

Pilot (now boarded up) still stands. Here, at the hotel bar, is where my grandfather spoke to some young United States Navy officers, inviting them to tea a few days hence. Subsequently, Lieutenant Frank David Higbee, USN, would meet the captain's daughter, Joan Amphlett Corfield. The rest is history. A special thanks to Barbara Turner-Vesselago, whose writing workshops helped me to write again after long silence. I also thank Sarah Greenwood, of This Ain't the Rosedale Library, a Toronto bookstore. She read the manuscript in early form and, returning it, urged "Go for the dark."

I am grateful for conversations I had with my two sisters over the years, as we tried to put pieces of the family jigsaw together. I wish, fervently, that Anne and Joyce had lived longer (in part, to see this book) and that there had been more communication among the three of us while they were still alive.

During the 1980s and 1990s, when a trip to England became an almost annual event, I was able to visit with my cousin Patricia Campbell on frequent occasions. We went through old photographs and she explained family connections. Our recollections of family history and of the time we spent together in 1933 often remain at variance, not so much in fact as in feeling. The other person who is still alive and who knew me as a child is Joanna Dimock Norris, in New London, Connecticut. She was able to remember names I had forgotten and to confirm the tragedy of Kate Morse's early death. Joanna is amazed by my account of the intramural segregation of Negro children at Harbor School. Although she does not doubt what I am saying, she has no memory of the New England disappearing act which rendered black children, attending school in the same building, all but invisible to us.

Which brings me to a final note – my use of certain words and capitalizations to describe people with whom I have shared my life and times on this planet: colored, nigger, negro, Negro, black, Black, brown, African-American, Afro-American. I have been calculatedly inconsistent, as I have tried to reflect who is speaking, where and when. I am sure I have not hit the right note every time, but that is the point of the exercise. The task is far from finished. We are still trying to get it right.

Toronto, Canada
August 21, 2000

THE MORNING OF THE WORLD

CHAPTER 1

The Glacier Knocks in the Cupboard

MY EARLIEST MEMORY IS of a shaft of light filled with shining motes, and the sight and sound of a six-inch silver dollar (fake) rolling on its rim across our nursery floor, *and* of my older sister holding her hands over her ears. She is screaming a high, piercing scream. Mother has come to the doorway.

The year was 1926. Mother was early-on pregnant with my sister Joyce, her third child. I was not quite three. Anne was two years older than I. Pale and feverish, with deep circles under her eyes, she had been in hospital much of her life. With no benefit from antibiotics, she had undergone three mastoid operations. She often suffered excruciating pains in her head and behind her ears. In all innocence I had rummaged in the toy box, had found the souvenir of San Francisco's United States Mint, and had sent the silver disc on its reverberating course along the path of sunlight. What was music of the spheres for me was agony for Anne.

If I were going to caption the picture I would have a balloon coming out of my mother's mouth: *Now look at what you've done!* I looked. I saw. I woke from my dream-time. From that moment on I continue to remember. *The moment just before* is the moment I seek to recapture.

Susan K. Langer, in her book *Feeling and Form*, discusses that time-space in life when a child is about to cross the threshold into language. Langer contends that a pre-verbal child lives in a world where, for example, the feelings of "heaviness" and "permanence" may be articulated by the

3

presence of the bureau across from his crib. Light coming through a window may speak volumes not only to him but for him.

The sculptures of Claes Oldenburg are, to me, voices from that same anteroom. Oldenburg says that his inspiration for enormous soft typewriters and gargantuan kitchen objects came from a scrapbook given to him by an aunt when he was very young and ill with fever. Immersed in those pages, he took it for granted that an orange could be as big as a house. When I behold his works I feel the tug of intimations.

Maurice Sendak, in his picture book *In the Night Kitchen*, shows a dream-like urban skyline composed of architectural salt-shakers, egg-beaters, and pop-art packaging, all in the style of the late 1920s, or early 1930s. The back of my neck prickles. The same sensation occurs when I come across a book I knew then. Or, at the flea market, when I happen upon a relic washed up from my personal Lyonesse, a landscape lost forty fathoms deep beneath the waves.

Langer stresses how important it is that the child have the chance to go back and back to explore the same objects in the same environment in order to check out the reality of her personal landscape. Myth emerges from landscape. Parents know, or are soon taught, how important it is to tell the same story in the same way, to look at the same pictures we looked at yesterday, and to provide the same blanket, the same toy. Because of my father's job in the United States Coast Guard, our family moved frequently. When my parents were young we often lived in rented apartments with rented furniture, but wherever we went the books and toys traveled with us. The toy box in which I rummaged was our sacred Ark of the Covenant, carried at the forefront of our tribal procession.

In the morning of the world we were living in a second-storey flat on a hill in San Francisco, overlooking the Presidio and the Golden Gate beyond. The Presidio was the original Spanish fort, built in 1776; in 1926 it was a U.S. Army base. There was a government hospital there, where Anne was taken when she was sick. In those days there was no bridge across the Golden Gate, only a circle of bare tawny hills and the strait where the Pacific Ocean broke through to form San Francisco Bay. On clear days we could watch the ferries, each trailed by a wake of white stitches, chugging their way from San Francisco to Oakland or Sausalito, and back to San Francisco again. In late afternoon we stood at the window, with Mother's reassuring presence beside us, and watched the mysterious fog roll in.

Father was second in command of the U.S. Coast Guard Cutter *Bear*, a unique and famous ship that had been built in the 1870s especially for Arctic exploration. A striding polar bear served as its figurehead. The double wooden hull was uniquely designed to bend but not break under the pressure of the ice closing in all about it. The *Bear* had three masts and a smokestack and could proceed under sail or steam. Father had no romantic ideas about sail. It was dangerous and hard on the men who had to swarm into the icy rigging. Nor did he admire the primitive steam engine on the *Bear*. To him, a diesel engine was tribute to the intellect and aspirations of mankind. A diesel engine represented progress. In the early 1920s, all progress was romantic.

The old-fashioned boilers that pushed the *Bear*'s propeller screw consumed huge amounts of coal. To save fuel for the final lap from Nome to the Arctic Circle, the captain had to order the crew to break out the canvas. Sometimes the ship was deliberately trapped for months so it could swing with the ice pack. Then the officers, the crew, and the visitors aboard needed the coal to keep themselves warm and to cook their meals.

The *Bear*'s home dock was in Oakland. One day Father took me (just *me*!) across the Bay on the ferry to see the animals that lived on the deck of his ship. Deep-freeze refrigeration was not perfected yet. The only way to insure a supply of milk, fresh eggs, and meat was to take live animals along. I remember the straw and the barnyard smells, which I liked. I saw a sow with piglets buttoned to her row of teats; I saw strutting chickens, a duck, a duck egg. I patted a goat. I doubt whether I had ever been up close to farm animals before. That such creatures were on the deck of a ship bound for the Arctic did not seem any more strange to me than the impression that I had walked into the pages of my nursery-rhyme book. My myth-maker was Mother Goose; my image-makers, the illustrators of children's books – Leslie Brooke and Randolph Caldecott. Language was my mother's voice. Myth, image, word, enhanced by feeling and experience, culminated in epiphany that magic day.

When we went shopping with Mother, Anne and I wore navy-blue sailor coats with brass buttons. Mother always bought boys' coats for us because they were better tailored and cost less than coats made for little girls. Anne had a real quartermaster's rating, I had a signalman's; they were sewn onto the left sleeves of our coats. We wore round flat sailor hats, navy blue. A ribbon spelled out U.S. COAST GUARD CUTTER BEAR in gold letters across my brow. People would stop us on the street and talk to Mother about the *Bear*, her whereabouts and well-being. In those days Arctic exploration was the equivalent of space exploration today.

Few people now remember the excitement and desperate competition of early twentieth-century polar expeditions. In 1908 the Norwegian explorer, Roald Amundsen, had purchased Fridtjof Nansen's *Fram* with the intention of drifting towards the North Pole and then racing to the Pole by sledge. The news that Robert E. Peary had anticipated him and had reached the Pole first made Amundsen turn his thoughts to Antarctica. He arrived just thirty-five days before Robert F. Scott, the fastidious British explorer, who insisted on hauling his personal sterling silverware with him and who died of starvation rather than eat his dogs.

By 1926, just as I was coming to conscious awareness, Amundsen, the American millionaire Lincoln Ellsworth, and the Italian airship designer, Umberto Nobile, set out to fly from Europe to North America in the dirigible *Norge*, crossing the Pole on the way. The *Norge* was bound for Nome, where a welcoming party stood ready. During the flight the radio failed. The whole world seemed to hold its breath as it waited for news. Meanwhile, the *Norge* was so depleted by ice and wind that the expedition came down at Teller, a village ninety miles off target. The airship was dismembered and packed onto dog sleds, while the *Bear* sailed into the perilous fringe at the edge of the ice pack to pick up crew and cargo. Newspapers worldwide had followed, or attempted to follow, the voyage of the Norgenauts. Bathed in the afterglow of adventure and romance, I was led to believe that my father was a hero who sailed on a fabled ship to fabulous lands. For better and for worse, I was imbued with the notion that I was involved in something larger than everyday life. I was part of the Cosmic Story.

The *Bear* went farther north than any other ship and took with her artists and scientists as well as the regular crew. Sometimes it brought back dangerous criminals or madmen who had fled to the Arctic. When Father came home, in the middle of summer, he brought with him special gifts from Santa Claus: beaded moccasins lined with white fur; a chunk of ice from an iceberg to cool our watermelon; crayons and coloring books that looked suspiciously like those that Mother bought at Woolworth's. The other treat was Eskimo Pies, new on the market in the 1920s, which could be purchased in the ship's galley. The coldness of them made a pain right in the middle of my forehead.

Father had hoped to bring us a polar-bear rug. There were photos of him stalking the bear, pictures of him with rifle to shoulder, pictures of him with foot on slain bear. However, neither he nor anyone on the ship had any idea how to cure the skin once it had been flayed. As long as the ship remained in latitudes where the temperature stayed well below freezing no one complained, but once the ship headed south, the crew approached the captain and said that either Father or the bloody fleece must go.

We did not, however, lack permanent reminder of Father's Arctic voyages. Roald Amundsen had given Father the steering wheel of the *Norge* and a section of the catwalk, the keel or backbone of the ship. The wheel was surprisingly small, smaller than an automobile's steering wheel. Its rim was of oak. The catwalk section, a little more than a foot long, was a hollow block made out of some kind of reinforced fibre, the cutting edge of technology. These relics, used as playthings, later as bookend and doorstop, were constants of my childhood, always there when we moved from one house to another.

The consequences of my growing up with the *Norge*'s keel and wheel so close at hand are inestimable. According to Greek mythology, when the Argonauts built their ship, the *Argo*, the keel and rudder were fashioned from Zeus's oak, the divine tree of Dodona. One of its attributes is that it can foretell the future. More important, it represents one of a number of manifestations of the Great World Tree: Yggdrasil, from Norse mythology; the *huluppu*-tree of Inanna; Eve's apple tree; the Christian cross; pillars and arrows; maypoles and magic mountains innumerable. Each in turn, along with hundreds of other variants, is construed in stories to be the Axis Mundi, the Pole that skewers the earth. Each is the pestle that grinds the heavens and swirls the starry meal into orderly precession.

Dimly I perceive that the direction of my course has been influenced by alignment with the World Tree. My life is based on an even keel. *Although great harm has come to me, no harm has come to me.* As in the Finnish epic, the *Kalevala*, I have descended into the Great Maelstrom, into the Maw, the Gullet, and I have been spat out. My seaworthiness I attribute to an awareness, perceived in my earliest childhood, that I am playing in a shaft of sunlight filled with cosmic dust, and that my playthings are bits and pieces of myth.

CHAPTER 2

Border Country

IN APRIL 1917 the United States, at long last, entered the European war. Frank David Higbee, already a warrant officer in the U.S. Navy, was immediately commissioned as a lieutenant. A few weeks later his destroyer was despatched to its wartime station in Cardiff, Wales. He and several other young American navy officers, when they were in port, often stopped to eat at a favorite pub, the Ship and Pilot, which stood on a corner near the elegant Coal Exchange building in Mount Stuart Square.

On this particular evening Frank Higbee and his friends fell to talking about their most difficult navigation feats. As they were discussing how to enter the Columbia River bar, an elderly gentleman at the next table was listening to their conversation. When they invited him to join them, he introduced himself as Captain William Reginald Corfield, owner of the Cardiff Steamship Line, at 51 Mount Stuart Square. Many was the time he had sailed his China tea clippers into the Columbia, he said, and he would be damned before he would pay the piratical fees charged by the notorious Columbia River pilots. As he was about to depart, he invited the young Americans to come to tea with him and his wife at his house on Cathedral Road. Only Lieutenant Higbee accepted the invitation.

I like to picture him, a few days later, as he leaped out of a cab, opened the little iron gate, and walked up the curving tessellated pathway to the doorway at Number 31. As he stood in the deep entry, waiting for someone to answer the bell, he may have contemplated the art-nouveau tiles that decorated the walls, or he may have studied the little flower bed he had just passed, edged by what, to his sailor's eye, looked like a manila hawser but, on closer inspection, proved to be a cast-stone replica. Or he may have gazed up and down the road, at the rows of other Italianate villas, with a flicker of surprise that a residence so new and flashy belonged to the old sea captain he had met in the Ship and Pilot. When the maid showed him into the living room, Frank was in for another surprise. The beautiful and fashionable young woman who greeted him was not, as he first supposed, Captain Corfield's daughter, but his wife.

Frank Higbee, a boy from Kansas City, had only read or dreamt about a room such as the one where he now stood as invited guest. Oriental carpets covered the floors and silken curtains hung at the windows. A hookah stood by his host's chair, freshly prepared for use. (There was no way for Frank to know that Captain Corfield was suffering from cancer. Opium, a habit he had picked up on his travels, helped him to bear the pain.) Every table, shelf, cabinet, and mantel was crowded with photographs and curios: ivory and jade from the Orient, grotesque pottery from South America, carved teak and shells from the South Seas. Among a collection of North American Indian artifacts Frank spied a photograph of his host shooting buffalo from a train. A man in buckskin stood nearby. Peering closely, he saw that the picture was signed "Colonel William F. Cody."

The one thing that drew him above all others, and seemed to steady him, was the photograph of a beautiful young woman. With the brashness of a young American, he asked who and where she was. Mrs. Corfield seemed amused rather than offended as she explained that the young woman was her stepdaughter, Joan, who was away in the north of England, driving an ambulance. She would be home on leave in a few days. Would Lieutenant Higbee care to come to tea again?

Frank Higbee was about to meet his fate.

Kate, my grandfather's third wife, was one of the beautiful Ray sisters. (I never heard the sisters referred to without the accompanying adjective.) Their mother was the daughter of a Chinese merchant prince, who had married an English sea captain. Kate certainly looked regal, with only the faintest hint of the exotic. Elegant and graceful, she seemed taller than she actually was. She wore her black hair coiled on top of her head and her exquisite neck was often accentuated by a high lace collar. Her clothes were beautiful and simple. She wore no jewels. Ever since the shipwreck of the *Avonmore*, off Peru, no Corfield woman was allowed to wear jewels.

Consider now my grandfather's three wives.

The first, Jane Sophia Gwyllm, was born in 1843 at Vowchurch Court Farm, in the village of Abbey Dore, in Herefordshire. Killed in a shipwreck in 1877, she was the love of my grandfather's life, forever young, forever perfect. Their eldest child, Rego, had been sent "home" to school, but three other children were aboard the ill-fated *Avonmore*: Bertie, age five, born at Chimbote, Peru; Mabel, two and a half, born at sea; and Gwendolyn Avonmore, named after the ship where she had been born five months previously.

While the ship was off Huanillos, Peru, an earthquake occurred and the sea began to recede ominously from the coast. Not only the captain but every seaman knew that the withdrawal would be followed hours later by an immense tidal wave that would rush ashore with height and force in proportion to its recession. The crew mutinied and stole the lifeboats, leaving aboard the captain, his wife, his three children, a nursemaid, and the Chinese cook. My grandfather tied his wife to the mast with the baby in her arms, but first he bedecked her with all her jewels, a fabulous collection of gems from India and China. Also, gold chains and pendants, rifled from Inca graves. These would restore their fortunes if they both survived the loss of the ship, or insure the welfare of his wife and children if he did not survive. He tied the nursemaid to the mast with Mabel, the second child, and he took charge of Bertie. The Chinese cook fended for himself.

When at last the enormous tidal surge reared to its height, the ship was lifted up, broken apart, and flung far up on the shore. When my grandfather was restored to consciousness, he found that Bertie had been drowned. He staggered along the strand, searching for the rest of his family. The nurse he found drowned, the little girl tied to her, drowned, too. Baby Gwen was drowned and his wife was dead. Dead but *not* drowned! She had been strangled with one of her golden chains, murdered for her jewels. Only the cook was missing.

The story gets murky here. Grandfather had the bodies retrieved, then shipped them, encased in guano, to England. They were laid to rest in the Gwyllm family plot at Abbey Dore, awaiting the day when they would be reburied with him, under one stone. The stone dates from 1919, the date of the demise of "Captain William Reginald Corfield, husband of the said

Jane Sophia." He chose to be buried with his first wife. No mention is made of his two other wives. The gravestone tells the story of the shipwreck, but not of the murder.

The window, inside the partially ruined abbey, overlooks the gravestone. Jesus Christ is portrayed as a seated figure. He holds Gwendolyn Avonmore on his lap. Bertie is kneeling to the right, an orange tree over his head, perhaps to indicate that he was born in South America. Jane Sophia and Mabel kneel at Christ's feet. Jane's hair is plaited in one thick golden braid that hangs down her back, giving her an air of eternal girlishness. An imposing house is depicted in the background – certainly not English. Perhaps a villa or hacienda. The names of the lost wife and children and the facts of the shipwreck are picked out in gothic-style letters, an intrinsic part of the design.

As soon as Grandfather had retrieved the bodies and arranged for their burial, he took off after the cook, who had left a noticeable trail of transactions having to do with emeralds and rubies. For two years he followed the unfortunate murderer and finally shot him down in the streets of San Francisco. When my sisters and I, wide-eyed, asked Mother, "What did the policemen do to Grandfather?", she said, "In those days, one merely bowed and smiled and explained one's self to the passersby. In those days, one Chinaman more or less was not important, at least not in San Francisco." We all agreed that the situation was deplorable. We only hoped that Grandfather had got the right man.

The second wife was Mother's mother and my grandmother, Margaret Frances. No one, including my mother, seemed to know much about her. She was born in Patagonia and lived her young life in the Welsh colony there. She must have been still in her teens when she was married to William R. Corfield, a sea captain almost twice her age. He was a man obsessed with grief for his first wife, and Maggie, isolated from all feminine companionship, spent the early years of her marriage on board a sailing ship, going back and forth between South America and China, often with a stinking cargo of guano below decks. Pregnant and seasick, she was at the beck and call of her husband. Two of her children, who died, were born at sea, as were Harry and Francis, who survived. But she never could live up to Jane Sophia. Even when her husband took her "home" to England, she still was not home. She longed for the pampas and for her close-knit colonial family. She would have more children, Doris and Roger,

Joan and Hubert. When she was expecting Joan, her health was so poor that her husband sent her to the Welsh coast, for the bracing sea air. On March 9, 1892, my mother, Joan Amphlett Corfield, was born in Aberystwyth. Despite Maggie's continuing ill health and warnings from the family doctor, Hubert was born just eleven months later. There may have been whispers. Even when she was very young Joan apprehended that there was something shameful about the proximity of the births; she used to pretend that she and Hubert were twins. Maggie faded out of the picture, took to a darkened room and died when she was still in her forties. I have never seen a photograph of her. My mother's only keepsakes of her mother were an intricately carved ivory brooch from China, and a copy of G. A. Henty's *Out on the Pampas.*

Mother, for years we complained: "Tell us about our grandmother." For years you claimed you could not remember; you had been too young at her death. We thought you were lying. I knew what it was to be nine years old. I would not have forgotten my own mother, forgotten YOU, for God's sake. Then, after years of asking, a palimpsest wavered through, things you didn't know you knew.

You didn't remember her, but you remembered being in her darkened bed chamber, being asked to fetch from the cupboard. A willing child, you ran to do the nurse's bidding. Something underfoot went clinking, rolling on the closet floor. Rows of bottles went down like dominoes. Quickly the nurse rose, strode towards you, encircled you with strong nurse arms. "Miss Joan, look at me. You are not seeing what you think you see. *Your mother is not a drinking woman. It's the pain, Miss Joan, the cancer pain.* Forget what you just saw!"

A good child, hypnotized, you forgot. The other memory, a sort of dredged-up snapshot, is of your mother, like Snow White's, sitting and staring out of a window frame. Was the landscape as bleak? On only one occasion have you let yourself speak:

"She was wearing a grey dress and a little cape. I seem to remember that the day was hot, but she looked as though she were cold. She sat hunched forward, her hands under her cape, staring. She didn't notice me. She was wearing a white cap, lace and linen. Women did in those days, old women. I thought she was very old, but she couldn't have been. She died in her forties."

Kate, the youngest of the beautiful Ray sisters, had come into the household when my mother, Joan, was about five, she about fifteen. Kate was young and merry, besides being beautiful. She and her sisters were wards of my grandfather. Grandfather betrayed that trust. He seduced her. Joan, seemingly abandoned by the bedridden Maggie, adored Kate. For Mother's older sister, Doris, however, the story was a different one. She had had time to know her mother better. Joan was protected from Maggie's illness and alcoholism, the boys were safely away at school, but Doris must have borne the brunt of the shame and gossip, as well as actual experience with an alcoholic woman whom she both loved and feared. She must also have been confused by the near-incestuous relationship that was developing between her father and his lovely ward.

William R. Corfield's fortunes were subject to wild swings. He experienced many financial ups and downs, but when Kate first came to Saint Lawrence, my grandfather was a millionaire. In a time when there was no income tax, he owned several ships, his mining investments were prospering, he had an office and a town house in Cardiff, and an impressive Georgian house with capacious grounds on the banks of the River Wye. It is understandable that he should want a young and beautiful woman with whom he could share his wealth and who would make him happy. Like most women, Kate's position was precarious. To marry well, as Jane Austen has explained to us, was the best, perhaps the only, recourse. Although it was known that she had rich and powerful relations in Hong Kong, Kate was part Chinese. Beautiful and British as she may have been, her chances of marrying at all were limited and, once she had come within W. R. Corfield's sphere, no other choices were allowed to present themselves to her. She was a hostage and she fell in love with her captor. Even in his fifties, William R. Corfield was sexually attractive, lusty, charming, and fun. The knowledge that she had bewitched so successful and worldly a lover must have been thrilling. And it must have been thrilling to my grandfather to know that he was adored by such a beautiful young woman.

To Joan, a lonely, neglected little girl, Kate was a godsend. Hardly more than a dozen years older than my mother, Kate was an amalgamation of sister, friend, and maternal presence. Perhaps Kate knew what it was to be a motherless child, to depend on her older sisters for love and comfort. She was as often at Saint Lawrence as she was in the town house at Cardiff. There is no doubt that she brought joy into my mother's life, although Doris seethed at her mother's displacement, and her own. When Maggie finally died, Doris refused to hand over the chatelaine keys (although she was only fourteen), and she burned Maggie's rare chinchilla coat in the furnace rather than let Kate become its possessor.

William R. Corfield had had enough of marriage; he was in no rush to marry Kate, although by now she had borne him a son, Rex. He went off to America, ostensibly to assuage his grief by shooting buffalo. However, mysterious forces in far away Hong Kong soon persuaded him that it was in his own best interest to marry their stranded relative. He could not just smile and explain to passersby about *this* particular Chinese family. Once married, however, Grandfather seems to have been whole-hearted in his decision. He settled down to be the squire of Saint Lawrence.

In 1904 Kate had another child, Joyce, who was the apple of her father's eye. In a family photograph, set against a background of a brick wall with espaliered fruit trees, William R. Corfield dandles his four-year-old daughter on his knee. It is a pose reminiscent of the portrayal of Jesus Christ in the stained-glass window at Abbey Dore. He and Kate are sitting side-by-side in garden chairs. To their left, at a distance, with his mother's back turned to him, sits Rex, utterly ignored by both his parents and everyone else in the photograph. He is wearing long trousers, so he must be at least twelve, tall for his age. To their right, quizzical and bemused, sits Roger, one leg dangling over the other, one hand on hip, the other against his cheek. Very Oscar Wilde. Standing to the rear, but fully visible in the space between his father and Kate, stands Rego, the eldest son who was away at school when the *Avonmore* was wrecked. His expression is inscrutable. To his right stands Doris. She grips the back of her father's chair and wears a fixed smile. Joan, my mother, stands on the other side of Rego, behind Kate. She must be about fifteen. I imagine a slight air of sadness. Her wavy brown hair is not yet "put up," but falls below her shoulders. She is wearing a big, droopy bow, too immature for her age. She is a child in a woman's body, gazing gravely and innocently into the camera.

My mother often claimed that she had had the happiest childhood anyone could imagine. Only as an adult did I come to realize that her estimation could not be entirely true, but when I was a child myself I could easily agree with her. She did not go to school but was taught by governesses who were hired for their prettiness rather than for their scholarship. Two of them, sisters, eventually married Harry and Francis, Mother's older brothers. There was also a French governess, but she quit in frustration because Joan and Hubert constantly eluded her. They discovered that M'moiselle was afraid of horses, so they would run down to the stables and hide in the stalls, sliding under the horses' bellies when she tried to reach for them. There were grooms and gardeners, cooks and maids, a coachman, and an old man who came once a week just to wind the many clocks, and to adjust the barometer.

In the Joseph Jacobs collection, *English Fairy Tales*, the story of "Mr. Fox" begins, *Lady Mary was young and Lady Mary was fair. She had more suitors than she could count. They all came down to her brothers' country house.* The whole point of the story is that Lady Mary was spunky (*a brave one she was*) and quick-witted, so was therefore able to save herself from the nefarious Mr. Fox. Because Joan Corfield lived in a scandalously disorganized household with no one actually in charge, she had far more freedom than most little girls of her time and place. She picked bluebells and primroses with the village children and climbed trees in the orchard. She had access to walled gardens and open gardens and greenhouses that supplied the household with vegetables, fruit, and flowers. Every year her father instructed the gardener that Miss Joan was to be presented with a bouquet of the first anemones, in observance of her birthday on March 9.

Like Lady Mary, Joan had her own horse and rode through fields and jumped hedges, or followed ancient forest paths overlooking the valley of the Wye and the Severn estuary. Sheep and cows and horses grazed in the fields, kept from blundering onto the lawn by a ha-ha, a sort of sunken fence or moat. Joan and Hubert could take the pony cart or walk into Chepstow, through the medieval town gate, where there were shops and a magnificent Norman castle to explore. Sometimes they went to the station, paid the requisite penny to enter the platform, and would sit for hours, watching trains. Sometimes Joan Corfield seems to me like one of those characters in *Castle Blair* or *The Bastables*, Victorian books written about middle-class English families who were blessed (and cursed) with freedom and neglect. They saved themselves from disaster and corruption by a combination of earthy common sense and by cleaving to ideas of romantic chivalry.

My mother's stories about her childhood continue to tantalize me with glimpses of another country where she and her lost brothers play eternally. Mother used to say that she grew up in Monmouthshire, a county on the Welsh border that was neither English nor Welsh. But what she was actually describing cannot be found on any map, not even an inch-to-the-mile Ordnance Survey. She was speaking not only of a place but of a time; not only of a time, but of a state of mind. I knew from the story of "Childe Rowland," in Joseph Jacobs's *English Fairy Tales*, that if you go around a church or a fairy mound widdershins (i.e. counter-clockwise), you become trapped in Fairyland. I knew for a fact that Mother's young and gallant brothers and most of their friends had disappeared into a fairy-tale-sounding place called "No Man's Land," where, perhaps, they still persisted in living out their lives in pre-1914 England. Or perhaps it was Mother who was trapped, unable to return to her own world. Always I was aware that the woman who lived with us in prosaic America at the same time had a foot in a parallel universe. Magically, sometimes, we could slip back and forth over the border; the way was through her stories.

Grandfather brought back curios and trophies and plants from all over the world. The greenhouse just outside the drawing room was famous for his extensive orchid collection, brought from the Amazon, one of the finest displays in England. He planted a redwood tree from California at the edge of the lawn, and he was among the first in the British Isles to plant a field of American maize. He seems not to have minded when farmers came to gawk. His aim was to enlighten by scientific experiment and example. But it was another story when workmen, digging a pit for the prize boar, came across a tiled floor, then an entire Roman villa. Mother kept a Roman coin in her trinket box as souvenir. When I asked what had happened to the excavation, Mother said that her father had had it covered up again. "He didn't want to be bothered by all those vulgar trippers," she explained.

Joan, with the inseparable Hubert, was incorrigible. She could whistle like a boy and continued to do so all her life. She played cricket with her brothers and was captain of the village girls' cricket team. But best of all, she was good with horses. I own a formal photograph of her, age four, sitting sidesaddle on a full-sized mare. She is wearing a long skirt, a velvet jacket, an Empire hat with feather, and she carries a little whip. Who bought her such an extravagant outfit? Perhaps it was Kate, who was much taken with the pretty little girl and showered her with presents.

When Grandfather was feeling particularly affluent he took members of the family on hastily devised trips. Once Hubert and Joan went to Ireland, where they kissed the Blarney Stone and rode about the countryside in a contraption called a dog cart. (It was actually pulled by a donkey.) Another time he hauled most of the family off to Switzerland, to enjoy the toboggan slides. Mother picked an Alpine edelweiss. For years she kept the thick-petaled blossom pressed between the pages of a book. Another time, for no explicable reason, Grandfather took Joan, Hubert, and Kate to Morocco. Perhaps the children were being used as a blind, to make him and Kate appear like a respectably married couple.

When Grandfather's fortunes were at the flood he was a profligate spender; he continued to spend even when he was heading for the rocks. However, he refused to give any money to the church for foreign missions. He told the scandalized vicar that he had traveled all over the world and had never yet come upon a society that did not have its own religion that, if observed, served its followers well and dispensed its own morality. "Where the Church should be putting its money," he claimed, "is for the relief and education of the wives and children of the English clergy." He thereupon set up a fund to pay for the schooling of the Tilley sisters, the vicar's three daughters. "They were better educated than I was," Mother said with some amusement. "And they all married wealthily."

A constant stream of visitors came to Saint Lawrence. A rajah arrived with his son for a few weeks and left him to the tender mercies of the Corfield clan while he went up to London. "That little boy was very spoiled," Mother told us. "He ordered the servants about and he thought he could just clap his hands to get what he wanted." Every few days gifts came by train for him, toys and books and boxes of chocolates. "We told him that if he was good he could play zoo with us. We were the bears, behind the stair rail, and he threw his chocolates down to us, one by one. We caught them and ate them until they were all gone." One morning the small guest from India was terrified when he woke to find that snow had covered lawns and fields. Joan helped him bundle up and took him outside to make a snowball. He was so pleased that, unbeknownst to her, he put it on the mantelpiece to show to his father, who was coming up from London by train. "Of course it melted. When his father arrived he went to show him his snowball, but there was nothing but a pool of water. He thought we had tricked him again. He cried and cried," Mother said. "And the grown-ups all laughed at him. I was so ashamed. I realized how mean we had been. Poor little boy! I don't suppose he ever forgave us. We were absolutely horrid. It wasn't his fault that he acted like a rajah prince. He was one."

The moral of the tale? The religious message I received from Mother was that God loves us all, not only the deserving poor but the undeserving rich and spoiled, too. I found this thought comforting, not because I was rich but because I was not always good. Another unorthodox view, held by my mother, derived from my grandfather, was that children are not born into Original Sin. "You may be naughty, but you cannot be evil," Mother told me when, prompted by an Irish Catholic neighbor, I anxiously interrogated her. "I may have to spank you sometimes, but little girls cannot be evil, however hard they try." I grew up happy in that sunny Pelagian heresy. On the other hand, Mother did believe that grown-ups could be evil. The newspaper proved that every day and she recognized evil when she saw it. She called such a state "wickedness."

Other children were attached to Saint Lawrence, sometimes for years on end, although they were mostly away at school and came to visit only during the holidays. There was a Mormon boy from Salt Lake City, a girl from Australia, a cousin from South Africa, Kate and her sisters from China. Empire builders treated their children with alarming casualness in those days. Also, a series of old ladies, distant relations, "some of them dotty, some of them absolutely potty," inhabited the upper reaches of the household, accompanied by maids and nurses and companions. For months or years William R. Corfield was at sea or abroad, untroubled by the results of a careless hospitality. "Send them to Saint Lawrence," he would say, letting the women he had left behind (Maggie, Aunt Amy, Doris, Kate) make provision and be responsible.

William R. Corfield had been a boy midshipman in the Crimean War and he ran the Union blockade in the American Civil War. He was ship-wrecked seven times, twice on cannibal islands. He dug up a fortune in gold in Australia and brought it to the coast under a load of sheep hides. He invested in railways in the United States and he owned a silver mine in Colorado, in partnership with William F. Cody, the famous Buffalo Bill of show biz, formerly of the Pony Express.

When Buffalo Bill's Wild West Circus came to England to perform before Queen Victoria, Grandfather invited him and part of his entourage to come to Saint Lawrence. Mother could remember how elegant Colonel Cody was, his buckskins as beautifully made as any suit tailored in London. He brought a trick horse with him. The horse could untie knots and open gates and let the cows out into the road. Red Indians set up camp in the field that lay just beyond the lawn; it could be seen from the drawing room. There the Indians practiced their riding and shooting acts, emitting strange high-pitched yelps as they rode bareback on their fleet Indian ponies. (The present owner of the property tells me that, when he was a boy, Chepstow's oldest inhabitants could still describe how, on winter days, smoke drifted from the tops of the wigwams.)

"The worst old sinners started coming to church on Sundays," Mother told us, "to see the famous cowboy." Mother confessed that, sitting in the Norman parish church of Saint Lawrence, she swelled with pride to be in such splendid company. She could not help glancing up at the carved stone knights in their niches overhead, to compare them with the glamorous self-styled Knight of the Plains.

When Joan was sixteen she went away to the Abbey School at Malvern. She liked school and found that, despite her haphazard education, she did well in mathematics and history – indeed, in all her subjects, except French. However, her studies were frequently interrupted by her father's telegrams, informing her that an old uncle or a second cousin had died and that the funeral would be held at such a time and place. The two sisters who were the headmistresses at Malvern Abbey were distressed at how Joan Corfield's relatives were dropping off like flies. Little did they know! The telegrams were coded messages from Captain Corfield, summoning his daughter to the local hunts.

Near the end of her second year at school, Joan rode in a steeplechase that would prove disastrous for her. At the corner of a field her horse leapt a hedge. Another horse, at the same time, leapt a hedge at right angles to hers. She was dashed to the ground under the falling weight and flailing hooves of both horses. Her mount had to be shot. The groom came up with another one and she rode home gamely, but she had suffered a grievous injury. Eventually she developed tuberculosis of the spine.

For the next five years, Joan lay in a spinal carriage, strapped to a board. Her father went off on yet another long voyage and she was shifted from hospital to hospital. Once, a convoy of nurses wheeled her across London. "I was young enough to enjoy having traffic held up just for me," she recalled. Another time she was sent to Brighton, for a new sort of cure. "The patients were wrapped in seaweed and wheeled out on a pier while the fog rolled in." This, for tuberculosis of the spine! After a while she was lost track of; no one in the family knew where she was. Like a mislaid package, she found herself flat on her back, physically helpless, in a nursing home, with no one paying the bills and no one answering her messages. "Everyone thought that someone else would do it."

Eventually she was rescued by "a sort of aunt or second cousin." Although she made light of it, the experience was searing. Far from making her obsequious, she learned to be simultaneously arrogant and gracious. She gave off an air of disguised royalty. To serve her was a privilege. Later in life, cleaning women, waitresses, the postman, the milkman, junior officers, and enlisted men fell over themselves to please her. It was not just because she inquired about their families, sent presents to new babies, and gave thanks like an accolade. People felt themselves privy to a secret: someone special had touched their lives and had made *them* special. My hunch is that she made them aware of their own nobility.

Partly because of the harrowing experience in her youth, she was genuinely sensitive to other people and forgiving of their fears and faults. However, to someone who should know better, she could be judgmental, imperious, and petty. She could spot shoddiness a mile away and she could discern value in the most unlikely people.

I remember you stopped the car, bade me get out, help her get in. She was carrying a load of empties. When she dropped her shopping bag, you got into the act, too. How those bottles rolled and rattled down the gutter, almost got away! You helped chase them, drove her to the liquor store, then offered to drive her up the hill again.

Too well-bred to watch while our passenger negotiated, we retreated to the car and waited. "Poor old dear," you said. "Rather valiant, isn't she, with that awful hat? Her hair, such a peculiar color. But she tries. She hasn't given up."

When Mother grew very old, in her eighties and nineties, she became a caricature of herself. Father would become furious as she ignored him, as she knocked herself out to charm a waiter or a hospital aide. The more charming she became, the more obnoxious Father would be. Going out to dinner with them was pure hell. My sister Joyce had more insight than I. She pointed out to me that Mother, nearing her death, and aware of Father's infidelities, was experiencing again that ancient feeling of abandonment, betrayal, and helplessness. She reverted to a means of elemental survival that had served her long ago when she lay on her spinal carriage, forgotten and unclaimed.

When the young Joan returned to Saint Lawrence she spent most of her time in the drawing room. French windows opened to the garden and, across a few yards of lawn, to the greenhouse. When she was in the drawing room she could look into the entrance hall and the library beyond, where she was often wheeled. She entered as fully as possible into the life of the household. "I even had beaux," she told us. One Christmas time, a season of charades and tableaux, she was rolled into the greenhouse to play the part of Sleeping Beauty to Hubert's Prince Charming. When the french doors were opened, the Prince ("Hubert said he felt like an ass") was seen to be leaning over to kiss La Belle Dormante, who lay languidly on her chaise, a wreathe of orchids on her brow, her long white dress draped from shoulder to hem with orchids pinned to colored ribbons. Other orchids, still growing, hung above her head. "There was a long, long silence and I thought something was wrong. I didn't dare peek until everyone broke into thunderous applause and shouted 'Bravo!'"

One golden autumn day Joan was rolled out to the lawn. As she lay there reading she heard the sounds of the hunt. As she watched, the fox came running across the lawn and jumped over her. Horses and hounds streamed after. With a tumult of shouts, a yelping of dogs and a sounding of horns, the fox was soon cornered and dispatched. Mother was presented with the brush, her forehead and cheeks daubed with blood. "Just as though I had been leader of the chase," she said. She refused to be abashed by our American sensibilities.

When the Corfields lived at Saint Lawrence, the drive from the gate went straight between a row of dark yews. Ships on the estuary could take a bearing off them. The yews were planted during the 1100s, in King Stephen's time. When the drive reached the house, it opened out onto a sunny expanse of gravel and a huge lawn. The house was early Georgian, set on the site of one of those medieval fortifications meant to nail down the border and keep the hated Welsh from spilling into England. The only reminder of the castle was the curve of the drive as it followed the line of the old moat around the house. The ditch had long since been filled in with gravel.

Mother told us a story about that driveway. The ghost of an old mail coach was supposed to come up the drive at two o'clock in the morning. If you stayed awake to listen and watch, you could actually hear the jingle of the harness and see pebbles jump and roll in the graveled drive for no apparent reason except that they must be stirred by the hooves of the ghostly team. The clincher to the story, which proved its authenticity, was that the ghost had never been noticed or reported until *after* the coach was withdrawn from service. The old coachman had died of a broken heart. It was his ghost who drove the spectral coach.

Grandfather was infuriated by the very mention of the ghost. Only the servants believed in such nonsense, he said. Grandfather had been born in 1841, just a few years after the famous voyage of the *Beagle*; he was a great admirer of Darwin. The young Darwin had actually visited a relative of his, Richard Corfield, in Valparaiso, when he was on his epic voyage, a gratifying fact that served to heighten Grandfather's loyalty and seal his identification with the cause of modern science. Grandfather would not abide superstition in his family. He proved, to his own satisfaction at least, that the sound mistaken for the jingling of coach harness was, in reality, the echo of a freight train several miles away, making its regular run between the hills at two o'clock in the morning. The sound of the particular train was made more pronounced by the silence of the hour. The coincidence of the old coach's cancellation could also be explained: its run had been stopped when the sweep of progress replaced it with the railroad. The mysterious movement of the pebbles happened because an unscrupulous builder, a century or more ago, had stinted on his contract to fill the moat adequately with layers of rock and turf and to tamp them down. The vibration of the train disturbed the loose rubble that undermined the gravel so that the pebbles in the drive rattled like peas in a jar.

And the death of the old coachman? "He was *old*, dammit. He was going to die of *something*." So much for the servants' ghost!

But there was another ghost at Saint Lawrence, Mother would sometimes (but not often) admit. A delicious tremor would run through us as we settled down to listen. We knew that, if we asked too many questions, Mother's lips would be sealed, so we learned to be grateful for whatever crumbs would be forthcoming.

There was the Lady in the Library or, rather, her ghost. She had come with the house, like bad drains. Grandfather was even more adamant that this embarrassment never be mentioned. No one knew who she was or why she had come, but the Lady wore a simple gray dress, surmounted by a white fichu or collar. Her brown hair was parted in the middle and drawn back into a coil at the nape of her neck. She was not frightening, she seemed rather ordinary, but whoever saw her died within the year.

Had Mother ever seen her?

"Of course not," Mother snapped. "I'm not dead, am I?"

Only once did she go on to tell us another part of the story. During a particularly lovely week in August, even more young people than usual visited Saint Lawrence. They had been invited to a week-long tennis party. The young men were dressed in blazers and summer flannels and the girls wore linen skirts and pleated blouses with leg-of-mutton sleeves. A tournament was organized; the courts were in almost constant use. When guests were not playing, they could hit croquet balls across the lawn or stroll in the gardens or find some other amusement. In the evenings there was talk and laughter at the dinner table and, afterwards, singing and dancing.

Joan had her chair rolled out to where she could watch the tennis players, but every afternoon, when the sun was hot, she retreated to the drawing room. "People were very kind," said Mother, "I never felt left out. They would come and talk to me there. So many people were coming to and fro that it was hard to keep track of who was who and how they had come to be invited."

Well, on this particular day, a young man who had been lingering in the library stopped to talk. "He was a nice young man," said Mother. "Rather shy and bookish." So when he asked about one of the pretty girls, she tried to be especially helpful, even though she knew of no one in the tennis party who answered to his description.

"When she comes in at tea time, point her out to me and I'll introduce you," she said. But the girl did not make an appearance. Nor did she come to dinner. "I had a new idea," said Mother. "I thought that she might be a companion to one of the 'dots and pots' who lived on the third floor. Maybe she would come down to the library to fetch a book for herself or for one of the old ladies. I was determined to keep watch for her."

At dinner time Joan managed to talk across the dinner table to the young man, to tell him how hard she had tried to find the girl he had seen in the library. She had spent part of the day there, and when she was in the drawing room she had left the doors open so she could keep glancing across the hall. Someone else, overhearing, asked for a description, which the young man willingly gave. "She was a little old-fashioned," he added, apologetically.

"I saw her," said Hubert. "I wondered who she was." Francis had seen her too, as had several other young men. "She was dressed in gray."

"Maybe she's the Lady in the Library," said Roger. "Maybe you saw our household ghost. Anyone who sees her dies within the year."

At the far end of the table there was an apoplectic roar as Grandfather rose to his feet. "Out, sir, out!" he shouted, pointing to the door. "This is an age of enlightenment, not of darkness. We do not live in the Middle Ages. This is 1914, August, high summer! I will have no more talk of ghosts or superstition in this house."

"Of course Roger had to apologize, but within the year or soon after, those young men were dead. Dead. Killed in the Great War."

I doubt whether my mother actually believed this ghost story. I think it had fashioned itself, mythologizing a traumatic event too large and painful for her to transmit to us in any other way. *In myth lies the truth, the truth that lies.*

CHAPTER 3

Women's Business

WHEN JOAN AMPHLETT CORFIELD came home on leave from her station in Yorkshire, her stepmother, as promised, invited Lieutenant Frank Higbee, USN, to come to tea at the house on Cathedral Road. Joan and Frank fell for each other "like a ton of bricks," Mother used to say, recounting to us wide-eyed little girls the history of the family romance. They saw each other only three times before Father's ship left Cardiff. Frank wrote every day, sometimes twice, and Joan wrote, too, although her father was dying of cancer. When the ship returned to Cardiff, the young couple stood by her father's deathbed and told him of their plans to marry. She liked to think that he had heard and understood.

The war had just ended when, for some inexplicable reason, Frank was sent overland to Poland with three other young officers, one of whom claimed to be able to speak Polish. He was lying, but the three of them had a grand and glorious tour across Europe, driving a Dusenberg confiscated from the Germans. When they reached Warsaw, they were ushered in to see the American ambassador to Poland, none other than Ignace Jan Paderewski. The great pianist, composer, and statesman showed gracious warmth and courtesy to his adopted countrymen, but he said he didn't have a clue as to why they had been sent. Then they turned around and drove back to Paris. The year was 1919. On the strength of this mad expedition, Lieutenant Higbee was considered an authority on Eastern Europe, including revolution-torn Russia. He was therefore ordered to Vladivostok, this time by ship.

Joan Corfield, meanwhile, decided to take passage on a Cunard liner and to wait for her fiancé in New York. She was invited to stay at the home of Captain and Mrs. William Grace. Captain Grace, whose family owned the Grace Steamship Lines, was her godfather. Off the coast of Newfoundland, almost at the same spot where, seven years before, the *Titanic* had met its fate, the liner hit an iceberg. The passengers took to the lifeboats and were subsequently landed in Halifax. Joan arrived in New York by train, outwardly calm but inwardly in turmoil, not because of such a trivial incident as hitting an iceberg, but because there were no letters from Frank. She had not heard one word from him since he took off for Vladivostok.

Joan Corfield stayed two months with the Graces, who tried to be kind but only added to her anxiety by their well-meaning questions and silent sympathy. They took it for granted that she was an abandoned woman. Timidly, Mrs. Grace suggested that the American lieutenant might be a bounder, already married, with six children. Perhaps Joan should book passage back to Britain? On top of these social strains, Mrs. Grace did not approve of smoking, a habit which Joan had taken up while driving ambulances under fire from zeppelins. Nor did she approve of Joan's bobbed hair, the latest style from Paris. Joan found her way up to the attic and spent hours hanging out of an upstairs window of the Graces' brownstone, smoking and thinking about what to do next. She decided that Mrs. Grace was very likely right, but she also decided that she would not go back to Britain to be held up as an object of pity and scorn. She wrote back to her family that she and Frank, ever so sensibly, had decided to get to know each other better before they settled down. Meanwhile, she would visit a married cousin in Salt Lake City. He had been a special friend to her and Hubert when, as a schoolboy, he spent holidays at Saint Lawrence. Her ultimate plan, not spelled out, was to proceed to Patagonia to see her mother's relatives, whom she had never met.

Joan had a wonderful time in Salt Lake City with her cousin and his young wife, who was a Mormon. Joan's impression of Mormon life was that it was continual round of luncheons, teas, balls, and shopping. She actually attended a fashion show, an innovation she had heard was popular in London and Paris but never expected to find in a desert wilderness. No one talked about the war. It was as though it had never happened. At first she was angered by the callousness and ignorance she discovered in Utah, but after a while she found the situation curiously restful. She danced and flirted and threw care to the winds.

Then a telegram came, from Lieutenant Frank D. Higbee, saying that he had arrived in San Francisco, read her letters, and that he was taking a train to Salt Lake City. Miss Joan Corfield wired back, told him not to bother. Frank Higbee ignored the message and arrived anyway. Joan Corfield sent him packing. His claim that he had written every day twice a day was not to be believed. In six months at least one letter would have gotten through! No sooner had Frank left than a special van from the post office drew up at the door. Bales of stained envelopes, smelling of mold and sea water, were carted up the steps and dumped in the front hall, all of them from Lieutenant Frank David Higbee. Telegrams flew. Joan Corfield took a train to San Francisco.

They were married May 5, 1920. Frank was a "mustang," meaning that he had not gone to the Naval Academy at Annapolis, but had come up from the ranks. When Congress cut military funds, Frank Higbee was among the first to be discharged from the U.S. Navy. He was heartbroken. He tried ranching, he tried selling insurance, he even dug ditches (which he said he'd rather do than sell insurance). He had a civilian Master Mariner's license, but the American Merchant Marine was in shambles, too. There were few American ships and no new ones were being built. The 1921 recession made any job hard come by, but at last he was offered a first mate's position on a freighter going to China and the Philippines.

Mother was left in Oakland, California, alone and pregnant. During that time she worked in a corner grocery store, to keep herself busy and to earn much-needed money. My elder sister, Anne, was six months old before her father saw her. When he left for sea again, it was with the understanding that his next home port would be Seattle. But no sooner did Mother move to Seattle than Father wired her to move back to Oakland.

Mother was glad to be moving away from Seattle. There had been a series of assaults on women in her neighborhood. She lived in a ground-floor apartment across from a high school. Her last evening in Seattle was on a Sunday. Her packing boxes had been hauled away, her telephone had been turned off. She sat in an almost-empty apartment, looking out on the closed shops and the deserted schoolyard across the street. She watched idly as a woman walked by; saw a man spring out of the bushes with a hammer.

Mother thrust Anne into the steep-sided empty bathtub, for safe-keeping, then ran outside. She yelled as she ran, pounced on the man, kicked and clawed at him so that he dropped his hammer. The victim was saved, but the man got away. Mother was afraid that he had seen the doorway from which she had come, and that he would return to seek her out. She dragged her mattress into the bathroom, which she could lock, and slept the night in the bathtub with her baby. Next morning she took the train to Oakland.

I was born in Oakland, in August 1923. About the same time the United States Coast Guard decided to grant six extempore commissions. The federal government needed an increase in their rosters to assist in the war against rum-runners. Accordingly, they sent out notices to officers in the Merchant Marine. There would be a series of examinations, set for a certain date at specified hours. Mother and Father, with a two-year-old and a new baby, were moving to a larger apartment in Oakland. Just before they left the old one, the mailman came by. Typically, Father did not look at the mail, but stuffed several letters into the pocket of his dungarees. A month went by before he found occasion to wear his work trousers again. He reached into his back pocket and hauled out the letters. One of them was an invitation to take the exam. Only then did he come to realize that he might have a chance, a very slim chance, to be commissioned in the United States Coast Guard.

The examination was to be given that very day. Indeed, it had already started. Father tore out of the house and took the ferry to San Francisco. On the way across the bay he met a man whom he had known in the Merchant Marine. The former shipmate was also on his way to take the exam. His ship had come in a day late from China, but he had special dispensation to sit the exam late. When Father asked him how he had managed that, he said, "Because my father is a captain in the Coast Guard and my grandfather was before him. I'm the black sheep who failed to make it into the Academy." Then, according to our family legend, he said: "Look here, Higbee. You come along with me and make a great row about my having special privileges. I'll back you up."

When they arrived the exam had indeed already started, and time counted. They let Father take the exam along with his benefactor, but Father was not allowed four extra hours to make up for the time missed during the morning. He passed with high marks anyway. His friend, alas, failed the examination.

Father and the five other officers extemporarily commissioned were referred to as the "ex-temps" to distinguish them from those officers who had graduated from the Coast Guard Academy. The Coast Guard was originally the Revenue Service, inaugurated by secretary of state, Thomas Jefferson, in 1790, to fight the Barbary pirates, who were harassing U.S. shipping off the coast of northern Africa. As such, it claims to be two years older than the U.S. Navy. It was a small, inbred service, hoary with tradition; in some cases the commissions seemed almost hereditary. The ex-temps were deeply resented by the regular line officers, who saw their hierarchy – and therefore their chance for command – threatened. Father and the other ex-temps were originally allowed into the Coast Guard on a temporary basis; in 1931 their commissions would be made permanent, but their right to be promoted was left in limbo. They were paid less than the Academy graduates, and transferred more often.

In 1927 Father was ordered to Astoria, Oregon, at the mouth of the Columbia River, as second-in-command of the Coast Guard cutter stationed there. Father, as usual in those early years, had gone ahead of us to choose a house to rent. He knew that he would be away at sea, on rum patrol, ten days out of every fifteen. Most of Astoria is built on a steep hillside, and we did not own a car. Mother still suffered from the serious back injury she had acquired as a young woman. She also had three small children. (My younger sister, Joyce, had been born in December, 1926.) Weighing all these things, as well as his finances, Father chose a house on the flat, reclaimed land near the docks. Mother could push Joyce's baby carriage along Commercial Street to the shops and the bank and afterwards walk down to the waterfront to see the ships and the spectacular view of the Columbia. The only drawback was that our house was in Chinatown, considered by nice families in town to be lower class, racially taboo, and dangerous. The house itself was small and neat, with a fenced-in garden in the back, just right for a young family. But because it was in Chinatown, no one except the other officers' wives came to call, and they did so with trepidation.

Somehow Captain Cherry, the British port consul, heard of Mother's plight. An Englishwoman, daughter of an English ship-owner, goddaughter of W. R. Grace, owner of Grace Steamship Line, was living in Astoria's Chinatown! Mrs. Cherry (Maitie) came to call, and the Cherrys took Mother under their wing. Fortuitously, two destroyers from the Royal Navy, on a goodwill tour of the Pacific, put into port. Dinners, balls, and receptions were held in honor of the visitors. Although Father was out at sea, the Cherrys made sure that Mother was invited. She went in their company and had a wonderful time dancing the night away with her countrymen. Captain Cherry may have whispered something of Mother's story into the proper ear. When the commanding officer proposed a little dinner party to thank the various pilots and port officials who had shown such courtesy to his officers and men, the invitations named Mother as special guest of honor. Now, after the ships left port, everyone who was anyone came to call at the little house in Chinatown.

What I remember most about Astoria is a sense of abundance. Blackberries and salmonberries grew wild in the vacant lots; raspberries and currants crowded the garden. The cream on top of the milk bottle was so thick it could be whipped. The old man who delivered our milk drove not a horse and wagon, but a new-fangled truck. He wore blue overalls, had a thatch of white hair, rosy cheeks, blue eyes. He actually owned the dairy farm, he told Mother, but now his sons ran the business. After his wife died he chose to drive a milk route simply to have something to do, people to talk to. One day he asked Mother if it would be all right if he came by on a Sunday to take us out to the country, to see his farm and to meet his family. My memory of that day is vague (except for drinking warm milk from a cow's teat), but in later years Mother told us that Maitie Cherry had been shocked to discover that Mother had accepted the old man's invitation. There was no way for Mother to know, Maitie said, but our milkman's mother had owned the biggest, fanciest whorehouse on Astor Street. She had bought land outside of town and set up a dairy farm. She hired a family to run the farm and to bring up her little boy, whom she visited often. When she died, she had left her son considerable wealth and property, but of course no one in Astoria society could have anything to do with him. She, Maitie, was only telling Mother for her own good. Mother's retort had been that our milkman was such a nice old man, gentle and kind and well-mannered, that he must have had a mother who loved him very much. As we grew older, and Mother told us the story, she would wonder aloud about what had driven that woman to enter a life of prostitution, and how she had acquired the business acumen, not only to own and manage a thriving whorehouse and a dairy farm, but to buy up hundreds of acres of Oregon property when it was going for a song.

Mother had a nodding acquaintance with most of the women in the neighborhood and made a lasting friendship with Mrs. Wirkila, Finnish, whose husband was a fisherman. Mother and she exchanged Christmas cards for the rest of their lives. There was also Mrs. Bronsky, whom Mother admired but tried to avoid. Mrs. Bronsky had walked across Siberia to Vladivostok, where she took ship for America. She was a very brave, very determined woman, Mother told us. But give her an inch and she took a mile.

Mrs. Bronsky was in the *schmatte* business. She spent most of her life slaving over a scrub board and hanging out rags in her backyard. Although she lived around the corner from us, her backyard abutted ours. She was an empire builder. She asked Mother if she could use our clotheslines, too, when Mother was not using them. Mother had diapers to consider, but she could not bear to say an unequivocal no to someone who had walked to Vladivostok and who appeared to be the sole support of a skinny, nervous little girl with huge circles under her eyes. She agreed that Mrs. Bronsky could use our lines on Thursday afternoons, but sometimes, no matter what the day, Mrs. Bronsky would whip into our yard as soon as Mother had left and pin up her wares.

We children were fascinated by the tattered ensigns that fluttered from our masthead. We quite looked forward to seeing what outrage she would pin up next. However, one day Mother invited all the officers' wives to tea. She was pouring from her best pink luster teapot, her back to the window, when she sensed that something was amiss. The other women were staring dumbfounded at the awful wash that hung on Mother's clothesline. Mother started to explain, then she began to laugh, as she saw the scandalized expressions on the faces of her guests. She laughed so hard she had to wipe the tears from her eyes. To live in Chinatown was bad enough, but Mother had compounded the sin. Had she no shame?

When Mother went out to the sidewalk to get wood for the furnace, she often bowed and smiled at the Chinese woman who lived across the street from us. Neither was able to speak the other's language, but somehow they communicated. When Mrs. Chan gave birth to her thirteenth child, Mother took us to see the baby, bringing with her some of Joyce's outgrown baby clothes and a little gift.

Ten years later, when we were living in Connecticut, and Father had just received orders to return to Astoria, Mother told us a story at the dinner table, a story none of us had ever heard before. She said it had happened when we were living in the little house in Chinatown.

One night, when Father was out to sea and we children were in bed, there came a knock at the door. Our neighbor, Mrs. Chan, was there, with her eldest son. Quickly, they slipped inside. The boy translated for his mother. Mrs. Higbee must be very careful the next few nights. She must not go out after dark on any account, not even for wood. There was a Tong war in progress. Battles would be fought, shots would be fired. Men would come out of the tunnels.

"Tunnels?"

Yes, there were tunnels that ran from Commercial Street down to the brothels on Astor Street and over to the docks. They comprised a maze of old streets and cellars that had been covered over when land was reclaimed to build the new part of town. The tunnels were inhabited by desperate men. A valuable cargo of opium had been dropped from a ship entering the river. Several Tongs were claiming it, including outsiders who would have no respect for Mrs. Higbee. Mrs. Higbee was not to impart to anyone what she was being told. Mrs. Chan was risking her life, and her husband's honor.

When Father finally heard the story, he was aghast and aggrieved. "Good God, woman!" he said. "You never fail to astound me!" This was the very reason that his ship had put to sea that night. The Coast Guard had been tipped off that a huge shipment of opium was going to be put overside by a ship entering the river mouth. Why had Mother not told him that the opium was already in Astoria?

Because, said Mother, she had already given her word to Mrs. Chan. If Mother had told Father, *his* honor would have been at stake. He would have been honor-bound to tell his commanding officer. Investigations would have ensued. Her neighbor and her neighbor's family would have been placed in jeopardy.

"Some things," said Mother grandly, "are *women's* business."

Father built an enormous sandbox for us in the backyard and hauled in the radio shack off an old ship to act as a playhouse for his three little girls. Cylindrical in shape, it was made of thick plates of steel held together by enormous bolts. It had a real brass porthole. Father painted the ponderous turret with an undercoat of navy red lead and an overcoat of thick white paint, like a ship. Then, incongruously, he painted the trim green and pink. For Mother he planted a hedge of sweetpeas in the same colors, to remind her of England.

By a trick of my memory, while the garden is always sunny, all the rest of Astoria is curtained in mist and rain. After living in southern California, Mother welcomed a climate that was so like England's. For the rest of my life I have thought of intermittent rain as a benison, perpetual sunshine as a bane. *The children sing in far Japan/The children sing in Spain/The organ with the organ man/Is singing in the rain.* Mother enchanted us with books that imbued us with a love for the English countryside we had never seen, might never see. Besides reading to us from *A Child's Garden of Verses* and *Mother Goose*, she beguiled us with a book, sent from England, called *Cosy Time Tales*, written and illustrated by someone who had only one name – Natalie. Our favorite story was about a family (English, just like us) whose father was often out at sea (just like ours). There were two little girls and a baby (not like Joyce, but a brother). The two little girls owned a dollhouse their father had made for them. Unlike our playhouse, which stood in the garden, their dollhouse was small enough to be placed by a nursery window. On stormy nights, "when the wind was crying aloud and ships were tossed at sea," the mother in the story would make hot cocoa for them (just as our mother did), and they would sit together in a big chair while she read to them (just as we did).

One such stormy night they heard a tapping on the window. When they went to look there was a fairy with a tiny baby in her arms. Of course they invited her in. She explained that she had been swept off her usual path by the storm and, just happening to glance through their window, saw the dollhouse. Was it to let? Of course the children were delighted to have a fairy as their tenant. They wanted to do everything they could for her but she was quite independent, even a little cross, when they would have interfered with her bathing the fairy baby in the doll bathtub. She could manage by herself, thank you! The storm lasted for three days and at the end of that time the fairy announced that it was time for her to go home again. They opened the window for her and, "hailing a passing leaf," she whirled away out of their sight forever.

The mouth of the Columbia River yearns toward the vastness of the sea. At tide's turn the Pacific, "the biggest thing on earth," Father used to say,

rushes upriver almost a hundred miles. At low tide we could see men standing on the shoals, hauling seines full of fish from the river. Mother used to
push Joyce's baby carriage down to the docks in order that she might buy
a salmon. In those days fishermen would sometimes haul in a salmon five
or six feet long. Mother would pay a dollar to the first man to bring in a
modest eight-pounder, the size that would fit exactly into her oval fish
poacher. She poached the fish gently in a bouillon made with a carrot, an
onion, and a few sprigs of parsley. Later she served it with a white sauce
containing lots and lots of parsley leaves chopped fine. Freshly cracked
white pepper was the secret ingredient. She put the peppercorns on a chop-
ping block, then smashed them with the bottom of her cast-iron frying pan.

Mother said that Columbia River salmon was *almost* as good as salmon
from the River Wye. This would infuriate Father. There was no more noble
fish than the noble Chinook! Mother would sometimes, in placating mood,
admit that the fish from the Pacific was very good, but she was swift to add
that Oregonians had no idea how to cook it. Sometimes, Clatsop Indian
fashion, they dug a pit in the sand, lined it with hot stones, wrapped the
salmon in seaweed, lowered it into the pit, then rebuilt the fire in order to
roast it. Granted, this way was romantic, but more often than not, after all
that fuss, the fish came out raw or overdone – or both. When they roasted
the fish in a civilized gas oven, she claimed, the results were dry to negli-
gible. What Mother and Father did agree on was that to fry a salmon was
a sacrilege. The salmon is a noble fish, a sacred one. A fried salmon is an
affront to God.

Mother had spent her childhood just five miles from Tintern Abbey, on the
River Wye. The ruins of the ancient abbey contain some stones on which
are carved pictures of salmon, so like those that swim in the peaty waters
a few yards away that they are instantly recognizable. These images,
carved by medieval monks, are more than nature notes. The fish is one of
the earliest symbols for Christ in story and legend, older than the cross.

The third morning after the Crucifixion, when the stone had been rolled
away from the tomb, some of Christ's disciples decide to go fishing in the
Sea of Tiberias. At first they are unsuccessful, but a mysterious stranger
bids them to throw their nets to starboard. When they haul in their nets,
heavy with catch, the stranger invites them to breakfast, and sets about,
matter-of-factly, to broil a fish over the coals of his fire (John 21: 4-14). The

enigma of the story is that Christ, who enjoined his disciples to become "fishers of men," was the stranger, but Christ was the fish also, of which they (and he) partook, in a meal as holy as the one where they drank the wine and ate "the bread of Christ." The story also evokes that one about the loaves and fishes, a mystery which foreshadows both the Last Supper and the meal on the seashore. *Take and eat this, in memory of me, for this is my body.*

Across the river from Tintern is an ancient forest, the Forest of Dean. There, some people believe, the early scenes in the story of the *Holy Grail* took place. Parsifal, whose name means "fool," was succored by his grieving mother, Heart's Sorrow. She had lost his father and all his brothers to tournaments and battle. Hoping to save her one remaining child from the violence of war and the corruption of the court, she fled into the wilderness. Alas! One day the boy wandered off, as boys will, else there be no story.

But there was another boy, related to Parsifal, who, years before, had also left his mother to wander in a forest. He was a prince, destined to become the Fisher King. In his peregrinations he came upon a camp, deserted by some hunters. They had pierced a salmon with sticks and set it to broil. (Despite my own mother's disclaimers, the Celts probably cooked much like the Clatsop Indians of Oregon.) Hungry and curious, the boy prince reached out to steal a taste. A vestige of salmon stuck to his finger. It was hot! Hastily he stuck his finger into his mouth. Before his soul and psyche were prepared for such a jolt he had tasted of the Salmon of Knowledge. At that very moment he was wounded in the thigh (his genitals) and forever lost his innocence. For the rest of his life (except for the last three days of it) he would suffer in agony, and the country he ruled would become a wasteland. *The* Wasteland! The only way for him to assuage his awful pain was to go fishing, fishing in the deep waters of the unconscious. The only way for him to be saved was if a simpleton entered the Grail Castle (where the Fisher King lay) and asked a certain simple question.

Parsifal was that simpleton. He came upon the Fisher King – fishing – and followed his directions: go down the road, turn left, cross the moat. That night he saw signs and wonders, but alas! He was too young, and therefore too "cool," to open his mouth and ask what the hell was going on. Thirty years had to pass before he, and the Fisher King, were given a second chance.

In Irish legend, the Salmon of Knowledge lives in a deep well. He swims around and around, waiting through the centuries for fruit from the hazel tree to fall into the water. Only when he eats thereof can the Salmon of Knowledge become the Salmon of Wisdom. *Knowledge comes but wisdom lingers*, as Tennyson was wont to say.

In Astoria, the forest primeval came to the edge of town. Huge trees, some of them more than a thousand years old, were carted along the roads. Log rafts floated down the river; timber for the world was piled on the docks. Downtown there was a wooden sidewalk that ran in front of the bank and the grocery store, past the Bee Hive Emporium. The wooden sidewalk was covered with a wooden awning, like in the old cowboy movies. All of the houses were built of wood, and each house had a pile of wood stacked on the sidewalk in front of it. We had a gas cooking stove but we burned wood in our furnace, just as all the other households did.

One day Mother received a mysterious package from England. She sent us to spend the day with another officer's family. When we came home her eyes were red from soot and tears. In the package she had received were her brother Hubert's bloody uniform and his other effects, sent by the British War Office. She had spent the day burning them in the furnace. Hubert had been killed at the Dardanelles ten years before. It had taken all those years for the package to catch up to her.

I saw my mother as being as much a hero as any man, courteous and noble as a knight, yet I saw her as the quintessential domestic woman. I did not know it then, but I have come to know that she was a descendant of Eleanor of Aquitaine, through Joan Plantagenet, daughter of Edward I, whose granddaughter married a Corfield. She taught me to be brave. I did not for an instant feel that stories of great courage or decision were not meant for me, a girl. My mother's brothers, killed in the Great War, and Parsifal's brothers killed in tournaments and battles, the Fisher King, the Forest of Dean and the forests of Oregon, the Salmon of Knowledge, the noble Chinook, the Christ salmon of Tintern, the recipe for parsley sauce, would, over the course of my lifetime, become fused forever in my body and mind, my soul and my psyche.

Joan Amphlett Corfield taught me to be ready, always, for signs and wonders. If, one day, a salmon should lift its head from the pan and speak to me, I pray that I will be neither too cool, nor too astonished.

CHAPTER 4

Golden Spheres

PEOPLE OFTEN ASK ME how I became a storyteller. I am convinced that travel – and therefore constant change – at an early age was an important ingredient; so was stability – life around the dinner table. Being put off-balance heightens and sharpens the senses. Words must be found to pin new awareness to the wall. When we traveled, what else was there for us to do but tell old stories, make up new ones? Travel put us at risk of having no sense of a self, of having no sense of "home." Stories gave us structure, a sense of permanence; they built a special place to go to.

Both of my parents had a strong sense of narrative and drama, plus a natural affinity for language. There was the danger, of course, of toppling over into mere self-dramatization. That happened, but not when they drew from the purest well, the Well at the World's End, where the Great Salmon swims. At its best, story was truth and beauty, story was courage, story was play, story was a way of making love to each other. As my parents went through the day, living moment by moment, each shaped and honed experience into a little work of art to be presented that night at the family dinner table. Their children were lucky enough to sit at the same board, to witness and partake. In return, we were expected to live *our* lives as story, to mix and knead and shape ourselves from everything we had seen and heard. How did I become a storyteller? We ate and drank stories for dinner. They were our mass, our communion.

We had lived in Astoria little more than a year when Father received orders to transfer to the new U.S. Coast Guard cutter now stationed back in Oakland. Father had to leave immediately. Once again Mother packed up all our belongings and, with her daughters, boarded a coastal steamer (Father was anxious that we support the U.S. Merchant Marine). In those days families who traveled together could talk together. We were not strapped into seats, facing forward like Easter Island statues. We sat where we could watch Mother's face and she could watch ours. On ships or trains or in railroad stations she entertained us by telling us tales from Mother Goose and Joseph Jacobs, the Brothers Grimm and Hans Christian Andersen, not reading them out of a book. (Our books were packed away.) She told stories about her childhood and, thrilling, about ours: *When you were just a baby.* How infinitely fascinating, to know that I used to spit up orange juice! She told us about the little boy who came to our house for lunch and, when his mother asked him, "What did you have?" he answered, "Spaghetti and lots of laughing."

Sitting in a railway station, I took turns with my sisters. The game was to tell stories about the other people who were waiting, a safe distance away. "I'll trade you that lady in the big flowered hat for the man with a string around his suitcase," I said. Anne refused to break the rules. We were supposed to take people in the order in which they came.

Anne's health had so improved that this time we did not have to be near the Presidio, across the bay in San Francisco. We rented a house in Alameda, close to Father's ship. It was one of those California craftsman cottages, slightly Japanese in concept. All the rooms were on one floor; a sunroom in the back led to an overgrown garden. Although northern California was almost as cold as Oregon, it was part of the California mystique to pretend that a house did not need a furnace; the gas fire in the fake fireplace in the living room was supposed to suffice. On each side of the fireplace was a book shelf with glass doors. They had tiny little window frames. Joyce still dug in the toy box, but Mother designated the book cupboards for Anne and me. I loved best the privacy afforded by the mullioned door, which could be shut or opened only by me, or only with my permission. Even Mother had to ask. *Privacy* was a concept that Mother regarded as fundamental, an essential for any human being, even (especially) for a small child. She guarded the territorial rights of each of us with fierce determination. Her daughters might have to share one bedroom, but each of us was given a separate and inviolate space for mind and soul.

Joyce was still at that age when she liked to play with real things – pots and pans and the forbidden daffodil-shaped telephone. Anne was learning to read, to wrestle printed letters into words and images. I was suspended in that state that precedes reading, where building blocks afford glimmers of grammar and syntax; small figures and toys (or twigs and pebbles) become three-dimensional hieroglyphics with which to tell a story. However, I was jealous of Anne and her newfound ability. So I cheated. I *pretended* that I could read. I seized upon Anne's primer whenever I had the chance. Solemnly I turned the pages and expounded the history of "The Little Red Hen," pointing to words, frowning over letters, keeping a wary eye on the pictures so I would know when to turn the page. Then one day I came across the same tale in another book, an anthology of folk tales, where the text was presented in entirely different layout and with only one picture, and I discovered that I had been fooling myself even while I sought to fool the rest of the world. I *could* read! I was off and running. A few months later I struggled through Hans Christian Andersen's "Snow Queen." *"I did it myself," said the Little Red Hen.*

Mother read aloud to us every night from the "big green books," a collection put out by the people who published *Saint Nicholas* magazine, which mother had purchased volume by volume from a door-to-door salesman. Or sometimes she read from "the big red book," a collection of about fifty of the tales from the Brothers Grimm. My favorite story was "Snow White and Rose Red." I liked best that part of the tale when the mother sits before the fire reading to her two daughters and a bear knocks at the door. The bear, in my mind, was Father. Had he not served on a ship named *Bear*? A photograph of it hung in our hallway, and then there was the family saga about a smelly bearskin. More significant was Father's gruff, burly, hirsute presence in our all-female household, reassuring yet upsetting. When the bear in the Grimm story came through the door, he was so covered with snow that Rose Red rushed to fetch a broom to sweep him off. Father burst into our lives sporadically, clothed in the myth of Arctic seas.

On rare and solemn occasions, Mother showed us her copy of *The Parade, 1897: A Gift Book for Boys and Girls*, edited by Gleeson White. (I would later learn that he had been editor of *The Studio*, the most influential art magazine in *fin de siècle* London.) She had been given it as a birthday present when she was only five. My favorite picture was an austere drawing by Aubrey Beardsley, illustrating "The Frog Prince." The picture was in black and white, except for a saffron-colored ball in the frog's mouth, and a saffron-colored sphere (golden apple? magic orange? Persephone's pomegranate?) on a tree by the well. Bruno Bettelheim notes in *The Uses of Enchantment* that a golden ball (or apple) represents the perfect sphere of childhood – which, ultimately, must be lost, else the story cannot happen.

Fritz Perls, the grandfather of Gestalt therapy, averred that dreams are projections of our many selves. *I am everything and everyone in my dream and everything and everyone in my dream is me.* In the 1970s, when I was training at the Gestalt Institute of Toronto, I developed the idea a step further: a folk tale is a sort of communal dream. *I am everything in the story and everything in the story is me.* I am the stone and I am the water that flows over the stone; I am the hand, and I am the sword that severed the hand. I am Hansel and I am Gretel. I am the good sister and I am the bad sister. As a child I accepted that the mother in "Snow White and Rose Red" (and hence my own mother) loved her daughters equally, both the adventurous, outdoorsy, aggressive Rose Red and the gentle, domestic, bookish Snow White. There were other stories ("Mother Hulla," "Cinderella," and the one about looking for strawberries in the snow) wherein there was a "good" sister and a "bad" sister. Deep inside my psyche my mother's voice confirmed that I was both of these, and that it was all right to be so. When all was said and done, at the end of the story, good would triumph (though not without a struggle) and evil would be dispatched (though not forever).

I started kindergarten in Alameda, California, in the fall of 1928. Mother could tell a story, and tell it well, but my teacher's way of telling was thrilling; it verged on the magical. At five years old, I fell madly in love with her. (Mother may have been a little jealous.) I like to think that my teacher learned storytelling from Gudrun Thorne-Thomsen, either directly, or a few degrees removed from her. Gudrun Thorne had been born in Sweden into a family of artists and intellectuals. Her mother was a famous actress, noted for her portrayal of Ibsen heroines, but a stronger influence for Gudrun was the storytelling that went on in the household. Everyone was encouraged to tell stories, even the servants – especially the servants, while they were working.

In 1888, Gudrun came to Chicago to live with an older sister. She attended Cook County Normal School, directed by Francis W. Parker, "the father of progressive education." When Parker's school became part of the University of Chicago, Gudrun Thorne-Thomsen (now married to her childhood sweetheart) was appointed to teach storytelling and reading. Young as she was, she had convinced her mentors (among them, John Dewey) that the best preparation for learning to read was by listening to folk tales and learning to tell them. Subsequently, she lectured throughout the United States, and joined the faculty of the Carnegie Library School in Pittsburgh. By the year I started kindergarten, she was principal of an experimental school in Ojai, California, just a few hundred miles down the road from Alameda. Her influence was still powerful, especially in the San Francisco Bay area. I like to think that I was initiated into storytelling by my mother. Because of her, I was able to appreciate the magical technique of my kindergarten teacher. I like to believe that I was put under a spell by someone who *may* have learned her art from Gudrun Thorne-Thomsen, and that I have basked in that enchantment ever since.

Not only did I fall in love with my teacher, I fell in love with a new story from the Brothers Grimm, one that was not included in Mother's repertoire. The story of "One-Eye, Two-Eyes, and Three-Eyes" is the only folk tale that I am aware of wherein the middle daughter is the heroine. *Two-Eyes is despised for being ordinary, but she is the only sister neither too rigid (one-eyed) nor too split (three-eyed) to see what is really going on.* I admit to owning within me elements of all three sisters, but perhaps because of the accident of actually being the middle child, a predominant part of me strove to be Two-Eyes. I determined not only to look, but to see; not only to see, but to own – by putting everything I saw into words. And I would live to tell the tale.

Two-Eyes is abused by her stepmother, and by her sisters, and given only scraps to eat. They assign to her the most menial tasks, and when she has finished, she must take the family goat up on the hillside to graze. One day, half-starved, she begins to weep. Her fairy godmother appears and shows her a magic trick: by twisting the goat's horn and singing a little rhyme, she can command a table to be set for her, spread with silver and crystal and linen napery, not to mention an abundance of delicious food. After she has eaten, all she has to do is twist the other horn, sing another verse, and ask the goat to take it all away.

The story has an epilogue. *When the jealous sisters kill Two-Eyes' little goat, her fairy godmother instructs her to bury the entrails in the garden. Next morning, she wakes to find a beautiful tree is growing outside her window, with leaves of silver, apples of gold. Two-Eyes climbs the tree and is picking the fruit when the sisters see, in the distance, a prince riding towards them. Quickly, they thrust Two-Eyes, and her apronful of golden fruit, under a barrel. The prince is astonished by the tree; he asks to whom the marvel belongs. Each sister claims it to be hers. The prince asks that the true owner climb up and pick a golden apple for him. First one, and then the other sister tries, but the branches seem to have a will of their own: they pull away from the sisters' grasps. The prince, impatient, voices doubt. He implores the true owner to reveal herself. Two-Eyes, from under the barrel, hears him. She rolls out first one, then another golden sphere, towards the prince. He lifts the barrel and finds Two-Eyes, a girl not only beautiful, but with a good head on her shoulders.*

I did not really believe that I was abused and given only scraps (except by the stepsister part of Anne, when she was in her most hierarchical mode). For the most part, I felt my mother's presence as a fairy godmother who provided me with endless abundance – spiritual, emotional, material. Over the years I gradually assimilated that aspect of my mother into my own psyche: fairy godmother became goddess-within, to whom I can turn to be nourished and satisfied.

In my old age, I have come to see the story as a code-story for women. A woman can go up on the hillside (withdraw from the mundane), and set her goat to graze on the hillside, both lofty and verdant. She can spread a feast for herself, which nourishes and satisfies her, intellectually and spiritually. Despite what she may have been told elsewhere, improving herself (and pleasuring herself) will not ruin her chance to enjoy marriage. Indeed, she will bring to her prince a lapful of golden fruit, not to be squandered all at once, but revealed and bestowed at her discretion. *When Two-Eyes moved to the palace, the tree followed her. She looked out of her window next morning and saw the tree was growing there, as beautiful and mysterious as ever.* By allowing herself time for music and art, stories and literature, philosophy and nature, a woman can learn to make a special, private place for herself which she can take anywhere, and to which she can always repair.

We had been in Alameda less than a full year when Father was transferred to San Pedro, the port of Los Angeles, which lies twenty miles from the city center proper. Although the federal government paid for our moves, changing households entails not only a toll on energy but extra expense. My parents were financially strapped, so this time we moved into an old house that had been made into a duplex owned by an elderly widow. As privacy was paramount, a doorway connecting the two apartments gave Mother cause for apprehension. Mrs. Van, our landlady, assured Mother that the offending door would never be unlocked except at Mother's behest. Mother had no way to know that she was about to be struck by disaster. Mrs. Van's accessibility would prove invaluable.

High on a hill, the house on Cabrillo Avenue had a wonderful view, not only of the working harbor just below us, but for miles down the coast, almost to San Diego. To the north lay the main part of Los Angeles, covered with haze. Beyond, so people said, were mountains. We would not be able to see them until after the rainy season began and cleared the air.

Anne and I could easily walk or run down the steep hill to Juan Cabrillo School, and we could walk in the other direction to the Point Fermin branch public library, situated in an old house. My parents still did not own a car and, anyway, Mother did not have a driver's license. (When she drove an ambulance during the war she had not needed one.) We were close to the discount grocery store (the post exchange) at Fort MacArthur, and close to the hospital there. But best of all, we could walk to the bus stop. Mother could take us to Cabrillo Beach several times a week.

Mrs. Haye, another officer's wife, lived in a cottage on the bluff. A profusion of nasturtiums hung from her garden, swaying like curtains over the cliff. A flight of rickety steps led from her house down to the beach. She and Mother would sit on a blanket and watch us play at the edge of the waves, or help us make sandcastles. When the tide was out, Mrs. Haye would take us around the point to clamber on the slippery rocks among the tide pools. She pointed out the creatures that lived there, and told us their names, as we crouched on our seaweedy perches. Mother didn't go with us to the point. She was pregnant again.

Mrs. Haye had no children of her own; naturally, we felt sorry for her. I am now inclined to believe that she *chose* not to have a child. She talked to Anne and me as though we were grown-ups, about what we were reading. She had gone to a college at a place called Bryn Mawr. At first

Mother thought she meant she had gone to school in Wales and was surprised to find there was also a place of that name in Pennsylvania. One day Mrs. Haye brought down to the beach some earrings she had made by prying the metal room numbers (a 3 and an 8) off the door of her college dormitory room. She had worn them to a party the night she graduated. She let me play with the three-dimensional numbers (maybe that's why I remember them so clearly), and I scolded her. Goody two-shoes that I was, I told her that stealing those numbers was not the right thing to do. She laughed! She told me that the night a person graduates from a good college she gets to break a few rules. Then, very seriously, she said that I must read as many books as I possibly could so I could go to Bryn Mawr when I grew up. Going to college, she said, was more important than getting married and having babies. Of course I didn't believe her.

When we were younger Anne and I used to be invited everywhere in tandem. Suddenly Anne was being invited to birthday parties without me. I screamed and yelled and did take on so! Mother made me sit on a small chair until I had calmed down. Then she came and sat at eye level with me. "Joanie," she said, "let Anne have what's hers. By the end of your life you will go to just as many parties as she will go to. *There's more than enough for everybody.*"

The rainy season began and, with it, fog. Day and night, hour after hour, we could hear the foghorn moaning from the lighthouse at the end of the breakwater, that long manmade finger of broken rock that protects the entrance to Los Angeles harbor. The Coast Guard warned ships not to put to sea, but a ship loaded with oranges disregarded the warning. The lubberly captain, fearing for his perishables and impatient after a week's delay, had barely cleared the harbor when he went aground on the toothy rocks jutting from Point Fermin. In happier times, this was the place of sun-warmed tidepools where my sisters and I had searched for sea anemones and pearl-lined abalone shells with Mrs. Haye.

Mother took us out of school early. Ever the quintessential picnicker, she poured hot cocoa into a thermos bottle, dressed us in our foul-weather gear so that we could stand on the headland, in wind and rain, and watch Father direct the rescue. Dimly, through spray and mist, we could see the wounded hull being pounded by the surf. We heard Father's voice give the order, heard the shot that fired a line across the bow. The cocoa lasted only the first hour. We waited, teeth chattering, until the last mariner was brought ashore by breeches buoy. Only then did we go home to supper and early bed.

In the night I woke to hear the silence: the foghorn had stopped. Mother was there to calm my unreasoning fear. When I woke again it was time for breakfast. We could look across the harbor, see Old Saddleback and all the other mountains marching north, sun glancing on snow. Although we were supposed to go to school, Mother said *Don't be silly*: it was such a glorious day that it would be positively wicked not to go for a picnic at Cabrillo. When we arrived, the tide was lapping at the grainy crescent that lies between Point Fermin's left thumb and the breakwater's finger. At fingertip, the lighthouse, its foghorn stilled, looked down on small, neat waves coming in from Catalina Channel. Pelicans flew along the line of surf, parallel to the beach. It was as though yesterday's storm and all the foggy days before had never been. The whole world, sharp-edged, flashed like knives.

The wrecked ship, out of sight and therefore out of mind, must have been lying in the cove just around the point; its tide-filched cargo was floating in the sea. What had happened the day before had no connection in my mind with what was happening now. To me, everything before the foghorn stopped was dream. Now I was awake. The sky was so blue I ached with its arch. The weather was too cold for anyone else but Mother to think *Picnic!* We were the only pebbles on the beach.

Such brilliant hues I had never seen before nor have I since. Fleet, I ran down to the edge of the boundless sea.

> *Grey goose and gander,*
> *Clap your wings together,*
> *Carry the true queen's daughter*
> *Over the One-Strand River.*

There, like a queen's true daughter, I found a golden ball, the perfect sphere of childhood, washed up at my feet, a gift from my mother. And another. And another. Dozens of them. Scores of them. Hundreds and thousands. All day I played with those golden apples from the magic orange tree. I floated golden balls, rolled, squashed, threw, paved a ceremonial way, dug tunnels to thread golden splendor through. Mother had told me the truth. *There is enough for everybody.*

Mr. Lincoln, the principal of Juan Cabrillo School, delighted in my ability
to read and spell. I beat all comers in the second- and third-grade spelling
bees, but I was more into jump rope than I was into spelling. I had my own
jump rope (Mother called it a skipping rope). I skipped to school and home
from school, around the house and through the house. I could stay in one
spot and jump one hundred times, red hot. I had finally been allowed to
enter into the long-rope game, the rope held at either end by two privileged
beings so high on the schoolyard pecking order that they ordained who
could play and who could not. I was learning to run in, jump up and over,
say a rhyme, do a trick, run out again without missing a beat.

Already I had my eye on the next hurdle, double-dip, which meant two
long ropes were swung in opposing directions. The only shadow on my
possibilities was that I talked funny. It was not just my accent (everyone
in the school had a different accent, including Mr. Lincoln) but that I used
so *many* words. Even so, although I was an unlikely candidate, I sensed
that I might still hope for a position in the inner circle, if I learned to shut
up, if Father did not get transferred first, if . . . I was happy at home, a
success in the classroom and, for the first time ever, about to be a power
on the playground.

Then everything changed.

One day Mother was not home when we came in from school. Mrs. Van,
from next door, was babysitting, but she was vague about Mother's whereabouts or return. Mother had taken Joyce to the beach while we were in
school, and Mrs. Haye had brought Joyce home. Neither Mother nor Father
would be home for supper. Bedtime came. Mrs. Van superintended us
through toothpaste and pajamas. We woke in the morning to find her
making breakfast in the kitchen. Mother was still not there – not in the
kitchen, not in her bedroom, not in the bathroom. Not anywhere. Mother,
said Mrs. Van, was in the hospital, and Father was with her. We went off to
school. I cannot say that I was full of foreboding. I involved myself in
schoolwork and play, but when I came home in the afternoon and found
that Mother had not returned, and would not return for any predictable
time, something shifted. My world went lopsided. Father appeared, but he
did not look like Father. He had not shaved, his clothes were disheveled,
he ate his dinner ravenously, shovelling in the food, chewing with his mouth
open. *Father, what big teeth you have!* He seemed angry. Mother, he said,

was very, very sick. She sent her love to us but she was too sick for us to go see her. He must get back to the hospital.

I went into the bathroom and sat on the toilet, watching him as he tried to shave. His hand shook. Blood ran down his cheek from where he had cut himself. If he hadn't been Father, and if he hadn't looked so fierce, I would have thought he was going to cry. When he was about to leave, Anne threw herself at him, clinging to him, screaming hysterically that she wanted to see Mother. Father disentangled himself as best he could, savagely prying her fingers off him one by one. He handed her over to Mrs. Van while he made his escape. Mrs. Van tried to comfort her, but Anne kicked at Mrs. Van's ankles and screamed all the more. I was both appalled by Anne and filled with admiration for her.

What had happened? For years, Mother erected a sort of force field around her that forbade us to ask. I was over forty years old before I forced my way into the forbidden garden. Even then the scene was veiled, confused, a tangle of weeds and vines. I finally established that Mother, five and half months pregnant, had taken Joyce to Cabrillo Beach. She was lying on her back on a blanket, talking to Mrs. Haye, when . . . *the first version was a lie. Something about some boys playing ball, stumbling over her.* . . . I had to come back again several years later, hammer at the gate, demand to know more. This time I was told that Mother had been watching Joyce play by the water's edge. Joyce suddenly ran toward her. Mother saw her coming but did not seek to protect herself. Joyce gave an exuberant leap and came down heavily on Mother's stomach, crushing everything inside. *I must swear never to tell Joyce what she had done to Mother!*

After Mrs. Haye rushed Mother to the hospital, she delivered Joyce to our doorstep as if she were a package. Anne and I did not ask questions about what had happened at the beach; we were utterly oblivious to our younger sister, who seemed all right. At the fatal moment, Joyce (age two and a half) *must* have been witness to, and cognizant of, the blood and agony she had somehow caused, and stored the memory in her psyche. For Anne and me, the perfect sphere of childhood was threatened, but it did not shatter. Mother did not die, although she was never the same again. In the days to come Anne and I acted out our fear and anger, but I can't remember any images of Joyce. I don't know if she even cried. I suspect that she became Mrs. Van's good little girl. *No trouble at all!* Joyce's perfect sphere had suffered a much more severe fracture. From that day onwards (although I was unaware), Joyce's mother was not my mother. Joyce had a different mother.

Obstetrical surgery was primitive in 1929, and San Pedro Hospital was not first rate. Mother's general practitioner performed a clumsy hysterectomy with the aid of several colleagues. Mother was not expected to live. Father did not tell us so directly, but he took us down to the hospital and held us up to a window. He told us to look and to look hard, so we would remember. Remember what? Mostly all I could see was a heap of bedclothes. The ugly person lying there was not my mother! I figured that Father was being stupid. He had taken us to the wrong window, maybe the wrong hospital. Far from me to be a tattle-tale, but when Mother came home, I would tell her how stupid Father had been.

Father slept at the hospital, although to do so was strictly against the rules. A sun porch near Mother's room had a large glider swing with elaborate awnings and canvas curtains that could be pulled down for concealment. Father tried catching naps on the swing, but at night the doctors and the nurses used it for amorous trysts. Father stowed blankets partly under and behind the swing and slept there as best he could, in short snatches, too weary to be bothered by thumps and pants issuing from just inches away. Passion at its height offered a good moment for him to slip out and steal into Mother's room. He stood over Mother's bed, talking and calling to her, then slipped away again when he heard someone coming. He was the Phantom of the Hospital.

The doctors have officially declared that Mother is dead. Now Father is standing over her, calling and calling. Mother is dreaming and dreaming. She dreams that she is climbing a ladder up to the sky. She dreams she can see her father and her brother Hubert. Her father and her brother are smiling and beckoning to her to ascend, but Frank's voice keeps calling her, distracting her. She looks down. *She can see her husband, and she can see Anne and me, lifting up our arms, imploring her not to go any further. Joyce,* "too young to be concerned," *is off to one side,* "playing with pebbles," *her back toward Mother. Mother turns and looks upwards again, climbs a few more rungs. She is full of joy and yearning as she gets closer to Heaven, but Frank's voice will not desist. He is saying her name over and over and over, pleading with her, ordering her not to leave him. She feels angry at him. Because of Frank's interference her father begins to recede.*

He motions to her that she must go back, return to earth, to the world below.
She hesitates, reluctantly takes a step downwards. When she looks up
again, Heaven's attic door is shut.

When Mother came home from the hospital she was weak and weepy.
Mornings were the worst time. The doctor decreed that she must have
breakfast in bed every morning. If Father was home, he boiled two eggs to
perfection and took them into the bedroom on a tray. I endowed that tray
with magic power, equated it with Two-Eyes's meal, spread on the hillside.
Always, the eggs were served the same way, in silver egg-cups from Saint
Lawrence, scooped out with tiny silver spoons. (They had to be polished
often.) Always, toast, butter, and marmalade, the toast in a silver toast-rack.
Always, the morning newspaper, two cups of coffee each and, until they
were in their seventies, two cigarettes. If Father was away, Mother made
breakfast for herself and retreated immediately into her room. We children
were not allowed to enter, except for a final goodbye kiss.

Since we were not allowed to ask for help to find things in the morning,
Mother helped us lay out our clothes the night before. Books and homework had to be firmly anchored, so there would be no panic. Mother could
not abide panic! It was hard to know ahead of time what would offend her,
what would send her into a hormonal rage. She and Father had terrible
arguments, which would end in shrillness and sobs. I remember being
frightened of her; at the same time I turned to her for solace.

When we were grown up Anne would tell me that Mother had asked
Father and the doctors not to let her know whether her unborn child was a
girl or a boy. Anne said that Mother mourned for the boy she had hoped to
have, to replace those brothers who went away to war. That was Anne's
truth, as valid as mine, though I, as usual, see the story differently. Mother's
grief for a son, I think, was a displacement. What she grieved for was her
lost sexuality and the implied loss of her husband. Our parents had been
married for ten years; they would be married for a total of sixty-three. I
don't mean that they never had sex again, but what had happened to my
mother's body must have made a huge difference to her sex life. Father was
an attractive, sensual, lusty man. Mother must have remembered, with trepidation, the plight of her own mother, ill with cancer of the uterus, groggy
with opium and alcohol, kept in a darkened room while Grandfather found
someone else to love, to make love to.

I am convinced that on some level Mother bore a deep resentment toward Joyce, all the more harmful because she never admitted it, not even to herself. In her dream, Joyce is described as "too young to be concerned" (Mother's words). In the dream, Joyce is seen *with her back turned toward Mother*. My hunch is that it was Mother who turned her back. I suspect that, even before she returned from the hospital, Mother determined to bear no resentment against the child who had almost killed her. A cardinal tenet, held by my mother, was that a child cannot be evil. Joyce was innocent by virtue of *being*. Mother would delight in her youngest child, convince herself that she loved her unconditionally, as much as she loved her other two daughters. She must have struggled hard to throttle the monster of resentment; she must have believed that she had done so. Mother had barely heard of Freud; the word Jung rang no bell. She knew nothing about the unconscious. How was she to know that another monster still lived? *Beowulf killed Grendel, but Grendel's dam still lurked, in deeper waters.*

In the years to come I lived three thousand miles away from Joyce and from my parents, so I am not sure when Joyce began to exhibit her paranoia toward Mother, when she did, in fact, *turn her back on her*. I think it was after she was divorced from her first husband, when she was in her late thirties or early forties. Father was allowed to visit Joyce at her apartment, but if Mother drove up to Pasadena with him she had to sit outside in the car. She was forbidden to enter Joyce's house. If there was a family gathering in San Pedro, Joyce would come for one hour, then leave. She never again would spend the night under her parents' roof. Piteously, Mother asked me, "What did I do wrong? How have I offended her? Just tell me, and I will apologize, try to make it right."

Joyce was just as puzzled. She told me that she believed that Mother was the only person she had ever known who was truly good. "She is the best person I know, the fairest of the fair. But when I am in the same room with her I think I am going to pass out. I feel I am in a room with a black curtain in front of me. I find an opening, and go through, but there is another curtain beyond. I keep going and going, through smothering, clinging blackness, and just when I think that maybe I can break out, I run up against a steel wall, black and shiny. No way to see over it, or get around it. It stretches up and out, forever."

I suggested that Joyce see a psychiatrist. She said she had. Then he became her lover. And her drug pusher. Besides using drugs, Joyce would punish herself with bad marriages, psychotic lovers, risky endeavors. Yet she was a loving mother, and a good one. Despite her complicated life, she was a first-rate teacher and, at the age of sixty, she became a lawyer. During her last marriage she cut herself off (or was cut off) from friends and family. She would die a lonely, painful death.

In one of my last visits with Joyce, I broke the taboo imposed by Mother. I told Joyce all I knew about what had happened at Cabrillo Beach so long ago, and about Mother's dream. She was furious at me (the message bearer) for telling her, and furious at me for not telling her years before. Actually, I had not been able to put the story together, as a whole, until quite recently.

In a Haitian folk tale, "The Magic Orange Tree," a little girl's mother dies. When her father marries again, the stereotypical stepmother is mean and cruel. The girl often goes hungry, so she steals some oranges that belong to her stepmother. When an orange pip falls from her lap, she plants it on her mother's grave. A green leaf sprouts. She kneels down and sings, to a haunting tune:

Orange tree,
Grow and grow and grow,
Orange tree, orange tree.
Grow and grow and grow,
Orange tree.
Stepmother is not real mother,
Orange tree.

Variations of the song are sung over and over. The line that never varies is *Stepmother is not real mother*. The substitute who replaced Joyce's real mother was not the stereotypical stepmother, mean and cruel, but something more insidious: a good woman trying to do the undoable, forgive the unforgivable.

After I told Joyce what I knew, after she had yelled and cried and stormed at me, we sat in silence while she lit a cigarette, inhaled deeply, blew a smoke ring. *I have always believed that I am evil*, she said. She broke my heart. Years later, I am coming to understand that her story is part of my story. She acted out my shadow. I am the good sister, and I am the bad.

CHAPTER 5

In the Belly of the Beast

SOON AFTER MOTHER MOVED to America and married Father, her stepmother, Kate, widowed in 1919, had moved to Cleveland with her two children, Rex and Joyce. Why Cleveland? I don't know. Despite sharing a continent, Mother had never managed the time or money to visit her relatives, nor had they journeyed to the West Coast to see her. Rex eventually worked in the advertising department of the *Cleveland Plain Dealer*, and Joyce became a librarian. Kate kept house for them in a big sunny apartment in Quaker Heights. In 1931 Father was transferred to New York, and we seized the opportunity for a visit. I don't remember Kate very well but I remember the *feeling* she engendered when, at last, we met her. She surrounded Mother with tenderness. I had never known Mother to be so cherished before. For the first time in a long time I felt my anxiety begin to seep away. Someone else was looking after Mother. I didn't have to feel guilty for not being able to cope.

Aunt Joyce was the most beautiful creature I had ever laid eyes on, tall and willowy with a strawberries-and-cream complexion and wavy chestnut hair. She had a beau, a young doctor, to whom she would be engaged for seven years before they married. ("Ralph always was so impetuous!" she was wont to say.) As for my sisters and I, all our feminine passion was focused on the dress that Joyce would wear to an upcoming ball. It was rose velvet, with an undefined waist, and barely reached her knees. Cut jaggedly at the hem like a petal or a leaf, it reminded me of a dress a fairy might wear. On the night of the ball she pinned a velvet rose to where her waist was supposed to be. I fell utterly in love with Joyce, with the whole idea of romance and glamor, with beautiful, sensuous clothes, with being a *girl*.

We stayed with these strangely familiar, yet unfamiliar, family members for six weeks. For the first time we heard voices that sounded like Mother's voice, heard turns of phrase, saw gestures and expressions mirrored not only by our mother but by ourselves. Uncle Rex, over six feet tall and very British, made us laugh and laugh. Better still, he made mother laugh in a way we had not heard for a long time. So this is how our other uncles, lost in No Man's Land, might have been!

After only a few days, Father went on ahead of us to join his ship, stationed at Stapleton, Staten Island. He chose a house for us in the village of New Dorp. True to his word, when we walked through the door we found that he had unpacked and put everything in its place. He had also bought new-to-us secondhand furniture. One of the upholstered chairs was so beautiful that Mother marveled. How could anyone bear to give up that chair at any price, much less a price affordable to us? Her guess (which became a story in itself) was that we had benefited from a family dispossessed by the Depression who had to sell their household goods out of desperation. Every time I curled up in the chair I thought of the lady who had once owned it.

In November 1932, Franklin Delano Roosevelt was elected president of the United States, but he would not be inaugurated until the following March. For four months after the election, the nation teetered on the edge of anarchy. To me, age nine, it felt as though America had been swallowed up by something mysterious and enormous, as had Jonah by his whale; we were waiting for the leviathan to regurgitate us.

Winter started early in 1932. After Thanksgiving, temperatures dropped to record lows. Day after day went by, each colder and drearier than the last. People no one had seen before appeared at the end of our street; they built fires in rusty oil drums. We called them the Potato People, partly because they were dressed in potato sacks and partly because Mother and other people on the block gave them potatoes to roast. Mother, ever the good hostess, also supplied them with salt and pepper and a pound of butter.

Dairy products were so cheap that the farmers declared it was not worth their while to deliver them to wholesalers. Farmers spilled milk on the roads of upstate New York, although people were starving to death in the city. Cheap though milk was, many people could not afford to buy it. Mother discovered from the milkman that some neighbors of ours (we played with the children) had canceled their order. We were not rich, but Father had a steady job. Although I had no inkling of it at the time, she paid our milkman to deliver to both households.

Mother was well pleased by the house. The only drawback was that the local school had been closed because of the Depression. We had to take the schoolbus over to Public School 41, in Grant City, two miles away. Joyce was in kindergarten, I was in fourth grade, Anne in sixth. Every morning we walked five blocks to a corner where the schoolbus was supposed to pick us up. After Christmas, the cold became almost unbearable. Not even snowsuits were on the market yet. Nylon had not been invented, zippers were still a wonder. We were muffled up to our noses in scarves and down to our eyes with hats. We wore mittens tied to our clumsy woolen coat sleeves, and we wore long stockings held up with little clips called "hose supporters." Even when they were not falling down, our stockings left gaps of exposed skin at the tops of our legs, too close for comfort to *down there*. The schoolbus was usually late; sometimes it didn't come at all. The Board of Education of New York City did not have the money to fix its buses or to buy tires; sometimes there was not enough money for gasoline. When the drivers were not paid they quit. Almost every week there was a new, disgruntled driver.

Mother was still a semi-invalid from her botched operation. She still did not have a driver's license and, when Joyce suffered a series of colds and earaches, she was stuck at home. Once we went out the door to school, it was difficult for her to check on us. Father was out at sea ten days out of fifteen, looking for rum-runners. We knew that he was worried about his chances of promotion, we knew that Mother was far from well. Our parents had enough troubles! Perhaps we wished to spare them any worry about the schoolbus situation. Perhaps we didn't tell them because our life on the schoolbus corner took on its own dreamlike dynamic.

The corner was near a vacant lot distinguished by a mound of dirt and old rubble which we called "the mountain." The bigger boys ran up the incline and slid down on an ice ramp that they had made. At first, only the big boys could play, then they allowed the girls and little kids to join in. Eventually they organized us all into ragged teams. One half of us would occupy the mountain and the other half would rush the fortress. It was a way of keeping warm and of whiling away the minutes and hours of waiting. There was a shallow pit beside the mountain, presumably where earth had been dug for the foundations of a house that never got built. Sometimes we huddled there to get out of the wind.

As weeks went by, the band of children grew smaller. Those of us who were left helped build a snow fort. Anne and one of the older boys urged us on. Every day we fashioned snow bricks with which to extend the mountain and encircle the pit. Now when we stood in the hollow the walls were over our heads. Any snow that melted froze again at night so that the walls, thus caulked and sheathed, became impervious. Several days, when the schoolbus never came, we kept warm by alternately hustling on the walls and huddling inside our ice castle. We ate our brown-bag lunches and went home in the afternoon. If we had to pee, we used the bushes. Waiting to go to school began to be our real life's work; it had more social substance than being in school.

One morning we arrived to find that the Potato People had moved in. As silent as ghosts, cloaked in grey shrouds, they lay in a heap in a corner of the castle. I was indignant. Grown-ups were not supposed to take over a children's game! But the Potato People did not care. They hardly moved. They didn't seem to have the strength to lift their heads. They didn't even talk to each other. They just lay there like sacks of potatoes.

Anne decided that we should walk the two miles to school. We set off in a straggling band. Some of the children, much to Anne's chagrin, deserted on the way. The rest of us, led by our Napoleon, marched on and on over the frozen steppes that lay between New Dorp and Grant City. What once had been farmland had been sold to developers who had planned to build houses, but had lost their money in the financial crash of 1929. A few houses and acres of vacant lots lay between the schoolbus corner and school.

When we arrived, Miss Colletti told us latecomers to take off our shoes and to drape our stockings along the radiators. She went out into the hall to consult with other teachers, then she went to the big cupboard at the back of the room and took out all the leftover colored kraft paper. She said we were going to study Indians. I was shocked. I knew that we were supposed to talk about Indians only at Thanksgiving time. Kraft paper was for Hallowe'en and Thanksgiving and Christmas (now past). The red paper had gone at Christmas, the rest was being hoarded for Valentine's Day. Otherwise, only khaki, puce, beige, tan, and gray were left, because nobody liked those colors. Miss Colletti had a glitter in her eye, an air of determination that I had never seen before.

Miss Colletti said she would help each of us make a pair of moccasins. Meanwhile, the rest of us could work on our spelling and arithmetic while we awaited our turns. She rationed out half-sheets of newsprint, so coarse yet so flimsy that we could see bits of straw pressed into the fabric. Every day all of our work had to be done on one piece of paper. If I made a mistake in arithmetic (which happened frequently), I might rub a hole through the paper with my eraser and, if the hole grew (which also happened frequently), there would not be enough surface left for my spelling and my penmanship. I lived in an agony of apprehension. I loved Miss Colletti with all my heart, and I did not want her to be cross with me.

Meanwhile Miss Colletti called first one child and then another up to her desk. While the pupil stood on a sheet of kraft paper, she drew a line around each foot. She folded and cut and pasted, then she gave the child a pair of scissors and some crayons so he or she could cut a fringe and color an Indian bead design on the completed moccasins. She even used up the red paper! Hours went by, and still my name was not called. I began to feel sad and hot. What had I done wrong? A tear trickled down my cheek and splashed on the paper; the paper was melting because of my tears and more tears were coming because the paper was melting.

Then Miss Colletti said it was time for us to get ready to go home. We would be allowed to leave the school early, but we would not have to walk. The one schoolbus that was working was waiting for us at the door. We were to wear our moccasins inside our shoes. A sob escaped me. Miss Colletti came over to see what was the matter. I was beyond speech, so she took me out into the hall. My moccasins! She had not made me any moccasins! She knelt down and put her arms around me. "I never thought," she said. "There wasn't enough paper to go around, and you were the only child who had a pair of decent shoes without holes in them. I had to think of something, I had to think of a way that would not embarrass the other children. Some of them don't even have proper socks or stockings, just rags. They had to walk all that way, almost on their bare feet. It's a wonder that none of them was frostbitten."

The last week in January, when Father came home from sea, he took a few days leave. One late morning, at almost noon, he happened to drive by the schoolbus corner and saw Anne and me playing with a gang of children at a place that was almost two miles away from P.S. 41, where we were supposed to be. Intermingled with us were the ghostlike Potato People. He brought the car to a screeching halt and ordered us to get in.

The clincher, for Mother, was when the school authorities sought to make it plain that she was an ignorant immigrant whose children must be protected from her influence. Many of the children we played with had parents who had immigrated from Europe to Brooklyn, from Brooklyn to Staten Island, a stone's throw away. The problem lay in the way we talked. Anne and I were fascinated at recess to hear the familiar jump-rope song sung out as "Keep the kettle *berling*, one, two, three." The word "girl" was pronounced "goil." But Mother was not at all fascinated when Anne, her eldest and most British child, was reported to have a language problem. Anne was placed in a corrective class, along with children who could barely speak English. "I am *not* an immigrant," said Mother.

Oh, but she was! The pain of it, for me, was that she kept on being unashamedly *Mother*, embarrassing me at every step of the way. She spoke differently, she dressed differently, and she dressed her children differently. And, since she had been brought up by governesses, she didn't have a clue about American public schools. I switched my allegiance from Mother to the new order. Anne, however, continued to trill the words of "God Save the King" when the rest of the assembly was singing "My Country, 'Tis of Thee," to the same tune.

Father, if he had cared to, could have made the argument that he was more of a New Yorker than anyone. His Dutch ancestors had come to New Amsterdam in 1630, and had eventually intermarried with the British. Obadiah Higbee had served with General George Washington.

Father argued that if we persisted in singing a travesty of the British national anthem we might as well not have fought the American Revolution. A friend of his, a little old lady whose social connection to us is lost, came several times to tea. There was no Social Security in those days. Father was trying to help Miss Key get a pension on the grounds that she was the only living direct descendant of Francis Scott Key, a man who had written a song impossible to sing. For several years Father had enlisted several congressmen and the Sons of the American Revolution in his cause to make "The Star-Spangled Banner" the official anthem and, at the same time, rescue Miss Key from humiliation and starvation. In the early 1930s the choice for the American national anthem was still up for grabs. Besides the partisans for "My Country, 'Tis of Thee" and "The Star-Spangled Banner," there were those who advocated "America the Beautiful" (which I still prefer). Family opinion was polarized: Anne and Mother wanted the comfort of the British tune, albeit disguised with the wrong words; I threw in my bid with Father.

When Mother's brother Roger arrived from England to look for a job in America, we children were enchanted. He was six feet four inches tall and had a charming British goofiness about him, a quality we adored, but which seemed rather off-putting to employers. Uncle Roger had attended school at Marlborough, where he learned nothing immediately useful. During the war he had flown a plane in the RAF, where he learned much more of the same thing. At least he had survived.

Uncle Roger had a friend, Marmaduke Jennings. I think they may have been lovers. They had gone to school together and had been in the RAF together. The difference was that Marmaduke was still rich. He had inherited properties not only in London but scattered about the Empire. The English Antique Shop on Madison Avenue was counted as one of them. After a while, Uncle Roger ceased his fruitless round of interviews and went over to Manhattan on the ferry every day, ostensibly to help his friend run a business that was bound, by its very nature, to lose money during the Great Depression. One thing that Roger and Marmaduke shared in common was a hatred of things Victorian. Marmaduke wanted to get rid of the shop on Madison Avenue but, if he closed it, not only Roger but several elderly people would be out of a job. Occasionally he would, in a bemused state, pick up an object, gaze at it, and say: "Hideous, isn't it?" Then, "Oh, dear!" as he let it fall from his nerveless hand.

Mother, for the first time in her married life, had a cleaning woman who came to the house once a week. Father was adamant that she not stay home, but take the ferry to Manhattan to have a day to herself. In late afternoon she would find her way to the antique shop and have tea with Roger and Marmaduke. They liked to shock and amuse her by playing diablo across the length of the display room, where table after table stood stacked with antique china. The trick is to set a sort of top to whirling on a string and then, suddenly, to hurl the top so it can be caught by the opposing player on *his* string and set to whirling again. It is quite a difficult feat, the very devil to play. People strolling along Madison Avenue stopped and gathered in a little crowd on the sidewalk outside the shop window, mesmerized by the sight of two six-foot-tall Englishmen dashing about, leaping and reaching, in a shop full of china, each doing his best to keep the volley going. No matter which of the two won, the results were shattering.

Father had always intended to send Mother, and her three little girls, home to England, on a visit. Now the time had come. Since Mother had sailed to America as a first-class passenger on a Cunard liner, she wanted to return to England on a British ship. She thought that, as the daughter of the owner of the Cardiff Steamship Line, and goddaughter of William Grace of the Grace Steamship Company, she would be treated with more dignity, even though she and her children traveled in third class. Father's fealty was pledged to American shipping. A compromise was finally reached: we would return from England on the *Majestic*, British White Star Line, but we would go to England on the *Leviathan*, United States Line.

Built and registered as the *Vaterland* in 1913, the *Leviathan* had originally sailed under the German flag. She was intentionally made to be bigger than any of the British liners and as luxurious as any of those she was meant to rival. In April 1917 the *Leviathan* had been moored at a dock in New York harbor. The crew, knowing that the U.S. was about to enter the war, sabotaged their own engines. The United States seized the vessel, replaced the engines, renamed the ship, and used her to carry American troops. After the war, the United States retained possession and refitted the hull with an eye to capturing the trans-Atlantic luxury trade for itself. But the *Leviathan* was haunted by its *Vaterland* past. More devastating, because of Prohibition, she was a dry ship. Although heavily subsidized, the *Leviathan* ran at huge loss. Fares were the lowest on the Atlantic run. Our sailing date was set for March 8, partly because that was the day before Mother's birthday, but also because March was the most unpopular month in which to cross the Atlantic. Fares would be at their lowest then.

Ever since Father had discovered us waiting at the bus stop, Mother and Father had decided to keep us home from school. When the truant officer knocked on our door, Mother invited him in. Patiently, she explained to him the laws of international quarantine. If any of her three children caught one of the common childhood diseases, now rampant, we would not be allowed into England. Moreover, the dreaded yellow quarantine flag would fly from the mast of our ship, and no one else, crew or passengers, would be allowed to go ashore. The ship would be held at anchor for a month in Southampton Water. In light of these circumstances, she would tutor us at home. Our being six weeks out of school would surely make small difference to the New York Board of Education.

Ah, but it would, the truant officer explained. If P.S. 41 did not keep its enrollment to a certain level it, too, would be shut down and all the teachers would lose their jobs. Some parents were not sending their children to school because the winter was particularly severe, and many of the children did not have proper clothes to wear. Mother pointed out that she was well aware that not only New York City but the whole country teetered on the brink of disaster. Her children were left for hours, unsupervised, on a corner frequented by men and women who, although to be pitied, were of unknown potential. This was legitimate cause for concern. The Lindbergh baby had been kidnaped the previous March, his battered body recovered in May. For months the papers had been full of the search for the kidnapper. She would, under the circumstances, be irresponsible to send us to school. All this was conveyed, with an air of sweet reasonableness, over tea and caraway cake, served with no hint of contrition, on her best pink luster. The law, no match for Mother, retreated in confusion.

Father received orders to report to Norfolk, Virginia. From there, come summer, he would be sent on International Ice Patrol – all the more reason for us to seize this chance to travel to England. Meanwhile, Mother was faced with the task of packing for England and packing for Norfolk. Most of our belongings would be stored in crates and sent to a warehouse, but items constantly had to be rescued to be put in our trunks and suitcases. Not only was our household swept into a whirl of change, but so was the nation. A few days before we boarded the *Leviathan*, Franklin D. Roosevelt was inaugurated as president of the United States. During his first forty-eight hours in office he shut the banks and took the country off the gold standard. Most of the rich people who had planned to embark on the *Leviathan* canceled their passage but, as Mother cheerfully explained to us, we were the sort of family that had so little money we had drawn it all out of the bank anyway, in order to make the trip.

Our exact social and economic status was always a matter of puzzlement to my sisters and me. We were not poor, we were certainly not rich, but we did things and knew how to do things that rich people do. One characteristic of the rich is that they are outlandish. Mother was outlandish: she dressed Joyce and me in overalls. In 1932 slacks and shorts did not exist for little girls. We wore short, short skirts and voluminous bloomers of pink, green, or blue flannel, which were not supposed to show but did. Mother sighed for the long skirts and pinafores of her own country childhood. She was convinced that they had enabled little girls born in the 1890s to be more active than little girls born in the 1920s. Unlike other mothers in our neighborhood, she never once told me that I should not climb trees, not swing on a trapeze, not lie sprawled across an armchair as I read a book.

One August day when Herbert Hoover was still president, a woman had knocked on our door to ask if Mother would buy fresh vegetables. She was accompanied by several shy, barefoot children of both sexes who were wearing blue-denim bib overalls and not much else. Mother bought corn and carrots, then asked where she could purchase such sensible clothing for her own three daughters. She had admired overalls on other children but, when she looked for them in the girls' department at Macy's, she had not been able to find them. The vegetable seller must have given her the answer, and Joyce and I took to overalls right away. Anne refused to wear them.

Much to Mother's annoyance, we were not allowed to wear overalls to school. As soon as we came home, however, we popped them over our short gingham school dresses, the kind with puffed sleeves and lace-edged collars. Denim overalls were like pinafores, only better, Mother said. They kept our dresses clean an extra day, they cut down on washing and ironing, and they enabled us to live an untrammeled healthy life, free of drafts *down there*. She could not understand why the school authorities were so much against them, even in the winter months. She perceived them to be a kind of American folk costume, invested with all that was good about America – sensible, practical. Blue-denim overalls, Mother explained to all who would listen, were *classless*. Or should be.

Dimly I perceived that, because our mother had once been very rich, she had license to dress us as though we were very poor, and we were supposed to feel proud about that, even though other children and even grown-ups made embarrassing remarks. Occasionally we met someone who complimented Mother for dressing us with such élan. Those people always turned out to be very rich indeed. Alas! The nature of the very rich is to be few and far between.

But overalls were a blessing aboard ship. During our March crossing, the seas were enormous and the winds almost scooped us off our feet. There were still stiff breezes, even when the *Leviathan* entered the Gulf Stream and the temperature turned springlike. We were permitted to run around the decks, to talk to the other passengers and to the sailors, as long as we did not leave third class. Because of all the cancellations, we were almost the only children aboard. We were obviously having such a good time that, every day, a couple of woeful children from first class crawled under a canvas barrier and came to play with us.

Among the passengers were half a dozen Russian Orthodox priests, wearing black cassocks, black hats, and full black beards, who paraded along the deck like a phalanx of Rasputins. One of them picked Joyce up, despite her kicks and screams, and planted a juicy kiss full on her mouth. Mother sprang at the man and beat him on the breast, yelling for help, pulling his beard until he let Joyce go. He was most offended, having seen himself (presumably) as Jesus Christ suffering the little children. *Never, ever*, Mother told him fiercely, pick up a child and kiss her against her will. *That is a wicked thing to do.* She was not so worried about germs as she was about her child's loss of sovereignty.

The first two days at sea I had been violently seasick, but the third morning I rose from the dead and could hardly wait for meals. The seas were so rough that wooden collars had to be fastened around the tables to keep plates and cutlery from escaping to the floor. We children thought the sight of a soup plate sliding down a tilted linen incline was absolutely hilarious, especially if it hit the wooden rim and bounced off in another direction. Mother had to caution us to lower our voices, but the sight of the stewards, keeping their faces Buster Keaton straight, staggering in with plates and tureens, would set us off again.

In late morning, a pale, salty bouillon, afloat with bits of stringy celery, was served to the rug-covered adults lying recumbent in oak folding chairs. The chairs were placed in rows along the sheltered part of the deck. They reminded me of giant water stalkers. Their balance was nicely calculated for a lady to lower herself into the seat between the armrests and then swing her legs onto the elongated leg rest. They were not made for children. If I tried to climb over a wooden arm, my weight tipped the whole chair towards me. When I tried to crawl up the length of the leg rest, polished brass hinges and panels of wooden slats took umbrage. Everything collapsed. Yet I knew those chairs were extremely strong and, because of their slats, buoyant. I figured that they would stay afloat better than a lifeboat.

Our family saga was full of tales of shipwreck. Now, because of what had happened to the *Titanic* in 1912, Father was on International Ice Patrol. His job was to watch for icebergs as they were being calved from glaciers in the Arctic. The Coast Guard would then track and report their whereabouts as they drifted south into the Atlantic shipping lanes, eventually to melt in the currents near the Gulf Stream. I might appear to be just a carefree, ordinary child, but in my mind I knew I was no ordinary lubber. I was constantly planning what to do when the *Leviathan* hit an iceberg. If the collision came during the night, I would waken Joyce, who shared my cabin, and instruct her to take up her bed (well, just her sheets) and follow me to the deck. Clad in bathrobe and slippers we would help each other corral half a dozen deck chairs, tear the bedsheets into strips, tie three chairs together with clove hitches, then tie three more. As the ship went down, each chair would spread out its wooden flaps and tentacles and float lightly as a water bug on the surface of the Gulf Stream. Thus buoyed, they would no longer resist our crawling across them. Each of us could lash herself into a center seat with her bathrobe sash. Even though the waves washed through the slats, we would lean back and wait to be rescued by Father and the United States Coast Guard. I figured that Mother, being who she was, would know how to look after herself. Anne, who enjoyed being brave, could go down with the ship.

As a champion of United States shipping, Father was determined to show Mother that she could enjoy herself as much on an American liner as on a British one. He also may have felt that his being on the lowest rung of the U.S. Coast Guard ladder made it more incumbent on him to show Mother how special she was to him, how lucky he was to have her. Before he paid our fares, he had visited the president of the United States Line in his New York office and told him that, in order to maintain American honor, he, personally, must make arrangements to prove to Mother that she was treated better on an American ship than on a British one.

The president of the United States Line made a noble effort to meet the challenge flung down by Father. The captain of the *Leviathan* was informed

of his responsibilities. On several occasions Mother was invited to dine at
the captain's table. Every day, fruit and flowers were delivered to our cabin,
and the captain came in person to make a formal call. Solicitously he
inquired after our health. Toward the end of the trip, when Joyce complained of a sore throat and swelling behind her ears, Mother asked the
captain if she could speak to the ship's doctor.

When the doctor came, Mother explained to him that all three of her
children had been exposed to various epidemics at school. She begged him
to please tell her, confidentially of course, whether Joyce had the mumps.
If so, she would keep her in isolation and not tell anyone. When the doctor
made another call he looked grave and stern. He told Mother *not to be an
alarmist*. He and the captain together had reached a joint medical opinion:
Joyce absolutely did *not* have the mumps. The next day the swelling had
gone down and Mother, more than willing to believe the doctor and not
wishing to be "an alarmist," let Joyce leave the confines of our airless cabin
and run about the deck among passengers and crew. The captain did not
call on us again.

Only after we arrived in Britain would Joyce's mumps blossom fully.
There is no way to know how many other passengers succumbed. I would
soon have swellings, too. So, eventually, would our English cousins. So
would Boniface, Marmaduke Jenning's butler. We can only conjecture
about the Russian priest.

Before we even left New Dorp, Father had had a jigsaw puzzle made for
us from a large publicity poster he had first seen hanging in the offices of
the United States Line. It showed a cross-cut view of the interior of the
Leviathan. Soon we knew the entire labyrinth from stem to stern, from
bridge to engine room. Father also made arrangements for the chief engi-
neer to take us on a tour of the actual engine room while the ship was in full
operation at sea. Born into a generation which unquestioningly celebrated
the idea of progress, Father wanted to give us, his progeny, an opportunity
to appreciate a triumph of the Industrial Age, a four-screw steam turbine at
work in the bowels of a great ship. We would not be denied the treat just
because we were girls.

For years afterwards I dreamed of that yawning cavern and its fearsome
ladders with widely spaced steps. Each space was wide enough for me to
fall through to my death. The ladders zigzagged down and down toward a
red glow five storeys below. I was terrified. As we descended, the vibration

and noise of the ship, plus my pride and good manners, made protestation impossible. There was to be no turning back. After what seemed like hours of sweaty hands clinging to slippery steel rails, we inched down to the floor of the engine room, the belly of the great leviathan.

I saw myself reflected in convex curves of polished steel, disturbing and disorienting as a mile of fun-house mirrors. There were valves and gauges and red-painted handles with skulls and fearsome warnings printed above them. Everything was shipshape and polished, yet filmed in oil. Giant horizontal shafts thrust and sucked in the background. I remember the heat, the sweetish smell of engine oil which almost made me sick, and the sweat and oil on the muscled arms of the men. They turned their blackened faces towards us in wonder and hostility as we, three prim little girls (two in overalls), trespassed into their Promethean realm. I was aware that I was supposed to feel inordinately privileged just to be there. I was aware that I had wet my pants.

The *Leviathan* had been provisioned for more than a thousand passengers, but because of Roosevelt's draconian economic measures, only 220 actually came aboard. There must have been a premonition that the ship would return empty. Given the primitive state of refrigeration, even in 1933, an enormous surplus of food would rot in the hold unless it was consumed on the voyage. A feverish recklessness predominated among the stewards and infected the passengers. The unspoken message was to use up everything before the world came to an end.

Among the many choices that were brought to our table was something black and salty, which I liked as much or more than peanut butter. It was called *caviar*. A great economic depression gripped the industrialized world. People were dying in the streets, starving on dust-bowl farms, while my nine-year-old self gravely dug into yet another mound of glittering beluga. Grownups gathered round me at feeding time, snickering knowing snickers. I must have seemed obscene.

On the last morning of the voyage, the elderly steward who served at our table put a plate of caviar in front of me. I glanced up at him, pleased but puzzled. I knew it was not on the morning menu. "Go ahead," he said, handing me the silver dish with neatly laid overlaps of triangular toast, "I want you to be able to say all the rest of your life, *When I was a child I ate caviar for breakfast.*"

CHAPTER 6

That Other Realm

IN *THE WOMAN WARRIOR*, Maxine Hong Kingston writes about life with her Chinese mother, and claims that an immigrant child has nothing to measure against. She can never be sure whether her mother's craziness is an individual craziness or a family craziness or a village craziness or Chinese-in-general craziness. I, also the child of an immigrant, had little chance of knowing whether Mother's peculiarities were due to her being herself, due to her being a Corfield, being of a certain class, or being British. Or maybe she *was* crazy. Now I would have the chance to find out. At Southampton, I, as Two-Eyes, walked down the gangplank into the enormous shadowy cavern of a covered pier. I devoured with eye and mind whatever I could see. Here and now I was in the promised land, where fairy tale and history and family myth would all come together. If I paid enough attention, I would be able to pierce the veil, bare the secrets, understand the mysteries.

As in a fairy tale, whatever I saw those first few days has bewitched me for the rest of my life. A huge, striding, red-coated Johnny Walker, an enormous White Horse, a giant's glass of Guinness towered into the struts and rafters of the pier. Back home in Public School 41 our principal had told us, in assembly, that, if the Democrats were elected, Prohibition would be repealed and the wicked people who were now gangsters and rum-runners would publicly advertise their wares. Instantaneous craving would cause people to foam at the mouth. A tavern would appear on every corner. Fathers would fall down drunk and women would be driven to deeds of

66

unspeakable evil. Little children would be sent to bring home a pailful of beer as casually as we were now sent to the corner store for milk. In America, although I had never seen a liquor advertisement, never to my knowledge passed a tavern, I had certainly seen people falling-down drunk. But here in England the porters and taxi drivers, the passengers and customs officials and the policemen, if they did glance upwards, seemed totally unaffected and apparently sober.

The train that would take us to Cardiff was so small that I thought it must be a toy. Inside the carriage, instead of sitting on seats set either side of a center aisle, we were packed into a cozy compartment with several other people, strangers to us, all facing each other but not in such close proximity as to be un-British. The railway tracks, miniatures of what was familiar, were not elevated on an artificial bank with yards of gravel on either side, as in America, but ran close to the earth. Bowling along through town and country I could look down from the train window, see separate and distinct flowers, see here a rabbit, there a partridge.

The train stopped outside a station. A band of workmen came along to do some sort of maintenance on the tracks. They were coal black! At first I thought they were colored people, but underneath the blackness they looked *just like us*. Give them a good wash and they could have been officers on Father's ship. They were British, with blue eyes and Anglo-Celtic faces shining through layers of coal dust that actually stained their skin. Back in New York, this kind of heavy, dirty work would have been done by Italians or Portuguese or Slavs; in California, by Mexicans. Not by people who looked like us! And not by colored people. Colored people were porters. (I know now that, although being a porter might seem easier and more genteel, it did not pay as well as working on the roadbed.)

At Cardiff we changed to a train for Bridgend, which took us about twenty miles farther, and the nearest stop to where we were headed. Aunt Doris's house, called Castleview, was in the village of Southerndown. We arrived there after dark, by taxi. The house was not heated; we slept with hot-water bottles. When I came down to breakfast next morning, I found the french windows in the dining room left wide open to the garden, even though the month was March. Ten days before, New York had been frozen by record cold, our whole world turned to shades of dun. Doors were shut, windows sealed, we wrapped ourselves in central heating. Here, there was hardly any line between outdoors and indoors. Spring sunlight made the outside air warmer than where we were sitting. *The air in fairyland is always warm.* I could lean out, reach my hand towards primroses, daffodils, wallflowers. Other flower beds, some incandescent with bloom, some with new-turned earth, lay beyond. A blue-green lawn, pied with daisies, stretched towards a distant wall. Beyond the wall was a hill, and on the hill was a castle. I thought I had fallen down Mother Hulla's well or entered a fairy mound. I was *inside* my books.

In the days to come I would discover that there was not just one garden at Castleview, but many, each giving way to another, through walls and hedges. Most of them had gone to seed and were full of nettles and dock leaves. Mother was sad to see them so, but to Two-Eyes they offered mazes of delight. Behind the house was a flagged stable yard, and beyond that was a kitchen garden; beyond *that*, chicken coops and hens. A few weeks later I asked for and was gladly given the job of feeding the hens and collecting their eggs. This was harder than I had thought, for there was no telling where or when the hens might lay; sometimes in their boxes, but as often among the nettles. Chickens do not date their eggs when they lay them. Some eggs were so new that they were still warm; some were not warm but new-lain that day; some eggs looked new but were not new: they were filled with a stinking mess.

I asked about chicks – baby chicks – and wondered why there were none. Uncle Will seemed amused, my mother and aunt embarrassed. There was no cock in the barnyard, therefore the eggs were not fertilized. A dozen fertilized eggs were purchased from a neighboring farm and one of our hens left to sit on them in peace. After six long weeks, hen and eggs were brought into the kitchen, near the stove. I watched in wonder as each chick chipped its way toward the light, emerged wet-feathered, grotesque, and bedraggled. Long, anxious moments ensued before the new-hatched bundles dried enough to be identified with those fluffy yellow creatures portrayed on Easter cards. But real life is not an Easter card. A few curled gargoyles lay dead in their shells and could not be resurrected. There was singular lack of comment from the grown-ups – scientific, philosophical, or spiritual. In another two years I would be menstruating, but no one seized the opportunity to discuss with me the mysteries of ovulation and fertilization, copulation and death. A fog of ignorance, good taste, and smirks from Uncle Will and Cousin Alan, hovered over the whole procedure, swallowing up my questions.

The house was filled with cousins. Margaret, the eldest, was in her early twenties. She went to work in an office in Bridgend every day, on the bus. If she were a few minutes late, the bus driver and all the other passengers would wait for her, urging her on from the gate. We were definitely not living in New York! Somehow, the country seemed more efficient, measured on a sensible human scale. One day, when Mother and I were coming back from Bridgend, the bus driver turned around and asked us, the passengers, if we minded taking Mrs. Jones up the hill to her house. The hill was steep, we could all see that, and we could see Mrs. Jones, laden with bags and bundles from market. The bus driver helped her down from the bus into her own barnyard, while cows, ankle-deep in mire, stared at us with bovine hauteur.

Alan, the only male cousin, was just back from Canada, where he had spent two years. Before that he had been at school at Cheltenham. When my uncle lost his business and all his money, he had yanked his son out of school, even though Alan was head boy, even though the school implored that he be allowed to finish his last term at their expense. An Isaac to his father's bankruptcy and pride, he was shipped off to herd sheep in the mountains of Alberta. He had lived in a cabin and subsisted mainly on flapjacks and sourdough bread smeared with sheep fat. He loved to talk about that at breakfast time, loved to make his girl cousins from America squirm and squeal with the horror of it all. Now he worked as a laborer at a neighboring farm and came home with straw and manure sticking to his boots. He wore American overalls; his face was red from sun and wind, and his hair was wild. He was an angry young man, and I was afraid of him. Never having had a brother, especially a sarcastic, wittily articulate English brother, I had no clue how to talk to him. I was relieved to discover that he and his father preferred their own masculine company; they usually ate by themselves at a table in the kitchen, talking about Mussolini and a man named Hitler who just a few weeks before had come to power in Germany.

Uncle Will had been a prisoner-of-war in Germany. Wounded, he was operated on by a German surgeon who did a clumsy job of it and left him with injuries, including a ruined colon, which were a source of embarrassment to him and to his wife. He had lost his business, and his physical condition cut him off from normal social activities. He was understandably a bitter man, but the strange thing about him was his attitude toward the Germans. He admired their efficiency (despite the butchering surgeon) and their industry. He shared their hatred of the Jews, who were all rich and had caused the Depression by sucking away all the money in the world. I had met a lot of Jews in New York but, as far as I knew, I had never met a rich one.

Mother had confidently promised the truant officer that there would be a governess at Southerndown, but when we arrived she discovered that there was no governess. Her sister had no money for school nor for teaching at home. Mother suggested that her own three little girls and Cousin Pat attend the village school. Aunt Doris was horrified. And adamant. We were English gentry. She would never lift her head again if we were allowed to mingle with the village children, who were common, and Welsh besides. What if we acquired their accent on top of the American one that we already possessed? Under no circumstances were we to play in the street with the village children or to wave to them from the garden wall. And if we came across a group of village children on the moor we must pass them by with barely a nod.

This was too much for Mother. She took us off to her bedroom and told us that, since we were guests, we must abide by the house rules but, *if* we were ever up on the moor, and therefore out of sight of house or village, we could play with whomever we liked. *Because*, she said, *you are Americans.* This was a revelation I had never expected to hear from Mother! As a matter of fact we would not have been allowed to go to school anyway. Joyce's mumps emerged in full bloom, and I came down with mumps, too. So did the two younger cousins, Pat and Anne. We contracted the disease chain-fashion, instead of all at once, and were quarantined for weeks and weeks. Meanwhile, even if we had no governess, we still had to be occupied and entertained.

A compromise plan was conceived. Cousin Jean, at seventeen, was betwixt and between being a grown-up and being one of us. She, too, had had to leave school when the money ran out, and had been home for several years. She had no skills, nor prospects for a job. (Later, she became a nurse.) Mother came up with an idea that was discussed and modified with the help of Aunt Doris. Mother would pay Jean a little something to be a sort of presiding governess. Jean would teach the older children: Anne (almost twelve), Pat (ten), and me (nine). The older children would teach the younger ones: Joyce (age five) and Little Anne (not quite five).

The curriculum would consist of history, geography, and much reading aloud from the extensive library in the unused wing of the house, and from the store of children's books that were in the nursery cupboard. Long division, the bane of my existence, was not even mentioned. Mother insisted that we should have American history and literature, too, out of loyalty to Father and to the fact that we were really Americans (this new truth that she was just beginning to apprehend). As consequence, we read yards and yards of Henry Wadsworth Longfellow. I liked *The Song of Hiawatha* and the one about the Viking tower at Newport, and *The Children's Hour*. I thought *Evangeline* was silly. Why didn't she buck up and marry someone else? I don't remember much Tennyson (except that Anne learned "The Charge of the Light Brigade" by heart, and broke down in hysterical weeping at "I'm to be Queen o' the May, Mother"). *Horatius*, by Lord Thomas Babington Macauley, was more generally admired. We learned to recite it in unison, and would do so at the drop of a hat, marching round the garden or over the moors to its thumping rhythm. Sixty years later, Cousin Pat and I, sitting in the old Granary restaurant in Hay-on-Wye, recited it with gusto over a good tea.

Rudyard Kipling was our favorite. Anne read *Kim* to herself, but she listened with the rest of us when Cousin Jean read *The Jungle Book* aloud as we sat around the dining-room table. Cousin Pat reminds me that Anne also used to hold prayer meetings in the garden and commanded all of us to attend. When I said that I didn't remember, Cousin Pat said it may be because I was a Dissenter. I absolutely refused to be a member of the Anne-glican church.

History was the favorite subject. We read about Boadicea and King Canute, Harold at Hastings, good Richard and wicked John, Edwards and Henrys innumerable. The story of the Little Princes in the Tower, murdered by their wicked uncle, produced a delicious chill. And the wicked Roundheads, who asked King Charles's little boy, *When did you last see your father?* The little Stuart was grandchild of James I, about whom is written: "The child of Mary, queen of Scots,/A shiftless mother's shiftless son." The boy said he had seen his father the night before, but only in a dream (which was a lie). And about George Washington, who never lied, and Admiral Nelson, who said, "Kiss me, Hardy!" Most of these historical gems came out of a book called *Our Island Story*, a lavishly illustrated history book with a gilded red and blue cover and pages thick as cream.

A School History of England by C. R. L. Fletcher and Rudyard Kipling, published in 1911, was delivered to us in person by aunts-by-marriage, Dolly and Mabel. They were the two sisters who had been governesses at Saint Lawrence, and had married two of mother's brothers, Harry and Francis. Francis had been killed in the war and Harry was "missing" (which turned out not to be true, actually; he had merely run off with a common shop girl, though in 1933 nobody yet knew). Dolly and Mabel had joined forces to run a school for girls in Leominster, Herefordshire.

When they came to visit us at Southerndown, I discovered that these aunts had already written a script for me. They claimed that they knew exactly what I was thinking, because I was a Yankee and they knew what Yankees thought, which surprised me because I never knew what I would be thinking next. The book was to be a correction to our American error. I still have the book. Messrs. Fletcher and Kipling present a text that is jingoistic, snobbish, racist, sexist, bellicose, outrageously opinionated, quirky, and vividly memorable. Each chapter ends or begins with a poem. I learned most of them, including the one that heads a chapter entitled "The American Rebellion and the Great French War":

> 'Twas not while England's sword unsheathed
>   Put half a world to flight,
> Nor while their new-built cities breathed
>   Secure behind her might;
> Not while she poured from Pole to Line
>   Treasures and ships and men –
> These worshippers at Freedom's shrine
>   They did not quit her then!
>
> Not till their foes were driven forth
>   By England o'er the main –
> Not till the Frenchman from the North
>   Had gone, with shattered Spain;
> Not till the clean-swept ocean showed
>   No hostile flag unrolled,

Did they remember what they owed
To Freedom – and were bold!

Kipling's irony was lost on me. I thought that he was complimenting us Americans for our cleverness.

One of the aunts, I could never remember which one, had a son named Ian who attended a Blue Coat school, founded for orphan boys by Edward VI in the sixteenth century. By the twentieth century the school cost a pretty penny and was difficult to get into, but the uniform was the same – bright-blue smock and saffron-yellow stockings. Our cousin Ian, the Blue Coat scholar, was destined for a university, but not a red-brick one. The aunts would rather die than that should happen. When I (a California child, acquainted with earthquakes) asked, a little anxiously, what was so wrong with red-brick buildings, the aunts ignored me and went on to talk about the ridiculous pretensions of North American universities with names like Manitoba and Ohio and, for all they knew, Medicine Hat. To which I added, conversationally, that I myself had heard of an English university named after a cow crossing. Mother told me later that she could have hugged me.

Meanwhile, our daily education continued. In early afternoon we ate our main meal at the round dining-room table (meat and potatoes, vegetables and pudding). Before or after luncheon we were expected to put on a play, to be watched by the grown-ups. The play, part rehearsal, part charade, would demonstrate what we had learned from reading history and literature during the morning.

Anne, who had been reading *A Tale of Two Cities* to herself, read parts of it aloud to us, determined to fire us up for a major production. I remember this play particularly, perhaps because this time the grown-ups abandoned their role as mere spectators and entered into our make-believe. Marie Antoinette was being dragged through the streets to the guillotine. As everyone knows, Marie Antoinette's hair turned white overnight when she was imprisoned in the Bastille. This detail held special significance to the present company of players, because Aunt Doris's hair had turned snow white overnight when she heard that her husband had been wounded and was a prisoner of the Germans.

The queen had been transported in a tumbrel, which (according to an illustration) was a rough cart, high in front and low in back. Anne stood on the seat of an old upholstered chair, clutching the back of it. Joyce, Little Anne, Pat, and I had attached ropes to each of the legs of the chair and were dragging it and Anne across the floor, which was liberally sprinkled with talcum powder. The chair, its joints groaning, its lion feet protesting, made a dreadful sound. So did Anne.

In the midst of all this ruckus, Mother and Aunt Doris appeared and demanded to know what was going on. We were commanded to let go of the chair and to get to the part about the guillotine *right now*. Two steps (borrowed from the closed off library) led up to the place where the queen would bow her head to the knife. Anne, protesting all the way, was dragged out of the tumbrel. She struggled frantically as Pat tried to force her up the steps. I, in my alternate role as Madame Defarge, now sat beside the steps to the guillotine. I was knitting. As an act of record and vengeance Madame Defarge had included the coats of arms of all the beheaded aristocrats into a dreadful coverlet. Relishing the prospect of regicide, she (and therefore I) set about to fashion the royal device. Anne was still shrieking when Aunt Doris's voice cut through the frenzy. "That is *not* the way a queen would behave," she said. Aunt Doris advanced upstage, as Anne, snapped out of her acting trance, stood by uncertainly. I went on knitting.

"A queen would not shriek and wiggle about, she would be proud and cold and dignified," said Aunt Doris. "She would show those commoners how a true queen goes to her death. Here, let *me* show you." Anne stepped aside in awe as Her Majesty, white head erect, slowly ascended the steps to the guillotine. We, the assembled multitude, fell silent.

"I would not flinch, I would not quiver," said Aunt Doris, through lips that barely moved. "I would not deign to look about me."

"Oh, I don't know," said an unexpected voice. It was Mother's. "If I were going to die in the next five minutes I wouldn't want to miss a thing. Here, let me have a go." Aunt Doris descended; Mother took her place. "If I were going to die," said Mother (who, not long ago, had almost died), "I'd notice everything." She gazed about her. "I'd notice that daffodil outside the window. I'd notice that bird on the lawn. I'd *especially* notice the people." She looked down at me, sitting below her beside the steps.

"You dropped a stitch," she said.

Perhaps memory plays me false but it seems to me that Anne *always* grabbed what were considered to be the "good" roles. She was royalty to my baron, lord to my sturdy yeoman, Cavalier to my Roundhead, *Princess* Pocahontas to my John Smith. Also, she had veto powers over which plays would be produced. I wanted to put on a play about Richard Arkwright and the spinning jenny and, more important, about the Luddites. I was perfectly willing that Anne be a wealthy factory owner to my factory worker, but being in trade was beneath her. She sabotaged the production, saying there were no interesting people in it, by which she meant no true upper class, no nobles or royalty. For the most part I accepted my lot philosophically. I did my method research and threw myself into the roles of people who, like Two-Eyes, may have been ordinary, but saw clearly. Thus was the twig bent, my political outlook eternally affected.

Almost every day, after lunch and theatricals, we walked over the moors and down to the sea. On the way Jean taught us the names of British birds and flowers we saw on the moor. I was already learning the names of birds very quickly; I collected Players Cigarette cards on which they were depicted. At the beach Jean pointed out to us the fossils in the rocks of the cliffs (if the tide was high) and mollusks in the tide pools (if the tide was out). The beach at Southerndown was strewn with huge boulders, each as big as a hay rick or a motor car. In the lee of each boulder, at low tide, was a scooped-out pool, warmer than the sea and warmer than the air surrounding us. Each of us could have her own private pool; some of them were big enough and deep enough for a child to swim across.

Surprisingly, it was Cousin Alan who told me the story about our beach, a story he told as fact. Perhaps he thought it amusing that I was so guileless as to believe him. He said that one night the lads from several villages over had come to have a drink in our village pub. (Yes, The Three Cups, just over the wall at the end of our garden.) After closing time they decided to save themselves the long way home on the winding coast road; they would go instead straight across the sands. The moon was full and the tide was way, way out, so they knew they would be perfectly safe. *As they were walking over the sands, though, they heard the sound of girls singing . . .*

They came around one of those big rocks and here were these beautiful girls without a stitch on them. Naked as the day they were born, some of them swimming in the pool and some of them sitting on the edge, singing and combing their hair. And the lads decided each to catch one of them and to keep her for his very own. But the girls were more than they had bargained for. Fast. Fast and slippery. They slipped and slithered away and each of them picked up what looked like her clothes from the rock, but it was really a seal skin. And they put those seal skins on and went flopping down the beach and into the sea. All but one. She couldn't find her seal skin because one of the lads, smarter than the rest, had seized it at once and hidden it under his jersey. So his girl couldn't become a seal again and she couldn't get away.

"What happened to her?" I asked. "*How* did she get away?"

"She didn't."

He threw his jacket over her and he took her home to his cottage. He lived by himself because his mother had died and his father had been lost in the war. So they were married and he taught her how to be a good-enough wife, though she always acted sad. They had kids, and she seemed to love her children, and looked after them as well as she could. But her husband had hidden the seal skin up in the rafters in the barn. One day, one of the kids came running in with it and showed it to his mother and asked her what it was. "It's mine," she said, "stolen by your father a long time ago," and she grabbed it out of his hands. She went running over the fields towards the sea and none of them ever saw her again.

I know full well now that many versions of this tale exist in books of folklore but I am convinced, by the immediacy of the telling, that the tale I heard from Alan was genuine *oral* tradition.

A treasure trove lay for the taking in the nursery cupboard. I discovered the Andrew Lang colored fairy books (blue, red, green, mauve, orange, olive – the entire set). They were anthologies of tales, not just from Europe but from around the world.

There were scores of others, many in beautiful editions. The heft, the feel, the *smell* of those books, has remained with me all my life. I remember, particularly, those with tipped-in illustrations by Edmund Dulac and Arthur Rackham. They gave me my first intimation of books being valuable, not just for the information or plots contained in their texts, but as objects of art and craftsmanship, worthy of veneration in themselves. There were also history books and nature books, old *Chatterbox* annuals, and the thoroughly modern *Rupert* annuals.

In the late afternoons, when the light was beginning to lower, I read fairy tales aloud to a spellbound Joyce and Little Anne. Mother rarely interfered with our reading, but one evening, when she overheard me reading

"Bluebeard" with inappropriate relish, she did say to me that she thought it better if I did not frighten the little ones with that particular story just before bedtime. Once I knew that tale was forbidden I could no more resist opening the book to that page than Bluebeard's wife, Fatima, could resist opening the door to the bloody chamber. Joyce and Little Anne and I would sit almost inside the book cupboard, the doors only part open, making a little house for us, while I read to them in a muted voice. Afterwards we would run down to the end of the garden and climb up on the wall (which was also a forbidden thing to do) and swing our legs over the road. Hand over brow, each of us sheltered her eyes and scanned the countryside. From our perch on the wall we could almost look down the chimney of the village pub. We could also look over the moor to where it swept up, up, up toward Dunraven Castle, on the crest above the cliffs above the sea.

"Sister Anne, Sister Anne, do you see anyone coming?" Joyce and I would chant in unison. Sometimes we fed Little Anne her lines:

"I see only the sheep on the moorside," or, "I see the red deer feeding." Reports of both these sights were perfectly true. But we were waiting for a more definite sign, something new and unpredictable, a car going up to the castle or the shadow of a cloud passing quickly. For the third time: "Sister Anne, Sister Anne, do you see anyone coming?" Then would come the voice of Sister Anne, straight out of the story:

"I see two horsemen on the road." That would mean that our gallant brothers were coming to rescue us, in the nick of time, from being beheaded by our husband, the dreadful Bluebeard, who would throw our bodies on a heap of others, in the bloody chamber.

I learned more in that year of no-school than I learned in all the years of schooling that came after. I learned more than in any other year of my life. I have made my living from what I learned that year.

Sometimes we took the bus and ventured further afield. At Ogmore we could reach the ruined castle only by crossing the river on stepping stones. They teetered in an exciting way. Straddling from one to another we were ever mindful of the chatter of the river as it issued from hills and leafy glens, and rushed on, toward the sea.

There were once two king's daughters lived in a bower and Sir William came to woo the elder of them, with glove and with ring, but then his love turned to the younger daughter, she with the cherry cheeks and golden hair.

One fine day the elder princess said, "Let us go down to the River Binnorie to watch our father's ships come in. So hand-in-hand they went down to the strand. And the younger daughter went out on a stone, half in, half out of the water . . .

We ate our picnic lunch in the ruined banquet hall, where vestiges of the fireplace still remained, surrounded by ancient carvings. The walls were rubble and the roof was open to the sky. Afterwards we ventured into the woods where bluebells flowed so thickly they seemed like water, between the trees and over the paths. As in a dream we waded through blue pools of bluebells. The inbred admonition never to walk on flowers was of no use here. We could not be good even if we tried.

On another sally, to the Gower Peninsula, I ran off to hide in the bushes. When rain fell, I burrowed my way into gorse and bracken, making a sort of cave for myself. After a while I heard terrible footsteps. *Thump. Thump. Thump.* Slow and deliberate. They came closer. Stopped. Came closer . . . then a sound for all the world like the gnashing of teeth. *Fee-fi-fo-fum* sprang instantly to mind. I could not ignore that something big was out there, coming closer. Curiosity won at last. I parted the bracken fronds. The rain had stopped and the whole hillside was covered with mist. Standing a yard or two away from me was a little moor pony, its rough coat a-spangle with dew. Sunlight seeped round the edges of a cloud and, as I watched, the pony snorted, shuddered, transmogrified itself into a kaleidoscope of rainbows.

We went up to London for a week. We stayed in a small mid-Victorian hotel and did the usual tourist things: the Tower, Hampton Court, the Zoo. In New York I had been made constantly aware of the Depression. In Southerndown, the grown-ups talked about the Depression, but for me its immediacy had receded. In London, the Beast was back again. Once more I was transported to a grey and foggy world, the Wasteland I thought we had left behind us. Everywhere I turned I saw pale, sad-faced men, often horribly mutilated. Men with legs cut off were sitting on little carts made with a few slats of woods, a bit of dirty carpet, and roller-skate wheels. They were begging in the streets. The grown-ups kept saying there would be another war. I began to have nightmares. At the movies I had seen an old newsreel of tank warfare in a desolated countryside in France. In one of the Mother Goose books at Southerndown was a picture meant to illustrate a seemingly harmless rhyme: *If all the world were apple pie/And all the seas were ink/And all the trees were bread and cheese/ What would we have to drink?* Something about the curve of that huge barren pie crust against the sky and the obscene transformation of the trees melded with the war films, haunted my dreams.

Mother took us to Weston-super-Mare, a seaside town near the Cheddar Gorge. We stayed there a week. Joyce and I begged to ride the donkeys that stood for hire on the sands. I fell off mine. We took a bus tour to the Gorge and to the famous caves, where I gazed in awe and delight at stalagmites and stalactites and crystalline cascades, all garishly lighted. I was disappointed that there were no cavemen to see, and no pictographs. At Castleview I had been reading H. G. Wells's *Outline of History*. On some dim level I already sensed that the message of the fairy tales and the thoughts of the ancients were somehow connected.

On the way to the Cheddar cheese factory the bus driver pointed out the rock cleft in the Gorge where a Victorian clergyman, sheltering from a storm, had dashed off "Rock of Ages," an all-time hit in the hymn books. I was more interested in the manufacture of poems than of cheese. I plied the guide with questions and finally elicited from the poor man that, fortuitously, the poet just happened to be carrying a notebook in his pocket. And yes, he had brought a pencil.

Anne went off to Leominster to attend the aunts' school for a month; at the end of the term Mother and Anne set off together to see Stratford-on-Avon and other cultural sites. Uncle Roger was now back in Britain. Joyce and I stayed at a farm where Uncle Roger was now living. I have never seen Shakespeare's birthplace but, thanks to Uncle Roger, I know a bank where the wild thyme grows. Joyce and I slept on straw mattresses in an attic (like Heidi, I thought) and looked at the moon out of an odd-shaped little window under the eaves. We could only look through it if we were lying on the floor. In the morning light the countryside rolled like a green sea below us. The River Wye wound through the fields and through a town (it must have been Hereford) where there was a cathedral. All through the day the throats of bells pealed the joyous hours. There were no toys, no books, no playmates, no schedule; nothing to do and everything to do. Joyce and I confiscated some barrel hoops and amused ourselves from morn to night by bowling them down a long country lane. Over and over and over. The run downhill must have been a mile or more. Magically the distance became less and less, became easier to run. To assuage our thirst we gathered blackberries as we walked back uphill. Our legs were like bands of steel and the August sun had bronzed our skins. "Like Red Indians," the postmaster liked to say, hopefully, to Uncle Roger. We were the first Americans he had ever seen. We did not have the heart to disabuse him.

Finally we went to Chepstow. We stayed in a hotel in town for a week while Mother ostensibly tried to make arrangements to visit Saint Lawrence. Meanwhile we took a bus tour to Goodrich Castle. Another day we went to Tintern Abbey, and saw "bare ruin'd choirs, where late the sweet birds sang," in Shakespeare's words. Mother told us how, when Henry VIII sent his hated minions to destroy the abbey, the monks got word of their coming and carried all the altar gold – chalice, cross, and candelabra – down to the River Wye and threw it all in. On the night of Harvest the full moon fits into the abbey's rose window exactly, and the ghosts of the monks can be seen walking down to the river, carrying their treasures. People used to come from all over England to see the sight, Mother said. She also told us about Grandfather's remark: all those people milling about on a moonlit night, anyone could claim he had seen anything! No ghosts for us, alas. We were standing in sunshine while Mother told us the story. Later we paid sixpence apiece to tour the abbey. The guide took us over to some stones, to see the fish the monks had carved there. He explained how the fish, an early symbol for Christ, was usually stylized so as to be nothing more than two overlapping circles. What was interesting about these, he said, was that whoever the stonecarver had been, he must also have been a fisherman, well acquainted with the famous salmon that still swims in the peat-stained waters of the Wye.

Later, we had lunch in at the Abbey Inn, an ancient building that had once been the abbot's house, but was now a restaurant. Mother ordered fresh Wye salmon for all of us. Served cold, with mayonnaise, it was not only delicious, but brought back to us the wonderful arguments that Father and Mother so enjoyed exchanging over the dinner table. For one magical, sacred moment, the Holy Salmon swam in the waters of the River Wye, swam across the Atlantic, up the river that Henry Hudson had hoped to be the Northwest Passage to Cathay, and into the Columbia River, where Father was waiting for it.

All this was by way of marking time. Quite suddenly, during the last few hours of the last day in Chepstow, Mother ordered a taxi and we drove out to Saint Lawrence, the house where Mother had lived as a child, where she had played with those brothers gone to another realm. I knew they were dead but I had also assumed that they were still alive, living in a parallel world in that house of many stories. Mother still lived there, too, but as a little girl. We were about to pierce the veil.

Mother had meant, she said, to call the people who were now the owners, to write to them ahead of time, to arrange a visit. *Meant to.* I remember getting out at the gate. I remember peering up the drive, trying to see more of the house. *Aren't we going in?* Mother didn't answer us. *Aren't we going in?* I turned to look at Mother. She had tears in her eyes.

"*I don't want to go in,*" she said. Later she told me that she was afraid that once she opened the gate, once she went up the drive, opened the door, entered the rooms, all the memories would flee. She would not even be left with the memories.

CHAPTER 7

Naomi

FOR THE FIRST TIME since the *Titanic* went down and the International Ice Patrol began, the Arctic ice cap calved almost no icebergs. Consequently Father, earlier than expected, returned to Norfolk to take up his new duties as second-in-command of a Coast Guard cutter stationed there. He was living a bachelor existence, while Mother and we three girls were far away in England, visiting our aunts and cousins. Father wrote to Mother almost every day, and was as romantic as ever, but I think she may have been apprehensive about leaving him footloose and fancy-free for too long, so she decided we would go home. Another reason for leaving England a few months early was that Father's pay was cut almost in half by the drastic fiscal reforms of the new administration. Franklin Delano Roosevelt, the new president of the United States, had decided that, in order to haul the country out of the depths of the Depression, everyone who worked for the government must sacrifice a percentage of salary – even the armed services.

We had been in England during the first months of Roosevelt's presidency and were unprepared for the changes that had taken place. Prohibition had been repealed. Liquor advertisements sprouted everywhere. Father and the Coast Guard no longer chased rum-runners. Now they turned their attention to other kinds of smuggling. Every grocery store or corner shop carried a blue-eagle sign in the window, to show that the owners supported the National Recovery Act. People's conversations and the front page of the *New York Times* (to which my parents subscribed, even in Norfolk) were studded with bewildering new references to PWA (Public Works Administration) and WPA (Works Progress Administration) and CCC (Civilian Conservation Corps).

At our new school every child was assigned to a miniature version of the categories devised in Washington. We wore green and yellow armbands (our school colors) with these same mysterious letters affixed. Picking up a piece of paper on the school ground was now a patriotic duty that would affect the nation's economy. I was convinced that any failure to do my share of good deeds would be close to committing treason. Mother viewed such zeal with suspicion. I think she was reminded of the missionary craze that had swept Victorian England, or perhaps she had seen newsreels of Nazi and Communist youth corps.

Loyalty and treason had been confusing issues in Britain; new confusion awaited in Virginia. People talked often about "the War," which, I began to understand, was not Mother's and Father's War. Nor was it the American Revolution (or Rebellion) I had been blamed for in an English nursery. Nor was it the War of 1812, with bombs bursting in air. While we had been away, the Americanized version of "God Save the King" ("My Country, 'Tis of Thee") had definitely lost the contest. Mr. Francis Scott Key's "The Star-Spangled Banner" was now in ascendancy. Father asked us how the teachers of Norfolk were introducing the new anthem.

"We don't sing either one of those songs," I reported. Every morning the teacher read from the Bible, we recited the Lord's Prayer, and we sang either "Carry Me Back to Old Virginia" or "Dixie." Father was ready to go to the school and complain; Mother deterred him. "But we *won* the war," he said. "We *beat* the South, dammit." When Father's father had died, he, an orphaned ten-year-old, had been sent to live with his grandparents in Iowa. His grandfather had fought in the Civil War and had been a hero, keeping up the morale of his men even when they were in Confederate prison. Father's Civil War was fought to preserve the Union. Freeing the slaves was secondary.

In first grade, in Alameda, California, there had been a little "colored" girl with whom I had felt particular affinity. She was as carefully brought up as I was, and had the same kind of Victorian good manners that I had. I felt safe with her on the school grounds, and I think she felt safe, too. I pointed her out in the class picture as my special friend, but Mother never suggested that I invite her to come play with me. In New York there were children at the school whom we called "Negroes" (probably with a small "n"). I don't remember even thinking about playing with any of them. There were Portuguese, Italian, Jewish, and Irish children with whom I played in the schoolyard and in the neighborhood, but no Negro children lived near us. There was a Negro man, though, who came to look after our furnace.

The other officers' wives once asked Mother about the advisability of having him come and go in our basement when Father was away at sea, but Mother said that Father had interviewed the man, decided that he was intelligent and reliable; moreover he had a family to support. The man had looked after the furnace for the family who had lived in the house before we did. To discharge him would have seemed unjust, especially since we would be moving on. She did not mention that the man had asked permission to use the toilet in the basement. He was miles from home, he held several jobs, and he could not use a toilet at a gas station or at the other places where he worked, something Mother and Father had never considered before. Mother was a creature of her country, class, and historical time. Her father, a Confederate sympathizer, had run the Union blockade, taking cotton to the mills of Manchester. Mother was culturally racist, but one-on-one humane. Of course that man could use our basement plumbing.

In Norfolk there was a toilet off the kitchen hallway that led to the back porch. Mother gave the mailman (who was "colored") permission to use it when he was on his route. Naomi, our maid, served him coffee in the wintertime and iced tea or lemonade in the summer. There was no store where he could stop to get a drink, and he could not even use the drinking fountain in the park. Before Naomi came to work for us, when we were still moving into our house, a colored woman had come from an employment agency to help Mother. The idea was that, after a few days' trial, Mother might hire her permanently. "Do you pay or do I tote?" she asked. Her accent was so soft and thick that at first Mother didn't know what she was saying, and then she didn't understand what she meant. Finally it was made clear that either Mother would give her money or she would work for nothing and take food from the larder and refrigerator. Mother, shocked, said she most certainly would pay.

Mother was a veteran mover, an old pro. She had marked every box and tagged every piece of furniture before we left for England. Our furniture had been shipped by the government and stored in a warehouse in Norfolk.

Now came the moment of resurrection. Mother directed the moving-van men to look for our metal beds and springs first thing. As one by one they emerged from the rubble, they were taken upstairs and set up. We three girls searched for the boxes that held sheets and blankets, and made the beds. We knew it was important to make the beds first so, at the end of an exhausting day, we could fall into them. However, much of the furniture and piles of boxes were dumped helter-skelter in the middle of the rooms that Mother designated for them. The van men just left them there, to be walked around and excavated gradually. Drama ensued when our new cleaning woman tried to lift a heavy sideboard out of the center of the dining room to where it belonged, against a wall.

"Oh, don't do that," Mother said. "You'll hurt yourself. We'll wait for Mr. Higbee to come home this afternoon, and then maybe we can all three do the job." The woman gave no heed; she went on lifting. Mother raised her voice: "Don't lift that. You'll hurt your insides. Women aren't supposed to do that kind of lifting."

"Nothing but an ol' colored woman," she said. "Don't matter none if I hurt my insides."

"It *does* matter," Mother said. "That's a terrible thing to say, that you don't matter! You should have more pride. And you're not so old. You might want to have more babies and, even if you don't, you should look after yourself." Mother saw the incident as having to do with gender, not race. The woman quit.

Hence Naomi. Naomi was small and slim and intense. She was dark and pretty and intelligent. She emanated self-respect and somehow, without saying so, let it be known that she would take no guff from anyone. Immaculate in her uniform, she arrived every morning at eight, as we three girls were having breakfast – by ourselves, sans parents. Each of us would have made her own bed before breakfast. After breakfast we dashed into the inner sanctum to kiss our parents goodbye. When the coast was clear, Mother had her bath and then got dressed, lacing herself into the all-important boned corset that supported her spine and "insides."

During the day, Naomi and Mother worked side by side, cleaning the house, washing, starching, and ironing for a family with three girls. (This was before the era of automatic washers and dryers.) At night one of us set the dining-room table with best silver and best dishes. Dinner was at 1800 hours; actually, at 1759 hours, but Father, being a tolerant man, allowed us sixty seconds' grace. Mother believed that family dinner-time conversation was too important and too intimate to be interrupted by an outsider, so Naomi did not serve us at table. Once she had brought in the vegetables, potatoes, and meat, she retired to the kitchen to eat alone and to put the pots and pans to soak. Only if Mother rang her little bell for more vegetables or ice water did Naomi reappear. At the end of the first course Mother rang the bell again. Naomi cleared the table and brought in the dessert. She left before our meal was finished. After dinner either Mother and Anne, or Mother, Joyce, and I, cleared the table and did the dishes.

Mother preferred to do most of the cooking, but she fully acknowledged Naomi's mastery of the native cuisine. We occasionally supped on food we had never tasted before, cornbread and Sally Lunn, succotash and black-eyed peas. We ate fried chicken and barbecued pork and would have had catfish, but Father rebelled. When Father was at sea, we relished green beans and spinach cooked with bacon, and collard greens cooked with ham hocks. Naomi made superb baking-powder biscuits, and gingerbread, and she introduced us to Cay-lime pie.

After school I often chatted to her in the kitchen and told her about what I had learned. She was a good listener. However, she did not talk much. She refused to tell me about her family, whether or not she had brothers and sisters, what she had been like as a little girl. She never let me give her a hug. She told me firmly that she did not like being touched by white people. A boy at school told me, "If you touch a nigger your hand will get stuck forever." Of course I didn't believe him. I knew that he must have read or been told the "Tar Baby" story from Uncle Remus, and that he was so dumb that he had missed the point, and got several ideas all mixed up. The boy's name was Robert Edward Lee Grant.

Anne set off for junior high school every morning and was happy there. She was invited to parties where the girls wore long dresses and danced with boys. I was in fourth grade. Before the term was out I was president of my class, and before the year was out I was president of the school. Reading was no contest; I read faster and read more than anyone else by far. History and geography were a snap for someone who had traveled as much as I had. I could run faster than any other girl and many of the boys. Also, I was not afraid to hit back. Mother warned me about being "too physical." My besetting sin was impatience.

My younger sister Joyce was in first grade. Like a possessive mother, I became ambitious for her, too. I went over and over her lessons with her and found an old MacGuffey's reader at the library, the better to instruct her. When she made a mistake I pinched her. Hard! When we were both grown up and had children of our own, I confessed. "I don't know if you remember," I said. "I suppose you don't. But when I was teaching you to read I used to pinch you . . ."

"I remember," said Joyce. "*I* remember very well." Her voice dripped with sweetness. She reached for a cigarette, lit it, inhaled. " 'But,' I tell myself, 'I've always liked to read.' " She leaned over and blew smoke full in my face.

Early in the year Miss Dabney, my fourth-grade teacher, decided we should do a project on cotton – how it was planted, grown, picked, processed, shipped to a waiting world. We planted cotton seeds, watched the shoots sprout and bear pink blossoms, watched them go to seed. When the bolls split, white and fluffy, we picked our crop. We had already read about Mr. Eli Whitney (who was a Yankee but not all bad), and we made a sort of cotton gin ("gin" is a very old word for "trap"). It didn't work, but I got the main idea. The teeth in the gin were supposed to comb the cotton and let the seeds rattle out to a tray below. Before Whitney's invention was introduced, slaves picked out the seeds by hand. It was slow, tedious work, as is everything connected with cotton.

Though this is not exactly the way Miss Dabney explained the situation to us, cotton is a notoriously labor-intensive crop, mostly stoop work. The gin, the one concession paid to industrialization, "freed" the slaves (children included) to spend more time plowing, weeding, weeding again, weeding again, and stoop-pick, stoop-pick, stoop-pick an even bigger crop to send to the mills in New England and Britain. By the 1930s the Emancipation Proclamation still hadn't made much change in the lives of the people who worked in the fields.

One day, toward the end of the term, we went on a class trip to a cotton-gin mill, a maelstrom of noisy, clanging confusion. Towering cumuli of cotton were trucked into a warehouse, divested of their seeds, and compressed into surprisingly small hundred-pound bales. A machine banded each bale with metal strips and wrapped it in jute. We followed the bales out to a dock where we saw colored stevedores toting them on their backs, up gangplanks, on to freighters. Returning from the docks I saw street after street of colored people, horrifyingly poor, sitting on doorsteps or street curbs. I saw youngish men with arms and legs cut off (I suppose from industrial accidents) sitting on little wheeled platforms. I was reminded of the of the war casualties I had seen in London. I was reminded of *A Tale of Two Cities*, the book we had read aloud to each other around the table in England; the book that had inspired my sisters, my cousins, and I to make that play about the guillotine. I thought of Madame Defarge.

Miss Dabney explained to us that the plantation owners could not have afforded to pay their slaves, even if they had wanted to. Actually, there was no need. The slaves were given food and clothes and cute little houses to live in. Their masters loved them and they loved their masters. Then wicked people called Abolitionists came and told the slaves they should run away. Where could they run to? They didn't know how to do anything. They had to be kept care of, like children. Some of them ran away and starved to death or were captured by slave traders who sold them to masters more cruel than their own. After the war many of the slaves had gone to live in cities; that is why their children and grandchildren lived in such poverty and degradation, all because of the hated and hateful Abolitionists. I loved Miss Dabney and I wanted to believe her.

I could hardly wait to get home to tell Naomi. Over milk and cookies I would tell her about what I had learned in school that day. Something in me bade me put Naomi (not Miss Dabney) to the test: I wanted her to vindicate Miss Dabney, so I could go on living my life without being troubled by the worm in the bud, the weevil in the boll, that nibbled away at my unsullied admiration. I was so taken by my tale that I tried acting it out: I grasped Naomi by the arm to show her how the Abolitionists came right into the fields to drag people away from their happy homes. I tried to drag Naomi across the kitchen floor just as, at Southerndown, my cousins and I, playacting, had once tried to drag Anne to the guillotine. Naomi was no Marie Antoinette. Naomi was Madame Defarge. *Naomi slapped me.*

I never told Mother or Father about the slap. It was between me and Naomi. After that, she talked to me in a new and different way. When she slapped me her hand had not stuck to my cheek, but perhaps she was stuck on me, in some other way. She made me think about things I had never thought about since I had sat knitting by the guillotine. She spoke to me, when we were alone in the kitchen, in a hoarse, urgent voice that was almost a whisper. The content was not as important as the tone and timbre of that voice. I knew that I was being told things forbidden, dangerous, vital. The same sort of hoarse urgency came into white people's voices sometimes when they spoke about colored people *or* the unspeakable subject that concerned *down there* and put a sly, shamed look on their faces. Naomi talked to me, her fascinated pupil, about power, not sex, but there's no doubt I was being told the facts of life. Power, sex, and race are connected by a certain tone of voice.

Miss Dabney read aloud to us every day. When she read *Sara Crewe*, by Frances Hodgson Burnett, I wept at how the dreadful Miss Minchin had treated poor Sara Crewe, just like we treated colored people, although Miss Dabney did not say that. Of course everything was righted in the end because Sara, after all, was white. She had lived in India and been very rich and she never forgot that she was really of very high caste, almost a princess. That was why she spent her last farthing to buy a bun for a beggar child. *Noblesse oblige.* But it had taken a Hindu servant, a black man who lived in the house next door, to recognize her true status and to save her from her plight.

I went to the library to look for more books by Frances Hodgson Burnett, and found *The Secret Garden*. Obviously it had been written especially for me. Here were moors and a moor pony, gardens full of flowers and gardens neglected, like those at Southerndown. The very earth of England was described in loving, glowing detail with mystical overtones borrowed (although I did not know it then) from the theosophical teachings of Madame Blavatsky. Mary Lennox was a much more believable character than Sara. I wanted to be like Sara, but in my bones I knew she was a little crazy, and even after she became rich again her life was suspect. Mary was Sara given a second chance. She was grounded by her nasty temper, by the earth she dug in, and by the Yorkshire people who surrounded her.

Yorkshire people were not servile, as Mary's servants in India had been. They were respectful and self-respectful, honest, sensible, and outspoken. On the first morning at Misselthwaite Manor the very young servant girl who came to look after Miss Mary was surprised and a little disappointed to find that her charge was not "black," and said so. Mary was furious and flew into one of her tantrums, although Martha's mistake was obviously an honest one made out of ignorance.

As any reader does, I portaged what I was reading into my real life; real life was used to test what people said in books. I went back and forth between the two worlds. In *The Secret Garden*, when Mary was living in

India, she hardly ever saw her silly, flirtatious mother, or anyone else of her race and class; yet, one inferred, most of the time she spoke in an upper-class British accent. She learned the servants' Hindustani dialect because she liked to learn, and used it sometimes, just as, in Yorkshire, she sometimes dropped into "Yorkshire." But speaking dialect was a matter of choice, and therefore further proof of power and arrogance. I had soon apprehended, in England, that *accent* was what kept the masses distinct and down; in Norfolk, Virginia, it was skin color.

Naomi was not an obsequious Indian servant, nor was she an ingenuous Yorkshire girl. Part of her self-respect came, I think, because she considered herself a *professional* housekeeper. She communicated her boundaries, yet she was, calculatedly, not outspoken. She was a mystery, yet somehow she was compelled to allow me glimpses of her mysterious otherness, the true source of her identity. Maybe it was because I had kept my mouth shut about the slap.

In Joseph Jacobs's *English Fairy Tales*, there is a story called "Fairy Ointment." *Dame Goody, a midwife, is called out at midnight by a "squinny-eyed ugly fellow" on a coal black horse. He takes her to his wife, who lives in a tumble-down filthy cottage, surrounded by a horde of ugly children. But the baby is beautiful. The mother hands Dame Goody a jar and tells her that when the baby opens his eyes she must rub his eyes with the ointment contained therein. Goody follows instructions but, curious, rubs a little ointment on to her own eye. No sooner had she done so, than everything seemed changed about her. The cottage became elegantly furnished. The mother was a beautiful lady, dressed in white silk, and the little baby was made more beautiful than before . . .*

Naomi revealed to me her pride in being black; she did not waste her time by talking about slavery or poverty. Instead, she dabbed my eyes with fairy ointment so I could see past the rags and misery, peer into a parallel world. She told me about churches and movie houses that were like palaces, bigger and better than any the white people had. She talked about debutante balls and beautiful gowns worn by beautiful women who would put any white woman to shame. She talked about doctors and lawyers and professors and wealthy businessmen, all black. She talked about ancient kings and queens who would have made the royal family of England envious with their pomp and grandeur and fine jewels. I never heard her describe her people as victims. They were rulers and conquerors! Whether

I believed or disbelieved was beside the point. I was privileged to be allowed to see what she saw. More important, I was witness to her outspoken scorn, of me and mine. I tried not to think about that!

We lived in a suburb that within a few blocks fell away into empty lots and woodland, then into swamps. About a mile away from our house I had come upon two grandiose gateposts or sentry boxes. They were faux medieval; their plaster had fallen off of them; chicken wire showed through – so I knew absolutely that they were only pretend. Perhaps some people had been going to build a house or several houses there, behind falsely impressive gates. Probably, like everyone else, in 1929 they had run out of money. There was no gate, but a broad driveway, which ran between the gateposts and continued a few yards, branched off into two tracks. The driveway was a mere prelude to a circular path which looped around a peninsula which stuck out into a swamp. The swamp smelled strongly of crude oil, mud, and raw sewage. That may have been another reason for builders to stop whatever they had planned to do.

Walking, I took twenty minutes to get there. At Christmas, when I received a bicycle, I could race to my secret garden in less than half that time. The bike was smaller than standard size. I liked to think of it as my moor pony. Mother said I could play wherever I liked, as long as I took Buster, our black-and-white Border collie, with me. Buster had a strong herding instinct and bad manners. He chased cars. Worse, when strangers approached, he had an embarrassing habit of leaping at them, teeth bared. I would have to catch hold of his collar and drag him back until he had calmed down, still growling.

When I got to the woods, I hid my bicycle under a curtain of honeysuckle which hung down from an old fence near the entrance. Ritualistically, taking the right-hand path, I ran three times widdershins (counterclockwise) around the entire peninsula. I probably ran a mile. Almost at the end, just before it reached the tip of the peninsula, the right-hand path was split by a fissure. At high tide, swamp water oozed into the crack, a long skinny finger wriggling into solid ground, tearing at its vitals. I could jump over that place without missing a beat. At the end of the peninsula the path ascended to a little headland, the Peak of Darien, from whence I could gaze out across a wide swath of swamp grass and treacherous silt to a Stygian stream beyond. After I had run around the boundaries of my kingdom I usually returned to the Peak and sat on a stump, which was like a chair, or throne. In the springtime, magically, a pink lily, fleshy and delicate, grew out of the rotted wood. My flower book said it was an orchid.

When water from the Chesapeake rushed up the inlet, the mud and foul water thus diluted did not smell so bad. When the tide was going out the waters gurgled and sucked among the tussocks. At slack tide the river pulled back to its narrow bed; a swift inky-black current ran between treacherous mud flats which extended far out from shore. Composed of quaking silt and oily slime, the flats were avoided even by wading birds. However, a multitude of small bird species did thrive among the grasses. Over a mile away, on the other side of the river, were more mud flats, what looked like more swamp grass, and a strange place that I could not make out through the haze of smoke and mist that hung over it. Huge fires burned there. It looked, quite literally, like Hell. I figured out that it must be a garbage dump, but people seemed to live among the heaps. People don't live in garbage dumps! Nor does music come from such a place. Sometimes I could swear I heard drums.

The peninsula was almost an island; its center mound rose well above tide-level and was crowned by a stand of towering pole-pines. Their trunks extended a long way upwards before they put out branches. Sun-warmed pine needles below acted as ground cover and did much to dispel the fumes from the swamp. Thickets of laurel and other brush reminded me of the gorse and bracken that gave cover on Welsh moors. I wiggled myself a hole through them, and found that the summit of the mount was a sun-dappled saucer, covered with pine needles, and surrounded with a wall of thick brush. No one could see me from the path below.

I could stay in this haven for hours. I stored my bird-watching book and my flower-identification book in a tin box so I did not have to lug them back and forth from home. I brought library books in my bicycle basket and lay in a root hollow by a big pine to read them. I read *Heidi* and *The Secret Garden* there, over and over. I vowed I would always read those books in the out-of-doors. I re-read the Mowgli books and discovered the Tarzan books. I read *The Flamingo Feather* and *Green Mansions* and *The Magic Forest*, *Swiss Family Robinson*, *Smugglers' Island*, *The Mysterious Island*, and *Robinson Crusoe* (Father's unabridged edition that *his* Father had given him). I read a series of books about the French and Indian wars by a man named Joseph Altsheler, a sort of watered-down James Fenimore Cooper. I longed to be a true denizen of the wild, who could amaze intruders by fading into the forest. To this end I made half a dozen bolt-holes in the brush, green tunnels that led from the main path into the pine clearing. Diving for cover became part of my daily ritual, as I circumvented my kingdom. I also practiced walking through the forest without crackling a twig. I still made too much noise, but I was getting better and better at placing my feet quietly. I had become adept at silence, not only when I was walking. I could sit absolutely still for a long time, not even reading, barely breathing.

Hardly anyone else ever came to my woods. The only child I ever played with there was Joyce, but since she did not have a bicycle, and was not as enthralled as I was, she did not want to come every day. I don't know why people didn't come more often. Sometimes I wonder if there was a taboo. Maybe something bad had happened there once. Or maybe people were just frightened by the silence and darkness of the woods and of the swamp beyond. Occasionally I heard voices, but always I was warned in time to dive for one of my bolt-holes. I could wriggle my way into the thicket and crawl through a green tunnel to the clear space under the pines. Once, I remember holding my breath as a group of older boys walked near where I was lying. They stopped to argue just a few yards from me. One or two wanted to stay and explore some more but when Buster came flying at them, seemingly from nowhere, they scrambled back to the main road, to sunshine, cars, people.

I know I must have played there almost every day for more than a year, because I remember seeing the pink lily twice. One day, during the second spring, I came through the gateway and found a large and luxurious car parked where the widest part of the road ended and the left path branched off to circle the peninsula. I was thrilled. In a flash I decided that the wealthy family, the very people who had had the gateposts built, had come back to visit the place where they once planned to build a house. Perhaps they had come for a picnic and to reconsider. Maybe their chauffeur had carried one of those wicker picnic baskets to the Peak of Darien and was even now arranging wool blankets (what the British called rugs) for the older members of the party to sit on. I hoped there would be children. Sara Crewe and I longed for them to be rich – rich and well-read.

Though the car had been parked on the left branch of the road, I took, as usual, the path to the right, so I could do my widdershins. When I got to the place where the fissure split the path I had to wait and wait for Buster to follow me. He scrabbled down into the crack and pottered off into the grasses, something he did not usually do. I noticed with relief that the tide was still high, though it was going out. I hoped the picnickers would not be put off by bad smells. I leaped the crack and after a moment's hesitation Buster came back to run silently at my heels. I slowed my pace and went into an Indian walk, one foot at a time put down softly. The pine needles were thick on the track. Nary a twig crackled. When I saw the man standing on the Peak of Darien, staring out to the farther shore, I came right up behind him before I said "How do you do?" in my best British manner. He jumped, which sent Buster into a paroxysm of barking. I had to hold Buster's collar firmly while I repeated what I had just said. Lord Greystoke could not have made a better entrance nor caused more of a sensation.

The man did not look rich, not like the rich people I had met. He was stocky and swarthy, not like a colored person but like an Italian, or a Portuguese, or a Jew. On the other hand there was the car. Even I knew that it was a very expensive car. Maybe this man was the chauffeur? But he didn't look like a chauffeur. He was wearing a pinstripe suit, not a uniform; on his head was a wide fedora, not a peaked cap. What really caught my eye were his rings. I had never seen a man wearing jewelry. This one even had a ring on his little finger. It sparkled like a diamond. No doubt it *was* a diamond.

I had to repeat my greeting, shouting above Buster's barking, before I got a response. Finally the man grunted, more to stop my inane chatter than anything else. When a loud staccato suddenly exploded in the treetops he jumped and glanced quickly over his shoulder. I could see that he was not used to being in the woods. Gently I explained to him that we were listening to a woodpecker. He seemed more interested in the red-wing blackbirds swinging on the swamp reeds. Maybe he was a bird-watcher – or a would-be bird-watcher. Red-wing blackbirds were very common, I told him, but common or not they were my favorites anyway. If he wanted something rarer he must go back along the path, into the woods, and listen carefully. He might hear a mockingbird. Then, not wishing him to think I was a charlatan who made false promises, I told him not to count on it. The conversation languished. The man continued to peer intently at the place across the river. By now I realized that he was not bird-watching. He was looking for something, waiting for something. I peered out toward the other shore, too, trying to penetrate the haze. I told him I had very good eyesight, so if he would just tell me what he was looking for . . .

He dropped his gaze and turned to consider me. He actually turned his back on the river. He was standing right next to the tree stump but he didn't seem to see it or what was growing out of it. I held my breath, waiting for his surprise and delight when he espied the pink lily. Finally I had to point it out to him. I explained that I had found a picture in my flower book that seemed to match. If this pink lily was really what I thought it was then it was a kind of orchid, the only one I had ever seen in my whole life. In England, before the War, my grandfather had had a whole greenhouse full of orchids, which he had brought from South America to his greenhouse in England.

I had caught his attention. "Are you rich?" he asked. That was exactly the question I had wanted to ask *him* but I was restricted by politeness. Obviously he was not. Either he was not well brought up, or he was so rich and so well brought up that he could break all the rules. I explained to him that my family was not poor but that we were far from rich, although my mother had been rich, I thought. But she wasn't rich any more. Her father had died and her brothers were killed in the War, so the family fortune had been lost. No one in our family was rich any more . . . *I could hear myself repeating myself* . . . not poor but far from rich . . . *I was no fool. I had caught the drift.*

I knew about the Lindbergh baby – what child in 1933 did not? This man was either a kidnapper or a gangster, or both, I decided. I remembered a movie I had seen about gangsters. They wore pinstripe suits and squashy hats. I began to talk about my father. I told the man that my father was an officer in the United States Coast Guard. I was about to say he had shot and killed many, many rum-runners, more than anyone else, but stopped myself in time. Not only would I be telling a lie, but I might make a person, a gangster by trade, feel sad. Or cross! I shifted ground. My father was going to pick me up in a little while, I said, brightly. So I had better get back to the gate. If I wasn't there he would have to come looking for me. I knew I was lying but I hoped that he didn't know.

"Goodbye," I said. "I've enjoyed talking to you." I tried to sound very grown-up, very British, as much like Mother as I could. Instead of continuing around the point I jumped down from the little bluff, back onto the path whence I had come. Buster followed me, then ran ahead to the boggy place, the place where the path was split. Bushes grew in profusion on both sides of the path, above my head on one side, below my feet on the other. Buster disappeared down into the swamp and began to bark. He did not come when

I called him, so I, following his barks and excited panting, jumped down the bank and ducked under bushes to see what he had found. I pushed through the undergrowth farther than I had ever gone before, and came out on a little beach of tar-stained sand surrounded by reeds. Lying on the beach was an immense, perfectly formed human stool, still steaming.

Two-Eyes squatted down like an Indian, or an African hunter. Two-Eyes, cool observer, gazed at the stool in total, non-judgmental awareness. Spoor! And brand-new. Whoever had made it must have been surprised in the act by Buster. Mr. Whoever must still be very close at hand, watching me. I took care not to appear to be looking for him among the reeds. I straightened up and, ostentatiously scolding Buster for being so silly, made my way through the bushes, back to the path. Just around the next bend I dove into one of my less-used bolt-holes, pulled myself through a scratchy tunnel, came out in the clearing under the pines. Even there I was careful to conceal myself among the pine roots.

I cranked my mind down to the lowest level of deep thought. The gangster had not followed me. No doubt he had taken the other path and was on his way back to the car, on the other side of the peninsula. He had been sort of scared of me, I realized. He didn't know how to handle an eleven-year-old female Lord Greystoke. The bad men in the books were often nonplussed on their first encounter with a Mowgli or a Tarzan but eventually they reacted. They wanted to either (a) kill or (b) capture the noble denizen. Maybe the gangster would think he had made a mistake to let me go, maybe he would come after me in his car. After a while I heard the car start, heard the sound of it driving off, but even then I did not stir. I decided to stay where I was for the rest of the afternoon. The gangster might be waiting for me at the gate. When I did not show up he would probably decide that he had missed me, that I was on my way home. He might try to catch up with me down the road, but he had the disadvantage of not knowing from which direction I had come.

So much for the gangster. Now I had to think about the human being who had defecated on the little beach among the reeds. He must have pulled up his pants in an awful hurry when he heard Buster coming towards him. My arrival must have been even more of a shock. Maybe he jumped into the water. Or into a boat – a rowboat or a canoe. He had probably sat watching me while I inspected his spoor. His *fewmet*. Its presence proved that at high tide a boat could come across on the flood and be poled or paddled through the reeds to the little beach. Up to now the possibility had never entered my head. The people on the other side of the river were fixed there forever, although the place was only a mile away. Washington had crossed the Delaware. The Normans in the Bayeux tapestry had crossed the English Channel, which is twenty miles across. The Vikings, along with Angles and Saxons, had landed in Britain and burned towns and farms, killing and pillaging. What kept those people living in the garbage heap? Why didn't they bring a fleet across the river, march up the road, burn our houses?

This particular loner had made the trip often enough to know exactly where to land in order to meet the gangster at an appointed time. I wondered what was so important as to bring them here. When I arrived on the scene I must have spoiled everything. The tide was just turning, going out. If he waited much longer the mud flats would be bared. He would be stuck in his boat in the reeds for hours and not be able to make it back. I knew without having to be told that if he were caught on our side of the river he would be killed.

At last I ventured out of my haven. Flitting from tree to tree, I kept a sharp eye out for threat or danger as I made my way toward the gate. When I got to my bicycle I did not pull it out from its place under the honeysuckle right away. Instead, I took advantage of the green curtain and crawled underneath, my back against the wall. After a long wait I scooted out and pedaled very fast all the way home, arriving just in time for supper. After supper it was Anne's turn to do the dishes; Mother went into the kitchen to give her a hand. I took my bicycle from out of the garage and made a few sweeps and loops out in front of the house, keeping one eye on the sunset. I was allowed to ride until dark as long as I stayed on the block. Almost as though it had a will of its own, my moor-pony bike took off. Next thing I knew (surely it wasn't my fault), I was flying down the road toward the woods.

I ran through the woods toward the point, as though I were being pulled by a magnet. When I reached the Peak of Darien I saw that the lily had been hacked off mid-stem. It lay on the ground, petals scattered, a victim of wanton destruction. Perhaps it was meant to be a warning, but I did not think of that until years later. I sat down on the stump and looked across the swamp. Streaks of red from the sunset were reflected by the river and even the mud flats were crimsoned. Fires in the dump were so high that they joined the glow in the sky and the mud-flat reflections below. Leaping about on the dump heaps were hundreds and hundreds of frenzied stick figures silhouetted against the flames. The beat of drums and the wail of wild music came from across the water. I wondered if this sort of thing happened every night, but I knew that could not be so, not with this intensity. Something terrible and wonderful had happened to make these people behave so. This was beyond celebration. The tiny leaping figures were powered by an energy that was phenomenal. I had seen a movie called *King Kong*. This was like the moment just before King Kong broke through the barrier. I shivered with an excitement compounded of fear, curiosity, and, yes, sex. If I was afraid, the fear was enjoyable.

Sunset gave way to darkness. The darker the sky, the better I could see the other shore, lit by flames. I was certain that what I was witnessing was connected to what had happened earlier in the afternoon. The gangster and the man in the reeds had finally met. This was the result, and I was taking a voyeuristic pleasure in the scene. I tore myself away and pedaled home. By some miracle I made my way up to my room without being discovered. When Mother came in to kiss me good night I was lying on my bed, reading.

Now next day happened to be market day, and as Dame Goody had been away from home, she wanted many things in the house. As she was buying the things she wanted, who should she see but the squinny-eyed old fellow . . . taking up things . . . here some fruit, and there some eggs . . .

Now, Dame Goody did not think it her place to interfere, but she thought she ought not to let so good a customer pass without speaking. But she couldn't finish what she was a-saying, for the funny old fellow started back in surprise, and he says to her, says he: "What! Do you see me today?"

"See you," says she, "why, of course I do, as plain as the sun in the skies, and what's more," says she . . .

"The ointment! The ointment!" cried the old pixie thief. "Take that for meddling with what don't concern you: you shall see me no more." And with that, he struck her on her right eye, and she couldn't see him any more; and, what was worse, she was blind on the right side from that hour . . .

I did not tell Naomi about what had happened. I had a feeling that she would be angry at me. Just by watching, I had filched something that wasn't mine. I did not tell my parents about the gangster or what I had found on the beach in the reeds, ever. Once I told my story they would never let me out of their sight again. I would be restricted to house, school, and neighborhood, I would be sentenced to playing with those little girls in my class who spent their lives dressing and undressing dolls, and talking about whom they would not invite to the next birthday party.

I could make no sense of what had happened, of what I had seen and experienced. When Father received orders a few months later, we moved to New London, Connecticut. Most of the time I did not think about what was, after all, a mere blip, an anomaly in my life. Years would go by. Then, during the sixties, when my son and my friends' children were into drugs, I would read an article about how, in the thirties, the FBI made a pact with the Mafia. In return for keeping drugs out of the white world the FBI would look the other way when the Mafia supplied drugs to the black world. During the Depression, J. Edgar Hoover and others were terrified of a black revolution. They figured the Negroes had nothing to lose and everything to gain by rising up against white society. Prohibition was over. The Mafia was seeking ways to diversify. Hoover looked upon the drug trade as the most effective way to keep the Mafia happy and to relegate King Kong to the garbage heap. The article also contended that Hoover was using the same calculated tactics to destroy the Flower Power generation. That made me wonder.

I never told my parents about Naomi slapping me. I know my mother would have been angry at her for doing so, but I am not at all certain that she would have fired her. Not in the depths of the Depression, not for one slap struck in anger. Mother knew how aggravating I could be. More than a slap struck in anger, my mother abhorred cruelty meted out in cold reason.

CHAPTER 8

Becoming Civilized

NEW LONDON, CONNECTICUT is a small city strung along the Thames, pronounced to rhyme with dames – so as not to confuse it with that other river that flows through another London. The river runs into Long Island Sound. We lived in officers' quarters at Fort Trumbull, the U.S. Coast Guard Station and Patrol Base, which stood on a promontory overlooking the mouth of the river. The house was at the end of a row of four attached houses, each house four stories high. They were built before the Civil War. The walls, almost two feet thick, offered deep window sills, which were perfect for curling up in with a good book.

First of the six extempore officers to have made the rank of lieutenant commander, Father now wore two and a half stripes, which made him a thorn in the flesh to many of those officers who were his contemporaries. Father's immediate superior, a three-striper, put him on call twenty-four hours a day. Finally Captain Stromberg, commander of the base, noticed that something was wrong. From a distance he had watched Father walking across the parade ground below his office window. Father was so hunched over that Captain Stromberg called him in to reprimand him for lack of military bearing. One close look, however, convinced him that he had a medical problem on his hands. Father was suffering from ulcers and from lack of sleep. Stromberg ordered Father to report to a doctor. Gradually, almost imperceptibly, the situation got better, but meanwhile my parents were living in a state of siege, under terrific strain. I think my mother developed a streak of paranoia. She sometimes became hysterical.

Sailors came and went at all hours, bringing messages for Father to sign and to act upon. Mother made our hall into a waiting room for them, with a chair to sit on, magazines to read, hot coffee to cheer. One of the men, as token of appreciation for Mother and admiration for Father, presented us with an excruciatingly patriotic candlewick table mat, the American flag in red, white, and blue, composed of hundreds of little knots, tied and cut. The backing was an old sail. Mr. Abrams, a signalman, had worked long hours on the project, whenever he was out at sea. We three girls thought it was embarrassingly ugly (the word "corny" had not been invented yet), but Mother put it on a table in the hall where she kept the brass tray for calling cards.

In Norfolk, age eleven, I had fancied myself Nature's child; in New London, age twelve, I yearned to become a social being. I wanted to be civilized. Anne went to Frances E. Willard High School for Girls (there was another high school, just for boys), which was in the center of town. Joyce and I went off in the other direction, to Harbor School, which was downriver from Fort Trumbull, towards Pequot Point. The houses on the Point were big, many of them grand; the houses near the Fort were modest, built for working-class families. For one little stretch I went through a Negro neighborhood; some of the houses there were some of the finest examples of eighteenth-century architecture in the city, with fanlights over the doorways. Now dark-skinned children clustered on the dilapidated steps. Although they must have attended the same school that I did, I did not recognize any of them.

Harbor School was divided into four streams. I don't know what excuse was used for the segregation; probably none was needed. One stream consisted entirely of Negro children, who were made almost invisible. Their classrooms were on a separate floor from ours, they entered through a separate door, and they had recess at a different time, or in a distant part of the playground. They had the same teachers that we had, on a rotating basis, so I pray that they got a good grounding in the three R's, even though the unvoiced message (for them, and for the rest of us) was that they were beings apart, not of our species. The next rung in the hierarchy was occupied by new immigrants, mostly Italian and Eastern European. The third rung was made up of the Irish poor, second-generation Italian immigrants, Jews – and me. The fourth and top rung was given over to children from Pequot Point.

Our teachers were the unmarried daughters of the New England middle class, not married because the men they might have married had been killed in the eighteen months of World War I, or because their men didn't have jobs, or had jobs that did not pay enough. Catch 22 was, if they were not married, they had to teach in order to earn a living; if they did marry, they would lose their job. Though they were high-minded, intelligent, self-righteous, and opinionated, not many professions, except teaching, were open to them.

Automatically, because I had come from the South, I was relegated to the second rung in a scholastic and social hierarchy. This was not the first bigotry inflicted upon me. The New England schoolteachers were rather like my English aunts, also schoolteachers, and had claimed to know what I was thinking *because I was a Yankee*. These New England ladies claimed to know what I was thinking because (and this was confusing) I was *not* a Yankee. Seventy years after Appomattox, the passions of the Civil War still seethed, not only in Virginia but in New England.

I did not have the wit or the will to point out the hypocrisy of the system. I was merely confused when I was told that, since I came from the South, I hated Negroes and treated them badly, while in the North the Negro was happy and was treated as an equal. I had no Naomi to correct me. A good child who wanted to please the grown-ups, I adapted my role as a Daughter of the Confederacy with the same relish that I had adapted my role as Roundhead and French revolutionary in the plays we gave at Castleview. It was easy to bone up on being Southern. Shirley Temple, playing the part of *The Little Colonel*, tap-danced with her dear old slave, Bojangles, on movie screens everywhere, and Margaret Mitchell's novel *Gone with the Wind* was becoming an overnight bestseller. I became a devil's advocate, which satisfied my teachers and made me the center of their attention. They thought my parents must think the same way I pretended to think. My parents were full of prejudice, too, but no more (and no less) than my teachers.

My parents were oblivious to my position on the totem pole. It was I who protested my second-class status. I may not have been good at arithmetic, but I knew that I was better at reading, at social studies, and at penmanship than anybody in the whole school, including the first stream. My rebellion began over the subject of penmanship. Just the year before, the schools of New London had switched to a new writing method, something called "manuscript," or "printed script." I wrote a fine hand, using the old-fashioned Palmer method. Not only had I won a certificate in fourth grade, which I produced to prove my proficiency, but all anyone had to do was look at what I wrote. Every word was legible, every letter! I argued my case: there was no good reason for me to change my way of writing. The next school I went to might not be using manuscript. I would end up not being able to write well with either method.

My adamancy must have been astonishing. I was reasonable, articulate, arrogant. The teachers backed off. I never thought to take my troubles home to my parents. My parents' very silence may have seemed ominous. Perhaps it frightened the teachers into allowing me to "graduate" to first stream. But they could not let me think I was getting away without paying a price. I would have to do a little neck-bending. The teacher's sentenced me to read *Uncle Tom's Cabin*, by Harriet Beecher Stowe. The kids who would be my new classmates had read the book the year before.

"That old thing? I've already read it," I said. I knew I was telling a lie. I had read only the first few pages. My guilt must have been palpable. The teachers smelled blood. Where? When? I said I had read *Uncle Tom's Cabin* when I was living in England. I had read a copy, signed by Harriet Beecher Stowe, which had been given to my grandfather when he visited Mrs. Stowe on her plantation in Florida. My grandfather had said that she was mean to her servants. The teachers were flabbergasted. This was the second time I had been caught telling a bare-faced whopper. Unfortunately, I had already announced to the class that, when my mother was a little girl, Buffalo Bill had stayed several months at my grandfather's house. My mother could look out of her window and watch American Indians camping in the meadow.

I was brought into the teachers' staff room and grilled. I was sent to the office and halfway brainwashed into belief in my own culpability. I broke down and cried. Possibly that was another reason why my parents were not informed. Worst of all, for me, was not the accusation that I had made up these stories, but the fear that my mother had made them up. If so, she was either bad or crazy. To protect my mother, I finally confessed: I was a liar.

My mother went to her grave never knowing how I had suffered for her. Or how, by even thinking she had lied to me, I had maligned her.

Aunt Doris, it was, who had showed me the book given to Grandfather by Mrs. Stowe. It was a small, cheap edition, printed on bad paper. There were no illustrations. The bindings were black, and the endpapers were black. It was a *gloomy* object. Aunt Doris flipped to the inscription on the flyleaf: "To Captain W. R. Corfield, Florida, 1868," signed by the author. Seeing that I was such a good reader, seeing that I was a Yank, I should read the book. She made it sound as though it would be good for me. She made it sound like a punishment. My mother explained that Mrs. Stowe had given my grandfather this copy of her book on the occasion of his being a dinner guest at her plantation in Florida, soon after the American Civil War. I had listened as the adults continued to talk over my head. Their father had told them that he had never known anyone to be so cruel to her servants, crueller than slave owners he had visited before the war. She was continually berating them for not behaving in ways which, by his lights, they could not possibly achieve.

My grandfather was a great admirer of Charles Darwin who, while embarked on the *Beagle* voyage in 1836, had become so seriously ill that he stayed several months with an old school friend, Richard Corfield, a distant relative of our branch of the family. Grandfather took a proprietorial interest in Darwin's theory of evolution. He thought that Stowe's attempt to civilize her black servants was not only cruel, but unscientific. Blacks were too low on the ladder of evolution to be expected to act like white people. He had often remarked that black crewmen on his ships were happier, and functioned better, when they were allowed to be themselves. Harriet Beecher Stowe, my grandfather reported to his family, had no tolerance, no sense of humor, no forgiveness in her soul. She was a thoroughly unpleasant woman. (Please note, I do not agree with my grandfather. Nor Mrs. Stowe. I am only the messenger here.)

Under the weight of this daunting recommendation, I had struggled to read the ugly little book. The florid Victorian style, combined with grimness of format, defeated my nine-year-old capabilities. Besides, instinct told me that I was being manipulated. I dug in my heels, refusing to drink from such murky waters. Now, in New London, I was being manipulated again. I resisted. I absorbed the whole sad tale of my accusation, along with my doubts about my mother, and built a wall around it. Like a dormant cyst lay the fear of discovering my mother's madness, or her wickedness. Then, in 1999, an independent historian, doing research on my grandfather, started sending me material to read and verify. Only recently it occurred to me that now, surely, it is safe for me to inquire into the life of the formidable Harriet. Everything else my mother told me, however melodramatic, has turned out to correspond to reality, in the most surprising detail. Why should the story about Harriet Beecher Stowe be any different?

Braving the computer in Toronto's main reference library, I found the most current Stowe biography: *Harriet Beecher Stowe: A Life*, by Joan D. Hedrick. Resolutely, I opened the book, took the plunge. Harriet had family secrets, too. Her son, Fred, who had failed medical school, was a problem alcoholic. Months after the end of the Civil War, he begged her to give him enough money so that he, with several other young men, could invest in a cotton plantation on the banks of the Saint James River, near Jacksonville, Florida. They were carpet-baggers!

In the winter of 1866-67, Harriet visited her son. She wrote to her friend, Mary Ann Evans (George Eliot), how delighted she was with the climate. She pointed out that, whereas Miss Evans went to Italy every year to escape the English winter, Harriet had found a balmy clime also, reachable by train or ship from *New* England. Italy held out the attraction of ancient cultures, which Florida lacked, but Florida offered unspoiled naturalness, which had its own charms.

Harriet Stowe was, perhaps, the first prominent tourist "snowbird" to migrate every winter. In 1867 she bought property near her son's, in Mandarin, Florida. According to Hedrick, Stowe saw herself as "a self-appointed home missionary."

In a letter written just two years after the end of the Civil War, she told of her efforts to civilize the "immature minds" of former slaves. She had chosen to use a system devised by the Anglican Church to train the "laboring class of England" (I surmise that this included the Irish and the Welsh) to become good servants, "at a time when they were as ignorant as our negroes now are."

My grandfather must have witnessed Stowe at this self-set task. He interpreted her constant reprimands and corrections as mean-spirited and useless. The problems remain with us today. Do we leave ghetto kids to their welfare fate? Do we aspire for them to become lawyers and doctors?

Do we hope they become lawyers and doctors by first training them to be on time for a service job at McDonald's?

At the end of the term, when I was told that next September I would be elevated to the top stream, I tried to explain to Father what it all meant, not only scholastically but socially. He told me that being happy was more important than having good grades. I did not believe him, thank God! I interpreted his remark to mean that now I was supposed to get good grades, and an A for happiness besides – and happiness meant *being popular*. If I weren't popular, I would never be married, if I never married I would never command a household, as Mother did. I might be popular if I didn't get good grades, but if I stopped working for good grades, I might be left with nothing – not smart and not married.

When summer came, Mother paid for me and my sisters to join the Osprey Beach Club out near Pequot Point, so we could play on the beach with friends we had made at school, and swim under the eye of a lifeguard. The beach, as compared to the beaches of San Pedro and Southerndown, was a sorry excuse – a thin strip of sand near the mouth of the polluted river, where it mixed with the pollution of Long Island Sound. Presumably, I was fit to be included in the in-crowd of the Pequot Point kids, which meant being a friend of Betty Morse. If asked individually, most of her classmates would have said that they didn't particularly *like* Betty Morse, but responding as members of a group they would have all agreed that she was the most popular girl in school. Further down the Road of Life, I would discover such a social dichotomy tends to be the rule, but I didn't know that interesting fact when I was twelve years old.

Betty Morse's father was president of the New London chapter of the Sons of the American Revolution (SAR); he therefore was acquainted with my own father. When Father's physician recommended that he find diversion beyond home and work, the shade of father's Revolutionary War ancestor, Obadiah Higbee, had been summoned. Father had joined the Sojourners, a branch of the SAR composed of commissioned officers, active or retired, descended from soldiers who had served in the American Revolution. Father enjoyed the company of other men in a relationship away from shipboard (or office), and he enjoyed the speakers who came from universities, museums, government, and business to lecture at monthly meetings. He enjoyed knowing men like Harry Morse.

The trouble was that, although by adult standards I had the qualifications to be a paid-up member of New London's in-group, I still didn't fit. Nor did part of me want to. I had had some idea that, when school let out, I could return to the role I had perfected in the Virginia pinewoods. I had discovered the *Swallows and Amazons* books by Arthur Ransome, in which English children in the Lake District played elaborations of my own kind of games. I thought, come summer, I could include some of my friends in such a scenario. Alas! That was the summer that my New London peers were mysteriously inspired to sit on beach towels high above the tide line and play bridge. Betty Morse and her older sister, Kay, were the center of the bridge-playing set. Betty was in my class, our parents knew each other, and we visited at each other's houses, so I hailed her as a friend. To her horror I came running up to the bridge party, dripping with dirty sand, to bid her come see the sandcastle Joyce and I had made. Poor Betty! She must have lost points for even *knowing* me.

Anne's best friend was Gloria Kaufmann, who was Jewish. The Kaufmanns lived across the street from Osprey Beach Club and owned, with their house, the right to use the beach, even though Jews were not allowed to belong to the club. The person who had sold his house to the Kaufmanns after the 1929 stock-market crash had broken Pequot Point's gentlemen's agreement. Gloria and her five-year-old sister were ostentatiously shunned by the bridge players. Anne, who sunburned easily and was self-conscious in a bathing suit, was happy to spend minimal time at the beach, so she and Gloria found refuge on the Kaufmanns' terrace in the garden behind the house.

Anne had also made friends with Alice Dimock, whose family's summer house, one of the oldest on the Point, was next door to the Kaufmanns. In Anne's Latin class the teacher had mentioned *Horatius*, then followed with, "I suppose no one knows that poem any more." At which Anne, schooled in the glorious tradition of Castleview and Southerndown, burst forth with

Lars Porsena of Clusium,
  By the Nine Gods he swore
That the great house of Tarquin
  Should suffer wrong no more.
By the Nine Gods he swore it,
  And named a trysting day,

And bade his messengers ride forth,
East and west and south and north
    To summon his array. . . .

At which Alice Dimock spoke up, and said, "I can say the whole thing in Pig Latin." And did! At which they fell, laughing, into each other's arms. The upshot was that Mrs. Dimock telephoned Mother to ask both Anne and me to tea, and sent her chauffeur to pick us up.

Alice had a younger sister, Joanna, who was almost my age. During the fall and winter the Dimocks lived in their eighteenth-century house in the center of downtown New London; Joanna went to a school nearby. In April every year the family decamped to their summer house, an unheated shingle masterpiece with an exuberant wooden sunburst over the door and a huge verandah. As an annual occurrence, Joanna was taken out of the downtown school and thrust into Harbor School for the last few months of the term, a move made possible because her mother was a member of the school board. Sometimes Mrs. Dimock, along with the rest of the board, came to inspect the school. She was the one with the lorgnette.

Joanna and I didn't meet until a week or so before the invitation to tea. I had hardly had a chance to speak to her. When I did, she volunteered that she had a pet rabbit named Hrothgar because, like his namesake in *Beowulf*, he was house-proud. He gloried in an outsize hutch especially made for him. Joanna is the only friend I have kept from my childhood. Now that we are in our seventies and my two sisters have died, she is the only person, except my cousin Pat in England, who remembers me as a child.

Being with the Dimocks was like being at Castleview. I felt at home and challenged at the same time. The house was not quite as old as Aunt Doris's, but the rugs were faded and the furniture was late eighteenth century and early nineteenth. I thought it was because the Dimocks, like the Corfields, had lost all their money. Mr. Dimock did not go to an office every day, so I thought he, like so many fathers after 1929, had no job to go to. The house was full of books but, unlike Southerndown, new books arrived every week or so, sometimes by the boxful. Mrs. Dimock was a Bunner. Her father, H. C. Bunner, had been editor of a literary magazine that had been an influence in the 1880s and '90s but had expired soon after the turn of the century. The magazine had been called *Life*. Now Henry R. Luce, the owner of *Time* and *Fortune*, was dickering to purchase the right to use that title on a pictorial news magazine he was planning as companion to his other publications.

During the next year and a half, as I got more acquainted with the Dimocks, I used to ride my new bicycle from Fort Trumbull all the way down to the Point, to stay with Joanna. I even had my own room, one of seven guest rooms, with a canopied bed and Currier & Ives prints on the wall – *The Sailor's Farewell* and *The Sailor's Return*. My favorite was the one showing horrified whalers being capsized in their dory. Mrs. Dimock told me that she had put some books by my bed to amuse me, signed by the author – who, with his wife, Vinnie, used to stay in the same room, sleep in the same four-poster bed. The books were first editions of books I already knew: *Tom Sawyer* and *Huckleberry Finn*. But the man who claimed to have written those books was a barefaced liar, a cheat, and a plagiarist! Everyone else knows that the books were written by Mark Twain (it even said so on the spine), but the man who had told Joanna's grandfather that he had written those books had signed himself "Samuel Clemens." I was too embarrassed for Mrs. Dimock to break the news to her.

Mrs. Dimock talked to me about books, and listened seriously to my opinions. When I said how much I liked the social-studies book, by Harold C. Rugg, which we used at school, she said how unusual it was for a child to like a school text. She suggested that I write to Mr. Rugg and tell him how much I liked his book. I never did. Writing the letter in my head was easy, but the task of making a perfect copy (which I thought I must do) on unlined paper, plus organizing envelope and stamp, seemed overwhelming. Also, I experienced a whiff of that same fear that had assailed Mother at the gates of Saint Lawrence. I was afraid to pierce the veil.

Authors belonged on the Other Side, safely dead, trapped in long-ago far-away. If you could commune with authors in such a mundane way, by attaching a U.S. stamp, was there not danger that you might summon their creations? I know now that many North American Indian tribes refuse to tell stories except in the dead of winter, when it is important to tell stories to keep the cold at bay. Winter holds the story-energy within a safe grasp, but stories told on a warm breeze let loose ghosts and tricksters, they give license to create havoc in this world. Whenever Mrs. Dimock asked me about the letter, I lied and said I had sent it. She was surprised and disappointed that I never received a reply.

I was a strange amalgam of child and (the term had not yet been invented) teenager. I had begun to menstruate when barely eleven; now, as I turned thirteen, my hormones were racing. I was crazy about boys, but boys did not like me. Books and movies talked about girls who were ignored by boys because they were flat-chested and wore glasses; I had huge breasts, and my eyesight, alas, was perfect, so I could not, with one sweep of my arm, take off my glasses and become beautiful. I was a child in a bumpy woman's body.

At night I went down on my knees and prayed that I would become popular, like Betty Morse. When Aunt Joyce came to visit from Cleveland, she was distressed by my preoccupation. I heard her whispering to Mother, in that special kind of voice, that the way girls got to be popular was by doing whatever the boys asked them to do. "Do *what?*" I shouted. "Just tell me. *What?*" I was furious with her for withholding the secret. The opportunity was there, wide open. Aunt Joyce could have been the perfect person to bring me (and my painfully ignorant mother) the vital information. After all, Aunt Joyce had waited seven years to marry her fiancé, a gynecologist-obstetrician. She must have known *something!* Because of my frank interest in sex, she left our household convinced that I was flagrantly immoral, headed for out-of-wedlock pregnancy. I was and would have been, except that no boy ever asked me to do whatever it was that boys asked girls to do. Aunt Joyce had told Mother that she must speak to me. Mother said that at Christmas time she would come and lie on my bed and tell me all about "it." That was in 1935. I am still waiting.

Mrs. Dimock, on the other hand, was determined to tell me about how babies are made. She was president of the local chapter of the Planned Parenthood Society and she had some pamphlets that made no sense and were of little interest to me. She also had an issue of the British magazine *Nature*, to which she subscribed. The U.S. Customs authorities had tried to keep it from coming through the mail to her, because, as in her illegal pamphlets, there was a photograph of a human embryo. I liked babies and I knew that people had them automatically after they were married, but it never entered my head that what Mrs. Dimock was nattering on about had anything to do with what I was experiencing. The blurred black-and-white photograph in *Nature* was indiscernible. In order to find out about I-didn't-quite-know-what, I scanned through women's magazines: *Good Housekeeping, Ladies' Home Journal, Delineator,*

Women's Home Companion, Cosmopolitan. Sometimes I found articles that purported to be about how to be popular, but they only told me to be a good listener and to use lipstick moderately and (a little more daring) to be sure to use an underarm deodorant.

The only article I ever found that seemed to apply to my way of *being* was buried in a syndicated column in the local newspaper, next to the "funnies"; I had taken to reading it every night. The columnist was a precursor of *Dear Abby*. Someone had written her a letter (it may have been planted) asking about how to bring up a girl to be a lady. The writer had raised six healthy, successful sons, but when a younger sister of hers was killed in an automobile accident, she was unexpectedly faced with the responsibility of taking care of a surviving child, a niece. She wanted to know what she and her husband should do differently with a little girl than they had done with their boys.

Much to my surprise the columnist replied: *Nothing. Bring up your niece as if she were a fine, upstanding boy. Bring up a little girl to be a gentleman – honest, brave, courteous, and intelligent. Encourage her to climb trees, play ball, take long hikes, and learn how to swim. Give her the best education you can afford, so she can work at a profession and earn her own money.*

I was infuriated. I was vindicated. I wanted to throw the article away, forget what I had read. Some other part of me (maybe it was Two-Eyes) clipped it and kept it among my papers for years. As I saw my situation, my problem was that I was already being brought up to be an officer and a gentleman, but I knew I was more than that. I was a *girl*! My father, in complete denial of reality, seemed to think his daughters were destined to grow up to follow the sea, as he had. Or, if we could not be captains, then we would be captains' wives – as our mother and our mother's mother had been. Failing that, his hope was that I become a glamorous secretary, airline stewardess, or nurse – all alternate versions of women who serve, who serve men. My columnist-mentor would have approved of my parents' other expectation: that I be intelligent, well read, well traveled, brave, and good. Neither of my parents gave a thought to my going to university, to my fulfilling myself with a profession and a way to make good money. Money represents sovereignty and power. So does sex. My parents never discussed either with me. This probably was what was happening in most other families, but other girls usually lived in one place long enough to observe their society over a period of time and draw valid conclusions of their own.

One of the scariest parts of my life centered around Mr. Garvey's dancing class, held every Saturday night in the ballroom of the Mohican Hotel. It was supposed to be an honor even to be allowed to join the dancing class, but I suspect that anyone who had the money was accepted by Mr. and Mrs. Garvey, who once upon a time had been professional ballroom dancers. They treated that time of their lives as a passing lark, and now presented themselves as models and arbiters of deportment for the young teenage society of New London. The fee was outlandishly high, but that was only the half of it. I would have to have several dresses made for me, and the right kind of shiny black shoes and a beaded handbag and a black velvet cloak. There were dinner parties beforehand, to which I may or may not be asked, and I would be expected to give at least one dinner party for eight (four boys and four girls) during the course of the season. I was wild to go. I begged and wheedled. This was unheard-of in our family. Whining was a sin. Once Mother said "We can't afford it," it was understood that we would never ask again. I was the problem child. I not only wanted more, I *yelled* for it.

Mother thought that the idea of dressing up little girls in long dresses and little boys in tuxedos was ridiculous, as was the idea of thirteen-year-olds sitting around a formal dinner table, aping the manners of grown-ups. "Like monkeys playing tea party at London Zoo," she said. But she did not have the courage of her convictions. We bought some god-awful shiny satin material (which I picked out) and my mother took me to one of those impoverished gentlewomen she always seemed to know. They abounded during the Depression and, alas, too often turned their hand to dressmaking. The other lady and Mother whispered about my lack of definitive waistline, the necessity to "cut on the bias." A garter belt would not be enough for me. Should I wear a girdle? I desperately needed a brassiere, a good one, but even to contemplate buying one would be to admit to my most serious problem, two huge problems, affixed to my front. My mother was terrified of my burgeoning body. I believed then (and am now convinced) that she and her accomplice were bent on uglifying me.

I was a wallflower.

I went to the movies almost every Saturday, searching for the "meaning of life." Even scarier than dancing school, but somehow related, were the Busby Berkeley movies. Before my eyes, hundreds of girl-women were reduced to being parts of a machine, cogs in a wheel, bits in a kaleidoscope. One moment they leered at me in close-ups, the next moment, they were folding in on themselves, being sucked into a void, or exploding outwards into a pattern of waving legs, of mechanized, impersonal sexuality. Those movies were nightmares to me, representing my worst fears of lost identity. They made me feel that the *me*-ness of me, my innermost core, could be snuffed out in the blink of an eye. (Later, I read that Albert Speer, official architect of the Third Reich, had used Busby Berkeley movies for inspiration in programming Hitler's huge mind-numbing Nazi rallies.)

The mounting tension of my sexuality, my competition for not only good grades but the best grades, my feelings of failure (as a girl-woman), the strain around my father's job, and my mother's outbursts of hysteria all caught up with me. The stress of adapting to new schools, new places, new cultures, within the space of a few years, caught up with me. The Royal Family and families in general, and a Jewish girl at school, whose mother had committed suicide because *her* mother, in Germany, had been killed by the Nazis, impinged upon my dreams. As did another sad little girl, who invited me to go with her to a meeting of the Children of the American Revolution. Mother said I had to accept, because the girl's father was in prison for embezzlement, and I must be kind.

Sometime in March I refused to go to school. When I did go, I said I had a headache, which was a lie. What I was feeling was worse than a headache. Again I broke all the rules. I threw tantrums. I shook pillars and foundations. I yelled for help *from outside the family*. Mother took me to the public health doctor on the Coast Guard base, the one who was treating Father for ulcers. He sent Mother out of the room while he talked to me. I don't know what I said through my sobs, but he listened. He called Mother back into the room. He said he would run some tests, but in the meantime I was to stay home. When Mother asked what to do about the truant officer, he laughed. "You live on federal property; the truant officer can't get through the gate." When Mother asked what to tell the school, he said, "Throw them a bone. Say that your daughter is having a nervous breakdown. She isn't, but she will have one if she keeps on the way she's been going."

So I never went back to school in New London. Nor, despite all the money spent, did I go back to Mr. Garvey's. Mother was puzzled, sad, frightened. She never chided me or said I told you so. She only wondered what she had done wrong. Anne was ashamed of me and tried even harder to be a good and uncomplaining daughter. She looked upon me as a coward and a quitter, sins to which I cheerfully admit.

I got up in the morning at a usual hour and had breakfast in the kitchen with Anne and Joyce and Alice, the maid. Alice was the wife of one of the sailors. After breakfast I made my bed, I rode my bike around the base, I went down to the docks or climbed the turret stairs in the bailey of Fort Trumbull's mock castle. I read. When Mother took her morning break to drink a cup of coffee and smoke two cigarettes, I sat and talked with her or listened to her talk woman-talk to her friends on the telephone. I read some more. When a patrol boat went over to the army commissary on Fisher's Island, I went along for the ride and to inspect the lighthouse with Father. I read. When Mother went into town to shop she took me with her. She left me off at the library, where I stocked up on more books. Now I was allowed to go into the adult library. I discovered Thackeray, and *Vanity Fair*.

But what I liked best were my parents' winter picnics. The doctor had told Father that he must get away from the base for a few hours every day. Connecticut was full of country roads, stone walls, old houses, ponds, rivers, woods, fields, and rolling hills. When my parents found a perfect view they would park and have a picnic, even in winter. Especially in winter. Father had made a plywood shelf with a slot in it to accommodate the driving wheel of our old Packard. Father brought out the thermos, he lined up the cups, the milk and sugar, and spoons. Mother brought out the sandwiches and we ate, admiring the view, pointing out the roof line of an old farmhouse in the distance, a flight of birds against the sky, a flame of bittersweet against a grey stone wall. Muffled to the gills, we used mittened hands to grasp our mugs. Our breath made fern leaves on the windows, but as long as we sat in our wigwam we would be safe. Our individual ghosts and demons were held at bay.

Mother spoke of Mrs. Morse as being "plucky." Hard times had come, but she taught tennis and bridge for money, and knitted strangely patterned sweaters for a posh shop in Manhattan. She was a Fitzgerald character, lost in the wrong novel, *After the Crash*. Everyone knew who the Morses *were*, they were Old Family, but everything else was conjecture and speculation. They were envied for living in a large and impressive mansion, but disparaged for living there for free, as house-sitters. (The Morses had connections.) When summer came, and the truant officer was no longer feared, I took to riding my bike over to Betty Morse's house. To my surprise, without her entourage of admirers, she proved to be a person whom I could like. She was bright and funny, and I sensed she knew more about sex than she was telling. But there was also something sad about her, sad and elusive. At the least push toward heart-to-heart conversation, she would shy off and become insufferable again. I suppose I was just as insufferable. We were at an insufferable age.

Mrs. Morse telephoned Mother to invite me and Joyce to go on an outing. She was taking her two younger girls, Betty and Sally, down to Newport, Rhode Island, for a day, with a friend. We would have a picnic lunch on the way and in the early afternoon we would arrive at the Vanderbilt cottage, the Breakers, where she and her friend had been invited to a party. The Vanderbilts' name had been much in the papers lately, because of the custody fight over a little girl, Gloria Vanderbilt, who was about Joyce's age. She was so very, very rich that her mother wanted her, but her grandmother didn't want her mother to have her. Because of so much interest in the family, pictures of the Breakers had been flaunted in the press. During the winter we had driven over to Rhode Island with Father, to inspect a lighthouse, and to see the Atlantic waves roll in at Watch Hill. As we drove past, Father pointed out the Vanderbilt "cottage." It was not really a cottage, but a mansion.

Mrs. Morse's friend was not another woman, but a tall, handsome, dashing man. (Mother told me, years later, that rumors were rife that Mrs. Morse was having an affair with him.) Before Mother could protest, or change her mind, we scrambled out of our car and into Mrs. Morse's, already revved at full throttle. We were off like a shot! Somewhere along the way, we stopped and had a picnic lunch, as promised. I am fairly confident, in retrospect, that Mrs. Morse's friend was gay. Mrs. Morse laughed and laughed, as did we all. I felt that she deserved to have a good time with her friend, just as Mother did with Roger and Marmaduke Jennings, of whom he reminded me. Unlike Mother, I am sure that Mrs. Morse knew that her friend was homosexual, and what that meant. Probably Harry Morse knew, too, although maybe he had doubts. I am still not certain why Joyce and I, as well as Betty and Sally, were so essential to the scheme. That we were party to some sort of plot and subterfuge, I am certain to this day. Perhaps we were window-dressing.

Almost as soon as we arrived at the Breakers, Mrs. Morse and her friend disappeared into mysterious upper rooms. We four little girls, told to stay downstairs, were left to our own devices. We wandered around in the hall, the billiard room (which was being used), an enormous living room, and dining room. Ghostly dust sheets covered the furniture, but we were soon drawn to a room with a rescued piano. Someone was playing show-biz songs. Young people, incredibly beautiful and handsome, were clustered around, singing so well that the thought flashed through my mind that they were show biz, too. Not quite real, the young women were wearing beach pajamas and fluttering flowered frocks. The men wore blue blazers and white trousers. They seemed almost as though they had been hired for the day, as Joyce and I, in a manner of speaking, had also been.

Joyce and Sally were bored, so Betty and I went outside with them and wandered among the uninspired flower beds. The grass was yellowy, the day hazy and hot. The sea, through the offshore mist, looked like heaving dishwater. In the back of the mansion, wonder of wonders, we found a child-sized thatched cottage, a replica of the one owned by the Duke of York's children. (I had seen it in the *Illustrated London News*.) The door gave to our touch, and we went inside. It was like a house that Goldilocks might find, or Snow White. There was a snug little living room with a real fireplace, a bedroom with two little beds big enough for a child to lie on, and a blue-and-white tiled kitchen with a gas stove. The gas was turned off.

After a while, Betty and I left the two little girls and went back to the main house. Hardly anyone was left in the drawing room, but I did find one or two young men who were almost desperately glad to play Ping-Pong with me. I was a demon Ping-Pong player. About to serve, I looked upwards and saw, above our heads, a ceiling of incredible blue. There may have been clouds or cupids or flowers painted there, but if so they made no lasting impression. What I remember most about the whole strange experience at the Breakers is the blueness of that ceiling. It made me think of bluebells in the woods at Ogmore, of oranges floating in a blue sea. It lifted my heart and helped me to get through what seemed like a feverish daytime nap from which there was no waking. Years later, I read that the sunroom had been painted by Italian artists who were brought over especially to make the space appear like an eternal sunny day in Capri, no matter how dull the New England weather might be just beyond the panes of glass. Everything else at the Breakers was mirage, but the blueness of that ceiling, meant to be a mirage, had its own integrity.

Hours went by. Sometimes Betty and I went out to the playhouse and played with the little girls. In desperation, I told them stories, then Betty and I recited "The Owl and the Pussy-Cat" in unison, doing a sort of soft-shoe dance: *"hand in hand, on the edge of the sand, they danced by the light of the moon, the moon, they danced by the light of the moon."* After a while we all drifted back to the main house, hungry, tired, orphaned, and abandoned. The two younger ones curled up in sheet-covered armchairs and went to sleep. Betty dozed off, too. I had, as usual, brought a book to read. But I didn't read it.

Inspired by the blue ceiling in the sunporch, I "magicked" myself out of the bleak present, went to a place where I would most like to be, a safe place. I slipped away to the woods of Ogmore, waded through bluebells. I stood on the shore of the One-Strand River, saw oranges bob in a blue sea. This was a trick (almost shamanistic) that I had taught myself, a sort of self-hallucination. To transport myself (trip out) I have to have been excruciatingly aware (completely in the here-and-now) of the earlier experience. In order to retrieve that time and place, I have to let go, hang loose, be playful, expect nothing. *How many miles to Babylon?* (To Baby-land; to the Land of Fable; to Heaven?) *Three-score-and-ten.* (A lifetime.) *Can I get there by candlelight?* (Before I die? Before dark sets in?) *Yes, and back again.* (One of the aspects of a shaman is the ability to come and go between worlds.) *If your heels be nimble and light* (if you "can become as a little child"), *you can get there by candlelight.* (Yes, and back again.)

Mrs. Morse and her friend reappeared, full of apologies, looking sleek and satisfied as well-fed cats. I suspected that they were a little tipsy. They may have been high. Tired and half-starved, we reached home well after bedtime. Mother questioned me sharply about the events of the day. I told her everything I knew about living the high life. *Vanity Fair* does it better.

Two years later, when we our family was living far away, in Oregon, Anne received a letter from Gloria Kaufmann. Gloria wrote to say that Kay Morse, Betty's older sister, had committed suicide during her debut into New York society. After an argument with her mother, she ran from the ballroom, entered the ladies' dressing room, ran to an open casement window, and jumped to the avenue below.

CHAPTER 9

Myth, Ritual, Sex

AT LAST, AT LAST, Father had received orders to assume his first command, the first of the extempores to do so. He was to report to the United States Coast Guard Cutter *Onondaga*, stationed at Astoria, Oregon, at the mouth of the Columbia River. Fishing and lumbering were still the chief industries, but the town now had cement sidewalks. This time we would not live in Chinatown, but in a sprawling turn-of-the-century house high up on the hill, with a breathtaking view of the river, the ocean beyond, and the forests on the opposite bank, in the state of Washington. The house belonged to two sisters. Although one was married and had a son, they were still known, collectively, as "the Allan Sisters."

The first day of school, Mother came with me to meet my new teacher. Kids were hopping over the desks, throwing paper airplanes, erasers, spitballs. I thought it a charming change from New England. Almost unconsciously I looked for Mediterraneans, Eastern Europeans, and Jews. There were no Negroes. (We would learn later that the only Negroes in Astoria were the old shoeshine man at the hotel and three hapless young sailors assigned to Father's ship.) Except for the Chinese kids, everyone else in the class looked more or less like me. My untutored eye could not discern the difference between Icelanders, Norwegians, Swedes, Danes, Latvians, Estonians. And Finns.

In England it had been the village children on the moor to whom we should not speak; in Norfolk the colored people were already segregated from us; in New London it was the Jews who had to be recognized and excluded. In Astoria, a next-door neighbor saw fit to warn Mother that, although Finns are nice enough people in their way, she would not want a daughter to marry one. *Finns!* I had to go up to my bedroom, to explode with laughter. Epiphany! There would, in every town I ever moved to, always be someone who was elected to be the outsider. Since I was also an outsider (although I looked like an insider), I was destined to spend the rest of my life as a spy among my own people. Two-Eyes would watch and weigh, and live to tell the tale.

At Lewis and Clark Junior High, we used the same history book (by Harold G. Rugg) that I had used the year before. In New London, the school budget had provided corollary workbooks for each pupil. In Astoria, only the teacher had such a workbook. I soon figured out that she did not write her own tests; she cribbed multiple-choice and short-answer questions, word for word, from the workbook. If she cheated, so would I – not so much to get a good grade, as to live dangerously. Although I had not written a fan letter to Mr. Rugg, I now wrote to his publisher, to request a copy of the workbook. They sent me one, no charge, no questions asked. To get an A, I didn't need to know the test questions ahead of time; I already knew Rugg's book by heart. A butter-wouldn't-melt-in-her-mouth sort of child, I was driven to empower myself by ritualistic stealing. As surely as any would-be gang member, I had to prove to myself that I could snatch fire from the gods.

I was a teenager. Ergo, I had a really nasty streak. I broke my mother's heart by refusing to learn how to smoke. Mother had begun to smoke when she was driving ambulances during World War I and was being bombed by German zeppelins. To her, a woman with a cigarette represented a woman who thought herself to be every bit as good as a man, a woman who could remain, quite literally, cool under fire. It meant that she was unfettered by stuffy elders who thought smoking was unladylike. It meant that she was dashing and sexy, a creature of her times, open to new ideas. Mother encouraged Anne and me to learn how to smoke under her supervision. Silver, brass, and cloisonné cigarette boxes were available all over the house, chock-full. We were free to smoke any time, providing we showed a sense of responsibility about fire prevention and cleaned our own ashtrays. She offered us cigarettes when she offered them to guests, as she offered us a glass of sherry. She even put a pack of cigarettes in my

Christmas stocking. Of course she had no idea of the medical danger to lungs and esophagus. If well-intentioned bystanders had told her she was killing us, she would not have believed them. Like my mother, I did not think that cigarettes were unhealthy, but out of pure contrariness I refused to smoke. My resistance was not noble or enlightened; I was just being a rotten teenager – truculent, sullen, sour. I didn't smoke then and I never have since.

Other peoples' mothers were less embarrassing than mine, partly because they were other peoples' mothers. The mother of one of my new school friends was a graduate of Wellesley College, in Massachusetts. She said it was one of the best colleges in the country, along with Vassar, Smith, Barnard, and Bryn Mawr. I jumped at this last name. Mrs. Boland was out to recruit for her alma mater, just as Mrs. Haye had been doing on the beach at Cabrillo, so long ago.

Mrs. Boland gave me a college catalogue. Wellesley required four years of a foreign language; the University of Oregon and Oregon State required only two. Because of that lost half year in New London, I had entered the last half of eighth grade in September (such anomalies were allowed in the 1930s). This meant that I started the first half of ninth grade in January, and was left hanging out to dry in June. I would have to wait through the whole summer, go back to Lewis and Clark junior high in September, complete ninth grade in January, transfer to Astoria High School, start tenth grade. Latin and French courses started only in September, so I would lose a year. Juggle my schedule as I might, I would never be able to crowd four years of language study into my last two years of high school.

The high-school building was just a block away from our house, straight up the steep hill. One April morning, I turned aside from my usual route, along Irving Avenue, and climbed up the steep grade to the high school. I walked into the office and asked to see the principal, Mr. Towler, then I sat and waited in perfect confidence, even though I knew full well that I would be marked late to home-room study period at my regular school. When Mr. Towler asked me why I had come to see him, I explained that I wanted to go to Bryn Mawr or Wellesley college, therefore I needed four years of language. I wanted him to plan ahead for September *now*, so he could make sure that beginners' Latin would be taught first period in the fall. Every morning of the fall term, I would stop off at his high school, participate in the Latin class, then run the mile to Lewis and Clark, where I would be taking the rest of my courses. Over the next three years, I would take Latin for a year, then I would take Latin and French, then just French. Four years of language instruction would be accomplished in three years. *Voilà!*

Mr. Towler knew who I was, who my parents were. He asked me why my parents, if they felt so strongly, had not come with me. I told him that the whole thing was my idea. It was not the sort of thing I bothered them with. (I did *not* tell him that my father did not approve of a child of his going to college, unless to Annapolis or West Point. I did not tell him that my parents did not have the money to send me to a good private college. I did not tell him that, even if they were rich, they would not send me.) What was going on in Mr. Towler's mind I don't know, but the next year's high-school schedule was tailored to fit my demand. I don't think I ever told my parents what I had done. If I had, they would have wondered what the fuss was about. Only Anne knew, and she was embarrassed.

By very definition, to be young is to live in a state of embarrassment. Not only was I fat (although not, judging by photographs, as fat as I thought I was), not only did I not know how to talk to boys, there were the little things to worry about. White gloves, for instance. Anne and I needed white gloves to go to church but, come Sunday morning, our gloves would be dirty, or one would be missing. Once, when Mother heard me spelling out conditions for Anne to borrow one of my gloves, she gave me a scolding. "If someone asks a favor of you," she said, "either say yes or say no. Don't whine about your sister being careful, or what she did last time, or might do in the future. If you do someone a favor, *do it with grace!*"

Mother's promulgations usually made sense to me. Anne's rules had to do with being in poor taste (wearing pink) or unpatriotic (letting the flag touch the ground) or irreverent (putting something on top of the Bible). She was especially well-versed in nuances of hierarchy. Tactfully, she broke the news to me that, since she was the eldest, I could never get married until she did. "What if you never *do* get married?" I asked. I was told that it would be poor taste and unforgivable for me to marry, or even be betrothed, unless she were first.

Far more serious than white gloves (or lack thereof) was having your slip show. These things were never actually spelled out, but somehow I gathered, through osmosis, that a drooping shoulder strap suggests a breast exposed (slut!); a drooping hem evokes anything that exists below the waist (slut!). Worse than the revelation that you were wearing a slip would be to have people think that you were *not* wearing a slip (slut!). Worse, worse, worse was to have a menstrual stain show, but that was so unthinkable that one would have had to retire from public life. *Not* to menstruate was reason for such worry that it was spoken about in whispers. Pregnancy was too terrible for contemplation. Girls who became pregnant disappeared from high school and were never spoken of again. Not to have a boyfriend was a terrible thing. To have too many boyfriends was a terrible thing. To have a regular boyfriend was a wonderful thing – except that girls who went steady sometimes ended up disappearing and were never spoken of again.

I discovered that basketball was the consuming passion of Astoria High School. Basketball was an indoor sport that could be played despite a rainy climate. Basketball was a sport that demanded strong legs. To go anywhere in Astoria, especially to the high school, you had to climb steep hills. Basketball also required strong arms. When Astoria boys were not climbing hills, they were pulling nets full of salmon from the river. No wonder they won the state championship almost every year.

Basketball was more than just a game. It was, I inferred, a sort of religion, a ritual sport like the ball games of the ancient Mayas. Confirmation was whispered among the girls who had brothers or steady boyfriends. Sexual initiation rites were here and now being practiced among the young warriors of the tribe. I overheard this fascinating bit of information when, inadvertently, I was hidden in a stall in the girls' toilet room. Each veteran member of the team was required to steal a discarded Kotex, and to force the new initiates to kiss the bloody object. I was not horrified or disgusted by what I had overheard. I was *curious*. Ever since reading Andrew Lang's blue, red, mauve, and olive fairy books, I had had a hunch that underneath the surface of perfectly ordinary ordinariness lies a quickening force, mysterious, powerful, dangerous, beyond mere rules. I couldn't put it into words; it was the something that lurked beyond everyday life, barely glimpsed in myth and ancient ritual. I had not expected myth and ancient ritual to surface in 1938, in Astoria, Oregon.

In the Dimock household, in New London, I had read parts of Sir James Frazer's *Golden Bough*, plus other books on the same shelf. At Southerndown, I had read H. G. Wells's *Outline of History*. Since then I had read as much as I could find on archaeology and anthropology. Now I discovered that my unlikely-looking classmates were participating in the kind of male initiation rites I had resigned myself to thinking happened only in the ancient world or on remote Pacific islands. With proper scientific detachment I longed to interview these Astorian boys – in the hall and in my classroom – about their state of mind while taking part in such a ceremony. I could not imagine any Astorian male willing to answer my anthropological queries for an article, perhaps entitled: *Sexual Initiation Rites Among Young Males of the North Pacific Rim.*

The act of kissing is, presumably, an act of love. If you are made to kiss something you hate, the act becomes a form of abasement. Were Astorian males acknowledging the superiority of a female power that they yet despised and feared? Why were the boys so angry at us? A Judas kiss (the Mafia uses it) marks the recipient for death or serious injury. Did the initiates' kiss mean they were marking us (girls and women) as prey? Did they hate us just for being female? Was I supposed to hate myself for menstruating? (My mother seemed to think so.) Or were the Astorians *worshiping* the bloody object that they kissed? Priests kiss the cross (once bloodied). True believers kiss the Pope's toe. The toe of the great statue of the Buddha is worn down by centuries of warm lips pressing against cold stone. The altar stones of the ancient world were once stained by bloody sacrifice, preferably of a freshly killed virgin. *In geography class, when the forty-year-old virgin teacher mentioned virgin forests, a ripple of cruelty ran through the class. And she blushed.*

Almost every house on Astoria's hillside had a framed chart that showed the shoals that comprised the Columbia River bar, and showed the wrecks on those shoals. There were more than two hundred. At low tide ancient hulls and masts were clearly visible. We grew accustomed to being told that a teak stair-rail, or an ornate lamp, or a brass oarlock (used as a hat rack) was from such and such a famous wreck. During Father's command, for the first time in over a hundred years there were no wrecks on the Columbia River bar.

If a bad storm were coming up, Father would call all hands and take the *Onondaga* out to sea, before the bar became impassable. A deep musical groan from the ship's funnel carried throughout the town. Sailors walking down the street or entwined with their girlfriends at the movies would stop whatever they were doing and run toward the ship. On stormy nights I would lie in bed listening to wind wuthering around the house, wind creaking in the holly tree outside my window. I slept fitfully, knowing what was to come: the ring of the telephone in my parents' bedroom, Father's voice barking orders, the *Onondaga*'s whistle blast. Anne would rush to the kitchen to make a pot of coffee, so Father, at one gulp, could be jarred awake. Mother would get the car out, and all of us would get dressed so we could ride down to the docks. The other Coast Guard families would be there, too, shivering in the rain and darkness, watching the ship get ready to cast off.

The wide-beamed *Onondaga*, pitching and tossing so that even Father was seasick, would face into the storm that drove the waters of the Pacific into the mouth of the huge river. The two contending forces battled it out across the shoals. Somehow the *Onondaga* would make her way out into the open sea and remain there on patrol, stopping any ship that might try to make it into the river and signalling, by radio, to any shipmaster who was inside not to even *think* of putting out to sea. Once, twenty ships rode at anchor for three days. If a captain protested that his owners had ordered him to take the ship over the bar, no matter what the danger, Father would tell him to wire back that the United States Coast Guard commander present would inform Lloyds of London that the ship had proceeded against all warning. No Coast Guard officer had done this before. Father was too impatient (and too suspicious) to wait for shipowners and desk-bound officials to sort out the matter while sailors' lives were in jeopardy. Having been in the Merchant Marine, having been an enlisted man himself, he held that seamen's lives were more important than any cargo.

From our house high on the hill we could see more of the river and see it better than a sailor could from the *Onondaga* at dockside. Every member of our family was loyally bound to keep a sharp lookout for outgoing freighters as they made ready to cross the bar. If a ship was overloaded, we were to call Father at once. With the aid of his old Zeiss binoculars (which he had purchased in 1919, on his epic drive to Poland), we could check the Plimsoll mark on the freighter hulls. (Samuel Plimsoll was one of Father's heroes. As a member of the British Parliament in the 1870s, he fought for laws which required that all British merchant ships have lines and mark-ings painted on their hulls to indicate the safe level to which the ship could be loaded. Later, most other countries consented to the same regulations.)

Our big bay window also allowed us to look toward Smith Point, where signal flags flew from a mast at the harbor entrance. One red pennant meant Small Craft Warning; various arrangements of flags and pennants designated wind direction. Two red squares, each with a blue square in the center, meant winds of hurricane force. Father made us study *Knight's Manual of Modern Seamanship* in order for us to pass the licencing examination for a small-boat operators license. His ultimate aim was for us to pass the Able Seaman exam, which would have been fruitless (even if allowed), since American women were not allowed to serve at sea.

Sometimes Soviet ships came into the river, their hulls shockingly rusty and dilapidated. We would scan the decks with special diligence and sometimes see what we were looking for – women crew members hanging over the rails, drinking in their impressions of America. Father, ever hopeful that one day his daughters would be as privileged as those seafaring Soviet women, quizzed us on the meaning of red and black buoys (red, right, returning) and running lights (green for starboard, red for port.) We also knew the meaning of the toots and whistles as ships made their way up and down the river, seeking not to run into each other in fog and darkness. (This was before the invention of radar.) A chart with a bright display of funnel markings was posted near the window so we could report not only the name of the ship, but the line to which it belonged. Another chart showed the flags of the world. In addition, I set myself the task of learning the names of all the rigging on a three-masted sailing ship: fore, main, and mizzen masts, main sails, top s'ls, t'gallants, skys'ls, moons'ls, and all the jibs. I know now that this collecting and cataloguing and memorizing of lists of useless information was a classic case of displacement. What I really wanted to know about was sex.

There is an age when knowledge for the sake of knowledge takes on a shimmering intensity. The young warrior *attacks* Latin declensions and the implementation of pi, the parts of the grasshopper, the symbols of the periodic table. He-she *wrestles* with ideas. Girl or boy, the young warrior throws a ball, swims laps, runs miles. Sexuality is sublimated, and learning becomes sexy. Learning is power, a way out of the family into adulthood. Power also rests in learning how to drive a car (not in my family), how to earn money (not in my family), how to relate to the opposite sex (not in my family).

The *Astoria Budget* reported that, in the state capital at Eugene, there had been discussion in the legislature about sex education in the schools. Oregon, I read, was one of the first states in the union to introduce sex education in a general science textbook. I was delighted to find that I owned such a book. There was a diagram about how to place an outhouse so it would not contaminate a well. There was a diagram (straight lines, no actual drawing) of the human digestive system. A diagram of how a door-bell works. A diagram (straight lines, no actual drawing) of something labelled "the female reproductive system." What did this have to do with the fluttering in my belly, the tingling in my breasts, my longing to reach out to touch, to be touched?

I may not have known the names of the parts of my body, but I liked myself *down there*. Sometimes, using a hand mirror, I looked at myself, looked at my lotus, the heart of the rose. I could masturbate to orgasm. I was confident that I could be a good wife, that I could make babies when the time came. I was now a virgin, a maiden. One day I would be a matron. I was vaguely aware that I was leaving something (someone) out of the picture. I thought it was the man who would be willing to be my husband. I refused to acknowledge my Aphrodite, knocking at the door.

Surely young girls deserve information beyond the ken of talks about menstruation and how the sperm meets the ovary and where babies come from. They need a *Cunt Owner's Manual*, written by women who under-stand female sexuality. What I got was my State of Oregon science book and *Knight's Manual of Modern Seamanship*. Mizzen masts and door-bells, indeed!

Much later, from 1979 to 1999, I would go to England every year in my role as a storyteller and therapist, engaged in one way or another in King Arthur and the Holy Grail. In the late 1980s, and through the 1990s, I con-ducted a tour called "A Winter's Journey to King Arthur's Britain." I led a dozen pilgrims, male and female, to places connected to Arthurian legend. I stood in wind and rain, under sun and moon, telling the stories where the stories may have happened. Gradually, a very personal female version of the Grail legend has revealed itself to me. Part of me is Parsifal, the young warrior, the fool, the questing knight. My *mother* is my Fisher King, the wounded healer, wounded in the groin. The Great War, the loss of Edwardian England, the loss of her sexuality, and fear of my father's infidelity, are her Wasteland. She is fishing for the womb-shaped Celtic salmon, Christ incarnate, who swims forever in a well, waiting for the fruit of wisdom to fall from the hazel tree.

Like Parsifal, I erred in that I did not break through all barriers, to ask the burning question of my Fisher Queen. She sent out a message, loud and clear: *Don't ask!* So I didn't. As a teenager, I was afraid that if I called her bluff (about sexuality), if I destroyed her pain, I would destroy both of us. When my mother could not, would not, let the question be asked, I could have turned to other women, to the Ladies of the Lake. Once again I failed.

In the mysterious barge that bears the dying Arthur across the lake to Avalon, there are, supposedly, three queens (three goddesses): Maiden, Mother, Crone. I now discern a fourth queen, too long obscured, who is also in the boat. She has many names, among them, Aphrodite.

The questing knight's job description says that he is here to rescue virgins. At one time the term *virgin* meant a woman who had autonomy over her own body and life, not necessarily one who had never had sexual experience. Autonomy suggests the ability to say no. It also grants the right to say yes! My warrior-self was there to guard me against the consequences of unbridled sex. My warrior-self engaged me in learning, as a way to divert and protect me, taught me to value my self-esteem, my intellectual identity. Out of fear of losing the sovereignty I had gained, I did not allow myself to trust my Aphrodite. I was too frightened to welcome her, to make friends with her, to be playful with her.

Aphrodite could have assured me of my worth as a sexual being, taught me to acknowledge the virtue of sexuality. She could have shown me how to arouse desire in myself, and accept desire in a man. Alone in my room, I had opened my woman's body to the possibility of pleasure; out in the world, I froze rather than meet a man's eyes, hold his gaze. If a man looked my way, I thought he must have made a mistake, that he was looking at the girl over my shoulder. I rushed to put him at his ease, to let him off the hook, with chatter. My mother's habit of deflection had taught me to ward off, too. Before any boy got near enough to be a threat (or for me to be a threat to him), I had already broadcast my subliminal message: *Don't even ask.*

The Sisters Allan, who owned our house, soon became fast friends with Mother. The sisters were beautiful, aristocratic, and charming. They wore hats they had bought in Paris in 1920, when they went there with their papa, just after the War. The hats were of such superior quality that they could be steamed and reshaped year after year. Each sister had a felt hat, to wear to church in winter, and a straw hat, refurbished annually with flowers and cherries, to wear in summertime. Zoe taught English at the high school and was not married. Mignon was married to a Mr. Cellars, a grey shadow in the background, who had provided her with a son, and Zoe with a nephew. Needless to say, the boy's name was Allan.

One day, just after school was out for the summer, the Allans suggested a picnic at Youngs River Falls, to see the salmon leap. We three girls were invited, too. Joyce elected to spend the afternoon playing at a neighbor's house, but Anne and I accepted the invitation. We were just pulling the car out of the sisters' driveway when Allan came running out of the house. He had changed his mind, he said. He would go with us to Youngs River after all. What Anne felt I do not know, but I was overcome with shyness and delight. Allan was a senior, I a mere sophomore. We were only a few minutes out of town before I knew that Allan knew he had made a grave mistake. He hated being in the car with us, hated the prospect of spending the afternoon with a gaggle of chattering women and two uninteresting girls. He was wishing that he had never come.

As soon as we arrived at the falls, Allan bolted out of the car, but his mother called him back. She asked him to carry the picnic basket down into the glen. The discussion as to where would be the best spot must have seemed interminable to him. As soon as he could, he set the basket down and disappeared along the path to the falls. The ladies opened the basket and took out a square of oilcloth, which they laid on the ground. Then, a linen tablecloth. Then, plates, covered dishes, china cups. Finally they produced a beautifully contrived brass trivet with a spirit lamp, over which they fitted a diminutive brass kettle. All during this time the Sisters Allan were wearing their Paris hats, the straw ones with nodding cherries.

Anne, who was probably as aware of Allan as I was, took no risks. A year older than Allan, she cannily allied herself with the grown-ups. I was left in limbo, neither child nor adult. I, too, wandered towards the falls. When I came to the pool I was not prepared for the sight, not prepared for the cruelty and wantonness of nature. The waters below the falls were a-boil with fish. Fish were leaping out of the water, falling back with a splash, hitting the rocks with a sickening slap.

Salmon returning from the sea stop eating when they reach freshwater. These fish had lost the jewel-like quality I usually associated with them. They were lean and muscular and desperate, and their skin hung in strips and fringes, rubbed off by the abrasive action of the fight upstream. Some of them had holes gouged in their sides; I could see the organs beating beyond the bones. Some floated belly-up. The pool was filled with blood and foam and fish eggs – death and fecundity. And still they leaped and leaped, gasped and leaped again, battering themselves against the rock face of the falls. Allan had made his way out into the water and was trying to catch a fish.

When young Tamlane was stolen away by the Queen of Elfland, his own true love and betrothed, Burd Janet, pled with him to tell her how she could win him back again. He told her that she must make for herself a ring of holy water, as she stood by the well at Miles Crossing, at midnight on Hallowe'en. There and then she must wait for him to ride by in the Elf Queen's procession. She would know him by his one hand, ungloved, and by the star on his crown. She must drag him from his horse into the ring of holy water and hold on to him, no matter what shape they changed him into, until he became a red-hot glaive (sword). Then she must plunge him into the cold, cold well.

I took off my shoes and socks and waded out into the pool. *First they changed him into a sheet of ice, then into a fire that roared up as if to consume her.* The shock shivered through all my body, opening every pore and aperture. I reached out for a fish. There were so many that at first I could not believe that I could not capture one. *Then they turned him into an adder that skipped and skipped through their hands.* I managed to drive one salmon into the shallows. It caught itself among some rocks, and I picked it up. *Then he became a serpent that reared up and would have bitten her. But still she held on!* I looked over at Allan. He was drenched, his clothes were molded to his body. Something was growing, swelling in Allan's crotch! I was drenched, too. My dress was clinging to me.

I clutched the fish to my chest and staggered across the pool. *Then they turned him into a snow-white dove that fluttered and fluttered between her breasts. But still she held on!* I had a crazy idea that I could help the fish by placing it higher on the rock face of the falls. *Then they turned him into a milk-white swan with a long neck that thrust and thrust. But still she held on!* I reached up as high as I could. The fish heaved out of my grasp, slithered down between my breasts, over my belly and between my thighs. *And then he became a red-hot glaive.* I was directly beneath the falls, gasping as it engulfed me. A shiver emanated through my entire body.

*When she plunged the glaive into the cold, cold well, then Tamlane was
restored to her, and he nought but a mother-naked man encircled in her
arms. She covered him with her green, green cloak and together they ran
back to the castle where they wed . . .*

"Would you care for a cucumber sandwich, dear?" asked Mother, from
the bank.

CHAPTER 10

The Great White Fleet

MOTHER DID NOT GO away to school until she was sixteen, but when she did go it was to the Abbey at Malvern, a boarding school of excellent reputation. We knew that she had studied history and French there, that she was good at math, played cricket and hockey, and that she had passed the university levels for Oxford. What interested us more was the extraneous knowledge she had acquired. Girls at Malvern Abbey were made aware that each and any one of them might find herself, sometime in her life, the only English woman for thousands of miles around. She might suddenly be called upon to entertain British royalty in the middle of the jungle. Or she might have to represent, by her decorum and behavior, the best of civilization under the most trying of circumstances. Therefore, it was incumbent upon her to know how to give herself a decent sponge bath.

One of the treats of traveling with Mother was to witness this fascinating process. As long as she had a bar of Pears soap and a good sea sponge she could give herself a bath in a teacup. We three little girls would sit in a row on a ship's bunk or a Pullman settee and watch while mysterious movements were made under an all-encompassing flannel nightgown. "The trick," Mother would tell us, "is to wash up as far as possible, down as far as possible, and then wash possible." Among other accomplishments learned at school, she could walk about with three books balanced on her head (so as to keep her spine straight), and she could lower herself into a deep curtsey (suitable for royalty).

131

One of Mother's dictums was that one should know and enjoy the fare of the country where one was living. Only the lower classes insisted on tins of bully beef while abroad. (I suspect she had already learned this from her seafaring family.) It was Mother's belief that an intelligent, well-bred woman, finding herself in a strange country, tours the local market and inquires of her cook (or her neighbors) about the foods that are obtainable and in season. She learns what game and meat is available, what fish are swimming in nearby streams and oceans. She is not afraid to eat strange fruits or vegetables, provided they have been proved safe for human consumption. However, the menu should not be off-putting. The trick is to serve a foreign repast in a reassuringly British manner.

In 1938-39, the Astoria winter, famous for its incessant rainfall and howling storms, was made even more dreary by the news on the radio. Mother's and Father's Great War was supposed to have ended wars, but there was war in China, war in Spain, and war in Ethiopia. For our family, all this paled into insignificance compared to what had happened at Munich in September: the British had humbled themselves to the Germans and signed the Munich Pact. To no avail, for almost as soon as Chamberlain returned to London, proclaiming peace, Hitler marched into Czechoslovakia. Hitler's deliberate insult to Britain burned our souls, but in April, when Mussolini took over Albania, our family hardly noticed. Albanians, Ethiopians, Jews, and even the Czechs did not, of themselves, rally much interest. We were only concerned with something called *British Honor*.

In April a large Italian passenger freighter put into port. There were no passengers aboard and the ship was already loaded, but it did not make any attempt to put out to sea. The Italian captain and his officers strolled in the town, called on various officials and were entertained by the Pilot Association. They provided a welcome diversion for Astoria's tight little society. Mother and Father had met the Italian captain at various gatherings. When they drew up a guest list for the next dinner party aboard the *Onondaga*, the captain and several of his officers were included.

Fujas, Father's Filipino steward, was in his glory; Mother had consented to his carving a magnificent swan centerpiece out of ice. He and Mother had a stand-off on the menu, however. Fujas had wanted something elaborate, to dazzle the Italians. Mother had insisted that he keep things simple and use local fare. The more simple, the more exotic, she tried to explain. Pickled salmon cheeks and shad roe were among the appetizers.

(Mother figured that the Italians had probably never tasted them.) She bypassed the obvious Columbia River salmon for good Oregon beef. Roast beef *au jus* and fresh vegetables without sauces (just butter, salt, and pepper) would hold the center. And for dessert, blackberry pies and hand-cranked vanilla ice cream.

The pies Mother would make herself, from wild blackberries picked the previous summer by her own fair daughters. The ice cream would be packed into individual molds, shaped like little U.S. destroyers, which were standard issue for the officers' mess on all navy and Coast Guard ships. When the ice-cream ships were unmolded and served, on mirrors, they were arranged to look like Teddy Roosevelt's Great White Fleet steaming down the length of the wardroom table. Teddy Roosevelt was one of Father's heroes. It was T. R.'s Great White Fleet (strong and pure) that had inspired him to run away and join the navy in 1912.

Father and Mother agreed that they liked the Italian captain, who spoke excellent English and who was a charming, urbane man. But Father was wary. The Italian ship was overstaying its welcome. Day after day, week after week, the Italians postponed their departure. It was as though they were *waiting* for something. Father sent a junior officer and some sailors to make a standard Coast Guard inspection. The sailors, dressed in blue dungarees and wearing no ratings, included an old gunner's mate who had served in the 1917-18 war. When he came back from the inspection and reported to Father he said, Yep, some of the overhead pipes on the Italian ship *did* look suspiciously like gun barrels. Father was privately convinced that this was no ordinary freighter, that it was designed for attack, and that the captain was a high-ranking officer in the Italian navy who had been sent on a special mission by Mussolini himself.

April passed into May. At long last the Italian captain invited all the people who had entertained him to a dinner party aboard his own ship. Doubtless it would be the social event of the year. Mother bought a new dress. On May 22, a couple of days before the dinner party, Mussolini signed the infamous Pact of Steel with Germany, promising to blink if and when Hitler marched into Poland. Now the lines of war were firmly drawn and underscored. Winston Churchill came on the radio to tell us that the hand that held the dagger had stabbed Britain in the back. Mother was saddened and enraged. She told Father that she could not possibly go to the dinner party.

For two days and nights they debated what to do. The official position of the United States was not the same as that of the British. President Franklin D. Roosevelt might personally want to join Britain in its imminent fight against the Germans, but the people of the United States were a long, long way from involving themselves in a war. Although his sympathies were with Mother's, Father would be representing the federal government of the United States. He had already accepted the invitation. He felt that for him not to go would put him, his service, and his country in an embarrassing position. Not to say his career. Mother's argument was that she was first and foremost herself, Joan Amphlett Corfield, not just Father's wife. She was a British subject. Fate had dictated that she take a stand. For her to go would be to deny everything that she stood for, that civilization stood for. She had been in training for this moment all her life.

A compromise was reached. Father would go to the dinner, but he would escort his eldest daughter, my sister Anne, an *American*, as proxy for Mother. This would show that there was no personal ill-feeling toward his host, either on his part or on Mother's. However, on no account was Father to lie about the reason for Mother's absence. She did not have a cold and none of the children was sick or injured. This was no mere domestic matter. Mother was playing her part on a larger stage, the stage of the world.

All went well – perhaps better than could be expected. Father introduced Anne and, when the captain asked if Mrs. Higbee were ill, Father said, "Mrs. Higbee sends her personal regrets. However, as you know, she is a British citizen. She feels strongly that, since the signing of a pact between your country and Germany she cannot dine with you and your officers. It is a matter of principle."

At which, the Italian captain rose and proposed a toast to Mother.

In late June, the *Onondaga* went upriver to Portland, Oregon, almost a hundred miles inland. The ship, which made the trip every year to go into dry-dock, stayed on to help celebrate the annual Portland Rose Festival. During the festival, the public was invited to come aboard for a tour, from the bridge to the engine room. On the final day, a tea for three hundred people was served on the fantail of the ship. The mayor of Portland and other city officials attended, along with senators, congressmen, and the Rose Festival queen. We three girls were pressed into service to help serve finger-sized sandwiches and petits fours.

At the end of the week, when the *Onondaga* cast off again, the officers' wives and children were allowed to stay aboard and enjoy the leisurely river trip back to Astoria. For a long stretch we passed only a few towns and villages. Mostly we stared into endless forest. Some places that we glimpsed had no way to get in or out, except by river. The *Onondaga* blew its deep, satisfying whistle blast as we passed, and children came down to the bank to wave to us. I suppose that, as far as Mother was concerned, we might as well have been up the Amazon or in Conrad's Heart of Darkness, notwithstanding that everybody we saw was white and most spoke English.

There were other ships to watch, and log rafts. Schools of salmon cavorted past our hull, headed upriver toward their spawning grounds. Occasionally an eagle would drop from out of the peerless sky, talons stretched to snatch a struggling fish. A sailor stood at the *Onondaga*'s bow, taking soundings with a plumb line, calling out a litany of marks, including the ever thrilling *mark twain*. Father had ordered this procedure both as precaution and as basic training in seamanship. The younger enlisted men, he felt, were being rendered lubberly by too much modern equipment. If war came within the next few years, who knew where and in what predicament these men might one day find themselves? *One of Father's other heroes (besides Samuel Plimsoll and Theodore Roosevelt) was Captain William Bligh who, when he was put overboard by his crew, sailed two thousand miles in an open boat.*

In late afternoon we rounded Tongue Point. The river was unusually placid, a mill pond. We could see the houses of Astoria sprawled on the hillside and we could look downriver to Desdemona Shoals and beyond, to where the river met the sea. We could also see that the Italian ship had left the dock. It was swinging at anchor, its reflection mirrored in the still waters. I could hear Father's voice cracking out orders, then there was a scurry of pounding feet on the deck. Coast Guard wives and Coast Guard children knew enough to jump out of the way. We gathered close together under an awning on the foredeck, watching and wondering as the sailors uncovered the big gun and swung it around towards the Italian ship. Nothing happened. Nothing at all. We steamed past the Italians, about a quarter of a mile away from them, and made our way to the dock. Tired and sunburned, we straggled home.

"What was that all about?" asked Mother.

"Just an ordinary drill," said Father. Mother must have registered her disbelief. "If Mussolini is asking for trouble," said Father, "it could just as well start here in Astoria as anywhere else in the world. I want the captain of that ship to know that, even if we have been dining out together for weeks, I won't be caught napping. He has his job to do and I have mine."

A few days later the Italian ship was gone.

I like to believe that if my father had been in command at Pearl Harbor in December 1941, the Japanese attack would not have been such a surprise nor so disastrous. However, Father became so obsessed with the idea of arming Tongue Point that he colluded with the local politicians on a pork-barrel deal. Not for any personal or financial gain, I hasten to make clear, but for bull-headed, egocentric reasons. His unbounded enthusiasm constituted his fatal flaw. He thought that, if he liked something or if he did something, his cause was imbued with virtue because *he* was a virtuous man.

When the Congressional committee members came to investigate the possibility of building a naval base at Astoria, Father took them out on the *Onondaga* and kept them there all day on one pretext or another, plying them remorselessly with Mother's famous blackberry pies, while the local politicians had at them. Finally, in desperation, they said they would build the Tongue Point Naval Base. Which they did, instead of spending the money on Guam. Historians now agree that, if Guam had been properly fortified, MacArthur might have made a stand there and the war in the Pacific could have been considerably shortened. Some of the more pedantic historians mention a place called Tongue Point (among hundreds of other boondoggles) as reason for lack of military strength in the remote Pacific. Tongue Point, several miles inland from the Columbia River bar, was but marginally useful during World War II. After the war, it continued to be an embarrassment to the defense department, which closed it down in the 1960s. I don't know if Father ever understood his culpability.

My parents were less than fifty years old in 1939. I am over seventy as I write this. They were good people but not, thank God, perfect. I no longer need them to be perfect.

THE SALMON
OF KNOWLEDGE

CHAPTER 11

The Almond Tree

BRITAIN DECLARED WAR on Germany on September 1, 1939. The terrible passivity that had deadened Britain was over at last. France had collapsed but it never occurred to us that Britain might do the same. The current of change thrilled through our household. Grown-ups said the worst thing that could happen was a war, but it is my observation that war (in the beginning) makes people cheerful.

Father was promoted to full commander (three stripes) and almost immediately received orders to report as second-in-command to the Coast Guard base at San Pedro, the port of Los Angeles. We drove down to California on Thanksgiving weekend. In the Cascade Mountains, most motels and restaurants were closed for the season, but in late afternoon we saw, through snow, a sign advertising roast turkey and homemade pumpkin pie. Father agreed to stop, but only for one hour. We were the only customers. Mother, discovering that our elderly hosts planned to eat in the kitchen, urged them to sit at the same table with us. Father and the old man rearranged tables and chairs, Mother and Anne helped in the kitchen, Joyce and I set the table. The old man said grace, Father carved, then we ate, and talked about the war. After dessert, like genii out of a bottle, our family cleared the table, washed the dishes, bade good bye, and disappeared forever into the darkness.

In San Pedro our windows looked down on a sprawling military-industrial scene. Freighters and naval vessels swung at anchor in the outer harbor, in the crook of the breakwater. The inner harbor, threaded by a maze of shipping channels, was crowded with dry-docks and cranes, warehouses and docks, navy and army installations, oil wells and oil-storage tanks. Most of these were on Terminal Island, across Cerritos Channel.

The largest population of Japanese outside Japan lived on Terminal Island. After school the Japanese kids walked down to the landing at the end of Ninth Street and took the little passenger ferry (no cars) over to where they lived. The island, which once had been a sand shoal, was flat as the deck of a ship, a dirty platform, largely covered with concrete and asphalt, with a few weeds growing in the cracks. Oil wells, oil tanks, oily sumps made it smell bad. In the 1890s, before oil was discovered, it had been a summer resort for people escaping the heat of Los Angeles, the city proper. Wooden shacks and cottages were now a mysterious hodgepodge of bath houses, communal laundries, Buddhist temples, and dwellings where the Japanese were suffered to live.

The Yugoslavians lived in Mediterranean-style houses on the hillside in San Pedro: white stucco and red-tiled roofs. They attended Mary Star of the Sea Catholic church. There had been a church of the same name in Astoria, with a gaudy statue of the Virgin out front. Every year there was a blessing of the Yugoslavian fishing fleet. Strong young men (some of them boys from the high-school football team) carried a flower-smothered cross down through the streets to the harbor. The priest sprinkled holy water and blessed the fishing boats, then the bearers threw the cross into the oily waters of the harbor, just as their ancestors had once thrown a bedecked effigy of Aphrodite, or the dolphin goddess, Atargatis, into the Adriatic.

I was used to the soft mists of Astoria. In southern California harsh light glanced off white buildings, bounced off sidewalks. My eyes were assaulted by a chemical mix not yet given the name of "smog." We had arrived at the beginning of the rainy season. The Los Angeles basin had become so built up that there was no place for runoff to go. When it rained in the mountains, dry concrete storm culverts, miles below, were hit by flash floods in a matter of minutes; they became raging torrents, overflowing drains and flooding the streets. People actually drowned. Part of the trouble was the nature of the clay soil, which did not absorb. Adobe mud in the vacant lot, where I took a short cut, stuck to my shoes; by the time I got to school I was teetering on platform soles.

A few Japanese lived on strawberry farms on Point Fermin, above Portuguese Bend. Mother, out driving with a friend, was shocked to see a woman in harness, pulling a plow driven by her husband. Mother stopped the car and went over the fence to protest. The Japanese woman explained that the hillside was so precarious that one mis-step would send the adobe soil, and the quartz shale to which it was attached, sliding into the Pacific Ocean. A mule could not do the work she was doing. It took human intelligence, experience, judgment, teamwork. She and her husband had established a perfect partnership between them. Every step had to be thought out carefully and discussed before she went forward. *And*, she wanted Mother to know, she had two sons who had graduated from the University of California at Los Angeles. The real reason to protest was lost on Mother: by law, a Japanese family would never be allowed to own the land they worked so diligently and astutely. Because of the racially motivated Exclusion Act, they could only rent it.

Astoria High School in Oregon had been built like a fortress, three stories rising straight up on the hillside. San Pedro High School was laid-back. Low buildings sprawled over a large campus of flower beds, courtyards, and outlying buildings. I entered by a back gate and passed by the auto shop where boys went early, to work on their own jalopies. Welding torches flared and knightlike figures in steel helmets loomed in the darkness. I soon learned not to look; to do so invited whistles, cat calls, remarks about my big breasts.

A little farther on, down a few steps, I came to the Japanese garden, my favorite place in San Pedro. It was surrounded by a chain-link fence; the gate had a strong lock on it. A bronze plaque informed me that the elders of the Japanese Society had designed and planted the garden as a gift to the high school. Almost every morning I stopped and looked over the fence. The little landscape, textured with dark green bonsai, gave an illusion of northern forests, for which my soul was starved. Soon after Christmas, a pale-pink almond tree came into bloom.

I was pleased and surprised to find so many courses offered at San Pedro High. I decided to take the journalism course. There was also a print shop, where boys could learn how to set type and also work at an old Linotype machine. I managed to talk myself into the printing course, and persuaded the office to make it count as substitute for a home-economics credit in sewing. The school paper, *Fore and Aft*, came out every week,

looking extraordinarily professional. Miss Mary Jane O'Rourke, the journalism teacher, came from a newspaper family. Her father had been an
editor and her brother worked for the *Rocky Mountain News*, in Colorado.
Miss O'Rourke had been a hot-shot girl reporter in the 1920s and 1930s;
now she had only one arm and had to earn her living as a teacher. How she
lost her arm I never knew.

English had always been my best subject. Since I was eight years old I
had written poems and stories with utter self-confidence. English was my
native language; in most places I had lived, my schoolmates came from
homes where another language was spoken. Even in Connecticut, among
the upper-middle class, I was praised for my writing, especially for my
book reports. One teacher told me she thought that, when I grew up, I
would review children's books for the *New York Times*. (Which I did.)

Now Miss O'Rourke was teaching me to tighten my prose, know a good
lead, pull it up to the first paragraph. She was tough and I was reduced to
tears, something I expected to happen to me only in math class. Miss
O'Rourke said that, if I wanted to be a journalist, I would have to learn to
take criticism; to be able to do so was more important than being a good
writer. I learned to take her pithy remarks without so much as a glisten in
the corner of my eye. By the next term (in January 1940) I was made editor
of the *Fore and Aft*.

Mr. Nicholas Zerotovich (later Dr. Zerotovich) was Yugoslavian. He
taught Contemporary History and was the first European intellectual I ever
knowingly encountered. Mr. Zerotovich told me that there were sources
beyond *Time* magazine and *Reader's Digest* I should explore. He made
the class read "The White Man's Burden," which, being a poem by Kipling,
I already knew by heart. To my consternation he tore Kipling apart, along
with the British empire. He made me look up the word "jingoism."

Mme. Colfax, who taught French, had lived in Paris and had been
divorced! At the end of the term she took six students uptown to the
Museum of Los Angeles to see, not the dinosaurs, but actor Edward G.
Robinson's loaned collection of French Impressionist paintings. Robinson,
who looked like a frog, often played gangster parts wherein he used a New
York (i.e. Jewish) accent. I thought that someone who, in the movies,
looked and talked like a gangster, would have to be also an uncouth boor in
real life. Robinson, who spent his early career in the Yiddish theater, came
from a long line of rabbis, had graduated from City College, and studied

law before he became an actor. He was a gentleman, a man of culture, a patron of the arts who had started his art collection barely a decade after the famous 1919 Armory show.

I thought culture came in another package, that it looked, and sounded, like Ronald Colman, one of my mother's favorite actors. Colman, who always played the part of an English gentleman, was not half as well educated as Robinson. (Nor were most English gentlemen.) Mother had never set foot in an art gallery, much less taken me to one. I had never seen true art before! That day in the Los Angeles Museum, I was bowled over, especially by the Gauguins. I did my best not to seem impressed. I would kick and scream all the way rather than admit to Mme. Colfax, or to anyone else, that I was being pushed willy-nilly beyond the boundaries of my family's shibboleths.

Moving from place to place so often had taught the members of our family to be both flexible and rigid. Our family history was a sort of jerky movie film, made up of short frames of time. Now the sprocket holes were beginning to fray. My parents were as ill prepared as their daughters. We were what is now called a nuclear family, completely isolated. Our adherence to codes and manners, more than slightly ridiculous at times, nevertheless had given us definition. However, it also made us fragile. My sisters and I had not grown up with anyone. I had no brothers and I had not watched boys, even from a distance, go from A to B to C. Nor had I seen girls going from child to girl to woman. *How* an American child became an adult eluded me and eluded my mother. My father had been abandoned by his mother (scandalously, she had run off with the Isadora Duncan crowd). His father had died when Father was ten. He and his younger sister, Agnes, went to live with their paternal grandparents (where he was happy), and then with some aunts in Kansas City (where he was unhappy). He joined the navy at age eighteen. As parents of young children, my parents had shown strength, courage, wisdom, humor, and great ability to love. They were wonderful with small children, clueless when we began to grow up.

When Anne graduated from high school there was no plan for her, no place to go. Father still did not approve of his offspring going to college. He had done very well without it! Mother thought that college was rather like finishing school, an unnecessary and very expensive frill. I think they both had counted on their daughters being attractive and marrying early.

They must have had some vague idea that we would work at an inconsequential job until some young man, preferably sea-going and of the officer class, came along and proposed. Alas! We were more at home with older people than we were with our contemporaries. Our parents' friends often remarked on our good manners and poise, attributes which only masked our underlying social ineptness. Now the day of reckoning was at hand. We were being pushed out into the world.

Anne adored Father and tried to do everything to please him. What she really wanted was to be able to join the Coast Guard, or go to Annapolis, or ship out in the Merchant Marine. She envied those women on Russian ships. Father had only contempt for women who became school teachers or librarians. He had grudging respect for nurses, especially navy nurses. And for airline stewardesses. He also liked secretaries, as long as they were glamorous and prepared to marry well. To marry well (and happily) meant to marry someone just like Father, or what Father thought he would have been if he had not joined the navy: a successful entrepreneur.

Anne graduated from Astoria High School in 1938. She decided to become a nurse, which she had heard was a prerequisite for becoming an airline stewardess or a stewardess on a steamship line. Astoria Hospital was a few blocks down the hill from us. When she walked in and said she wanted to begin training, they took her without further ado. The second day she was sent into the operating room, told to take out a bucket with a severed arm and to scrub the bloody floor. I would have quit then and there but, being Anne, she lasted three more months.

I knew I could not be as brave as Anne. I was perceived as being uncharacteristically generous when I said so. My remark gave Anne the opportunity to bask, and may have been a comfort to her, but what I had meant was that I thought it silly to be brave just for braveness's sake. Eventually, the true nature of my attitude was revealed. I was not exactly shunned, but I was viewed with suspicion by Anne and Mother. In the fall Anne went up to Eugene, to attend Oregon State College. She was rushed by a sorority, but she lasted only six weeks in Eugene. A dean telephoned our parents to say that Anne should be withdrawn from school. I don't know what had happened; I only knew that Anne was terribly unhappy. I had read an article in *Reader's Digest* about something called "psychiatry." I suggested that Anne go see a psychiatrist. Mother was furious at me. Our family could handle its own problems, thank you. She told me that there was nothing wrong with

Anne so often that I began to suspect that something terrible had happened. I would have been relieved to hear that Anne was pregnant.

Meanwhile, we moved to San Pedro. Anne decided to go to Katherine Gibbs Secretarial School. She moved up to Hollywood and lived with other Gibbs girls in a hotel. She lost weight. She learned to put on makeup, wear high heels, choose black or navy-blue secretary suits, wear white blouses, white gloves, secretary-type hats. She quit the two-year course before the first year was out, in order to take a job as a switchboard operator with the Los Angeles Harbor Department. Mother was relieved to have Anne living at home. She had almost no social life and never went out on a date, but she knew everything that went on in the harbor. Father gave her grudging approval. They could talk shop together. Anne and I no longer communicated. Indeed, we had not been able to carry on a real conversation for years, and never did so again.

What I gleaned from Anne's experience was that my parents could not be trusted to make decisions about my future. Instead of trying to find out what they wanted me to do, *I* told *them* what I was going to do. I was going to go to college – a good college, like Bryn Mawr or Wellesley. The high-school principal summoned me into his office to tell me that I should go to Stanford, where he had gone. The head of the English department (with whom, because I substituted journalism, I had taken no courses) sought me out to tell me to consider her alma mater, Pomona College, fifty miles away from San Pedro. She set up a reading program for me to follow during the summer. I would return to high school in the fall of 1941, graduate in January 1942, and take the entrance exams in April. Going back east was a fantasy, I knew; Stanford was more expensive than Pomona and seven hundred miles away. Pomona was a good college, "the Oxford of the West," and had more Rhodes scholars teaching there than at any other small liberal-arts college. Despite Mr. Zerotovich's best efforts, I was still a snobbish Anglophile. I decided to go to Pomona.

As editor of the school paper I belonged to the Pep Club. So did the head cheerleader, the president of the Home Economics Club, the leader of the girls' Japanese club, of the Business Studies Club, and the secretary of the student body – about sixteen girls in all. Mother suggested that I invite them to our house for afternoon tea. We set the date for the first Friday after Christmas vacation, two weeks before I would graduate.

On a boring Sunday afternoon, when I was doing my homework, Father phoned from his office down at the harbor. His voice was sharp as he asked for Mother. Turn on the radio! The Japanese had attacked Hawaii! They might be on their way to Los Angeles! And, by the way, he would not be home for supper. We spent the rest of the day and a good part of the night glued to the radio. That night (or was it the next?) planes flew over San Pedro. The guns at Fort MacArthur upper reservation, just blocks farther up from where we lived, boomed heavily into the darkness. Father telephoned to tell us (order us) to go down to the garage, which was buried under the hill below our house. We left the wide garage door open and sat on folding chairs by the back wall, watching the searchlights sweep across the sky. There were planes overhead and unidentifiable globes of light (not searchlights) that streaked suddenly from horizon to horizon. Years later I asked Father what they could have been. He said he did not have any idea. For a while I assumed they were unidentified flying objects. I still don't know what they were.

On Monday morning, December 8, I went to school. I was short of sleep. As usual, I entered the campus by the back gate. I walked past the auto shops and toward the flight of steps near the Japanese garden. When I looked through the fence a wave of nausea swept over me. The stone lanterns, the arched bridge were pulverized. The bonsai had been uprooted and reduced to straw. The almond tree, almost ready to bloom, had been felled and hacked to pieces. When I tried to tell Miss O'Rourke about the almond tree, she was impatient with me. More important things were happening! The Japanese students had called a special meeting. Only three teachers were allowed to attend, and no other students – except me, the editor of the *Fore and Aft*. She had wangled that privilege, only to have me be late to class! I must run over to the auditorium *now*, or I would be locked out.

I entered the auditorium and sat down near the front, the better to take notes. The president of the Japanese Students' Society got up to talk. He pointed out that, from now on, every Japanese-born student and every Nisei (someone of Japanese descent, but born in the United States) must be careful not to speak in Japanese, no matter where he or she was. People would equate Japanese speakers with spies. Also, people would be waiting to pounce on any Nisei or Japanese student who broke the law. They all knew that, when they went down to the ferry after school, they had a tendency to jaywalk at the foot of Ninth Street. They had played tag with the town policemen for years and had been heckled, even given tickets, on that account. What had been seen as annoying teenage foolery could be exaggerated into an act of treason. They all knew that Japanese students were criticized for sticking together, not mingling with the rest of the student body. Now they must resist that tendency. They must circulate among students of different nationalities. *I thought of the ruined garden.* Someone raised his hand to ask what would happen if other students attacked them. A teacher got up to speak. Not to worry, he said. *I thought of the stone lanterns, smashed to smithereens.* Someone else asked if they would still be allowed to live on Terminal Island. And what would happen to their fishing boats? The teacher answered that those who were United States citizens had nothing to be apprehensive about. The government would look after them. *I thought of the uprooted bonsai.*

After the meeting I went into a girls' washroom. Some Japanese girls were there, combing their hair. They stopped talking immediately. I went into a stall; when I came out they were still there, obviously waiting for me to leave so they could continue their conversation. Some demon in me would not let them off the hook so easily, would not let *me* off the hook. If we were supposed to mingle, here was our chance. "Have you seen the Japanese garden?" I asked. One of them shook her head. No. I knew that they had probably come in by another gate, had probably *not* seen. "Someone has smashed it to pieces," I said. "They even hacked down the almond tree." Still no reply. No change of expression, except that their faces became more wooden. Dammit! We were smack dab in the middle of history! My sense of occasion was outraged. Finally I blurted out, "*I don't see what that poor little almond tree has to do with what's happening in Hawaii!*" All three girls began to cry. One of them, through her tears, managed to say, "We didn't think anyone else would feel that way. We didn't think that any of you would ever speak to us again!" Unwittingly, by getting angry, I may have done and said the kindest thing.

Miss O'Rourke grew impatient when, once again, I tried to tell her how upset I was about the wanton destruction of the Japanese garden. To me, this was the most important thing that had happened that day, the key to the whole situation. Miss O'Rourke was preoccupied. She did not merely edit my piece about the assembly; she tore it down and rewrote it, running back and forth to the office to consult with the principal and a hastily-put-together committee of teachers. Paranoia must have been rampant. Some of the teachers may have been afraid of accusations of being too friendly to the enemy. When I saw what was supposed to be my article in print, I barely recognized it. All the bones were taken out. I wondered why Miss O'Rourke had bothered to send me to the meeting. She could have written the piece beforehand, with her eyes closed. Contrary to everything she had ever taught me, she *wanted* the article to be vague. And she wanted my name on it.

Miss O'Rourke probably believed that she was breaking her own rules for someone else's good. She and the principal were terrified that whatever had been said, or asked, in that student assembly, could be turned to disadvantage, not only against the Japanese students but against the Japanese community. Also, the high-school administration might be criticized for even consenting to such a meeting. My editor, whom I had always trusted before, and who had seemed to trust me, struck out anything concrete that I reported, turned the article into patriotic mush. There was not anything about the Japanese students' fears, only a mish-mash about how much they loved the United States, how they deplored what the Japanese had done at Pearl Harbor, how they wished to offer their most abject apologies. I wish, now, that I had written about the Japanese garden. I could have compared the wantonness to Kristallnacht.

Father had been made captain of the Port of Los Angeles a few months before. After Pearl Harbor was attacked, we did not see him for the next few days. And nights. He slept down at the harbor. When the French liner *Normandie* had been sabotaged, burned at its moorings at a New York dock, he ordered that all vessels coming into Los Angeles harbor be turned around before they tied up, to face out to sea. If there was fire or explosion they would be able to cast off "with all due expedition," get under way without benefit of tugs.

Harbor security had long been Father's passion; now he flung himself into the cause with greater intensity. He went into covered piers all over the harbor and screwed big hooks into posts and walls. At night he took his hammock, a remnant from his early days at sea, and slept where he could keep an eye on what was actually going on. In the darkest hours, when least expected, he made sudden inspections and forays to prove how the harbor was, or was not, being secured against sabotage. A guard standing at the gangplank was not good enough. To prove his point, the captain of the port sometimes took a small boat and, at 0200 hours, boarded larger vessels from the seaward side, away from the dock, causing fury and chagrin. He was so appalled by the lack of alertness that he had a business card printed up:

Frank D. Higbee
Arsonist, Saboteur Extraordinary
Thirty years experience
Always at your service.

On Sunday afternoons, so like that one of December 7, Father would don civilian clothes and set out on one of his missions. Sometimes he took one of his daughters along. It was the only chance we had to see him, and I suppose we acted as camouflage. It seems incredible now, but in the early days of the war we could go to the gate of a military site or commercial storage yard and actually have to seek out the watchman or sentry supposed to be posted there. Father would say that he just wanted to show his little girl around the place where he used to work, and hand the man one of his calling cards. He always wrote down the time we had entered on the back of it. Sometimes the man would read the time; rarely would he turn the card over and read the inscription. Even then, he might not react. Father and I would stroll through the gate, find a remote and sheltered spot, and wait. Frequently Father would doze for half an hour or so on a pile of lumber or a heap of cargo nets, while I read a book. (I never went anywhere without a book.) To shut out the light he wrapped his necktie around his eyes. When I looked up from my reading I was struck by how worn out, and how vulnerable, he was.

Usually we waited one or two hours. When (or if) someone finally ferreted us out and came to see what we were doing, Father would congratulate him for his initiative, then remind him how many minutes we had been inside the installation. He would also point out that we should not have been allowed through the gate in the first place. On one occasion someone apologetically explained that he had sounded a general alarm but, since it was Sunday afternoon, there was no one else to respond. On the occasion I remember most, I could not fail to notice how nervous the sentry looked when Father and I approached the gate. The kid, no older than I, was wearing a brand-new uniform. Father gave him a card, with the time written on it, then we ambled through the entrance gate. After an hour Father decided that he had work to do at his office, so we went back to the gate. The young man stopped us, scared but resolute. "I read your card," he said, "and I called my lieutenant."

"Well? Where is he?" asked Father.

"He says he's heard about you, and he knows who you are, and what you are up to, so there's no need for him to come down here on a Sunday. He told me to ask for your identification." Father pulled out his wallet and displayed a few cards. The boy looked them over, then turned to me. "Where's yours?" he asked. I didn't have a purse or wallet, only a few coins shoved into the flaps in my penny loafers. No one of my age, in those days, went around carrying an identification card. I didn't own one, and I said so. Father walked over to his car, got in.

"Goodbye," he called.

"Hey, wait for me!" I said, and started toward the car. The boy jumped in front of me, holding his rifle across his chest. It looked like a toy. It *was* a toy. The army did not have enough real guns to issue to all the new recruits, so they had handed out wooden dummies. "You can't go unless you show me identification," he said. I looked toward Father, expecting help. Father leaned out of the car.

"Young man," he said, "you can have her. I've got two more at home. Feed her, clothe her, house her, educate her . . ." He started up the motor; the car actually started to move away. The boy and I stared at each other, wildly. We were in this together, but obviously he didn't want us to be together always. I had been set up for yet another rejection.

"Dammit!" I yelled to Father.

"Have a good life, dear child," he said. The boy suddenly made his own decision. To hell with his lieutenant. "Take her! Take her!" he implored. *I hated Father.* Eventually the newspapers got wind of Father's anti-sabotage tactics. *Time* magazine carried an article about him: "Barrel chested, gimlet eyed . . ." the article began.

"But he has *nice* eyes," said Mother.

Mother and I had almost forgotten about my graduation tea for the Pep Club girls. It was to be held on a Friday afternoon, a few weeks after Christmas. I had also invited several teachers. After some preliminary chatter, conversation failed. San Pedro girls did not thrive on caraway cake and cucumber sandwiches. Coca-Cola and tacos would have been more welcome. In desperation, Mother suggested that, going around the circle, each girl tell what her plans would be after graduation.

War had changed everything. Shipyards and airplane factories were already advertising for workers; there would be jobs for everyone. Two of the girls thought they would be getting married sooner than they had planned; their boyfriends would be going off to the army or navy. The three Japanese girls sat together, almost clinging to each other. When their turn came, the first one murmured that she didn't know. We had to strain to hear her. There was an awkward silence. One of her companions spoke up instead. She said that she and the third girl were engaged to men in Japan. They had been sent over to San Pedro to attend an American high school before they were married, so they could learn to speak English. Now they would go back to Japan.

I was astonished. These two girls seemed more Americanized than most Nisei, who were born in the United States. They had adapted themselves so well that, in a short time, they had been elected officers of high-school clubs. They were acknowledged leaders, members of Pep. Now, within a few days, they would be returning to Japan on the liner *Gripsholm*, which we could see swinging at anchor in the harbor below us, flying the blue and yellow flag of Sweden. The hull was painted with the same colors boldly displayed, the better to be recognized by warships and submarines. Both the Allies and the Nazi Axis found it useful that Sweden was a neutral country. During the past few years they had relied on the *Gripsholm* to carry out certain delicate international tasks. Just this morning I had read in the newspaper that she would be used to transport important members of the Japanese consular and diplomatic corps back to their own country, along with their families.

I suddenly realized that these two girls probably came from homes and backgrounds more wealthy and important than mine. I could have kicked myself for not getting to know them better, not because of wealth and position, but because I ached to ask them about how they had become betrothed. Had their parents arranged the marriages? Had they ever met the men they would be marrying? Did they think they could be happy with their parents' choice? If so, I was inclined to envy them. How comforting to know, absolutely, that you were going to be married. How useful to know *when*. I had failed Senior Prom. No boy even came close to asking me to go with him. Did that mean I would never be a wife? Never learn about sex? Never have a baby? If only I could dispense with the excruciating uncertainty that seemed to overshadow everything else. If the marriage question were safely settled, there would be no need for me to feel that, because I did not know how to get asked out on a date, I was destined always to live my life alone, pitied or despised. If a young man's parents had already signed a written guarantee that he would marry me, I could relax, get on with my life, turn my full attention to learning how to be *me*.

The front door burst open with a bang. Father, in full uniform, gold braid, panoply of ribbons, gold-encrusted hat, stood on the threshold. He hadn't been home for several days now. He paused in the doorway, groggy from lack of sleep. The consternation on his face gave way to horror, weariness, anger, weariness, despair. He had come home in the late afternoon to collapse, and found the house full of a gaggle of young girls.

"Damn!" he said.

I glanced at the Japanese girls. They were paralyzed with fear. Mother took Father's arm and they went off to the kitchen. A few minutes later he came into the living room and stood quietly by while Mother introduced him. He started around the circle, formally shaking hands with each young woman. "How do you do. How do you do." The Japanese girls were on the far side of the circle, behind him. As he worked his way toward them they became more and more frightened; everyone else was watching tensely. I don't know what Mother had been saying to Father in the kitchen, but he was absolutely unprepared for a Japanese guest. His eyes widened for only a fraction of a second, then he recovered. Simultaneously he became both more formal and displayed more warmth. He clicked his heels and bowed deeply to each young woman. Perhaps he saw the fear. "You are welcome in my home," he said, his uniquely rough, deep voice clear enough for all to hear. Then he continued around the circle.

The party broke up not long afterwards. Father went off to his bedroom and the guests went home. A week later I watched the *Gripsholm* steam out past the lighthouse, make for open sea. A few months later all the Japanese-Americans in San Pedro, United States citizens though they might be, were forced to pack up and move out to camps in the desert or to remote places in the mountains. Father said it was for their own safety.

Remembering the almond tree, I decided to believe him.

CHAPTER 12

Mrs. Warren's Profession

I WANTED TO BE A journalist, but I didn't go to the *San Pedro News Pilot* and ask for a job. Miss O'Rourke would have given me a good recommendation and, during wartime, the editor would have been lucky to get me. Part of my reluctance came from not wanting to be trapped at home, as Anne was. Also, I didn't think I was worthy. I had read that, to become a *good* journalist, one needed four years of college, which meant a rich background in the humanities and a graduate degree in journalism from either Columbia University or the University of Missouri. I did not want to be second rate.

I had passed the exams to go to Pomona College. I had convinced Mother, at least, that my plan was worth the staggering expense. Meanwhile, I took a job as a messenger at Henry Kaiser's California Shipyards, familiarly known as Calship. The pay was so high as to seem obscene. I would be able to pay a good part of my own college fees. In the dawn hours, I packed sandwiches and thermos in a humpbacked lunch pail and hurried down to the ferry at the foot of Ninth Street. I had to get there well before 0700 hours to stand near the front of the line. The toylike passenger ferry was the same one the Japanese kids had used before their families were sent off to camps. Once aboard, I raced for the stern, partly to escape being packed into the crowd, mostly because I admired the little bench installed there. Curved slats, artfully steamed, were fastened together with wooden pegs; salt spray had weathered the teak to silver. (Years after the war,

Father found the bench in a salvage yard; he paid a few dollars to take it home to use in the garden.)

Now I owned an identification card with my picture on it. I flashed it at the gate, punched my time card, then walked more than half a mile to the mail room. My job was to run between the various offices, carrying messages, waiting for them to be initialled, picking up messages to be taken back to the mail room and rerouted. This, my first job, was fun, varied, active and lucrative. Down-yard, torches flared day and night; the sound of rivet hammers never stopped. Henry Kaiser, determined to launch a ship every twenty-four hours, produced ships by template, on an assembly line. They were Landing Ship Transports (LST), sturdy, blunt-nosed, ugly. The bow was designed to be seaworthy enough to cross thousands of miles of ocean, then to act as a ramp from which troops, tanks, and Jeeps would disembark on some Pacific island.

Mother was pleased to be asked to launch an LST. She swung the bottle of champagne with gusto and aplomb. The ship was named *Juan Cabrillo*, after the Spanish explorer who first discovered San Pedro. Cabrillo Beach, where Mother had suffered her grievous accident years before, was also named after him. I doubt if she recognized any irony. She received a string of pearls in a silver box, engraved with the date and name of the ship, and a photograph of her was affixed to the bulkhead in the captain's cabin. The close-up captured Mother's happiness and exuberance so well that Father asked for a copy. (A few years later, in the middle of the Pacific, an embarrassed sailor asked to speak to Father privately. He didn't know if he should mention it, but he had lately been in the captain's cabin on an LST, where he had been startled to see a photograph of Captain Higbee's wife hanging over another man's desk. We three girls thought the story was hilarious. The very idea of either of our parents straying was beyond imagination.)

A net to keep out submarines was pulled across the entrance to the harbor, anchored between San Pedro breakwater and Long Beach breakwater. Yachtsmen were furious because they could not take their boats to sea nor sail over to Catalina. When small private vessels were confiscated for the war effort, many yachtsmen, hoping to get a commission, joined the Coast Guard Reserve. Since San Pedro is the port of the City of Los Angeles and Hollywood is part of the same city, Mother and Father found themselves being swept into a whole new social life. They were asked to Hollywood parties and some of the English crowd (Basil Rathbone, Ian

Hunter, C. Aubrey Smith, Charles Laughton, Elsa Lanchester, Madeleine Carroll, George Sanders, et al.) were delighted to claim Mother as one of their own. Zsa Zsa Gabor (who was Hungarian) was then married to George Sanders. Odd as it may seem, she and Mother took to each other. When Mrs. Sanders telephoned our house "just to talk," her accent was unmistakable. She was lonely, Mother said, and terribly worried about her husband. When George Sanders committed suicide (because he was so bored, the note said), people blamed Zsa Zsa, which Mother thought was utterly unfair. Mr. Sanders was a bitter, moody man who would probably have committed suicide no matter whom he married. Mother said she liked Zsa Zsa because she never pretended to be anything other than what she was, a professional courtesan.

I knew all there was to know about being a courtesan. I had immersed myself in the writings of George Bernard Shaw and had lately read *Mrs. Warren's Profession*. Mrs. Warren had, as a young married woman, made a fatal slip. Her seduction discovered, she was subsequently flung out of her marriage and barred from seeing her child. From that time on she had made a profession of pleasing others, meaning wealthy men. Then one day she saw a young girl about to make the same mistake, *and that girl was her daughter!*

I was also reading Oscar Wilde, Somerset Maugham, the Burns Mantle Best Plays of any given year, and Aristophanes. Shakespeare's plays were harder to read and understand than the plays of the ancient Greeks, because he was not translated into modern English. Shakespeare's poetry was more important to me than the plots of his plays. I tried to figure out how he crafted his images, so clear to my eye and mind.

Father had made friends with a Hollywood writer, Malcolm Boylan. Malcolm wrote film scripts, and stories for *Liberty* and *Saturday Evening Post*. He gave me a copy of the *Viking Portable Book of Poetry* and was encouraging about my efforts to write. Malcolm was Irish, a hero-worshipper, and a romantic. He admired Father as he had probably admired Barrymore, and attached himself to him, following him around the harbor whenever he had the chance. Mother was torn between being charmed and being jealous. Not since he was a boy had Father had a male friend with whom he could feel free to talk about anything and everything. He could be open with Malcolm as he could not with any of his colleagues. Nor with his wife.

One Sunday afternoon Anne and I, waiting for Father in his office, went for a walk along the docks. We met Malcolm and a nicely dressed middle-aged woman walking there, too. I assumed that she was Mrs. Boylan, but Anne, who knew everyone connected with Father's work, said she wasn't. Malcolm returned our greetings with unaccustomed curtness. He did not introduce us to his companion.

"It must have been Letitia," Father said, when Anne reported our encounter, at the dinner table. When Anne asked who Letitia might be, Father hesitated so long that Mother replied for him. "Letitia is Malcolm's mistress," Mother said. "And that's why he didn't introduce you to her. Malcolm is old-fashioned. He wouldn't deem it proper to introduce the daughters of his best friend to a woman with whom he is having an affair. And Letitia is European. She would understand completely."

Father seemed discomfited, but Mother was not to be deterred. "When I was a girl," she went on, reminiscently, "if I met a friend of my father's walking along the street with a beautifully dressed young woman, there would be a little maneuver. A man normally walks on the *outside*, near the curb, you know. But in this case he would suddenly drop back and come around behind the young woman to walk beside her on the *inside*. That would be a signal that the lady was not a lady, that she was his mistress, and that I was not to greet him or expect to be introduced. He would do this as a courtesy to my father, and to my respectability."

"My God!" said Father. "This woman never fails to astound me." Then, "How did you know all that? I thought you were young and innocent!"

"Unlike *some* who are present," said Mother, "*I* was not brought up in Kansas City." And then, to us: "I used to go on a little way and then look back. It was the clothes I wanted to see. The latest thing from Paris."

In the fall I went up to Claremont, to attend Pomona College. I lived in Blaisdell Hall, the girls' dormitory. Most of our male classmates expected to be recruited in a few months, but among the young women there was little interest in the war, none of the immediacy that I was used to. Meanwhile, in San Pedro, all windows had to be blacked out at night. When I came home for Thanksgiving the air was filled with blimps, huge balloons that were meant, rather pathetically, to foil a Japanese air attack. Sometime later a Japanese submarine fired shells at the oil wells at El Segundo, a few miles up the coast, and Commander Robert Bartlett of the U.S. Coast Guard torpedoed and sank a Japanese submarine in Catalina Channel. Father telephoned Mother from his office to tell her to drive Marijka Bartlett out to Point Fermin, to witness the battle. The two women stood on the same headland where, years before, we children had watched the breeches buoy rescuing the crew of a wrecked ship, the one that was carrying a cargo of oranges. Some people said that Bob Bartlett had just imagined a submarine was there, but twenty years after the war he was vindicated: the hull of a Japanese miniature submarine was discovered lying on the ocean floor, not far from the harbor entrance net.

Pomona College was nestled among orange groves with snow-capped mountains almost on campus. The name, of course, means fruit, or apple, evoking the goddess of fruits and the golden apples of the garden of the Hesperides, blown by western winds. A preponderance of the founders were old China hands who had been missionaries or entrepreneurs in the Far East. They hoped that Pomona would become the Yale-Harvard-Oxford of the West, yet face toward Asia.

I was too busy studying to listen to the news on the radio; besides, anything but Benny Goodman bothered my roommate. My professors did not quite know what to make of me. I was unevenly erudite in history and geography, but I had gotten my highest score in chemistry, which was not saying much. My reading had been random and unsupervised. I knew fairy tale and myth and children's books better than anyone, but I had not taken an English course in high school (except for journalism) and I had not read systematically in the Classics. However, I knew Aristophanes and Herodotus. I had read modern drama, but not modern novels. I had read reams of Victorian poetry on my own and I had won the California state-wide poetry contest. When Dr. Holmes, my freshman college counsellor, looked at my scores and said he thought I should aim to be a chemist, I just stared at him. I finally talked him into letting me take my electives in English history and Victorian literature. What neither of us had bargained for was that my very lack of a "good" education in "good" schools would make me take to cultivation at a deeper, a more truly radical, level than students from the weeded gardens.

Before I finished my first year of college Father had received orders to Greenland and Anne had joined the SPARS, the women's branch of the Coast Guard (the name is a derivative of *semper paratus*, "always ready," which is the Coast Guard motto). At last she had found her proper niche in the universe! I was happy for her, but we were still not able to communicate. She asked me when I was going to join up. When I said that I didn't know, she muttered something about white feathers.

Mother had decided that to stay in San Pedro was foolish, in view of the blackout and restrictions on gasoline. We lived on a steep hill. Just to buy a loaf of bread involved jumping into the car. In Claremont she would be able to walk everywhere. Besides, Claremont was inland; there was no blackout. Mother, Joyce and I rented a house from Dr. Helen Marburg, who taught French at Pomona College. Helen, with funds frozen in Europe, was happy to rent to us, since she had already moved into cheaper quarters. She and Mother became good friends. Helen was German-French-Jewish, from a wealthy family. She became an ardent convert to Anglicanism when she took her first job, teaching in a girls' school in England. There, she had been seduced by the headmaster. For that reason, she told Mother, she could never marry. She would not respect the sort of man who would marry a debauched woman. Her only recourse, therefore, had been to be always a mistress, never a wife.

I don't know what sort of message Mother gave to such women as Helen Marburg and Zsa Zsa Gabor, or how she managed to do it. *They* assumed that she was worldly; *I* knew that she could not name the parts of the body, especially *down there*, and didn't want to learn. By this time I was reconciled to the fact that she would never tell me the facts of life, because she didn't have a clue. She talked a good talk. She was all for sexiness in theory, as long as it was divorced from the reality of the body. She had a medieval nun's horror of the crotch. She was broad-minded and forgiving of those who strayed down the primrose path, but such tolerance was never tested within her own household. Our sensuality was turned toward food. We talked about recipes instead of sex. We learned how to cook, not to flirt. Perhaps her tolerance (for other people's error) came from her love and acceptance of Kate, her father's mistress, who had cherished her when she was a needful child. Her denial was mixed up with the fear and shame (and grief) about feeling she had lost her own sexuality.

In first-year English class Dr. Holmes gave us a list of modern books and novels to choose from. I chose Vera Brittain's *Testament of Youth*. It had been on Mother's shelf for years; she had urged it upon me to no avail. I was amazed to find that my professor thought that it was an important book. The first chapter was heavy going, but suddenly I was caught up in the struggle that Brittain had had to go through to persuade her father to let her go to Oxford. Her brother would go as a matter of course, but her father wouldn't send Vera because she was a girl. I told myself that, in our family, the situation was different: money was the problem. But for the first time I had my doubts.

A considerable part of Brittain's book speaks of the loss of young men that she had known, her brother, her fiancé, friends she had grown up with. They were all killed in the war. This sounded like Mother's story. Then came the part about driving an ambulance. This, too, sounded familiar. Mother had driven an ambulance. She had brought the wounded from the docks to hospitals inland, sometimes under heavy fire from zeppelins. No wonder she treasured this book! She must have welcomed Vera Brittain's voice, the only one at hand to confirm her own experience.

But for me the most important part of *Testament* was Brittain's perspective on her own time and place in history. She felt passionately the call to be part of her own generation. Not to answer that call would be a betrayal of the dead, not to take part would be a deadening of the self. I had also, that year, been set to read Plato, and so discovered the metaphor of the Cave. I knew that I would leave Pomona, much as I loved being there, because my life among the orange groves of academe was mere shadow of the real world. Much as I wanted to stay, I also wanted to experience what was going on out there. It was time to toss my golden ball (my perfect sphere of childhood) down the well. As in the "Mother Hulla" story, it was time for *me* to jump down the well, not knowing what would happen next.

When I told Dr. Holmes that I wanted to enlist, he was horrified. He confided in me that he felt responsible for letting me read Brittain's book. It was supposed to be an intellectual exercise. I was not supposed to *act* on it. He was afraid of what my parents would think, that he would be considered at fault for putting silly, dangerous thoughts into my pretty head. I tried to reassure him by explaining that my parents had imbued me not only with a sense of history, but with being a *part* of history. About to be drafted himself, he became angry at me when I told him that my parents and my older sister were ashamed of me for not joining up. If I had any backbone I would stay in college! I promised him, and myself, that I would not leave until I had finished my second year. I also decided to enjoy every minute.

Dr. Frederich Mulhauser, who was just a year or two out of Yale, carried an eighteen-inch ruler while he was lecturing, which said *Mack's Barbershop, New Haven* on it in big black letters. When he handed back a story or essay I had written he would tap his ruler on an offending paragraph and say, "Full of pus. Drain it." I was lucky to have had Miss O'Rourke as his predecessor, otherwise I might have collapsed in tears. Dr. Mulhauser was also waiting to be drafted.

I allowed myself to take two courses from Dr. Frank Pitman, who had taught me in Western Civilization the first year. (Drop a pencil, you lose a century.) Dr. Pitman, who had grown up in New Haven, as well as going to college there, was the very epitome of a New England gentleman. He seemed out of place in California, although he had taught at Pomona for over thirty years. He was ready to retire, but because of the war he had been asked to stay on. Some students complained because he preached and rambled, which was the reason I liked him. Pitman had written his Ph.D. on the triangular trade (slaves-sugar-rum) in the late eighteenth century. He told the class how, when Paul Robeson had come to sing at Pomona, the College Inn had made it clear that this particular performer could not stay there *because he was a Negro*. Dr. and Mrs. Pitman had immediately contacted Robeson's agent to say that they would be honored to have Paul Robeson as a guest. The agent thanked them, but replied that Mr. Robeson would be staying with friends in Los Angeles. I had come to believe that whatever had not been settled by the Civil War and the Emancipation amendment had to be tolerated forever as the "Negro problem." I had never heard racial discrimination discussed in a classroom before; I had never heard of anyone who thought to do something practical about it, in the present.

Dr. Pitman also told us about being in Germany a few months before the war started. What surprised him was that the *old* people he met failed to speak up against the Nazis. He said he could understand how the husband of a young family might keep his mouth shut, but old age gives one the license, the duty, and the luxury to be courageous. I was astonished by that idea. Until then I had thought, in my youthful arrogance, that courage belongs to the young. *Old* Dr. Pitman was the only professor who supported my intention to join the army.

In sophomore year I requested special permission to take Miss Ruth George's poetry-writing course at Scripps College (with Pomona, also part of the loosely amalgamated Claremont University). The seminar was usually reserved for third- and fourth-year students. Helen Marburg suggested that I remind the faculty committee that I had won the state poetry prize and, also, that I was planning to enlist.

Miss George was a wispy lady with wisps of white hair falling from the falling braids coiled around her head. Dressed in shawls and patches, she hurried into class clutching sundry books and bags, which were always slipping away from her. She spoke airily of her literary correspondence with dear Mr. Eliot, and with Sir Arthur Quiller-Couch. I lived and breathed the *Oxford Book of English Verse* and the *Manual of English Prosody*. She told us how, when she graduated from Bryn Mawr, she had planned to go off with her dearest friend on a walking tour through Tuscany, but her family had disapproved. (I surmise, now, that she was a lesbian. Perhaps her family had an inkling of that.) Eventually she made the tour with a young nephew. They had walked along dusty roads, slept in hay mows and barns, subsisted on bread and cheese, olives and tomatoes, which they bought from peasants in the fields. I decided that, when the war was over, I wanted to be just like Miss George. Miss George took care to tell me that she did not approve of my going to war. She was a pacifist.

She was also an ardent suffragette. To let us know the perils of being a woman writer, she assigned to us Virginia Woolf's *A Room of One's Own*. Having read Vera Brittain's book just a few months before, I was wide open to the radicalism contained in Woolf. I especially loved the part about Shakespeare's sister. What if Shakespeare had had a sister as talented as he was? What if she had come up to London to hang about the theater? She would have got pregnant, that's what. And even if she tried to write, the baby, ill health, hostility, and prejudice against her, not to mention frustration and depression, would have dragged her down into oblivion. The reason that women have not become great artists, musicians, writers, is that biology is against them and because they have had no time, no space, no room of their own. Not to mention *no money*. This was the part I found confusing. Mother had brought me up to think that knowing about money was vulgar and unnecessary. Virginia Woolf and Miss George both thought that women should know how to get money and how to use it, preferably with no man involved.

Another part of the essay that remains with me forever is where Virginia Woolf is contemplating some lines from Milton. As a writer she was curious to know if he had written them off first crack, or whether he had written and then rewritten. She was walking across a college green at Cambridge at the moment and suddenly realized that she was nearing the very library that housed that very manuscript. She could actually walk into the library, ask to see the original! Which she did. Only to be told that she could not go any further because she was a woman.

My third important foray into new ways of thinking occurred when Helen Marburg invited Mother, Joyce, and me to go to hear the farewell sermon of a certain Episcopalian minister. He was a youngish man, married, with children, who was leaving to go into the army. His mother had been a famous suffragette, which fact, Helen advised me, had influenced him for the better. That Sunday he preached on the famous and puzzling passage from the Gospel of Mark wherein, when Jesus is healing the sick, his mother and brothers show up. When someone tells him that his family is waiting outside, Jesus says he won't come out to them. He says to tell his mother that he is busy doing God's work. A well-brought-up son acting like that? His mother was probably angry and embarrassed. What would other people think?

The thrust of the sermon was that you have to make your own direct relationship to God. If you have been such a good parent that your son (my son the doctor) got into Harvard, that doesn't make you any closer to God. Being a good wife or a good husband or a good daughter does not cut any ice, does not guarantee that you will sit on the right hand of . . . You can't get there through someone else. You're not even supposed to try! I felt an enormous relief. I no longer had to waste time and effort figuring out what my parents or Anne wanted me to do. I no longer had to be a credit to my father, or uphold the Corfield honor. I could just be *me*, a good me, I hoped, answerable only to the Creator. (I don't know the name of the man who preached that sermon. I don't know if he came home from the war. But I am grateful to him. He lifted a heavy stone off my spirit.)

I knew that I would not join the SPARS. That was a given. I didn't want to be patronized by Anne, nor did I want to play the role of my father's daughter, wherein a script would be written for me, or I would think that one was. In late 1943, recruiting officers came to the campus from the WAVES (Women Accepted for Volunteer Emergency Service) and the WAC (Women's Army Corps). I talked to both of them. The WAVE officer, tall and slim, kept telling me that, if I joined the navy, I would be among women of my own ilk, that I might even become an officer. The WAC lieutenant was short and round, like me. The WAVE officer had insinuated, by her anxious concern, that I couldn't take it ("it" being real life); the WAC officer, by not treating me as a special case, showed respect for my strengths. I thought of Vera Brittain; I thought of Virginia Woolf; I wanted experience; I wanted a room of my own. I wanted to go out into the world; I wanted to stay in Claremont, which seemed to me like very heaven.

Sitting around Blaisdell Hall with my former dormitory mates, I found myself having to defend my decision to join up. My particular friend, Rosemary, said, "You always want to be different from everyone else, so how come you are thinking about marching around in uniform, having to obey orders? I could never do that. I feel too unique." The others, concurring, all shook their heads in unison. I was the only non-unique person in my class.

In June 1944, I went off to WAC boot camp at Fort Des Moines, Iowa. In the fall, Joyce went away to Occidental College, about twenty miles away. Mother, except for our family dog, was left alone. She moved out of Helen Marburg's house, into an upstairs apartment in another old house. Unexpectedly, she decided to apply for a job at the town drugstore. She had seen an advertisement for help in the window and, on impulse, had gone into the shop to discuss it with the pharmacist-owner. She said she would take the job as long as she never had to work at a soda fountain. The owner assured her that he did not have one; her job would be to count pills in the back room and to serve in the shop only occasionally. He was glad to get Mother, since students were unreliable, and everyone else was in the service or had a job with the war effort. Mother loved working at the drugstore. She got to know almost everyone in Claremont and they got to know her. Also, she was earning some money of her own.

Mother once told me that this was one of the happiest times of her life. She was all alone but she was not alone. She was having a social and intellectual life unlike any she had ever experienced before, but for which she was ready. She was earning her own money. She felt useful and free, yet she could bask in the glow of being the wife of an important, glamorous man. By this time Father had been transferred to the Pacific and had been promoted to four stripes. Mother wore a discreet little silver pin that had been designed for officers' wives to show their husband's rank as a captain. At one time she would have thought such a display vulgar, but she wanted people who saw her behind the counter to know she was not just an ordinary clerk. Father, as usual, wrote to her almost every day, even though he knew that his letters would be delayed and would likely arrive in bunches. Her real and secret triumph was in knowing how much her husband loved her.

Alas.

An envelope arrived, addressed to her, but with a letter inside written to Malcolm Boylan. Frank wanted Malcolm to know the good news. He had followed his friend's advice. At last he was having an affair with another woman! He had met her at a posh party in Australia, where American officers were treated like heroes. He must admit he had had more to drink that usual! This particular woman was married to an Australian army officer who was a prisoner-of-war in a Japanese camp. She was elegant and charming and experienced, and Malcolm was absolutely right. He, Frank, was not meant to live the life of a celibate.

Freud was no fool: part of Father must have wanted his wife to know that he was being unfaithful. I can forgive the infidelity. In fact I am happy for my father that he found a way to find sexual fulfillment, and that Malcolm helped him to be relatively free of guilt. But I find it hard to forgive his Freudian slip. He did feel guilty, and he took it out on my mother. She was devastated. When she told me the story years later, her eyes were so full of pain that I could hardly bear to look at her, much less to listen. She had been alone when she received the letter. She must have been swept with anger, sadness, fear. Even if her married life was not over, her absolute trust in her husband was gone. She had been betrayed. She had been made a fool of. And Frank was even more of a fool, she thought, easily beguiled by a woman who was probably just a few removes from being a prostitute.

Joan Amphlett Corfield telephoned her boss to say she would not be in to work the next day. She had to go into Los Angeles on business. Next morning she dressed in her going-to-the-city clothes. I can picture her: dark silk print, seamed silk stockings, black sandals (with a pump heel), a small straw hat, good purse, white gloves. Gas rationing was in full force; she was used to taking the bus into the city, although the ride took almost two hours. When she reached the bus terminal, she walked out onto Sixth Street, into the heart of the red-light district. She sat down on a bench and waited.

"What were you waiting there for?" I asked – much later.

"I wanted to talk to a prostitute. A professional one."

Eventually, after waiting several hours and sizing up the people who came and went, Mother spoke to a woman who sat down on the other end of the bench. "She was a little older than the others."

"What did you say?" I asked.

"I said, 'Pardon me, but are you a prostitute?' She acted a little surprised, but after she had taken a good long look at me, she said yes, she was."

I wasn't there. I cannot report exactly what transpired. I can only give you the gist. My mother told the Park Bench Lady the story about her husband's infidelity, but what she really wanted to talk about was the role of women – all women. For years, without knowing it, she had been a prostitute herself; or, at least, a kept woman. If her husband didn't love her, then all she was to him was someone to keep house, be a perfect hostess, and be there to have sex with. When she wasn't around or couldn't function, he found someone else to fulfill his needs. Which made a mockery of love. Which made a mockery of marriage. She had thought she was in full partnership. Now she discovered that she had been a mere convenience, fed and clothed and given a roof over her head in exchange for service. Lately she had been earning her own money and talking to women who had lives outside of marriage. It had made her think. If her husband was going to treat her like a prostitute, she might as well go into a life of professional prostitution. That might be the more honorable choice. What did her new acquaintance have to say?

After careful consideration, the Park Bench Lady spoke. She told my mother that she agreed with her about a wife being not much better than a kept woman. However, life is not perfect. We make the best choice we can under the circumstances. Somewhere in the conversation Mother had described her husband in terms glowing enough to make the Park Bench Lady see that he was, for a man, a good man, as far as men go. She advised Mother to reconsider her new career choice, even though she could understand how angry and fed up Mother was. It was a little late to become a prostitute. The Park Bench Lady herself was thinking of retiring, getting a war job. Be that as it may, her advice was to return home and put up with what she had. There are some things worse than infidelity. Mother seemed to her like a strong woman. She would survive and more than survive. She might even be happy again. Not *as* happy. But there are some things better than happiness.

Mother offered to pay for time spent, but the Park Bench Lady said she had enjoyed the conversation. It was on the house.

CHAPTER 13
Disobeying Orders

ON THE DAY OF MY induction into the army, Mother, Joyce, and I took the bus up to Los Angeles. The bus smoked and wheezed and finally broke down near Pasadena. When we arrived, two hours late, a woman sergeant gave me hell and told me that I was technically AWOL (absent without leave). No excuses. Mother, in full sail, all spinnakers flying, demanded to see an officer. The roly-poly lieutenant who had enlisted me appeared, much relieved to see me. She, too, had been given hell when I failed to turn up on time.

I was given a number on a white tag, the kind used for waiting in line at the butcher counter, only now I was waiting for my medical examination. Mother became tearful when she looked around and saw the women and girls who were going to accompany me to boot camp. No one looked like *us*. One by one the enlistees were being called into an inner room. Some of the younger girls emerged in tears. One of them collapsed into her mother's arms, sobbing. I could not imagine what all the fuss was about. Her mother looked at my mother and said, "My daughter has been raped." She had a hillbilly accent. I could tell that my mother did not believe her. I didn't believe her. How could anyone be raped in broad daylight, surrounded by nurses, doctors, sergeants and lieutenants? I still was not sure, technically, what being raped meant. Like most of my contemporaries, I knew that rape hurt, was embarrassing, and involved *down there*.

At last my name, rank, and serial number were called. I went into another room and was told to undress entirely, then put on an army raincoat. The day was hot, there was no air conditioning. My body glistened and then poured with sweat. I had eaten nothing since early morning. I thought I was going to faint. I was swept into the routine of eye chart, finger pricks, urine samples, knee thumps, take a deep breath, stethoscope, heartbeat. My throat was peered into and a doctor felt for swollen glands. My breasts were lifted up, peered under, probed. Then I was told to proceed into still another room, get up on a narrow table. A doctor came in, sighed a deep sigh, told me to put my feet into stirrups. He sighed again, asked me how old I was. He told me he was about to give me an internal examination. I didn't know what he was talking about. He thrust his hand up my vagina and into my pelvis. It hurt. A lot.

So this was what the other girl had been crying about! Unlike her, I did not equate this clinical experience with rape. I was able to intellectualize that this must be some sort of medical examination and therefore must be for a good purpose, like winning the war. I did not cry or whimper, and returned to my mother dry-eyed. Nothing to report. I did not know then that every month I would have to line up with my sister enlistees, naked except for raincoats, and undergo the same act in order to see if I was worthy to be paid. Toward the end of my enlistment, a young doctor, recently returned from overseas, said to me, "I don't understand why you women don't object, make a big stink about this humiliation." He said that the reason we were examined made no medical sense. He was right.

That young doctor was talking to the wrong person. I was brainwashed into numbness. I didn't have the requisite sense of outrage. I was lucky, I suppose, in that I was so benighted that I did not equate love or sex or even violation with a hand up my vagina. It hurt more – but meant about as much – as a stick down my throat or a drill in my tooth. The little girl from the mountains of Kentucky, unlike me, resonated with feeling. She had been ravaged because she had been taught by her mother what it meant to be ravaged, mythologically and physically. My mother had never discussed rape with me. Now, when someone told her that *it* was happening in the next room she, usually so brave and spontaneous, made no inquiries. Technically, of course, I was not raped – by an army doctor, or by anyone else. But I had been so desensitized by my mother that my body did not seem to be attached to my head. Much less, to my feelings.

We arrived at Fort Des Moines, Iowa, in a heat wave. When my uniform was issued to me, it came as a shock to realize that I would have to wear what I was told to wear, no matter what the temperature. In a huge warehouse we were handed khaki towels, washcloths, slips, underpants. The slips and underpants were a good brand (Hanes), made of high-quality nylon, better than anything we had been able to buy in civilian life for the past few years. The elastic was of good quality, too. How many rubber tires had been sacrificed to go to war with the WAC? No brassieres, though. The army could not face up to choosing breast sizes and shapes for each of us. No nightgowns. Two pairs of real nylon stockings were issued, with the warning that once they wore out we would have to buy our own, on the civilian market.

To wear now, for summer, we were issued shirts, skirts, neckties, narrow hats, all in light-colored cotton khaki. For winter, we would wear dark wool skirts and jackets, styled by the famous designer Mainbocher. Our uniforms were individually fitted by expert tailors, men drafted from god-knows-what exclusive shops and salons, to help win the war. Somewhere along the line I was handed the WAC emblem, a small brass medallion superimposed with a likeness of Athena, to affix to the collar of my jacket. Our winter overcoats were double-breasted with brass buttons, reminiscent of the sailor coats my sisters and I used to wear when we were little girls.

Our uniforms were augmented by "fatigues," i.e. work clothes. We had two brown-striped seersucker dresses, and a green denim one-piece jumpsuit with a drop seat, which buttoned down the front. The drop-seat design was of no practical use for a woman. When we went to the latrine, we had to unbutton the front and take the whole thing off at the shoulders, down to the knees. However, in fond remembrance of the overalls I had worn on the *Leviathan*, I liked my jumpsuit best of all, and also the squashy round wide-brimmed fatigue hat that went with it. When I glimpsed myself in a mirror, I knew I looked cute and fetching.

After hours of standing, it was a relief to sit down, to be fitted for brown laced shoes, of excellent leather, with a one-and-a-half-inch heel. I had convinced myself that I could wear only saddle shoes and loafers, but these GI shoes were of finest quality, comfortable and, if not exactly stylish, not unstylish. Classy. We were also issued heavy field boots. The men who fitted us were experts; they knew exactly what they were doing and took serious care to see that each of us was well shod for "the Duration."

The Duration! Everyone talked about this accordionlike, amorphous unit of time, so huge, so indefinite, that went on and on and might go on forever. We had almost stopped talking about "the war." "War" had a ring of excitement; "Duration" was something you had to live through, like "the Depression." I could hardly believe my ears, therefore, when, a few days after I had joined the army, we were summoned to the Parade Ground, called to attention, put at parade rest, and read a proclamation just received by the commanding officer. The date was June 6, 1944. The Allies had landed in Normandy! They had struggled up the beaches, climbed the cliffs, and were proceeding inland. The war in Europe was not over, but the beginning of the end was in sight.

In between learning how to take a thirty-inch stride, how to march in formation, how to do push-ups, clean latrines, make square corners on our beds, we were subjected to lectures on discipline and to propaganda movies about the meaning of the war. In one class we were asked what we would do if ordered to march over a cliff. The officer pressed for an answer. Some of us (including good-little-girl me) said we would continue to march. Wrong! We were chewed out by the lieutenant. "That's what the Germans would do," she said. "You are *Americans*. Mostly you're supposed to obey orders, but you're also supposed to be able to use your common sense and know when it's more important to *disobey* an order." This idea was not just the personal eccentricity of a particular lieutenant. It came straight out of a GI (government issue) training manual. Such manuals were written by professors of philosophy and education, who had also been drafted into the army. The seeds of the arguments used at Nuremberg were being sewn among us. If an officer orders you to shoot village women and children, or to burn people in a gas chamber, you have a moral right and responsibility not to follow orders.

I made one of the first adult decisions of my life when we were subjected to a battery of cognitive tests. I remembered how, when taking entrance exams for Pomona College, I had overcompensated for my low chemistry grade by studying chemistry harder than I studied English. As consequence, I had almost been sentenced to life as a lab assistant. I knew that the army merely wanted to know what I was best at, so they could use me to best advantage. When "time" was called on the English section of the exam, I proceeded, as ordered, to mathematics. As the math problems became harder I experienced an epiphany: I didn't want a job doing math!

It was up to me not to let it happen. So I cheated. I abandoned math, flipped back to English, finished the whole section, even correcting errors I may have made earlier.

I am proud to relate that, within a few short weeks, I had begun to understand the essence of being a real GI. *Take the war seriously, but not the army.* To survive and more than survive I must become a trickster hero, responsible for my own welfare and happiness. When the interviewer asked me, "What did you major in?" I lied. Blithely I invented a non-existent undergraduate major: "Writing Poetry," I said. I was assigned to the Signal Corps, to be trained as an 805, i.e. a cryptographic technician. The recruiting officer had assured me, earnestly, that I would learn a useful trade. Most days, cryptography isn't. The most useful thing I learned in the army was to know that sometimes, in order to win a war, it's okay to disobey orders.

I was sent to Camp Crowder, the huge Signal Corps center in the Ozarks, near Joplin, Missouri. Two hundred WACs were stationed there, along with two hundred thousand men. However, when reveille sounded and I fell out for roll call, my name was not on the roster. I trailed along with my sister WACs to attend lectures and typing class. I was soon discovered to be a stray, but no one was quite sure what to do with me. Meanwhile, my name was being called across camp, in another company, as *John* Higbee. Since I did not show up there, I was listed as being AWOL, maybe a deserter. I still don't understand why no one noticed that my serial number, A920270, was quite different from any man's, but this was the army. Meanwhile, although I would *sleep* in the women's barracks, and *eat* in the women's mess hall, I must march with the men's squadron, to which John Higbee was assigned.

Among the men in my squadron was a Chinese pathologist, an M.D. from Berkeley who had been doing research on the biological causes of homosexuality. He, too, was a misplacement, who had ended up in the enlisted ranks of the Signal Corps because, he said, "My grandfather insisted that I study not only Mandarin and Cantonese, but every rare Chinese dialect he could find a teacher for. This is all my grandfather's fault." The Allies were preparing for a major thrust in the China-Burma-India area, where, he was told, he would be invaluable. He did not want to be invaluable, only valuable enough to be made an officer! Otherwise, he was convinced, he would be mistaken for the enemy and perish by friendly fire. He did not know whether his plight came about because of an army snafu (situation-normal-all-fucked-up), or because of simple racism. He had given up trying to make his way into the Medics, where pathologists were a dime a dozen, but he was determined to be commissioned before he went off to the CBI. My ludicrous presence in his squadron cheered him up considerably, although I am not sure why.

The group of soldiers I hung out with were mostly Jewish, from Brooklyn, in their late teens and early twenties. A few years later, thanks to Dr. Seuss, they would have been called *nerds*. I was instantly stereotyped, assumed to be a WASP (White Anglo-Saxon Protestant, or – in my case – Princess), doubtless a prom queen and cheerleader, whose father never questioned the money spent to send his daughter off to Pomona College, the very name of which caused loud guffaws. Since this was the role in which I was accepted so wholeheartedly, who was I to disabuse them? I found that Shelley and Wordsworth cut no ice, but when I discussed T. S. Eliot there was sudden interest – not about Eliot's verse forms and imagery, but about his anti-Semitism. I thought then, and I do now, that this is a One-Eyed way to read poetry. Miss Ruth George had raised the same question once, and dismissed it in the same sentence: *Dear Mr. Eliot did not mean what he appeared to be saying.* She was wrong, but so were my newfound friends. Eliot is a great poet.

Daily newspapers were hard to get, but *Stars and Stripes* reported that a bill called the Serviceman's Readjustment Act was coming up before Congress. After the Duration, after we were discharged, the government was supposed to pay our tuition to any college or university that would accept us, and provide a living allowance to boot! This bonanza was beginning to be referred to as "the G.I. Bill." Hardly anyone believed that something so enlightened would actually become reality. There must be a catch!

Among the enlisted men I knew, the thirst for knowledge was insatiable. These young men, most of them who had been led to believe that they would never have a chance to be educated beyond high school, were determined to seek out what was rightfully theirs – access to contemporary knowledge. Books and magazine articles were read and shared; brought to the group, they were worried like a bone. For the first time I heard the name Joseph Campbell. He had co-authored a book called *A Skeleton Key to Finnegan's Wake*. I had read *Portrait of the Artist as a Young Man*, but steered well clear of *Finnegan*. Another name bandied about was Ludwig Wittgenstein. Norbert Weiner was another. No one had a copy of their books, but reviews were pored over. I was allowed to hang out on the fringes of this hotbed of erudition. I shudder to think what might have become of me if I had been made an officer and had spent my time in the company of officers. I doubt if I would have found myself involved with a group so high-minded and eager, so bright and idealistic. The level of conversation was as good, often better, than what I had been getting in the dormitory at Pomona.

At last I had a boyfriend: George Sidney Handler, Jewish, twenty years old, from Brooklyn. I called him Mint Julep, I suppose because, in his green fatigues, he looked tall and skinny and raw-boned, like the caricature of a Southern hayseed. We were regarded, with some amusement, as a dating couple. The idea of our becoming lovers never occurred to us, and would have shocked our little circle. I discovered that there was an outer circle, made up of older men who acted as mentors. In their thirties and forties, they spent off-duty hours kibitzing and playing cards at the PX. We called them the wise guys. Some of them had been Hollywood writers. A couple of them were gag writers for Bob Hope.

When Mint Julep and I went into Joplin together, on a Saturday-night pass, I came home at two in the morning to find that the wise guys were still up, still playing cards, on the porch of the PX. As I walked by them, on the way to my barracks, one of them said, loud enough for me to hear: "We can go to bed now." Another one called out: "We were waiting up for you, Private Higbee. If that young nebbish had kept you out all night we would have had his hide."

As I write this, the story seems impossibly Andy Hardy-ish, especially in light of the sexual harassment that is going on in the modern army. When I joined the army, however, women were so few that they posed no threat. Deplorable as the situation may be, women knew their place. Male anxiety was not centered on the issue of having to rely on female ability in a front-line situation, nor in a high-tech job skill such as flying off the deck of an aircraft, nor in competition for jobs and promotion. There was little competition, male-female or male-male, because hardly anyone in his or her right mind considered the army as a lifetime career. The world was turned inside out. All the world was in the army – *in* but not *of* it. Ordinary people were in the army. Extraordinary people were in the army.

During the Vietnam War, the average age for draftees was nineteen. In World War II the average age for draftees was thirty-something. A thirty-two-year-old who came into the army in 1942 had been born in 1910, was eight years old at the end of World War I, lived through the boom times, Prohibition, Teapot Dome, and gangster headlines. He turned nineteen the year of the big stock-market crash. If middle class, he had witnessed his parents' dashed hopes and despair during the Depression. If he was from a farm family, he experienced the blight of the Dust Bowl on the plains. Or he may have faced unemployment in the factories, and had strong feelings about the union movement. He watched the rise of Mussolini, Hitler, and Stalin, and beheld the erosion of British power. He may have been an isolationist Republican, but, since he was old enough, he was more likely to have contributed to the landside votes for Franklin D. Roosevelt. When the Japanese bombed Pearl Harbor, he was probably married, had one or two kids, was grateful to have a job. By the time he was drafted he was old enough to have developed both a personal and an historical perspective. World War II was waged by grown-ups who had not grown up in the army culture.

Red tape eventually untangled itself, and I was fully restored to the bosom of the WAC. We attended most classes and some daytime maneuvers with the men, so my friendship with Mint Julep and his friends continued. The women in my company tended to be counterparts of the men in the company – Jewish working-class intellectuals, well read and politically astute. They, too, had tested well in language ability, and had probably done better in math than I had. They also regarded me as a rare specimen of what they had always been warned against, a freak from the upper classes, a WASP to be educated.

No one wanted to be on kitchen police (KP) duty with me because I was so slow and clumsy. I barely knew how to sweep a floor. And I failed mustard pots. (The war was won by lining up all the mustard pots on all the tables the length of the mess hall, with a piece of string.) I had become acquainted with a foul monster, called Grease Trap, who lurks beneath all mess-hall sinks. A slimy coagulation from all the dishes and pots and pans floats there on top of yesterday's dishwater. At four A.M. every morning a hapless KP is lowered, head down into the pit, to skim off the slime. Since I was not much use for anything else, the job usually fell to me.

I had never in my whole life gone to bed without reading before I turned my light out. Lights-out time in the barracks was mandatory at nine P.M. After that, the only place to read was in the shower room, so I went there. A little committee, well-meaning I assume, came to warn me that I could be raped. I thought this was too ridiculous. Did men really creep into our barracks at night? No. They were warning me about the "dykes" who had their eye on me. I considered the matter. I said I would rather be raped than give up reading. I continued my hour in the shower room. I became peripherally more aware of some of the behavior and conversations that went on there but no one approached or bothered me sexually. However, I was too tempting a target to be left alone entirely. The same committee came to ask me what I knew about Karl Marx and Communism. I said I knew everything, I had studied about him in Victorian Philosophy and in English History, second year. I had had to read the *Manifesto* twice. Boring. They asked me what I knew about lesbianism. I said I knew everything. I had read Tennyson's poem about the lovely isle of Lesbos and I had read some of Sappho's poetry. Next question?

Their efforts were not all in vain. Every hour of the day what I thought or took for granted was mercilessly challenged. I was made to think and, impossibly, expected to justify myself. About why no Negro women were in our barracks, about what Hitler was doing to the Jews, about lynchings and the Triangle Shirtwaist fire. They also pressed upon me certain Communist novels, smuggled through customs, that I had never heard about, much less read. I did manage to finish the one about passionate comrades building dams in Siberia. I read it for the torrid, yet prudish, sex. Sex between comrades is a good thing. Sex with someone who is not a true believer is sordid and demeaning. Sex with a member of one's own class is the stuff of literature. Sex with a gamekeeper gets the book banned. My English aunts had told me that I was a Yankee, and they knew what Yankees thought. My barracks-room aunts told me I was rich and decadent, and they knew what WASPs thought. They were trying to educate someone who had starred as Madame Defarge, and championed the Luddites! They didn't know about my experience with Naomi, with Zerotovich and Pitman. They did not know that I had had to fight to go to college. Their mistake was that they tried to tempt me with a Russia that was mirror to Kipling's England – rigid, exclusionary, snobbish, naively jingoistic. Even from a distance I could smell the smugness, the familiar essence of *Don't play with the village children.*

Clearance. That was the new watchword. We were all waiting for "clearance" before going on into training as cryptographic technicians (805s). Meanwhile we practiced typing hour after hour. I was content to improve my typing skills. After all, I planned to be a writer! On Tuesdays and Thursdays we were required to wear gas-mask kits slung over our shoulders and to learn how to don them properly at sudden command. The kits were handy for carrying Kleenex and Kotex, even a book, so some of us elected to wear them every day. Kleenex comes in handy when you are putting a message on a shitting pigeon's leg. We also learned to make messages on the ground for overhead planes to read – by tramping out SOS in the sand or spelling it out with white strips of cloth. The manual said we could use our underwear if need be, but that seemed useless, since our general issue was expressly designed *not* to be seen. Among ourselves we discussed the delicious possibility of being marooned on a Pacific island, doffing our white brassieres, stringing them together in fancy loops and spirals to signal a friendly plane – in script.

Preparatory to being sent on bivouac into the Ozark bush, we were taught to read contour maps. The training manual had as its frontispiece a photograph of Betty Grable. "Run your hand over this photograph," the caption told us. "Yes! It's flat! But you know that Betty Grable isn't flat." I wonder how the real Betty Grable felt about that? Armed with map and compass we were sent into the Ozark woods. Shots were fired over us as we wiggled along on our stomachs, constantly being urged to keep our butts down. At one point we were solemnly shown, with help of a dummy, how to sneak up behind a Japanese soldier in the Malaysian jungle, how to cut off his head with piano wire. "Who has piano wire?" I asked. I was told it would be issued. Also, be careful to catch the head while it is falling so it doesn't make a noise as it hits the ground.

Real soldiers, acting their parts with gusto, had distributed themselves in tasteful repose throughout the bush. They wore bloody bandages or exposed fake bloody wounds and moaned as we passed by. We were taught to rifle their packs for fake sulfa powder (bright green), and to sprinkle it on the wounds. At lunch time, the dead and dying joined us for lunch. We were each given a tin containing C rations. The whole adventure had the air of one of Mother's picnics, except that the main course looked like dog food, tasted like corned-beef hash. A tiny chocolate bar (chocolate was rationed in civilian life) was included "for morale purposes" and to give a shot of quick energy. Drinking water was dispensed from an enormous canvas bag (a Lister bag) hanging from a tree. We filled our canteens from what looked like an udder. Evaporation kept the water surprisingly cool.

Now came the time for clearance to be announced. I had thought that the term meant something like grades and report cards, but clearance was more complicated than that. All these weeks, while we were training at Camp Crowder, our backgrounds were being checked, in order to see who was – or was not – trustworthy enough to be initiated into the mysteries of the code machine. Rumor had it that it was one of the most secret of secrets developed by the Allies.

When the lists of cleared names were posted I noticed that the women who seemed (to me) most likely to be a shoe-in for 805 training were turned down. When I expressed amazement (they were so smart!) they explained that IQ was not important. What the army and the FBI were looking for was whether they had ever belonged to the Communist Party, or been active in a union. My life seemed short and blameless, if that was the criteria, but I did not receive clearance either. Several weeks went by. My barracks-mates seemed more concerned about me than I was. My case was much discussed. The consensus of the most knowing was that I was being held back because of the company I had kept since I joined the army. Maybe I really was tainted by association, maybe it was just Communist paranoia that made my barracks-mates think so, maybe it was another case of snafu. Whatever. Tardily, my clearance finally came.

I remember surprisingly little about my training with the SIGABA, the War Department code machine. I suspect that I was hypnotized into not remembering. We were told that we could never discuss SIGABA nor describe it, even after the war. Everything we learned must never go past the code room. However, during the last fifty years, I have read articles and book reviews describing SIGABA in great detail, and have seen a movie on PBS about its inventor. The little machine was developed by the Germans, stolen by the British. Small and clumsy, it looked like a very old-fashioned typewriter, the sort that Samuel Clemens might have invested his money in. Actually, SIGABA was a very early computer sans electronic chips. We had to turn the drums by hand in order to set the "teeth" that would catch the electric impulses that realized the code. Almost immediately someone in our company dubbed SIGABA "Sigababy."

We were taught not only how to use the books that contained the code *du jour*, but how to destroy them. They were kept in a safe. If the Germans or Japanese broke into the code room, we were to fling ourselves in front of the safe, fight off the enemy, and ignite the fuse that was attached to a flat black slab underneath. It was a magnesium bomb. We must be prepared to blow ourselves up with the code books, if need be. Some people thought this was hilarious. I did, too, on one level. But cursed with a *Girls' Own Annual* type of honor, I knew that, if need be, I would sacrifice my life to save civilization as we know it. In 1944 most of the other people who trained with me would have done as much.

My orders came in October. I was posted to the War Department Code Room, Pentagon, Fort Meyer, Virginia, Military District of Washington. Our barracks were in a boggy hollow, separated from the Pentagon by a complicated cloverleaf in a broad, busy highway. We walked to work through a tunnel underneath the road, entered the main foyer of the Pentagon, then walked up enormously wide ramps to the fifth floor.

Sometimes, on the way to the mess hall during the wee, small hours, I would stretch out my arms like a bird, half-running, half-sailing down those ramps, wheeling and pirouetting as I went. The corridors were so huge that, outside our office, there was space for a messengers' bicycle lane, a pedestrian lane, and for us to make a military formation three ranks deep. We worked in shifts around the clock and fell in for roll call ten minutes before the shift began. In order to make the code room more secret, there was no number on the door, but as far as I know no other office in the Pentagon advertised itself by having its members stand formation three times every twenty-four hours, in the public corridor.

On my first day, an officer shouted us to attention, shouted to us to stand at ease, ordered us to turn our heads to the right. "Do you recognize the person standing at your right?" The answer came thundering back: "Yes. I recognize the person standing to my right." Attention! At ease! An order to look to the left. "Do you recognize the person standing to your left?" Back came a voice crying, "I do not recognize the person standing to my left." The voice was speaking of me! I was ordered to step forward, give name, rank, serial number. My name was found on the list, I was asked to show my orders, then we went into the War Department Code Room, the nerve center of the war.

The door shut behind me with a *click*, as though I were entering the Dark Tower in the story "Childe Rowland," from *English Fairy Tales*. The room was long and narrow, really a series of rooms opening one on the other, separated by glass partitions, but open to an aisle. A colonel's office was the only one fully separated from the rest. We walked past the desks of lieutenant colonels, majors, first lieutenants, second lieutenants, master sergeants, first sergeants, and plain old three-stripe sergeants, to a room with no aisle, filled with corporals and enlisted men, first and second class. Such was the proliferation of rank that the table where I worked was no more humble than an officer's.

The Pentagon mess hall, buried in the bowels of the basement, was lovingly reconstructed to look like a mess hall in the field. There was even a grease trap! We were allowed out of the code room only to go to the mess hall and to the latrine where, paranoid persuasion had it, people listened to our conversations through holes drilled in the walls. No one who was not a member of the code room ever entered our office. Our world was hermetically sealed. There were no casual passersby – no messenger boys, no generals. No one.

Baskets of decoded and un-decoded messages were brought to us and dumped on a table in the middle of our space. Incoming (coded) and outgoing (not yet coded) messages looked like telegrams, with yellow tape pasted to the page. To send a message I would set the SIGABA to encode mode, look up the day's key word, set drums, type out a second prescribed word, note result, set drums to match, start typing the message. Somewhere across the world, the text of varied English words I was typing would be coming out of another SIGABA machine in five-letter, nonsensical increments. For a letter received, I would set the machine to decode, set the five-letter key of the day, look at the first five-letter word. The words were nonsense. Sometimes runs of them could have been made into poetry, but I was not there to have such thoughts, I told myself sternly. Miraculously a sensible sentence would spiel out. Or maybe not. I may have made a mistake in the first or second step. Or the 805 clerk in Europe or Asia, while encoding, may have transposed when he or she set the drums. Or maybe he or she – or I – had placed fingers on the wrong keys. Or maybe there had been a sort of static in the atmosphere and the message was scrambled. The messages that were beyond my ability to redeem were sent over to the editing table.

Sometimes the editors could figure it out. They also proofread letters that were badly written or misspelled. I longed to be an editor. To say, airily, one day, after the Duration, "You're asking what I did in the war? Oh, I was a code department *editor* in the Signal Corps," would sound much grander than admitting to have been a clerk. It might be a way to put my foot on the great ladder leading toward a literary life.

During the summer, while I was in training, I had barely paid attention to the war, although heavy fighting continued in Normandy, and the Allies had made a secondary landing in the south of France. By October, when I arrived in Washington, our armored divisions had reached the Rhine, and the Soviets, from Baltic to Balkans, were pushing to the west. On the other side of the world the Allies were hopscotching across the Pacific, toward Japan. Mint Julep was in New Guinea. I don't know where my friend the pathologist was. Anne was living in a hotel in midtown Manhattan, but she was stationed at the Battery, overlooking the Statue of Liberty and Governors Island. She had been made a quartermaster, one of only two women to hold that rating. Her job was to instruct convoy captains when to zig and when to zag as they crossed the Atlantic. We were all proud of her. She was born for the job! Father, on the other hand, was stuck in Greenland, chafing to get into the action in the Pacific.

The WAC barracks at Fort Meyer were getting colder and damper with every passing day. A perpetual miasma hung over us; moisture ran down the walls. Not only did we pull KP duty in the Pentagon but in the WAC company mess hall as well. The food became increasingly worse. When other people complained, I thought they were being unreasonable. After all, our families at home were being rationed, and the troops at the front fared far worse. Soldiers had griped about their rations since the Crusades, and probably before that. That's what our officers told us. Just to prove their point they appeared suddenly in the enlistees' chow line. When I looked at the menu that day, I had to admit things weren't so bad, better than usual in fact. But when next I pulled KP I became inadvertent witness to a felony.

At 0500 hours a two-ton truck brought, among other things, crates of meat and grapefruit and butter to the back door. We helped carry the load inside, while the cook checked off each item on a list. Her responsibility was grave. Food was rationed; in civilian life, such food was worth its weight in gold. At 1000 hours we were all given a break at the same time, and told we could go to our barracks for twenty minutes. I, slow as usual,

Members of the Corfield family, 1907: Roger (left, seated); (standing) Doris, Rego, and Joan; (seated in centre) Captain W. R. Corfield and Kate, his third wife. Joyce sits on her father's lap. Rex sits slightly behind his mother.

Joan Amphlett Corfield, 1896, age four, sitting sidesaddle and wearing a velvet riding habit.

United States Coast Guard Cutter *Bear* in Arctic seas, 1920s.

(Above left) Joyce, Anne, and Joan aboard *Leviathan*, 1933. (Above right) Joan with Joyce.

Tea in the garden, Claremont, 1943. Mother is seated. Joan and Joyce stand on either side of a visiting friend.

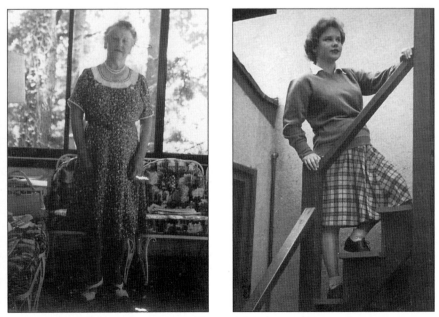

(Above left) Mother, Claremont. (Above right) As a college sophomore, already enlisted in the army and waiting to be "called up."

Staff Sergeant Joan Higbee, Fort Mason, San Francisco, 1945.

Captain F. D. Higbee at Leyte.

(Above left) Corporal Joan Higbee, cryptographer, Signal Corps, Women's
Army Corps, and Quartermaster third class Anne Higbee, U.S. Coast Guard.
(Above right) In fatigues, Camp Crowder, Missouri.

Mr. and Mrs. John Charles Bodger signing the marriage register, June 10, 1947. John's father (J.C.) peeks over the minister's shoulder.

(Above left) Father, Joan, and John. Joyce is bridesmaid. (Above right) Standing in front of a converted barracks apartment in Shanks Village, 1949, five months pregnant with Ian.

Passport photo, 1958, for the trip that inspired *How the Heather Looks.*

Daphne Milne (Christopher Robin's mother) at left, with Pooh, Ian, Lucy, and Piglet in the Milne garden at Cotchford Farm, Ashdown Forest.

Lucy, Ian, and Thames swans. The island where Ratty and Mole had their picnic, in *The Wind in the Willows,* can be observed in the background.

Lucy and Ian with Lucy's antique rocking horse, Dobbin.

(Above left) Christopher Diver and Ian (front), Katie Diver and Lucy (on couch), 1959. (Above right) Lucy (left), with her best friend, Esther Bromberg.

was washing out a mop in the utility sink, behind the kitchen. When I emerged, I noticed that another army vehicle had pulled up to the door, and three or four men jumped out, including the cook's boyfriend, a fat supply sergeant. The butter, meat, and grapefruit that we had carried *into* the mess hall was being hustled *out*, into the truck.

So befuddled was I from lack of sleep, and my own brand of cluelessness, that I did not put things together until weeks later. By that time we had a new mess sergeant. I remember standing in the mess line and seeing that the bread cage was open. I reached in and stole half a loaf, intending to take it back to the barracks to share with my mates. This had become SOP (standard operating procedure). Not to steal when I had a chance would have been selfish, a discourtesy to my fellow soldiers. This time I was caught in the act! The new mess sergeant, far from being the screaming tyrant we were used to, asked for an explanation. She shook her head in sorrow. "To think you had to steal a loaf of bread," she said. I felt like a character out of *Les Misérables*. By that time I had become a hardened criminal. I stole pencils as I walked past officers' desks, in order to do my work in the code room.

As winter solstice loomed, our work at the Pentagon increased from eight to ten to twelve hours a shift. A record-breaking fog lay over Europe, unexpectedly delaying transportation on war-torn roads. The Germans bombarded the main supply port of Amsterdam with their newly developed V2 rockets, and at the same time pushed troops back into Belgium. The newspapers dubbed the contest The Battle of the Bulge, for so it appeared on the maps. The Allied lines, swiftly laid down, now lacked supplies to hold them steady. I remember handling messages that begged for coats, socks, blankets. Our men in the Ardennes were dying, not only from artillery fire, but from the cold! Day and night, hour after hour, a sign blinked in the foyer of the Pentagon, enumerating the casualties. I saw hulking Russian generals, in enormous overcoats, stop to contemplate the sign. I saw Douglas Fairbanks, Jr., incredibly handsome in his navy uniform, pause for a moment. The tide was finally turned after Christmas, but not without a loss of almost eighty thousand Allied men.

In January, my day off happened to coincide with Roosevelt's fourth inauguration. I stood in the dirty snow with two or three hundred other people and watched the president being wheeled out to the back porch of the White House. I had had no idea that he was so frail, so shrunken. Usually, in the photographs, what we saw was his leonine head.

At Fort Meyer, long hours, lack of vitamins, and damp barracks took their toll. By February, sooner or later, most of us were down with flu. I succumbed a little sooner and came back to work when others were off sick. My first day back to the code room, I discovered there was a shortage of editors. Eagerly I volunteered for a place at the high table. Messages, all incoming, all flawed in the decoding, were dumped into the center of the table. I put my hand into the grab bag and pulled out a message about a place spelled Yalta. Obviously a mistake! I changed the Y to M. There was something about a wheelchair. A red carpet. Conscientiously, I changed the Ys to Ms. *Who had ever heard of a place called Yalta?* I knew about Malta, the British navy base. Mother had a lace tablecloth from there. By afternoon, as the same mistake continued to be made, I began to feel uneasy, but I kept on grabbing the Yalta/Malta messages as fast as I could. I began to feel like I had when, at five years old, I had cut my hair with manicure scissors, and had to keep on cutting to make things come out even. *A Very Important Naval Personage was miffed because he had counted on having the ground-floor suite for himself, but someone, without so much as a by-your-leave, had grabbed it for the Wheelchair Person . . .*

From where I sat, at the editors' table, I could look down the length of the code room – all the way to the colonel's office, near the front door. No one ever came there except members of the code room. Yet now I was vaguely aware of a knot of aliens, four or five generals, coming out of the colonel's office. The colonel was behind them, looking woebegone. He pointed to the lieutenant colonels. There was a brief consultation, a waving of papers before people's noses, then the lieutenant colonels pointed to the majors. The majors pointed to the lieutenants who pointed to the sergeants. Now the phalanx was coming close enough that I could recognize faces. I had seen them all, on the covers of *Time* magazine. There was General Marshall and General Grove and . . . They arrived at the editors' table. I knew what they wanted. I knew *whom* they wanted.

"It was I," I said, before they had a chance to ask.

General Grove leaned down and looked into my upturned face. What did he see? Pink cheeks? Green-blue eyes? Curly hair? Ignorance, innocence, and good intentions, no doubt. "Oh my God!" he half-whispered.

Because I changed the Y to M, planes had changed their flight plans. Because I changed the Y to M, ships in the Mediterranean had changed their course. Because I changed the Y to M, a certain wheelchair went astray. Because I changed the Y to M, the Yalta Conference almost didn't happen. Well, not at Yalta. Maybe I was meant to be an instrument of God. Maybe, if those three wartime leaders had met in Malta, Roosevelt would have listened more to Churchill, less to Stalin. Maybe he wouldn't have presented to the U.S.S.R. – on a platter – the whole of Eastern Europe, chunks of Mongolia, and strategic islands off Japan. Maybe Roosevelt and Churchill would not have made secret deals concerning most of the civilized world. Maybe the Iron Curtain and the Cold War would never have happened. Maybe . . .

Shoot me at dawn? Send me to Leavenworth? Demote me? I was an Enlisted Man first class, about the lowest of the low. What I had done concerned matters so secret nothing was ever said to me again – nor, probably, to anyone else outside of the highest high command. I was ordered to return to my SIGABA right away. Meekly I complied. Even the colonel was not made privy to the exact nature of my sin. He had never spoken to me. Now he went out of his way to avoid me. I was dangerous.

March dragged by. April came, with no leavening of my spirits. I had gone to the latrine and was just leaving the lounge when a voice on the radio said, "We interrupt this program . . ." President Franklin Delano Roosevelt had died, at Warm Springs, Georgia. I rushed back to the code room. Startled, stricken faces marked the progress of the news, spreading along a fuse running the length of the room. I arrived at the far end just as the full force exploded. As we marched into Washington, to participate in the funeral parade, I looked down and saw the cobblestones beneath my GI leather shoes when we crossed Lincoln Memorial Bridge.

In May we marched again, this time to celebrate VE Day, the end of the war with Germany. Already men were returning from Europe. Some of them were sent on to the Pacific, some of them were being discharged forthwith. It was strange to see young and youngish men out of uniform.

Once, when I was coming back from town, a young bus driver, as required, stopped the bus in the middle of the Lincoln Memorial Bridge. He intoned the usual announcement: "Ladies and gentlemen, we are now entering the state of Virginia. The law demands that I order all colored people to move to the back of the bus." Then he stood up, that young veteran, and faced us. "Ladies and gentlemen, I am just back from the war in Europe, where I thought I was fighting *against* this kind of malarkey. This is my bus, and I say no one moves unless he wants to, no matter what

the law of Virginia tells me. I'm gonna do this every trip until they fire me."
No one moved. No one argued or complained.

And no one applauded. I seem to remember touching the bus driver's
shoulder as I left the bus, leaning down to whisper something congratula-
tory, but I did not make a spectacle of myself. It is not enough to harbor
brave thoughts privately. I failed to be spontaneous when spontaneity could
have counted. I could have said "Hear! Hear!" or "Three cheers!" or burst
into applause, so that other people would know that young man did not
stand alone. So he would know. In my old age I am aware that being brave
usually involves the risk of appearing foolish. In 1945, at the age of twenty-
one, I did not have the kind of courage evidenced by the bus driver's singular act. He must have been about my age. A generation later, in the
1960s, our children, dressed like clowns and fools, taught me to be braver.

Unexpectedly, Father arrived in Washington. He had come from Greenland
to Washington in order to persuade Coast Guard Headquarters to send him
to the Pacific. Now that there were no German submarines cruising the
Atlantic, he felt he was irrelevant. We commiserated, Father and I. I had
never felt so close to him, but I did not tell him about Yalta/Malta. To do
so would have been to explain the workings of the code room. Besides, I
was ashamed of my stupidity.

Father's determination paid off. He received orders to command a
flotilla of LSTs, the very kind I had watched being built at Calship. He
would be part of a huge naval attack on Japanese-held islands, the names
of which he could not tell me. Neither of us discussed the danger.

Three weeks later I received orders to report to the Signal Corps code
room, Fort Mason, San Francisco Port of Embarkation. Knowing that
Father had pulled strings I was filled with guilt – and exultation. The War
Department Code Room must have been just as exultant to get rid of me.

Father was appointed Beach Master for one of the Pacific landings.
This meant that he and a couple of radio signalmen would leave the relative safety of their ship, jump into a small boat, and be first to go ashore.
The navy, using their biggest guns, had been bombarding the island for
hours. They reported that there was no possibility of anything on the
beach being left alive. As Father stepped ashore, the first thing he saw was
a huge water buffalo; it rose from behind a log and lumbered away along
the tide line. Also, he soon discovered, scores of Japanese were holed up

in the dunes. Father crawled up to the log, settled into the hollow left by the beast, and directed the landing from there. For this, he received an official *well done* from Admiral William Halsey, and was promoted to the rank of rear admiral.

Meanwhile, I was enjoying myself in San Francisco.

CHAPTER 14

Love and Marriage

GERMANY SURRENDERED ON May 8, 1945. Japan surrendered on August 14, the anniversary of the date that marked the beginning of World War I. The need for cryptographers stationed in San Francisco became minimal. Early in 1946 I was shipped to Sacramento, where I was kept busy in a typing pool, helping to process army discharges. Not until June 1946 did the army hand me my own honorable discharge.

I took the train "home," to where my parents were living, temporarily, in a house in Palos Verdes, overlooking Santa Monica Bay. The train was excruciatingly slow. Even though the war was over, our cars were repeatedly sidetracked for others with higher priority. Almost everyone aboard had just been discharged. Stalled between stations, we were left to stare for hours at the sun-blazed vastness of the San Joaquin Valley. There was little conversation. Like divers, we were emerging from one world into another. Soldiers who had been stationed away from home for years were especially susceptible, imperilled by the equivalent of emotional bends. They may have welcomed the long delays.

Somewhere along the line, I got off the train and walked up and down the platform, swinging along with my thirty-inch stride. A voice hailed me from behind: "Sergeant!" I stopped, turned on my heel. A man, a second lieutenant, caught up with me. "I've been watching you," he said. "You can't keep on doing that, you know; you can't keep on walking that way."

"What way?"

"The way the army taught you." Ovenlike though the San Joaquin Valley might be, I felt a chill run down my spine. "Do you ever want to get married?" he asked. I must have nodded, maybe I muttered "yes."

"Let me give you some friendly male advice. When you get home, forget all about the army. Don't ever mention you were in the WAC." He had written a letter to his wife, he said. He was coming home to take care of her. He wanted her to quit her job so she could stay home, take care of the kids, which he was confident they would soon be having. "Buy yourself some high heels right away," he told me. "Practise. I can see that you're going to need a lot of practise." Part of me knew he was talking nonsense, part of me believed him.

Someone shouted for us to get back on the train. Advice-giver ran for his car, I ran for mine. On a superficial level I was not offended by what he had said to me. If you had asked me then, I would have said he was "just trying to be nice." He probably thought so, too, yet that chill down my spine had split bedrock, helped prepare the way for my consciousness to be raised twenty years later. At the time I saw my inability (or decision) not to wear high heels as further proof not only of my lack of sexual desirability, but also of willpower. I could not stand the agony; just wearing the damn things left my feet bleeding. And when I tried to walk, I made a fool of myself, even with practise. I chided myself for not being able to make sacrifices that other women (good women?) made in order to gain the greater reward of marriage, children, the privilege of running a household.

I knew I would not shut up about being in the army, about being *me*. My story grew within me, irrepressible as a watered shoot. Pregnant with my own sovereignty, I yet felt as sad, guilty, and frightened as if I were about to produce an illegitimate child. I knew I should throttle the child (my sovereign self), and I knew I would botch the job. I lacked strength of character.

In September I went back to Pomona College to complete my last two years toward a bachelor's degree.

I had looked forward to wearing civilian clothes again, but I soon discovered that having to decide, every morning, what to wear was an unexpected aggravation. Once I had worked out a color scheme for skirt, blouse, and sweater, I tended to wear the same skirt and sweater every day for the ensuing week. My dormmates noticed and were mildly amused. They were also amused by my underwear, which, although it was khaki-colored, had real elastic, a commodity not yet back on the market.

In the army, I had dreamed about returning to Claremont and the college campus. I loved the eucalyptus trees, the clambering bougainvillea, the smell of orange blossoms. I loved the green quad (discreetly watered at night), the hidden courtyards where we picked camellia blossoms, floated them in the plashing fountains. Because I knew what it was like to "police the area" for cigarette butts, I knew now that someone had to clean those petals out of the drains. As in those trick Gestalt cartoons in my psychology book, figure against ground was reversed. Now I noticed the Mexican gardeners. I wondered how much they were paid, what they thought of the students who passed them by as though they were a bush or a garden hose. Most of them were old; they had probably worked on campus all during the war, but how about the younger men? I don't think I sentimentalized them, but I did identify with them, as fellow enlistees, not as faithful retainers. I knew they loathed the likes of me, and so they should.

In the dormitory, our rooms were cleaned twice a week by almost-invisible older women who stripped the beds and left clean sheets once a week. I, who never did learn the knack of making square corners perfect enough for inspection, stripped my own bed and rolled up the mattress, so the person who was cleaning could more quickly sweep and mop, get on to her next job, maybe the latrines. I knew the panic of having too much to do, too little time to do it. I would never forget that I had been the slowest person on KP.

Both my dormmates and my professors took it for granted that I was more worldly than the other women students. In a way I was; in a way I wasn't. Except for the brief time at Camp Crowder, when I dated Mint Julep, I had not "gone out." I had worked mostly with women, and I lived in a women's barracks, but, curiously, I don't remember much helpful talk about men, at least anything that pertained to me and to my situation. Either the sex proclaimed was so outrageous that it frightened me, or it was spoken of as something that would happen in the distant future, or had happened in the distant past, back home. I was afraid of getting pregnant (every girl was then), but since I did not date, there was not much danger of that. I was more afraid of being swept away from my moorings, from caste and class and family.

If I had stayed several years in the dormitory at Pomona (if I had stayed *anywhere* for more than a few years) I would have heard more talk about "ordinary" dating, about how far to go on a date, about what actually *happened* – or didn't happen. I could have observed the unfolding of other people's love stories: first meeting, dating, courtship, sex (?), engagement, sex (?), marriage. Sex. I could have observed and assessed my social peers to learn where I fit in, how to fit in. Great waves of desire waxed and waned in my body. I would be pretty if I weren't so fat; I knew I was sexual, but I did not know how to be "sexy." I did not know how to learn to bear the pain of wearing high heels.

I continued my double major in English and history, but decided to take honors in history, which meant, among other things, attending a small tutorial seminar. That's where I met John Bodger. He was five years older than I. In the ordinary course of events, if there had been no war, he would have left Pomona before I ever got there. John had been stationed in Australia and New Guinea as an enlisted man. If he had been an officer, I doubt if I would have wanted to have anything to do with him. An officer's war was a different war, to be looked upon with suspicion. John, like me, was back in college, on the G.I. Bill of Rights. He had just one more semester to complete before he would go off to Columbia University, to get his Ph.D. in American history.

We started walking across the campus together. Sometimes I met him by chance. Sometimes I *pretended* to have met him by chance. We hung out in the history section of the library, sat on the library steps to talk. We were both half-English (his father; my mother) and we both had been in England in the early 1930s. As with all young lovers, we were bowled over by the force of coincidence. We knew that we were meant for each other when we discovered we had both (each, separately, at different times) fallen off a donkey while riding on the sands at Weston-super-Mare. We became engaged over Christmas.

John's father (John Charles Bodger II) had immigrated to California when he was twelve. John's grandfather (John Charles I) had been apprenticed as a gardener on the estate of the Duke of Somerset, where he had proved himself clever with flowers, inspired in the art and science of hybridizing. Eventually he had left service and set up a greengrocer shop in Weston-super-Mare, where he continued to experiment. Craving more land, he sent his three eldest sons abroad, to Australia, Africa, and the Americas, to find a climate that was both temperate and sunny. Word came back that southern California offered a non-tropical countryside, blessed with cool nights and an average of 128 continuous days of sunshine, good not only for growing seeds, but for drying them. Furthermore, land was cheap. The greengrocer left his shop and younger children, including John Charles II, in the care of his wife, and set out for California.

When John Charles, John's father, was nine years old, he was watching some ladies practice archery on the village green. An arrow went astray; he was hit, and blinded in one eye. The country doctor said that, were he to stay in a darkened room for a couple of years, his sight might be considerably restored. Accordingly, he was not sent to work in the fields, like his brothers, but stayed home with his mother and sisters, who kept the house and tended shop. In a darkened kitchen they taught him how to cook, by touch and smell. He could not go outside and play. Instead, he became his father's confidante, a special relationship that was to last until his father died. The brothers knew about land and plowing, about growing standard and new varieties, about supplying the shop with produce, about harvesting and drying flower and vegetable seed to be sold in packets. Meanwhile, from an early age, young John Charles eagerly grasped the concepts of development and marketing, of borrowing and investing. He knew about banks, taxes, and accounts. A Joseph to his father's Benjamin, he came to be the leader among his brothers. He must have annoyed the hell out of them.

The country doctor had been right. John Charles did regain part of the sight in his blind eye. His father, already farming near Los Angeles, sent for his wife and the younger members of the family. They took a ship across the Atlantic and arrived in New York. John Charles, bored with being cooped up for a month, went ashore to explore, confident that he could easily find his way back to the harbor by just looking for ship masts. He had forgotten that Manhattan is an island, in those days surrounded by ships. He almost didn't make it back to the docks in time to help his mother, sisters, and younger brother get to the railway station. They crossed the continent in an immigrant car, which meant a car with benches on either side and a stove for heating and cooking in the middle. Mrs. Bodger had contracted an illness aboard ship; as the days went by her fever grew worse.

Once aboard the train, she lay on a hard bench, impervious to what was going on around her. Neither her children nor any of the other immigrants were able to help her. Desperate, John Charles hatched a plan. He had noticed, when they stopped at stations, that a man dressed in a white hat, white suit, and white boots would emerge from the private car attached to the end of the train, and walk up and down the platform, smoking a cigar. At the next stop a brash twelve-year-old, surrounded by rosy-cheeked siblings, walked up to this man, so obviously rich and powerful. Speaking in broad Somerset, he said: "Sir, our mother is very sick. She is going to die unless we can get help for her." The man in the white hat went to see for himself, summoned his minions to remove the woman to his private car, and telegraphed for a doctor to board the train further along the line. By the time the immigrant train reached California, Mrs. Bodger was restored to health, and to the bosom of her family. Years later, J.C. hired a detective agency to find out who his mother's benefactor was, to no avail.

The Bodgers not only worked the land. In 1890, their patriarch set up a business, Bodger Seeds Limited. John Charles I sold flower seeds wholesale, worldwide. The only time that John Charles II left his father, and the seed company, was during the Klondike gold rush. He shipped as a cook on a coastal schooner going to Alaska. The ship was so ill-favored that most of the crew, including the cook, jumped ship at Nome. Tales of the hardships on the trail and in the mining camps convinced the young adventurer that there might be safer ways to make money, rather than panning for gold. With sharp business acumen, John Charles II studied the market, and soon perceived that, like himself, some of the people who had come to the Yukon not only wanted to get rich quick, they wanted to know how to *act* rich. Advertising himself as an Englishman who knew the ways of earls and lords (had not his father worked for the Duke of Somerset?) John Charles set up a school to teach manners to miners. When he had collected enough money to pay for his passage home, he returned to southern California, and to Bodger Seeds Limited. In a few more years he would become president of the company. To distinguish him from his father (and, later, his son), friends and family took to calling him by his initials: J. C., which was pronounced as one word: Jaysey. John, who did not like his father, once said to me: "J.C. really likes those initials. He thinks he's God, walking on water."

John urged me to attend a meeting of the American Veterans Committee (AVC), which was forming a chapter on campus. The members were all ex-service men – and one woman. Me. I blessed the conversations and arguments I had been involved in, or overheard, in my barracks, and among Mint Julep's friends at Camp Crowder. They had educated me to look at life from the other end of the telescope. It was not mere fatuousness that made me agree with John and the other veterans I was meeting on the Pomona campus.

"Citizens first, veterans second," was the AVC motto. We were determined not to become like members of the American Legion, or the VFW, sentimentalizing their war experience, stuck in the past. We saw the AVC only as a temporary expedient, soon to be discarded as cheerfully as we had discarded our uniforms. We wanted to get on with our lives. We believed in the United States *and* we thought we could make it better. We deplored militarism, yet we wanted to put to use our hard-gained war experience and savvy. We had come back to college wiser and tougher, full of optimism and ideals. In 1946 we were convinced that our generation could socialize medicine, equalize opportunity, rub out poverty, abolish racism. Educated and enlightened, we would save the world from making the same mistakes that our parents' generation had made in 1918: instead of wreaking vengeance, we would avert economic depression by rebuilding Germany and Japan. Politics infused the air we breathed.

John asked me to attend an AVC-sponsored debate with him. This was our first real date! The meeting would take place in the courtyard of the Student Union. Pomona students were mostly conservative Republicans, or their parents were. Our campus chapter of the AVC hoped to educate them, draw them toward the light. Accordingly, we had decided to invite both the Republican and Democratic nominees for Congress to speak in our presence. I was somewhat fuzzy as to who was who, what the issues were. John awed me by his knowledge, his relish, of politics. I could feel his tension as he sat beside me; he radiated electricity. I was excited by it. Excited by him.

Jerry Voorhis was the Democratic candidate. He had taught sociology at Pomona and then gone into politics. He had been a liberal congressman for ten years, but was now under attack not only from the Republicans, but from the far left of his party. The Left, along with the barely formed American Labor Party, was trying to divide and conquer the Democrats by splitting off from President Harry S. Truman, who had not been elected, but came into office on the death of Franklin D. Roosevelt. John told me there was a rumor that the left-wing Democrats would rather an unknown Republican be elected, in order to prepare the way for a more radical Democratic candidate in 1948. John was for Jerry Voorhis, but Voorhis had just been given the Judas kiss by the Political Action Committee of the Congress of Industrial Organizations (CIO), which purported to endorse him.

The Republican candidate was from Whittier, a sleepy little Quaker town twenty miles away. Whittier College was our big football rival – the Sage Hens versus the Poets! This was the first time that this particular candidate would appear on a public platform, running for office. There was a restless stir among the members of the AVC when he walked in wearing his navy officer's uniform. *Didn't he know? Hadn't he got the message?* There was an even bigger hum of dissension when the inept visitor, all tricked out in gold stripes, tried to appeal to us enlisted men as his "fellow veterans." Perhaps noting the cold reception, he tried a few football jokes. His name was Richard Nixon. Sometime during his speech, Nixon pulled out a copy of the *Pasadena News* (many students came from Pasadena, and from San Marino, its wealthy suburb). He waved the paper in our faces, and recommended that we read an editorial which described Jerry Voorhis as "a tool of the Communist Party." In a hoarse, choked voice, Nixon harangued us about the dangers of Communism. I was willing to listen with an open mind to the thread of his argument, but I found myself lost in a labyrinth. I thought I must be stupid, not to understand what was so earnestly being expounded. Searching for a clue, I turned to the courses I had taken from Miss Ruth George, in poetry and prosody. I broke down the sentences, analyzed the man's syntax. Am I the first person to notice that Richard Nixon spoke in triple negatives?

Over the Christmas holidays I met John's family, and he met mine. His mother, *née* Bertha Stanton Jones, was tall and imposing, dark-haired and dark-eyed; she was almost Spanish in her looks. She must have been beautiful as a young woman, but now she dressed somberly and *was* somber. She was a Christian Scientist who suffered from diabetes, and perhaps from medical depression. Her parents were from New England; her mother was related to Edwin M. Stanton, Abraham Lincoln's secretary of war. She had grown up in Los Angeles; her parents had owned a house and kept a cow on what is now Wilshire Boulevard. She was the only person I ever knew who could recall that Hollywood was so named because the surrounding hills abounded in native holly.

In 1906, the year of the San Francisco earthquake, Bertha graduated from Stamford University and took a job as a teacher in a small town near Santa Barbara. She lived in a boarding house, with other teachers. One late afternoon, when a bevy of young women was sitting on the commodious front porch, John Charles Bodger drove past in his new automobile. All the young women rushed to view the wondrous machine. J.C. offered a ride to the first girl daring enough to volunteer to go for a spin with him. Only the beautiful Bertha Jones took him up on his offer. And so they were married.

Bertha had wanted to be a writer, but she was soon deeply involved in the seed business. She sat on the board of directors, composed of Bodgers and bankers. Bertha was renowned in the company for her placatory skills, reigning in J.C., smoothing feathers ruffled by him. J.C. respected her acumen and intelligence, but even more he appreciated her unswerving adherence to the family caveat: *There is only one God and his name is J.C.*

John had a brother, Howard, two years younger than he. Howard had married his high-school sweetheart, Pat, before he joined the army. Now that he had returned, he was working with his father, presumably as heir apparent. John had no interest in working for Bodger Seeds, but even if he had, his father would not have allowed him in. There was a deep-rooted antipathy between them which, at first, I thought might come from the difference in their politics. Later I came to see that J.C. had no respect for his elder son; he regarded him with suspicion. He thought John was clumsy, incapable, a loser. Now he had chosen an eccentric, unpredictable young woman to be his wedded wife. Even though I was an admiral's daughter (perhaps *because* I was an admiral's daughter), I was a loose cannon on deck. I talked too much. I was too plump. I did not dress well. I did not manicure and paint my nails. Often, I forgot to wear lipstick.

Consternation ensued when I said that I did not want an engagement ring. Maybe the Bodgers thought that my indifference meant that the engagement was not for real, that I was going to take off at any time – which J.C. half expected. Who would want to marry John? Surely not someone in her right senses – except, perhaps, for the Bodger money. John had already told me that very likely there would be no money, that his father would disinherit him, but perhaps his parents did not know he thought so. I was too embarrassed to say that one reason I didn't want a ring was because I was afraid I would lose it. I knew I was careless with watches, with any trinkets or baubles I had ever owned. More important, my mother did not wear an engagement ring, only a plain gold wedding band. I regarded wifehood as a career; my mother was my career model. On a deeper level still, there existed another reason, the wreck of the *Avonmore*, and the murder of my grandmother, the first Mrs. Corfield. Among Corfield women there was a taboo against wearing gemstones. On the most primitive level, I equated my wearing an expensive jeweled ring with an invitation to shipwreck.

During the months while John was away, Mrs. Bodger arranged for a series of meetings with me. She also gave a ladies' luncheon in my honor, at Pellegrino, a famous Hollywood restaurant. She invited a half-dozen or so of her own friends, my mother, Pat, Pat's mother. During one of our little private chats, Mrs. Bodger actually asked me whether I was bothered by the fact that Pat was so much more attractive than I was. I did not think of myself as being as sexy as Pat, but I did believe that, in a girlish way, I was prettier. I was mildly amused. I wondered if Mrs. Bodger were being ingenuous or whether she sought to sow dissension between me and my future sister-in-law. I told Pat about the conversation and my thoughts concerning it. I hoped she would consider the situation as funny as I did.

What most disconcerted the Bodgers, however, was my irreverence for J.C. I respected him, I quite enjoyed him – especially when he told stories of his childhood in Somerset, and of his early days in California. I accepted him as being on par with my own father, who was also an important man in his own sphere, prone to extravagant statements and strong opinions. But my father had a wife who said, "Frank, you run your ship and I'll run this house!" He had three daughters whom he expected to be spontaneous in their relationship with him. (I am not so sure he would have been so sanguine with a son.)

The first year we were married, John and I were summoned home to spend Christmas with his family. Fifty-two Bodgers were invited to turkey dinner. Heads were counted. Woe to anyone who failed to show up! The next day, Boxing Day, was maids' day off. John and I, Howard and Pat, Mrs. Bodger and J.C. gathered for a meal left ready for us in the refrigerator. At the end of the meal, J.C. said he would wash the dishes – with our help, of course. He went on to say that, having been a ship's cook, he could wash dishes better than anyone. All this ebullience I took as fun and games. About to dry a dinner plate, I noticed a smear of gravy. "Look here," I said. "I thought you were supposed to be such a great dishwasher. A little less boasting, a little more attention." There was a terrible silence. Everything went into freeze frame, then J.C. flung down the dishcloth and left the kitchen.

On that same visit, Pat and Howard had talked to us, confidentially, about how hard it was for them to be parted so often. J.C. was determined to teach Howard the ropes of the seed business and to introduce him to clients, contacts and contract growers all over the world. Consequently, Howard had been away for most of the year. He and Pat were young. They had been parted for several years because of the war. They wanted more time together. I suggested that they talk to J.C., that they explain their feelings to him. I thought his romantic soul would be pleased to know that they were truly in love and that, once they had shown him there was a problem, he would back off, give them more slack. Howard was not so sure it was a good idea to confront J.C. Pat, fed up with prolonged waiting, was willing to entertain the notion of talking to her father-in-law, *but* . . . She gave an anxious glance at Howard. In my view, not asking was a form of disrespect; *not* asking turned J.C. into an ogre, which I did not think he was.

The last evening before John and I returned to New York and Columbia University, J.C. and Mrs. Bodger took us out to dinner at the prestigious Jonathan Club, an old-fashioned place very much like the senior officers' section of the Navy Club on Terminal Island, where my parents went almost every week. However, after dinner, unlike the husbands and wives of the navy, men and women at the Jonathan went their separate ways. Mrs. Bodger led Pat and me to the elevator, which took us to the ladies' drawing room. Somehow Pat disappeared and I found myself cornered in a curtained-off alcove with Bertha Bodger.

Grave and sorrowful though she may be, she felt obliged to tell me that I had behaved very badly. First, no one ever criticized J.C. At first I didn't know what she was talking about until she mentioned "gravy." But that had been a week before! I must have stammered something about my words being meant in fun, that it was the sort of thing I might say, lovingly, to my own father. She stared at me, uncomprehending. I had made another blunder: I assumed that J.C. was an ordinary mortal, subject to being treated on the same level as me and mine. Beyond that, even more damning, I had sewn seeds of insurrection. Howard (a reluctant Howard) had confronted J.C. about the matter of travel. On having his arm twisted, he confessed that Pat had persuaded him, against his better judgment, to plead for more time with her. Pat, when called upon the carpet, had tearfully admitted that she had gotten inspiration from me. I had made her do it! Also, under further questioning, she had squealed about my accusing Mrs. Bodger of trying to make trouble between us. I did not make reply. I was too hurt, too dismayed, too confounded, too uncharacteristically *cautious* to do anything. I am glad to state that I did not apologize. I only muttered that I would think about what had been said to me.

But I am ahead of myself. We had planned our wedding for the following summer, but meanwhile John's courses were beginning at Columbia. After John left for New York, he and I wrote to each other more or less regularly, spinning bright aspirations for our future. John had sublet a room in a large apartment near Columbia. His landlady, a widow, rented another room to a married couple, Philip and Joanna Norris. Joanna turned out to be my friend Joanna Dimock, whom I had known in New London. She told John that she and Philip would soon be moving to veterans' housing, presently being constructed in an old army camp, Camp Shanks, on the other side of the Hudson. The army barracks there were being converted into apartments for the use of G.I. Bill veterans attending colleges and universities in and near Manhattan. On George Washington's birthday, when the university and libraries were closed for the holiday, John took a bus across George Washington Bridge and journeyed fifteen miles north to what was now being called Shanks Village, near Nyack, New York. He wrote to tell me that he had put down money, signed up for a studio apartment: one large room, a bath, and a kitchen. I was thrilled. Our imagined future was becoming a reality.

We were married on June 10, 1947, in one of the gardens at Pomona College. The bride wore white; the wedding was reported in the *New York Times*. About a hundred friends, family, and classmates attended. On the morning of my wedding I received a telegram from my father: GREETINGS, GOOSEBERRY NOSE. IT WILL BE HARD TO GIVE YOU AWAY. Father had a horror of big weddings, fearing they might trap a young person into going through with a marriage that was not meant to be. Just before we were to step forth to strains of Lohengrin, he, splendid in medals and admiral's dress whites, whispered in my ear: "If you get up to that altar, and look at that young man, and decide not to marry him, just give me the word. You and I will about face and march back up the aisle together."

I thought my father was crazy. Could he not that I was marrying the most wonderful man in the world? John was over six feet tall and, if not exactly handsome, had a kind face and expressive brown eyes. He had been in the army, as I had; he had attended Pomona College, as I had. He laughed at the same things that I did, and he wanted to do good in the world, as I did. He was imbued with integrity, which to me was (and still is) the most sexy attribute a man can have. John was well bred, well read, well educated. In a few more years he would have a Ph.D., and be asked to teach in a university. I was certain he would receive accolades and fellowships, that we would travel to Europe together, where he would lecture and do research (even though his field was U.S. history!). With my love, my intelligence, my support, John would write brilliant papers and brilliant books and have a brilliant career. Like many another young bride, I suffered from hubris. I confused my ambition with my husband's. I took it for granted that what I wanted, he wanted.

We spent the first night of our honeymoon in an old Spanish-style inn high in the hills above Santa Barbara. We were not experienced lovers, but I thought things would get better (that *I* would get better) as our honeymoon progressed. One of the reasons I was so optimistic was that Mrs. Bodger had given me a book by Marie Stopes, an Englishwoman who taught botany at the University of Berlin, and was an early proponent of birth control. The book was about sex. Published in 1918, its revelations were considered daring at the time. It was still daring in 1947. I don't know how Bertha Bodger got hold of a copy. It was banned in most states.

Stopes cautioned that probably, on the first night, love-making might not go well, but the young couple should have patience. Things would work out, given time and loving understanding. She advised that, if the young husband became too roused, and thus frighten his bride, he should buy a set of dumbbells and perform certain exercises morning and evening – see illustrations. There were also drawings of the male and female genitals and suggestions how to use them. The suggestions were rather vague, but Mrs. Bodger had supplied me with more information than my own mother ever had. I don't know if John knew much more than I did; if he did, it wasn't happening.

By the time our car crawled into Carmel-by-the-Sea, we were both exhausted, suffering from sleep deprivation. We had reservations at the Highland Inn. Built shortly after World War I, it was both American mountain-rustic and Japanese in style. An attendant led us to our cabin, showed us the fireplace, pushed back the curtains. We were situated on a hillside immediately above Robinson Jeffers's house. (Jeffers was a California poet of the 1930s, now almost forgotten except for the unique sculpture he contrived, of stone and driftwood, to be his dwelling place.) Beyond, framed by the twisted pines of Point Lobos, lay the Pacific Ocean – swelling, heaving, powerful, yet dearly familiar to me – as my bridegroom should be.

Our second night was no better than our first. Worse, perhaps. Neither of us had had any sleep the night before and John had been driving all day. We tried to make love again but, beyond fumbling caresses, without completion. John finally fell into troubled sleep, while I lay wide-eyed and wired beside him. When I finally dropped off, he thrashed about so that my own precarious sleep was constantly interrupted. Finally I took my pillow, and a couple of extra blankets, and slept on the floor. Next morning a maid came blundering in and stopped, astonished, trying to make sense of the scene. She was terribly embarrassed – more so, I think, than if she had come upon us in the act of love. I was not embarrassed, not angry, not tearful. My ignorance was abysmal. Maybe this was what happened to most people, I told myself. My body ached with desire, but I put my emotions on hold. I would rather remain in a state of denial about what was important than to spoil what was the unimportant part of our honeymoon. We spent the week having a lovely time being tourists on the Monterey Peninsula.

CHAPTER 15
Shanks Village

WE SPENT THE SUMMER at the University of Maine where, to meet his language requirements at Columbia, John was registered for a crash course in German. In August, we drove down through New England to New York. I loved being with John, especially traveling with him. Unlike my father, he would stop to read every historical marker. We talked endlessly, getting to know each other's past, projecting John's brilliant future.

When we arrived at Shanks I was pleasantly surprised to find that, although it had been an army camp, the village area was full of mature native trees left standing among the barracks. In the fall the leaves would turn to glory; in the spring the dogwood would bloom. The converted barracks were one-storey buildings, covered in pink and green asbestos. (In 1947, we were blissfully unaware of health implications.) Since John and I had no children, we were given a studio unit, unfurnished, for thirty dollars a month – one-third of John's GI allowance. The space was more than twice the size of what we had put up with in Maine. Besides, we had a separate kitchen, with shelves and cupboards, and there was a real gas stove (not a hot plate) and an icebox (alas! not a refrigerator). A large space-heater, which had to be replenished from an oil tank by the back door, squatted in the living room. We did not have a bathtub, but shower, sink, and toilet were new and in good working order. Renovations had been slapped together in a hurry. Painted sawdust lingered along the baseboards, curled in the cupboards. A neighbor found a cigar butt painted to her floor.

Our apartment was a long uphill walk from the bus station, on the last street in the village. Beyond us were woods, then fields of high brush. In the silence of the afternoons, when John was reading history, or studying his German, I became increasingly aware of a steady roar of human voices, like a football or baseball crowd, that seemed to come from the end of the street. Or, I told myself, it was the sound of a waterfall, or of ocean waves breaking against a shore, then scolded myself for silliness. Several times I walked to where the pavement ended, pushed my way into the woods. There was no path. Beyond the trees, fields of high brush sloped downwards. Sumac, poison ivy, goldenrod, Queen Anne's lace, mulberry, and chokecherry towered over my head, giving way to bulrushes and bog. Defeated, I turned back. For my pains and curiosity, I got a case of poison ivy, a further deterrent to our sex life.

In October, when the leaves dropped, there emerged, less than a mile distant, an enormous many-towered building, Byzantine in architecture, incongruous in its setting. This, we came to learn, was Rockland State, the largest mental hospital in the nation, where patients from Manhattan and the surrounding area were sent. Thousands of profoundly disturbed human beings pressed against the window bars, milled in the yards below, shouting, moaning, chanting, wailing, yelping. In 1947, chemical psychiatry was waiting to be born. There were no drugs to calm chemical imbalances in a human brain. Not until 1952 would two French psychiatrists administer chlorpromazine to schizophrenic patients. The song of Bedlam nagged in minor key beneath the harmony of our early months of marriage. I did not know then that the voices were prophesying.

John resumed his classes at Columbia, in Manhattan. I was accepted at Barnard College, across the street, signing up for a writing seminar and a course in the modern novel. To get there took almost two hours. A bus from Nyack stopped at Shanks. The Palisades Parkway was not yet completed; the bus wound out of New York State and through towns in New Jersey, before it crossed George Washington Bridge to Manhattan. Then we had to buy another ticket to take the A train from 168th Street to 116th Street and Broadway, where the university was. Already, the expense was killing us.

Within months the bus fare jumped by eighty per cent. The reason given was that, by our very existence, we had caused the company to lay on extra buses. Shanks Village came into its own! We discovered amongst us lawyers and law students, and sent them down to Washington. Because the bus route took us out of New York State, into New Jersey, and back into New York again, our plight came under the heading of interstate commerce, a constitutional issue. We decided to boycott the bus company. Meanwhile, we had to get to Manhattan. Some people owned cars, so it was possible to form car pools. Our lawyers pointed out that it was illegal to charge for rides without possessing a license. However, there was nothing to keep us from paying twenty-five cents toward the George Washington Bridge toll, or we could contribute to the price of gas. Pick-up points were established throughout the village, and a return station established at Broadway and 120th Street. Every evening, around five o'clock, a mysterious line would form: cars drove up, people stepped forward, boarded, drove off. (There was a sort of urban folk myth, about a New Yorker so curious that one night he decided to join the line, get in a car. When he came to the end of the journey he found himself abandoned in the wilds of Rockland County, at a place called Shanks Village, not even on the map.)

Car pools threw us together, mixed us up in pressure-cooker proximity. Passengers came from every state in the union. These were men who had been in a wartime army, who had slogged through Europe, landed on isles in the Pacific. They were not kids, nor cloister-bred academics. Instead of the forty acres and a mule offered to Union soldiers after the Civil War, the G.I. Bill was opening a new frontier by offering tuition and a living allowance to veterans who wanted to further their education. The benefit was not only personal. It would change the nation.

I rode in car pools with men who, in a few years, would be running the world. Jim Hendry would be working for the World Bank; Owen Roberts would be with the diplomatic corps in the Ivory Coast; John Plummer would be a curator at the J. P. Morgan Library; Sloane Wayland would become a dean at Teachers College, Columbia University; Dan Toan would design houses, public buildings, a space shuttle; Joe Kantor would become a Broadway set designer. (When he painted flagstones on the kitchen floor of his Shanks apartment, his wife complained of the cold.) Pat Suppes would teach physics at Stanford and devise, for good or ill, something called "new math." (Pat made sure that a proviso be written into his contract with Stanford: that every year he could go down to Oklahoma to help his grandparents at hog-butchering time.)

Living in Shanks Village was somewhat like living in a frontier society.

Everything was new, waiting for us to make it happen. The war experience had made us acutely conscious of our responsibilities as American citizens. We divided the village into districts and proceeded to elect a village council. Eventually, I ran for council, and was elected. Members of the Shanks Village Council took themselves seriously, took the world seriously. I remember one evening in May 1948, being asked to consider a petition to the president of the United States to recognize the State of Israel. Passions reached a fevered pitch. We took it for granted that Harry Truman was eagerly awaiting Shanks Village's opinion. Then, just as passionately, we debated the next item on the agenda: should the Good Humor man be forbidden to ring his bell during afternoon nap time? Which raised a thornier question: should nap time for all children be limited to certain hours, and those hours only? Indignant cries of "Fascism!"

One of the council's earliest and most ambitious projects was to approve the setting up of a co-op grocery store, within walking distance of everyone in the village. This disturbed the merchants of Nyack, who were already convinced that we were a hotbed of socialism – or worse. We also started a co-op nursery school. Wanda Hiestand, Marilyn Landgraff, and several other nurses joined with a group of social workers to set up the Health Committee. They persuaded Rockland County health officials to conduct a well-baby clinic, once a month, and to bring an X-ray trailer to the village for regular tuberculosis check-ups. They also advertised for a resident doctor, and were pleasantly surprised by the number and quality of the applicants. A nutrition center led to a canning kitchen; experts were found in our midst, to give lessons on how to grow and preserve food. The committee also gathered medical equipment – bed pans, breast pumps, canes, crutches, a wheelchair – the kind of thing that is expensive to buy, and used only temporarily. The items were kept in a loan cupboard and checked out as needed, like books from a lending library. That idea was written up in a medical journal.

John went into Manhattan every day. I went two or three times a week to attend my courses at Barnard, or to work in the library there. Thumbing through the Columbia catalogue I was electrified when I noticed that there was a course in storytelling offered at Columbia University's Teachers College (TC), across the street from Barnard. I had a vague idea that Celtic bards and troubadours learned their craft through a twenty-year apprenticeship, but had always assumed I was two thousand years too late to enroll. I had never entertained the notion that, in the modern world, a big university would seriously offer a graduate course on children's literature and on storytelling. I had regarded myself as a writer since I was eight years old; now I was reminded that I had always been drawn to books and stories containing a tale-spinner, a harp-singer, a minstrel, a bard, a troubadour. What I really wanted to be was a storyteller.

Barnard students were allowed to take courses at Columbia. I signed up immediately to take TC English 161K, "an interpretive and critical study of literature suitable for children," and TC Ed233K, Language Arts and Storytelling, "an examination and appraisal of practises and materials in the language experience of children. Special attention is given to storytelling."

My professor was Dr. Jean Betz. Born in Canada in 1888, she had studied at Yale and at New York University, and held a Ph.D. from Columbia. Before becoming a professor at Teachers College, she had taught at Horace Mann, the laboratory school there, and was a great admirer of the philosopher and educator John Dewey, who had transferred from the University of Chicago to Columbia in 1904. She assigned us to read his *Art as Experience* (1934). Besides Dewey, we also read *Education Through Art*, by Herbert Read, the works of Susanne K. Langer, and Johan Huizinga's little book on the nature of play (*Homo Ludens*). In class, we discussed the settlement-house movement in Chicago and New York, where nursery rhymes and storytelling were used to teach English to immigrant children and their mothers.

Betz communicated the excitement and passion of the late 1920s and early 1930s when Anne Carrol Moore taught at Pratt Library School and, later, became director of children's services for New York Public Library. Moore became interested in the power of storytelling when she went to hear Marie Shedlock, late come from England and France, tell stories at Schrafft's restaurant on Fifth Avenue. Later, she would also commission Gudrun Thorne-Thomsen to train librarians.

At Brooklyn's main library, Jean Betz told us, children waited for free tickets in a line that stretched around the block. Under Moore's influence, whole cycles (Robin Hood, King Arthur, Siegfried, Roland) were committed to memory by teams of dedicated librarian-tellers, who told them to rapt audiences, fourth grade and up. Each teller learned one piece of the story, perfected it to a fare-thee-well, then told that section and that section only, on circuit. Tellers traveled the city, and outlying boroughs, by bus and subway, each weaving her (yes, *her*, there were no men children's librarians until the 1950s; no Negro librarians until the late 1930s) particular swatch into the larger whole. Faithful listeners, by attending every Saturday for six or eight weeks, could eventually contemplate a whole tapestry unrolled.

I discovered that I knew more than I thought I knew. Professor Betz made me see that what I had regarded as childish things – to be kept secret or put away – possessed scholarly value. All those years of my mother's reading aloud to me, plus my experience in England (where I had read and re-read fairy tales in their original editions, and had acquainted myself with famous illustrators), won the respect of Dr. Betz. Even my account of how my sisters, cousins, and I had skipped school and acted out what we had learned every day impressed her. Betz confirmed that many things I liked to do for my own pleasure and amusement, and had discounted as frivolous in the sight of others (though not in mine), carried intellectual worth and weight. Indeed, they gave me a specialty, something on which to build a reputation. There was much more to know, if I were to become an authority on children's literature, but I was already well on my way. Betz assumed that I would want to take on such authority – and the years of study implied – in order to earn higher degrees. I did want to know more, I did want to study, but I was not here to become a teacher, a pedagogue. One Ph.D. was enough for the family! I wanted to be a storyteller, a bard. And I wanted to have a baby, become a mother.

Although I desperately wanted to be pregnant, there were others who hoped, just as desperately, not to. Once, when I was riding in a car pool, some doctors and medical students were discussing a new kind of birth control, a miraculous pill, being developed at Columbia Presbyterian Hospital. The other passengers in the car were incredulous. *Are you guys serious?* The medical students assured them that they actually received money from a pharmaceutical company, for just allowing their wives to take a little pill. (I knew at least one of those wives; she would die from cancer at an early age.)

As fall approached, and the 1948 elections, another federal case had to be addressed by Shanks Village. When we sought to register to vote, Rockland County officials refused to recognize us as resident citizens. They regarded

Shanks Village as a hotbed of Communism, and claimed that we were not adults, but students temporarily domiciled in college dormitories. A few miles north of Nyack, the Hudson Palisades reach a peak at High Tor, the very place where Rip van Winkle took his famous nap. Rockland County had been sleeping in splendid isolation ever since. Until 1957, there was no bridge from Rockland to Westchester County, only a tiny passenger ferry on an erratic schedule. Although Jim Farley, Franklin D. Roosevelt's campaign manager, was from Haverstraw, just upriver from us, Rockland County had no Democratic Club. John and other Shanks people set themselves to remedy the situation; they went door-to-door, registering voters. To John's chagrin, almost half of the Shanks Village veterans proved to be Republican. Meanwhile, the lawyers we had sent down to Washington came back with the news that the Supreme Court had thrown out the case. Of course we could vote!

The post-war climate was about to turn politically toxic. In a few more months, Joseph McCarthy, the senator from Wisconsin, would begin to savage the liberal establishment, the China lobby, and the Constitution. In September 1948, someone in my car pool asked, plaintively, "Who the hell is Whittaker Chambers?" The name had been bandied about in newscasts, but no one, except me, had even a crumb of information to offer. I waxed eloquent. Whittaker Chambers? In the 1930s, he had translated a little-known children's book by Felix Salten, from German into English. The book was about a family of deer, and belonged to that genre of post–World War I nature writing – poetic, pacifist, and mystic – also exemplified by *Tarka the Otter*, which was written by an Englishman, an ex-soldier suffering from shell shock who had lived "rough" in Exmoor. Salten's book, sensitively translated by Chambers, was called *Bambi*. No one else in the car seemed to find my remarks particularly helpful.

In November, against high odds, Harry Truman won the 1948 presidential election. For months, the House Un-American Activities Committee (HUAC) had been flinging charges against high-placed officials in the Democratic administration. Alger Hiss, head of the Carnegie Endowment for International Peace, had until recently worked for the State Department. In August 1948, Whittaker Chambers, a *Time* magazine editor and self-confessed former Communist spy, accused Hiss of being a traitor who funneled secrets to the Soviets, using Chambers as courier. If proved true, this information could be used as powerful evidence against Hiss, against the

State Department, and the administration. In late fall, Chambers led reporters into his garden, singled out a hollowed-out pumpkin, lifted the lid – and revealed a roll of documents he said he had received from Hiss.

When I did get pregnant I had a miscarriage. A few months later I had another one. The doctor told me that, if I wanted a child, I should stop going into Manhattan; the bus and subway ride was too rigorous. I decided to stay home and write a children's book, a historical novel based on material from John's Ph.D. thesis, *Immigrant Loyalties in the American Civil War.* I invented good characters and a good plot, but did not have the discipline to carry through. When I was by myself in the apartment, I could not stand the loneliness. Perhaps I was affected by the dull roar from Rockland State. I would run out-of-doors, walk to the grocery co-op, or pester my neighbors by going to visit them at inconvenient hours. I talked incessantly. I read incessantly – Henry James, George Eliot, T. S. Eliot, George Meredith, Arthur Koestler, Eudora Welty, William Faulkner, Iris Murdoch. We subscribed to the daily *New York Times*, and seemed to be able to afford several periodicals: *Partisan Review, Harper's Magazine, The Atlantic Monthly, The New Yorker*. I suspect that magazines were cheaper then; their advertisers had not yet switched to television. *The Lonely Crowd* was big news, much discussed; so was Kinsey's report on *Sexual Behavior in the Human Male*. I remember how John and I struggled to understand an article on something called "Gestalt therapy"; we wanted to know what was causing all the intellectual excitement. I read aloud from *Partisan Review* while John ironed shirts; he read aloud to me while I pared vegetables. We both admitted that the article left us as mystified as ever. As did the article about Jean-Paul Sartre, in *The Paris Review*, about something called "existentialism." I was unaccountably frightened by a now-forgotten book by Robert Graves, *Wife to Mr. Milton*, which was a catalogue of missed opportunities for connection, sex, and understanding between husband and wife. And try as I might, I could not finish any of the much-admired novels of Virginia Woolf. There was something shimmering just beneath the surface of her prose (I presume it was her madness) that I could not bear, just as I could not stand the sound, like waves breaking on a distant shore, from Rockland State Hospital. Both, I now believe, were intimations of the day to come when I could no longer deny John's intermittent mental illness.

Rather than sweep, dust, scrub, I cooked. My weight ballooned. I cooked childish things – brownies, gingerbread, sponge cake, macaroni, a casserole made with hamburger, rice, and Velveeta cheese. But most of the time we lived on spaghetti. Part of the reason was because of our limited budget, part was because of the paucity of choice so soon after the war. For my mother, ravioli and spaghetti came from a Chef Boyardee can. I knew better: I had lived on per diem in the Marina district of San Francisco, a neighborhood of many Italian restaurants. I made spaghetti sauce from scratch or, in winter, from canned tomatoes creatively augmented. Craig Claiborne, the new food editor at the *New York Times*, waxed reverent about something called *oregano*. (Claiborne had used his G.I. Bill money to go to a school in Switzerland, to learn how to be a chef.) Who, except our neighbors Bob and Maria Minnicello, had ever heard of oregano? We devotees of the *Times* put pressure on our co-op grocery store to stock the exotic elixir. I sprinkled it on everything I cooked, until John cried out for mercy.

In my frenzied state of doing anything but stay home, I started a library for the children of the village, in an empty storefront down near the railway tracks. I wheedled some money out of the village council to buy books. I held a weekly story hour, mostly attended by children, but I attracted grown-ups, too. Now I could put into action what I had learned from Dr. Betz – or, more specifically, from a book she had recommended: *The Way of the Storyteller*, by Ruth Sawyer. The book was originally published in 1932, and I still believe it to be the best treatise on the art of storytelling. Sawyer, who was from a well-to-do New York family, has described a year of her childhood in a prize-winning book, *Roller Skates*. She had studied folklore at Columbia University, revised myths and tales for telling to children, and practiced on the pupils at Horace Mann, the lab-school at Teachers College. From Columbia, she went on to other experiences, both abroad and in the rich storytelling culture that was proliferating all around her, fostered by Anne Carrol Moore and Marie Shedlock, who had come to teach at Columbia.

The most important chapter in *The Way of a Storyteller* is called "A Technique to Abolish Technique," in which Sawyer advises that the way to learn a story is not word-for-word, but image-by-image. She also stresses that everyone must find a style and a method that fits the life and voice of the individual teller. I learn stories visually (not everyone does). I see the story scene by scene, frame by frame, cinematically. I see more than I tell, forever aware of each story's Plimsoll mark, its load line. I jettison surplus adjectives and adverbs, sacrifice character dimension (a folk tale is not a novel), yet include such ballast and precious cargo as to make the voyage worthwhile for me and my investors (my listeners). Imagery must be kept spare, yet unforgettable: an arm issuing from the lake, *clothed in white samite*; Owl's face, *striking and fierce*, when he takes away his hat. Such details, vivid and isolated, illuminate a landscape, a dark corner of mind and heart.

In certain parts of west Africa, when a storyteller walks into a village, he shouts, "I see! I see!" The villagers, running towards him, shout: "See! See! So we may see!" The better I see, the better my listeners will see. Even when I am not telling, or not consciously working on a story, it is incumbent on me to live my life, as much as I can, in acute awareness, all my senses tuned to the here and now. Perhaps my storytelling began when I was two years old, and the fake silver dollar rolled across that nursery floor. *"See!"* a voice said. And the Two-Eyes part of me saw.

There is another aspect to storytelling, which may seem a contradiction to the idea of relying on one's senses. It is the concept of creation, of making something out of almost-nothing. Through story, both teller and listener become godlike: they create a universe, people a world, set that world to wagging. Steven Pinker, in his book *The Language Instinct*, argues that language is not learned. "People know how to talk in more or less the sense that spiders know how to spin webs," he writes.

Making a baby should surely be instinctive, too, I kept thinking. Why was I having such a hard time making one? One of the best books about storytelling is not, ostensibly, meant to be about storytelling: *Women's Work, the First 20,000 Years: Women, Cloth, and Society in Early Times*, by Elizabeth Wayland Barber. Although the book was not published until 1994 (when I was seventy-one) it has affirmed my hunch that spinning, weaving, pattern-making, storytelling, making babies, *creating*, are all somehow connected. What is the double helix but a sort of spindle, wound with DNA?

Barber could not write about one aspect of women's work without writing about the rest. She has made me see that to tell a story, to listen to a story, I hark back to my wandering paleolithic ancestress. Strands and tufts and filaments she plucked along the way, she fashioned into spiraled string, by rubbing almost-nothing between her palms or against her thigh.

She learned to tie a string of yarn around her waist or neck, to hang things from it, add or subtract from it – as need, use, or sense of design might dictate. She may have strung beads to help her count the days in her month, count months in a year. Only time will tell how she came to tell time, to give form to nothingness! Eventually she learned to spin string into thread, learned to weave thread into patterns. Even to make tapestries.

Barber speaks of "the women of the courtyard" who gathered to cook, watch children, make cloth, make babies, "spin yarns," i.e. tell each other stories – all at once! In some respects she is describing life around the sandbox in Shanks Village. Although I had no child of my own, I sat with the other women and watched the kids play together in the space between the barracks. Like birdwatchers, we *observed*. Commented. Philosophized. Watching what was going on in the sandbox, we evoked Arnold Gesell and Benjamin Spock, Ruth Benedict and A. A. Milne. We also spoke of Virginia Woolf and Iris Murdoch, Shirley Jackson and the new young writers at *The New Yorker*, Capote, Updike, Cheever.

The women of Shanks did not look upon themselves as second-class citizens, even though their lives were attuned to the schedules of small children: meals, naps, play, sleep. Hard-working, educated, intelligent, well-informed, they did not scorn what they were doing; neither did their husbands. There were a few racially intermarried couples in Shanks; that the husbands were attending university on the G.I. Bill was a strong component for commonality. Some local veterans lived among us who were not allied with any school or university. Because of the nationwide shortage, they and their families qualified for government housing. Some of these families were Negro. I will not say that there was no racism (racism always exists), but as far as integration goes we were probably as close to Utopia as any place in the United States. The sandbox circle accepted everyone as an equal, white or black, from whatever cultural or economic level.

Occasionally we got ourselves into Manhattan, to go to an art exhibit, or we met our husbands in the city, to go to a play. *Talk* kept our minds sharp, connected us to the world, connected us to one another. We discussed endlessly and enthusiastically what we were reading, thinking, experiencing. Margaret Mead, who was teaching anthropology at Columbia, was fascinated by us. Several times she came out to Shanks Village, to sit around and talk. There were so few elders among us as to be almost non-existent. We were women in the process of inventing ourselves as we lived from day to day. Talking with our friends enabled us to support each other, to struggle through situations our mothers would have gone to their graves rather than discuss, even with a friend. Especially with a friend. We gained strength and perspective by being open with one another, allowing ourselves to tell our stories until we didn't need to tell them any more.

The first time I was pregnant, John and I had applied for a larger apartment, and even though I had a miscarriage, our name remained on the list; eventually we moved, this time closer to the center of the village. Lyn Hendry lived across the street from me. Immediately after World War II, Lyn applied for a teaching job in Peking. There she met Jim Hendry, who had been studying in the Oriental Languages School at Fort Ord when the war ended. As soon as he was discharged, Standard Oil hired him as a junior executive. Lyn, whose father was an economist who had been part of FDR's original brain trust, disapproved of Jim's working for the "enemy," but she fell in love with him when he sang "Bye Bye, Blackbird" at a party. I gathered there had been many parties, until the Communists came, then there was blackout and curfew. The Hendrys had just been married, and there was nothing to do at night except talk and make love. Lyn became pregnant right away. When their baby was born, they managed to escape under cover of darkness, on a river barge. Jim had already been accepted at Columbia. They came straightaway to Shanks Village, so he could begin his term. I was awestruck – not only by Lyn's intellect and energy, but by her ability to keep house. I had been trying to persuade myself that intellectuals don't dust.

Anita Winston also lived across the street. She was from Brooklyn, had graduated from Barnard, and was studying for a degree in architecture. I also got to know Rachel Pochapsky, Millie Greenfield, Charlotte Plummer, and Bette Diver. Some of us decided to start a book club. Once a month we would choose a book, read it, meet for discussion, then choose a book to read for next time. I invited my childhood friend, Joanna Dimock Norris, to join the group; a few months later, Lyn Hendry invited someone she had met in the grocery store. Her name was Valerie. She and her husband had just moved to the village from Wisconsin (which seemed a little odd, since we were in the middle of a term). She wanted to involve herself in anything that was intellectual and stimulating, she told Lyn.

Our newest member arrived wearing a pinstriped suit, spike heels, bright red lipstick; she looked a little like Joan Crawford. Valerie took over the meeting. She asked a lot of questions and gave forth statements that seemed to have only a tangential connection to *You Can't Go Home Again* by Thomas Wolfe. She was critical of the United States (we all were) and very down on Truman, whom she castigated for dropping the atom bomb on Japan (we could agree with that). I wanted to get back to the novel, but during tea and cookies, Valerie insisted on prolonging a discussion on the China policy with Lyn Hendry.

I remember feeling bored, but far be it from me not to appear intellectual. I was willing to be polite, keep my mouth shut, even when Valerie boasted she was an anarchist and that she thought the whole structure of government should be destroyed. Not so Joanna! She actually leaped up, shouted "No!" I had never seen Joanna so furious. "Things may not be perfect," she said, "but I don't see a reason to destroy everything that it has taken ages and ages for people to think about and put into practise. Parliaments and literature and art and Aristotle and Voltaire and the Constitution. I think you are being stupid!" I was embarrassed by Joanna's ardor, by her naïveté. By her rudeness. A few weeks later Valerie and her husband disappeared from the village as quickly and mysteriously as they had appeared. I hoped it was not because we had hurt her feelings. Months later, perhaps a year later, we discovered that she and her husband had been agents of Senator Joe McCarthy and his House Un-American Activities Committee, sent to penetrate the inner sanctum of intellectual radicalism in Shanks Village. The ladies' book club. Us!

In 1949, I discovered that, if I took the credits I had earned at Barnard and Columbia, plus three extra ones allowed me for being in the army, I could take courses during the summer and wind up with a B.A. from Pomona College. John urged me to get a degree, although I was not particularly interested. I argued that reading on my own, and taking courses in things that interested me from time to time, was better than gaining a piece of paper to hang on my wall. My ambition was to become an amateur scholar, a writer. I wanted to be a Jewish intellectual – all the more erudite for pursuing my own path. I was beginning to perceive, however, that if I never did have children, then I might want (or need) a job. The G.I. Bill was making possession of a college degree more attainable to more people; at the same time, the Bill was making the state of not-having-a-degree a serious drawback.

We went to California for the summer. We were able to rent Helen Marburg's house in Claremont, and I enrolled for the requisite courses. We visited our families, John worked on his thesis, and I finished my bachelor's degree, graduating from Pomona. We returned to Shanks Village at the end of August. Our front door was piled high with purple-ink-smudged fliers of varied political persuasions, from Trotskyite to Republican. Photocopying had barely been invented; mimeographs prevailed.

The village was in an uproar over what was happening in a town across the river from us. Peekskill was close enough to New York City to attract summer residents and weekenders, who had bought second homes there. Most of these "outsiders" were Jewish. The year-round population tended to be blue-collar Irish. The situation was not unlike the relationship between Shanks Villagers and the long-time residents of Rockland County. What was causing all the furor was that the summer people had arranged to have Paul Robeson give a concert in a local park, for the purpose of raising funds for the Harlem chapter of the Civil Rights Congress.

Robeson had sung there twice before with little or no trouble, but now McCarthy's House Un-American Committee had inflamed public opinion against him, and against Jews. To most Shanks Villagers, Robeson was someone to admire: the son of a former slave, he had attended Rutgers University in New Jersey. He had played football for his college, but he was also a member of Phi Beta Kappa, he held a law degree, and he was a famous singer, actor, and activist. Because of his outspokenness on racial issues, and because he had chosen to live in Russia for a year, he was now being regarded as un-American and a traitor.

Robeson's concert had been scheduled for August 27, but when he arrived in Peekskill he was met with such hostility that the concert was rescheduled for September 4. The local chapters of the American Legion, the Veterans of Foreign Wars, plus the *Peekskill Star* and members of the local Catholic Church all promised that there would be violence if Robeson appeared in Peekskill. Death threats were rampant, not only against Robeson, but against those who supported him. Anti-Semitism, fanned by the HUAC hearings, emerged full blown in Peekskill. Jews were equated with Communists, and were therefore enemy aliens who should go back to where they came from.

A few days before John and I arrived home, a meeting had been held to consider inviting Paul Robeson to conduct his concert at Shanks Village –

instead of Peekskill. Now the organizers of that meeting were asking Shanks men, especially veterans, to attend another meeting in order to devise tactics. Since I was a veteran, I attended too. I was immediately struck by the military savvy of the men – men, not boys – soldiers, hunkering down, deploying troops. The people with whom I rode in car pools really *were* veterans; they had taken Italian hill towns, landed on islands in the Pacific. The meeting was sober. We were about to place ourselves in harm's way. We must expect and prepare for drive-by shootings. If we were serious, we must start right away to construct sawhorses to waylay cars, deflect direct routes through the village. Platoons and patrols must be organized, but there would be no weapons. Some voices raised the issue of putting women and children at risk. John and I had taken for granted that there were no weapons in the village, but found we were wrong. A few ex-officers still possessed sidearms. Several men with Southern accents said of course they had guns; would anyone in his right mind go off to Manhattan all day and leave his wife without a gun in the house? This scared the committee. Violence would only beget violence! Efforts must be made to bring the local police on side; a delegation would drive up to Albany, to enlist the help of the governor. Press would be invited as witnesses. Shouts and boos! We knew that the police in Peekskill had not only stood by when people were being stoned and dragged out of their cars, but had taken part in the assault. The politicians were keeping their distance. Even the *New York Times* was waffling.

Despite our invitation, and our planning, Robeson went to Peekskill after all. A few people from Shanks Village drove across Bear Mountain Bridge and up to Peekskill to attend the concert. As Robeson had promised all along, he sang songs from his usual repertoire, and did not deliver an address of any sort. Although he was flanked by hundreds of union members, he and his protectors were attacked by a frenzied crowd. Bystanders were pulled from their cars, clubbed, and dragged through broken glass, while the police stood by, or arrested those being attacked. The press, including the timid *Times*, branded Robeson and his supporters as troublemakers. The incident, which became known as the Battle of Peekskill, is recalled in chilling clarity in *The Book of Daniel*, a novel by E. L. Doctorow. This is the stuff of which myth is made!

In November 1949, I became pregnant again. This time the pregnancy stuck, even though for the first few months I suffered such body-wrenching nausea I was afraid I would lose the baby. Then, in the fifth month, I felt better than I had for years. I was full of energy. I went for long walks (I remember almost dancing!) and I actually lost weight.

The women of Shanks prided themselves on talking about Jean-Paul Sartre or Lionel Trilling rather than babies' bums and Pablum, at least in front of me. But now that I was pregnant I rather wished that there could be more talk on a less elevated level. Sitting around the sandbox, or over cups of tea, I found it was not difficult to steer the conversation. I wanted to know and I didn't want to know about what happened in the delivery room. My mother had had three breech births. She was adamant about the use of anesthetic: only a stupid, superstitious woman would believe she was meant to suffer! Even Queen Victoria had espoused the cause of oblivion.

Lyn Hendry had an entirely different slant on childbirth. When she was living under the Communist regime in Peking, she and Jim worried that they might have to leave before the baby was born. There was a good chance that Lyn might have to deliver without benefit of a doctor. An English woman gave her a copy of *Childbirth Without Fear*, by Dr. Grantley Dick-Read. Lyn asked her doctor, an American-trained Chinese woman at the Rockefeller Clinic, whether she knew how to deliver a baby "naturally," i.e. without anesthetics. The doctor was amused. "Mrs. Hendry, the women of China have been having their babies that way for thousands of years."

Dick-Read's book was not available in America. Lyn lent me her copy to read, which I did with great interest – academic interest. When she got pregnant a few months after me, I commiserated with her that it was too bad she couldn't have her second child by the Dick-Read method. And that I couldn't have my first baby that way, either. Secretly I was relieved. But I had not counted on Lyn's energy and enterprise. She consulted with Marian Landgraff, the nurse who was head of the Health Committee. Together they decided to start a training group for women who aspired to natural childbirth. Lyn was apologetic. Marian had said that, absolutely, she would not accept anyone beyond the third month of pregnancy. I was graciousness itself in the face of rejection. However, two weeks after the class started, Lyn came to me again and said that by unanimous consent the group had decided to include me *and* they had talked Marian into changing her mind.

By this time I was six months pregnant; everyone else in the class was only three or four months along. This meant I would be the first (except for Lyn) to go through with natural childbirth! It would be my task, Marian informed me cheerily, to persuade my doctor to read Grantley Dick-Read's book, and to educate the nurses of Nyack hospital to help me use his method. I would not only be an inspiration and example to the other women in the class, but it was up to me to set a precedent which might reverberate nationwide. The year was 1950.

As it so happened, when the chips were down, only Lyn and one other woman besides us would go through the birth process "naturally." My big-bellied sisters and I attended class twice a week, did stretching exercises, learned about the stages of delivery, practiced how to breathe and pant. What proved most helpful to me was a field trip the group made to the hospital. Otherwise I might have panicked when I was wheeled into a brightly lit, blindingly white delivery room with tools and instruments hung on the wall – saws, forceps, and God knows what. In July, a few weeks before delivery, I was found to be suffering from toxemia; even so, the doctor vowed he would help me keep to my chosen path if at all possible. He put me in the hospital a week early. The Hudson Valley sweltered in tropic heat.

Lyn's parents had sent money for her to go away to Myrtle Beach for a month, with her first-born Nancy. Marian had disappeared, I knew not where. My doctor was basking in the Hamptons. However, when the moment came, he braved a thunderstorm to fly back to Nyack, in a private plane. John it was who remained constant and reassuring. He read to me and talked to me all through the sweaty, smelly week. He remained behind in the ward while I was being wheeled away from him, down the hall. (In 1950, the idea of a husband being allowed to be present during a birth was beyond contemplation, even by the likes of Lyn and Marian.)

I had to explain to the people in the delivery room that I did not want any anesthetic. Only then did I discover that my doctor had not apprized the staff of my ambitious and audacious plan. Fortunately, the anesthetist was recently from Switzerland. As I was doing my panting, he cried out: "An American woman, and she knows what to do!" An older nurse leaned over me and said: "I'll try to help; I'll tell you when to push, when to stop." By the time the doctor arrived, the worst was over – except for the last agonizing push. I had been warned about that by Marian: she compared it to a quick burn on a hot iron. Reward came when the nurse put my damp and naked little boy across my damp and naked abdomen, while everyone stood about discussing what to do about the placenta. "According to the books, the afterbirth should come out by itself, all in one piece," said the doctor, somewhat doubtfully. We waited. And waited. Meantime the doctor was massaging my stomach. "Maybe we should do something else," he said. The Swiss doctor counseled him to wait. So did I. We waited. Then, swoosh! "Look! Look! It's all in one piece," the doctor said. "Just like in the books." The staff was more excited by the placenta than they were by my perfect child.

CHAPTER 16

The Crystal Mountain

DAYS AND NIGHTS BECAME a blur of changing diapers, bathing, feeding, burping, and consultations with our well-thumbed copy of Dr. Spock. In 1950, ex-soldiers considered being able to change a diaper a macho skill, a step up from replacing a spark plug, or taking a gun apart. John, like most Shanks fathers, took his fair share of responsibility for his new baby, but despite our efforts, Ian did not thrive. The resoluteness that had carried me through natural childbirth continued through my attempts at nursing. The trouble with breasts is that they are not transparent, and they do not have "oz." marks on them. It's hard to know how much nourishment the baby is getting. I tried not to worry about what the scales were saying. The books said that babies often lose weight when they first come home from the hospital. Ian cried day and night. My nipples were so sore they bled.

We bought a washing machine, a Thor, which (a wonder!) spun-dried the diapers. Final drying was accomplished with aid of wind and sun outdoors, or chairs and wooden racks around the space heater. One freezing day, when I had had no sleep since I could remember, I hung out a line of diapers on the clothesline, then started on a second row. In that brief time, the first row had frozen. A wind came up and, ignominiously, I was hit over the head by a frozen diaper – so hard that I actually saw stars. I turned my face up to the sky and shouted: "Dammit, God, I'm *trying!*" I was like a soldier in the trenches, suffering from battle fatigue. I had lost my capability of judgment. I listened to the doctrine of the truly converted: whatever happens, never let the baby suck from a bottle. The new pediatrician, who had just come to Nyack, concurred. He refused to see me until the next appointment. I felt my life, my baby's life, and my husband's were all spinning out of control. Nothing connected any more. We were entering a period of anarchic transition.

A delegation arrived at my door, waking me from fitful afternoon sleep. A coven of neighbors, young mothers themselves, had had an eye on me, and on my baby. They had called a meeting, compared notes, decided that Ian was losing weight at an alarming rate. Now they were bending over Ian's crib. Despite what they had preached to me about breast-feeding, they said, this was no time to be doctrinaire. Something was very wrong! They called the Health Committee, which called Columbia Presbyterian Hospital, to arrange for Ian's immediate entry. They had acted in the nick of time. Ian was in the hospital for three weeks. I felt like a fool, an incompetent mother. I felt like a monster. Even now, I can't write about what happened (almost happened) without tears.

John had postponed an important research trip because of my pregnancy, postponed it again when Ian went into the hospital. By late November Ian was home again, giggling and gurgling, eating well from a bottle, although he never did sleep through a night. John set out to complete the research for his thesis, *Immigrant Loyalties in the Civil War*. He had long planned to tour the Middle West, in order to explore local libraries and dig into newspaper archives, especially foreign-language newspapers. Weather reports were ominous when John set out. Winter came early that year: snow and ice and terrible driving conditions. John did not suffer any accidents (although he had many near-misses), but six weeks on the road, by himself, left him in a state of anxiety and depression. I was too engrossed to notice the immense strain he was under as he strove to finish his thesis. I thought that anyone and everyone could see how brilliant my husband was. I was like the princess in "Old Rinkrank," a story from the Brothers Grimm. With my loving, intelligent help, how could he fail to scale the heights of Academe?

There was once a king who had a daughter, and he caused a glass mountain be made next to his palace. The surfaces of its sharp-edged prisms sparkled so, that ordinary folk below called this edifice (erection) *"The*

Crystal Mountain." This image reminds me of a glass-windowed office tower. The tower (the mountain) is a metaphor for a society concerned with hierarchies: corporations, universities, the church, army, politics. In such a paternalistic (phallic) society, rank and degree are recognized as the ultimate values, always to be reached for.

The king proclaimed that, if any man would come and climb over the mountain without falling, he could have the Princess to wed and half the kingdom besides. Dukes and princes and wealthy merchants came, but not one of them was able to scale the heights. Then came a Lad who said he thought he'd like to climb the mountain. The Princess found him comely to look at, and good to talk to, for although he was often merry he listened seriously to what she had to say. She offered to go over the mountain with him, and promised she would hold him up if he were about to fall. Nowadays, after years of training as a therapist, I see a folk tale as a communal dream. According to Gestalt therapy, everything in my dream is an aspect of me; I am the dream and the dream is me. I am both Princess and Lad: he represents that part of me that is lively, ambitious, and merry, yet takes myself seriously. The Lad is that part of me able to climb the mountain on his own. The sucky Princess is the part of me that will not take responsibility for her own power, her own ability to accomplish. She prefers to manipulate, then bask in reflected glory.

March, 1951. Although John had often told me that he hated his father, and even wished him dead, when J.C. actually died, John went into lugubrious mourning. Full of guilt and anxiety, he insisted on wearing a band of black crepe around his arm, an anomalous custom straight out of Dickens. He did not fly out to California to attend his father's funeral. He was afraid that this would be misinterpreted by some members of the Bodger clan, but the truth was that John's exams were scheduled and, also, he had to appear before a panel of experts to defend his thesis – everything he had worked to accomplish during the past four years.

John passed his exams and made his defense, but the recommendation that Professor Alan Nevins wrote for him was, at best, lukewarm. Nevins was John's advisor, but did not choose to be his mentor. John never received a graduate teaching job, nor did he make a special relationship with any of his professors, nor network with his peers and contemporaries. This made it difficult for him to find a job, although he wrote scores of applications.

At home, with me, he embarked on harangues and talking jags. I tried to follow the leaps from one non sequitur to another, the twists of irony and sarcasm, the contradictions – perhaps followed by a question that I was supposed to answer with a simple yes or no. I soon learned whichever answer I gave would be the wrong one. I felt useless, cut off, although "communication" was ostensibly unceasing. *So they set out together, to go over the mountain, and when they were halfway up, the Princess slipped and fell, and the glass mountain opened and shut her up inside it . . .*

In June we drove across the country, to California. Ian was eleven months old, a handful in the car, although he was not walking yet. His first real word was "map." John finally found a job, teaching history at a private school. With some money that had come in from the Bodger estate, we bought a house, a modest duplex, at Hermosa Beach and lived in the back apartment. There was only a tiny living room and kitchenette, and a closet big enough for Ian's crib. However, the garden was enclosed (ideal for a small boy) and there was a sort of house, or cabin, at the end of the garden, which John could use as his study. We rented the front part to a couple who were of mixed race – Negro and Filipino. This did not make us popular with our neighbors.

By the end of the year, John was advised to look for another job. The couple who owned and ran the school drew me aside, told me that John should see a psychiatrist. I did not have the wit to ask them what they could see that I could not, nor did I think to ask them how one goes about finding a psychiatrist. I would have ignored the conversation entirely, but the ophthalmologist who tested us both for glasses told me that my husband was sick and exhausted; I must show him more consideration. I didn't know what to do, where to turn. I was terrified. I went into denial. Maybe things would get better over the summer. I deemed it disloyal to report the situation to either my family or the Bodgers. Besides, John's brother, Howard, had enough to cope with. John's mother, suffering from the complications of diabetes, was very ill. She died in May, 1952.

John, courageously, wrote scores of letters, received scores of rejections, wrote more letters. At the very end of the summer he was offered a job in Corcoran, a farming community, in the middle of the San Joaquin Valley, noted for its vast cotton fields. Corcoran's crop was the last one to be picked in the whole country. Migrant workers followed the picking season, from the old Confederacy, into Texas, across New Mexico and Arizona, to wind up in Corcoran, where they spent the winter. Their children would be John's pupils. Thirteen millionaires lived in Corcoran; one of them had a huge house across the street from the school. When John asked, in the faculty lounge, whether the owner of the house had any children in the Corcoran schools, there was a long silence. "Not any legitimate ones," he was told.

We decided to keep our apartment in Hermosa Beach. A true Persephone, I would live in Hades only part of the year, and miss the worst of the valley's heat during the summers. John taught at Corcoran for two years. Adlai Stevenson, who was running for president, warned the nation against the fallout from the atom bombs being tested in the Nevada desert. John Hersey's *Hiroshima* had taken up a whole issue of *The New Yorker*, but the full scientific (not to mention the moral) implication of the atom bomb had not yet penetrated my psyche. The import of what Hersey, and now Stevenson, was trying to tell us was unlike anything that had ever been described before. My world was already full of danger. A black widow spider had bitten me. I had become a binge eater. A doctor gave me "uppers" to help me lose weight; maybe that was why I had another miscarriage. Or could it have been because Corcoran was a few hundred miles downwind from Nevada, where the atom bomb tests was being held? I made no connections: unless a bomb was dropped directly on top of us, what was there to worry about? The fallout from John's anxiety was far more threatening.

John was still writing letters, applying for jobs as far afield as the American University in Beirut and a university in Bangladesh. Although we were willing to go anywhere, our lives, our marriage, and John's career were going nowhere. When we went down to Hermosa for the summer, I happened to drive by an old house I had long admired, just as a real-estate agent was pounding a "For Sale" sign into the lawn. I lusted for that house. Built fifty years before, by an English couple, it stood just across the road from an esplanade that ran along the sea wall in Redondo Beach. The house felt like an English cottage, and was surrounded by gardens, kept beautiful by a family of Japanese gardeners. The couple who were selling the house were happy to go on living there, paying us rent, until their condominium was finished. The house by the sea became the Holy Grail to me, the cauldron of plenty and rejuvenation, the virgin's womb, where I would conceive (and keep) a baby. Unlikely as it may seem, I talked John into buying the house for me. We had enough money if we sold the duplex in Hermosa, added capital from his inheritance. Cart before horse! I would write a script for us, spin a fairy tale, make my story happen by sheer willpower! If I knew that I owned a place somewhere in the world, a place that was beautiful and near the sea, I could bear to go on living my life in Corcoran – or anywhere John took me. The decision to buy was crazy. A suitable name for the house could have been *Folie à Deux*.

There was no library in Corcoran. I ordered books by mail, subscribed to the Sunday *New York Times* (it came two weeks late) and yearned to have someone to talk to. *Meantime the Princess had fallen deep down into the earth, into a great cave, and saw, in the shadows, a little house was there. An old fellow with a very long gray beard came to meet her, and told her that, if she would be his servant and do everything he told her to do, she could be his housekeeper, but if she didn't cherish him, honor and obey him, he would kill her.* (It is not John who should be cast in the role of demanding husband. If anything, he was indulgent. My royal Princess-self, having introjected society's idea of what a wife should be, pulled me under. My way of acting out my terrible anger was to throw myself into being a martyr and a household drudge.) *In the mornings he took his ladder* (his phallus) *out of his pocket, and set it up against the mountain and climbed to the top by its help, and then he drew up the ladder after him. Every day the Princess slaved away at the housework until her husband came home again, bringing with him a heap of gold and silver.* (I interpret this as meaning not just his paycheck, but news and experience from the outside world, which she could only enjoy vicariously.)

The first year in Corcoran, I had balked when someone asked me for which church I would be teaching Sunday school. (That's what teachers' wives were expected to do.) The second year I vowed to myself that I would participate in anything going. I taught Methodist Sunday school, I took a Bible course on the book of Jeremiah, and I went to a revival meeting (held in a tent). A few months later I went to another meeting, in the same tent, where the speaker described his personal experience of being kidnaped by little green men who came out of a spaceship. I felt that the person I used to be was about to rot away. *When they had lived together for some years, her husband said she had to call him Old Rinkrank.* (I must face up to my illusion: my long-cherished concept of being married to a brilliant and successful man stinks!) *And from now on, he says, he will call her Old Mother Mansrot.* (The outlines of my old self must rot away, become mulch, so something new can grow.)

All small children are delightful, and Ian was especially so. He was end-lessly busy. I sent to Scribners Book Store on Fifth Avenue, even to Blackwells, in Oxford, for boxes of books to read aloud to him. I sent to F. A. O. Schwartz Toy Store to buy toy soldiers and knights, and to Creative Playthings, on West 23rd Street, to purchase nursery school "unit" blocks for him, the beautifully crafted unpainted kind. He referred knowingly to the names of shapes: square; rectangle; double rectangle; triangle; Roman arch; Gothic arch. He built castles and roads and made up games and stories to act out with his miniature figures, his Dinky toys, and objects he drew and asked me to cut out of cardboard.

Ian liked to draw, and even at two or three years old could render a sur-prisingly effective impressionistic sketch of a complicated piece of farm machinery. But mostly he drew pictures of knights and soldiers, castles and armor. When my sister Joyce came to visit, she said: "I am a schoolteacher. If you showed me those pictures and said your four-year-old drew them I would say 'Uh huh,' and know you were lying. But I am your sister. I know you can't draw worth a damn. Besides, I've watched him. Sometimes, I'd swear, Ian sees something just under the surface of a blank piece of paper. All he has to do is press his pencil, and something pops out from the page."

But once again John's job was in jeopardy. His principal complained that he could not keep discipline in the classroom. John decided that he would give up trying to teach; he would become a librarian. "If you put a book on the shelf, it stays there," he said, somewhat ruefully. He applied to the School of Library Science, University of California at Berkeley, and was accepted. In the fall we moved to the Bay area and found an apartment within walking distance of the campus. The apartment house was an old turn-of-the-century wooden building, a fire trap, but we lived on the first floor. On the floor above us was a little boy just Ian's age. His name was Mark. His mother, Phyllis, was English, a townie from Oxford. His father, a Rhodes scholar, was an American who had made a local Oxford girl pregnant. Her father was a postman who, on hearing the news, had said:

"Do you love him?" When she said she did, he went round to see the randy young American, and put the fear of God in him. Rhodes scholars are not permitted to marry, so Bernard applied for a Fulbright scholarship instead, and they moved to Italy. In Florence, they lived in an apartment house with an American family, also on a Fulbright. It eventually dawned on me that we were talking about the Diver family – Bette, Bill, Christopher, and Katie, our friends from Shanks Village. I knew they had also been in Florence that year.

In Berkeley I discovered a co-op nursery school, the oldest in the nation, where I enrolled Ian. I worked there two days a week and made friends with women who were mostly university wives. I also became acquainted with Leona Garvey, head of children's services, Berkeley Public Library. She was fascinated by the fact that I had been taught by Jean Betz, and also by my knowledge of the history of children's literature. Berkeley Public Library no longer had a regularly scheduled story hour, but Miss Garvey arranged for me to tell at a special session. Inspired by my interest and enthusiasm, she decided to resume teaching a course she had let lapse at the U.C. Library school, a course on children's literature and storytelling.

Meanwhile, in response to an advertisement in the newspaper, I attended an estate sale, where I was able to purchase some remarkable bargains in rare books for children, among them first editions of Joseph Jacobs's *English Fairy Tales* and *More English Fairy Tales*, with thick, creamy pages still uncut. I also discovered an edition of the *fin de siècle* art magazine *The Studio*, with an article by Gleeson White, which preceded his publishing of *The Parade, 1897*, the book given to my mother when she was very young. Those purchases became the basis for my future collection. Miss Garvey was quite envious, not to say cross, because I had not thought to inform her of the sale. I felt badly, because the collection of rare books that Miss Garvey had already assembled had educated my eye, made me even more knowledgeable. She had accumulated a large amount of background material on children's literature: biographies of authors and illustrators; the history of publishing and criticism. I browsed to my heart's content and felt, for the first time in a long time, the tug of creativity. I knew that one day I would write about all this. Meantime, I told stories to Ian, and to Mark.

In the spring, my parents said they were going on a trip, and asked if we would like to use their house in San Pedro while they were away. I leaped at the chance, because I had wanted to bring Phyllis and Mark down to southern California, to enjoy the beach and sunny weather. I had never met anyone like Phyllis before. She was brave, and deliciously common. When Bernard had received an invitation to be interviewed for a position in the English department at Berkeley, he had left her and Mark in Italy and proceeded on his own. There was apparently some doubt whether he would send the money for her to follow him. Eventually, she had booked passage on the Italian liner *Andorra* (soon after, shipwrecked off Nantucket). She cheerfully announced to me that she had flirted with one of the cabin boys and had had great sex with him all during the voyage. Maybe it was her frankly sensual-sexual conversation, acting as an aphrodisiac, which stirred me to welcome John with open arms (and thighs) when he appeared. We went to bed, made love, and *I felt the moment of conception!* Counting on my fingers, I figured: we would be having a baby early in 1956.

The house in Redondo was about twenty miles away from the new University of California campus being built in Long Beach. John applied for and was offered a job in the UCLB library. Since the university was new, special effort was made to arrange lunches, teas, and lectures where the faculty wives could get to know one another. Some of the women I met became my lifelong friends, especially Margo Herman, whose husband was a writer. A private in the Infantry, he had slogged through Italy, survived unscathed, and used the G.I. Bill to enroll in the Iowa University writing course. I felt like I had come home: the Hermans were from Shanks Village, without ever having been there.

By September I was in the fifth month of pregnancy. I could feel the baby quicken: one evening, when I had balanced a book on my belly, and settled down to read, the baby kicked the book out of my hands. Every day I walked three miles along the beach, picking up shells and bits of polished sea glass left by the tide. I had not felt so well for years, not since my last pregnancy. Ian was happy, too. The Raglan family, three boys and a girl, lived just around the corner from us. I told stories to them and to the other kids in the neighborhood, and to the Episcopal Sunday school. I especially enjoyed telling stories to families waiting hours to see a doctor at the Los Angeles County hospital. Some of them were wetbacks (illegal immigrants) unchecked by a doctor when they came over the line from Mexico. I quit, reluctantly, when my doctor warned me that I could catch measles, rubella, even smallpox, from my undiagnosed listeners. But I had been rewarded: an Irish grandmother informed me that she had not heard such "real" telling since she left home in the 1920s.

Jimmy Raglan was just Ian's age; they were supposed to walk to school together. "Ian had an idea," said Jimmy. "I don't think it was very good idea." Unbeknownst to me, my son had found some blue paint in the garage. He painted himself blue all over and arrived at school announcing that he was an early Briton. His teacher was not amused. She was an experienced teacher, an old hand, about to retire. Perhaps she no longer gave a damn about trying to be merciful. She told me that Ian had no power to concentrate and that he would probably never finish school. She predicted that he would either end up on the street or in jail. The school psychologist came to visit me. I told him how Ian could spend hours building with his blocks, looking at books, drawing, playing with soldiers. But there was something wrong. Ian did not fit in. He hated school. And school didn't know what to do with him.

Lucy was born on February 1, 1956, in San Pedro hospital, the very one where my mother had almost died in 1929. Like my doctor in Nyack, the doctor present had never participated in a "natural" childbirth, a birth where the mother *chooses* to be conscious. This time, John was allowed to stand just outside the delivery room, separated from the scene by a flimsy curtain. In the first stages of birth, I talked to him, but further along I was too involved with the birth – and with something else that was happening to me. Along with the pain, I was experiencing the greatest orgasm ever to roll over me, through me, from the roots of my hair to the tips of my toenails. I must have indicated something of the sensations that were flooding my body. My yells of pain were punctuated by cries of sexual ecstacy. The staff seemed embarrassed, not wanting to believe what they had seen and heard. (Years later, I discussed my experience with a gynecologist. I was blushing as I spoke, but I had to know whether I was the only woman in the world who . . . The doctor said he had read that some primitive women experienced birth orgasm, but he himself had never before talked to a woman who was willing to admit such a thing had happened to her. Of course, most of the women he dealt with had been under anesthesia.)

The twenty miles between Redondo Beach and Long Beach University was not a long drive by southern California standards, but it proved to be a

mistake for John. The road passed through Signal Hill, one of the oldest
and richest oil fields in the nation. Even after fifty years, pumps were still
working, penetrating ever deeper wells. The stretch smelled of oil; it was
lined with truck stops, sleazy bars, strip joints. Hardly a blade of grass
grew along the way. Color was supplied by garish signs and, at night, neon
lights, jiggling and jerking spasmodically. To me, it was just a place to be
hurried through, but to John it became a trap, a snare. Years later he told
me how, after dark, he would get lost there. As he withdrew from me, I
withdrew from him. As I sought solace in my children, my house and
garden, and the beach, he sought solace elsewhere. At the time, the idea of
fastidious John stopping off to watch strippers at work and play was so
ludicrous that I would not have believed it if someone had told me. If he
had told me.

*Then once, when he was out, she shut the doors and windows all fast, and
there was one little window through which the light shone in, and this she
left open. When Old Rinkrank came home, he knocked at his door and
cried, "Old Mother Mansrot, open the door for me," but she would not.
Then he said,*

> *"Here stand I, poor Rinkrank,*
> *On my seventeen long shanks,*
> *On my weary worn-out foot,*
> *Wash my dishes, Mother Mansrot."*

*"I have washed your dishes already," said she. Then he sings the song
again, ending with a demand that she make his bed. "I have made your bed
already," she says. Then, a third time, he sings the song, ending with the
sexually suggestive: "Open your door, Mother Mansrot." To which she does
not answer.* (Actually, I would have been thrilled if John had asked me to
"open my door.")

I knew that something was very wrong. I knew that we had lost touch
with one another and that John was suffering from a terrible anxiety. I
could plainly see that he was unhappy and I blamed myself. What seemed
obvious to me was that he did not really want to be a librarian and that he
was deeply disappointed that he was not teaching history at a university. I
decided, on my own, that he resented my friendship with Margo Herman,

whose husband was doing more or less what John wanted to do. I did not check this out with him. I was writing my own script again, projecting my own theories. I thought I was showing my love by *guessing*.

I did not know where to turn, whom to talk to. I blamed myself for being so selfish. I had talked John into buying the house. In a way, I had tricked him – and now God was punishing me, for getting everything I had ever wanted out of life. If it would make John happy, I would give up the house. At my urging, John started writing letters again. In March 1957, when Lucy was a little more than a year old, we left her in the care of her devoted Estonian nursemaid and, taking Ian with us, set out on a tour of the Midwest and the eastern seaboard, so John could be interviewed by those few colleges that had responded. Rejection followed on rejection. At last he was offered a job in a small Lutheran college in New Jersey. He would be teaching history. I was ecstatic. John would be doing what he was born to do, and we would be living less than fifty miles from Rockland County, where many of our Shanks Village friends now owned houses.

We sold the house in Redondo Beach. We bought a turn-of-the-century house in Maplewood, New Jersey, in a neighborhood of other old houses, old gardens, good schools. Most of the men went into Manhattan every day; it was just a short train ride to Hoboken, and a subway ride through Holland Tunnel. I would be able to go to museums and art galleries, spend time in the famous Children's Room at the 42nd Street Library. John talked about taking a trip to England. We would go by ocean liner, take the kids, show them places we had seen when we were children. I had an idea for a book; I wanted to seek out places described in children's literature. It would be sort of a detective story, a treasure hunt for a literary landscape, described through children's eyes.

I had read a book by Annis Duff called *Bequest of Wings*, which was the sort of book I wanted to do. She had written about her husband and children, her family's love of books. I discovered, when talking to the librarians at 42nd Street, that her husband had died quite young, and that she was now working as an editor at Viking Press. I wondered how to approach her. Meanwhile, I wrote an article on children's books for the *New York Times Book Review*, which was accepted, and another one for *Horn Book: The Magazine of Children's Reading*. I was establishing a track record.

In June 1958, we took the children to England. Ian was eight years old, going on nine. Lucy was two and a half. John was of inestimable help in renting the car, making reservations, poring over maps, planning routes. I had spent years reading not only children's books, but biographies and histories, which gave inspiration for the journey. Tired as he might be, John was obviously having fun. We had almost no sex; we might as well have been brother and sister. Ever amicable, ever pleasant, courteous and civilized, we must have seemed like a nice couple, a loving family. Which we were.

When we returned to Maplewood, I set about writing the book. I set the alarm for four-thirty A.M. and would spread out my work on the dining-room table. Utterly congealed, I took the first half hour just to thaw myself out with coffee. I was excited about my writing; I was making progress. The time I gave to myself in the morning, to be my old true self, was pure heaven. I felt as though I were ten years old again, back in my private kingdom, the pine woods in Norfolk. I had made friends with Evelyn Bromberg, a neighbor whose back garden adjoined ours. Jules Bromberg was a radiologist and, I discovered later, a renowned diagnostician. Evelyn said that, when she came into her kitchen at six-thirty every morning, she could look across our yards, see my light, know that I was at work on my book. She said it gave her a wonderful feeling of peace. And of strength.

Around seven o'clock I would try to wake up John, to roust and organize Ian. Try as I might, John was always late for work, Ian was always late for school. Finally, on the insistence of Ian's principal, Ian and I were each assigned a therapist at the West Orange Clinic. Ian saw a psychiatrist; my therapist, Jane Weinricht, was a psychologist. She spent the first two months on the getting-ready-in-the-morning syndrome. She showed me how John and Ian sabotaged me, had me running in circles. I learned to stand at my post and to say: "I'm frying this egg. You find your socks." Although I protested vehemently about going to a clinic, this tiny glimmer of light afforded the beginning of an understanding of what therapy might do for my family. What it might do for me.

Ian once asked me, "Is Lucy famous?" When I inquired what had put that idea into his head, he said it was because, if we went into a restaurant, everyone stopped, forgot to eat, turned to look at Lucy. He was right. Lucy was beautiful. Her coloring was peaches-and-cream. I am not making it up when I say that she seemed to give out a special light. Her hair was red-gold, her eyes violet. She was funny and articulate and, unlike the rest of the family, she had a scientific bent. Her favorite book was a big picture dictionary, published by Golden Books. The names of birds and trees were like poetry to her. She liked to say "igneous rocks" just for the sound, the crunching of teeth.

A dry brook bed made a steep ditch between our yard and the Brombergs. Our two families shared the expense of having a little bridge built across the ditch. Esther Bromberg and Lucy could go back and forth between the two houses; they were equally at home in either. The Brombergs had a back stairs, going up from the kitchen. Lucy and Esther played make-believe games there. I was made privy to tales of Mrs. Broom, who lived halfway up the stairs, and Mrs. Mop, who lived on the landing. Dustpan and Bucket were their children.

Lucy could spell almost anything phonetically; she wrote before she could read, but she also liked me to write things down for her. For a week or so she dictated to me a list of terrible-awful threats: *If you are mean and bad to me, I won't call you to see how far I can climb up in the cherry tree; higher than you think. And* (to her father) *if you aren't nice to me, I won't let you read* Alice in Wonderland *out loud to me.* To both of us: *I won't watch the sunset with you, no matter how red it gets. And when you call, I won't come running, running, running to see the first star.* Her aim was unerring. Her father would stagger back, as though pierced by an arrow, pleading: "Oh no, no, no! Anything but that!" while Lucy collapsed into giggles.

Despite these moments of family happiness, by the spring of 1959, John was in an almost constant state of agitation. He was in several small car accidents, caused by tailgating other cars, and he got lost driving to and from work. His classes complained of his lectures, and the exams they wrote proved that they had learned nothing. He began to talk wildly of plots against him. I took him to our family doctor, who almost boasted that he knew nothing about mental illness. He sent us to a clinic where John was given electric shocks. (I would never allow such a thing now, but I knew no better in 1959. Neither did the doctors.) I promised John that, whatever happened, I would not send him to a hospital.

When summer came, I sent the children to stay with my mother and father in San Pedro while I tried to cope. John accused me of turning the knives on the kitchen counter in a direction fraught with meaning; he accused me of upending the milk bottles in the dish-drainer, to test his sanity. He talked unceasingly. When he lost his job, I thought the college had been unjust, but when John assured me that the mailman was a KGB spy, and that the barber was stealing his "essence," I began to divest myself of my illusions. I turned to Bette Diver for help, asked her to ask around about how to find a good psychiatrist, and finally John and I were able to get an appointment with Dr. Lawrence J. Hatterer, a Harvard graduate with an office on Fifth Avenue in Manhattan.

I did not have the will or strength to move house again. There would be no gain in doing so. Eventually, John seemed to be helped by medication and talk therapy; he got a job in South Orange Public Library, near to Maplewood. He would hold that job for two years. I worked on my book and spent more and more time driving up to Rockland County to be with Bette. Her children and mine were like close cousins. We spent Thanksgivings together, and the day after Christmas (which our English mother called Boxing Day) the Diver children always came to stay with us. We played charades, and the older kids built an enormous fantasy city using blocks, toys, books; then they added tins, odd-shaped jars, bottles, vases, as towers and pinnacles. Even in winter, Bette and I took our kids for long drives and picnics, exploring the countryside that lay from the Hudson River to beyond the Delaware. An amazing number of square miles remained as wilderness. Whenever a plaintive "Are we lost?" came from the back seat, I had a standard retort: "We are not lost. We are merely having an adventure." On George Washington's birthday (February 22), then still a national holiday, we would take the kids to Valley Forge, and to the embarkation site of Washington's famous crossing of the Delaware. If we were cold and miserable, then so had been the noble patriots! The difference was that we could roll on to New Hope, Pennsylvania, consume hot chocolate and cinnamon buns.

I became ever more appreciative of my neighbor, Evelyn Bromberg, who was warm, and kind, and scholarly. She shared my love of history, and respected my passion for language, especially as it relates to creativity. On Wednesdays, when John and I went into Manhattan to see our psychiatrist, she encouraged me to use the opportunity to stay on, to visit libraries, lectures, museums, while she looked after Lucy and Ian. She had a housekeeper and a cook, so I knew she was not overburdened, but her offer was nevertheless generous.

So it was that in April 1962, I went into Manhattan to attend the annual conference of the Child Study Institute of America. Lucy was not well (although she had no fever) and the weather was so stormy that I considered not going, but I had paid out a hefty sum just for that one day. The extravagance was already inexcusable! Evelyn urged me to go; she would be home all day and would see that Lucy was well cared for. I had made check marks in the program, for several seminars on language and creativity, but I would arrive too late for the beginning remarks by the main speaker of the day, someone from Mississippi; his subject did not seem immediately pertinent to my obsessions. As it turned out, because of the storm, his plane was late coming into La Guardia and the whole program was behind schedule. The audience had been waiting for him almost an hour when I picked my way towards a still-vacant seat. A young man, in army captain's uniform, came rushing into the hall. His hair was sopping wet; so were his clothes. His name was Robert Coles.

Born and bred in Boston, graduated from Harvard, Coles was trained as a child psychiatrist. He admitted to being resentful when he found that he was ordered to spend two years of military service in the deep South. He had regarded himself as a young man going places; surely this exile was only a bump, a mere swerve, in the road! He had regarded himself as an intellectual liberal, but in 1958, when he saw a middle-aged Negro woman being set upon when she tried to swim at a white people's beach, he wondered what she was making such a fuss about, when she could swim at her own beach. But he was disturbed by the way she was treated (watch broken; glasses stepped upon). He began to notice what he had not noticed before, not only the obvious, but the subtleties of racial separation in the South.

When four small Negro children walked between lines of screaming white people, to integrate the schools, he suddenly realized that the most important event in child psychiatry that would happen in his lifetime was happening underneath his nose. He was sitting on top of a situation crying out to be studied in depth. His especial genius was that he not only interviewed the four Negro children and their families (a very delicate transaction in trust), but he paid as much attention (and compassion) to the few white children attending, and to their families. When his two years of military service were finished, he elected not to go back to New England, but to stay in the South, and to dedicate himself to research in this field.

(Eventually, he would receive foundation grants. In 1964, he would publish the first of the five-volume *Children of Crisis* series, *A Study in Courage and Fear*.)

The remarks that Robert Coles made that were most pertinent to me *personally* concerned the subject of anger. Someone asked him the question that I wanted to ask: were not the Negro parents doing great harm to their children, to let them face such danger? To which Coles replied that he had thought so at first, but he had come to see that the danger was already there for these Negro children; now it was made manifest. Instead of fighting with shadows (which is crazy-making), they could see and have confirmed the palpable anger in the people threatening them, and they could act out their own justifiable anger by insisting that they be granted their rights. He thought that walking through those lines was a healing process. *Justifiable anger is healthy.*

Old Rinkrank (my false ideal of John) *was dead. The Princess stole his phallic ladder and climbed up out of the Crystal Mountain. She found the Young Lad, who had been waiting for her, and married him.* (I would no longer live my life through John. I would assimilate, integrate with, *become* Princess-Lad, willing to own my own power, seek my own success.) One doctor told me that John was ill because I insisted on being in competition with him. Another doctor told me his illness was due to my being overweight (not sexy enough) and because I was not a good housekeeper. (Look more closely at what is left of Old Mother Mansrot. Her rot is turning into experience, which is becoming mulch. She can't stop sprouting, even if she tries. *Wild orchids spring from rotted stumps!*)

Providentially, I had read a minuscule article in the *Times*. The deans and registrars of seven women's colleges (Barnard was among them) had held a conference to discuss the phenomenon of women graduates (and nongraduates) who refused to confine themselves to home, husband, and volunteer work. As their children were getting older, these women were demanding that their alma maters help them to use their education to earn professional degrees, develop businesses, publish, and perform. The word "networking" was used in the article. Women were urged to turn to their colleges for help in making contacts, garnering professional advice. The network would not be confined to the woman's own college; all seven colleges would work together as a sisterhood. I wrote a letter to Barnard, then went in for an interview. The earth shook! Someone from Bryn Mawr, who worked at Viking Press, approached Annis Duff in the hall as she was going to lunch, and made a pitch for my book. The next thing I knew I was invited into her office on Madison Avenue, to talk about it. Viking was definitely interested!

When John lost his job in South Orange, I was not surprised, nor particularly dismayed. He found another library job nearer to the New Jersey–New York line. We sold our house in Maplewood and bought a house in Rockland County. We would be living in Piermont-on-Hudson, a block away from the Divers. Helen and Burroughs Mitchell were the owners of the house, which had been built by a ship captain in the late eighteenth century. It looked rather like a New England saltbox: slanted roof, clapboard siding, slatted shutters. The front door entered into a center hall; a parlor, or keeping room, went off to each side. Burroughs was fiction editor at Scribners; he had replaced the famous Maxwell Perkins. Helen told me that James Jones had lived in the left-hand parlor for several months, a self-imposed imprisonment, while he was writing *The Thin Red Line*. The idea had been to keep him writing, not drinking. The Mitchells had added a dining room behind the kitchen, and built a guest bedroom above it. Sir C. P. Snow (*Corridors of Power*) and his wife, novelist Pamela Hansford Johnson, had been the first to use it. The room was small and cozy; ideal for Lucy.

I hoped that John would last a little longer in his new job. Perhaps Ian would find happiness in a new school; certainly he would enjoy being close to Chris and Katie Diver. Even Lucy had been having trouble in kindergarten. Her teacher complained that she wet her pants and she "pretended" to be always tired. I took her to see the family doctor. He thought she might have a stomach virus. I took her to see the pediatrician. He thought she was reacting to my writing a book. "Mothers should not work," he said.

Moving day, July 1, was rushing towards us. On a beautiful Sunday morning, I was packing dishes, wrapping them in newspaper, sticking them edgeways in boxes, as my mother had taught me. I could see Jules Bromberg in his backyard, reading the *New York Times*. Lucy, having trudged down our lawn and crossed the bridge, was so weary that she stopped to rest on the edge of Jules's chaise. I saw him talking to her, pointing to a bird up in the tree. Now I watched Jules leap up. He was heading for our yard, holding Lucy by the hand. What had Lucy done? Why did he look so . . . grim? He came into my kitchen. He had been observing Lucy for the past few weeks, he said. He wanted me to see a specialist. He had already made an appointment, for tomorrow afternoon. "But Lucy is going to a birthday party . . ." Of course I took her to see the doctor, a neurologist. He informed me that Lucy was seeing double. I didn't know what that meant. "She is suffering from a brain tumor," he said. She was to be operated upon immediately.

CHAPTER 17
The Crack in the Teacup

LUCY'S FIRST OPERATION for a brain tumor occurred in July, 1962. The operation took five hours. Sometimes John, who was under sedation, dozed. When the doctors came out, in their green suits, they spoke in tired voices. Lucy was resting quietly, they said. When we asked if they had got rid of the tumor, if our child was going to be all right, they didn't answer.

John and I drove home, I at the wheel, because his medications made it hard for him to drive. We had called ahead to Jules and Evelyn Bromberg, who were looking out for Ian these days. News that Lucy had lived through the operation must have traveled through the neighborhood. As we turned into Hickory Drive, doors burst open all along the winding street. People we barely knew crowded into the house. Someone had brought champagne. They told stories about Lucy I had never heard before. In the hubbub, only Jules was silent. I went over and sat beside him. "Jules?" I touched his sleeve. "She has about a year," he said.

Next day, when I visited, Lucy's head was swathed in bandages. She was drinking through a glass straw, bent at an angle. "Just like the Romans," she said. "Lying down and drinking at the same time." She cracked a crooked smile. She was being funny. Then, matter-of-factly, *"Did I almost die?"*

Awful temptation: "Who gave you that idea?" or, "Don't worry. You're going to be all right." Instead: *"Yes. You almost died."* Lucy sighed, satisfied. Perception confirmed! "It was like in 'Childe Rowland,'" she told me. *In the Dark Tower. The big ruby turning and turning in the warm air . . . I* had filled her mind and Ian's with stories for a rainy day. That-which-could-not-be-talked-about came tumbling out in nuggets of imagery – fairy gold! Coin of the realm, it was the only way to make exchange, to communicate the enormity of what was happening to us.

In August, a month after Lucy came home from the hospital, we moved to the house in Piermont, and John went into one of his cycles of agitation. We went to see the Fifth Avenue psychiatrist. "Call me if he begins to hallucinate," he said. Before the week was out, I called. The doctor recommended that John sign himself into Payne-Whitney, the Cornell University hospital in Manhattan. I could visit him on Wednesdays and Sundays. Otherwise, I was to be left alone with the children from September through most of April.

Ian hated his new school, but he had hated the last one, and the one before that. The good news was that now he lived half a block away from Christopher and Katie Diver. The kids swirled back and forth between our two houses. He also made a new friend, Steven Bordwell, who lived farther along River Road. The commodious attic on the third floor of the Bordwells' Victorian house had been turned over to their three kids. Steven's father owned a collection of lead soldiers, World War I vintage, which he allowed Steven and Ian to use. They painted maps of various battlefields on the attic floor in order to wage campaigns that sometimes went on for days. Tottering out to get my *New York Times* early one morning, I found an envelope, heavy with sealing wax, on the doorstep. It was addressed to Ian. When he opened it, he found a terse message: *Troops move at dawn!* For once, Ian was out of bed like a shot.

Lucy was not well enough to start first grade but the principal suggested that she come for the Hallowe'en party. He was a kind man. "We'll assign a desk to her," he said. "So the children will call it 'Lucy's desk.' That way she will always be part of the class." Lucy started planning her Hallowe'en costume in September. She would go as a pirate, she decided, using the black patch she had had to wear over one eye just before the operation. I hated the black patch and had thrown it away. Meekly, I went out and bought another one.

In late October, the voices on the radio warned that Castro would allow the Russians to bomb New York from Cuba. Meanwhile, Bill Diver had walked out on his marriage. Bette Diver and I, with four children to care for, faced the world alone and together. We wondered if and when we should drive west to the Mississippi or north to Canada with the kids. Or should we head for the Catskills, before everyone else started pouring out of Manhattan? We did not comprehend that, if the bomb dropped, no one in the eastern part of the United States would be left alive. Meanwhile, my furnace broke down, necessitating frequent trips to the basement. I found myself eyeing the eighteenth-century walls, wondering. Would they would be thick enough to ward off radiation? Would I be so lucky that the bomb would drop before my check bounced?

The money was running out. I don't know why, but it never occurred to me to ask my parents for financial help and it never seemed to occur to them to offer. Only Joyce asked me if I needed money. I said I'd let her know. Anne sent her prayers. Meanwhile, doggedly, I continued to work on my book, *How the Heather Looks*. I went into town to talk to Annis Duff, who was now my editor at Viking. She told me that, since this was my first book, there could be no advance until I had finished the entire manuscript. Although I couldn't afford to, I hired a typist.

I telephoned John's brother, Howard, in California, to ask if he could find a way to borrow from the Bodger family fortune, from John's trust fund, so I could get my hands on some cash. I had decided to go to library school, so that I would have a way to earn a living if John was unable to work when he came out of the hospital. Howard said he had to have time to think about it. When he called back (or, rather, when I called him) he said that the answer was no. He had noticed that, when a wife went to work, the marriage usually ended in divorce. He would not be party to the dissolution of his brother's marriage.

Bette told me that another woman in the neighborhood was writing a book – a sort of update of Virginia Woolf's *A Room of One's Own*. Her name was Betty Friedan. She lived just down the street from us; her little girl was in Lucy's class. I telephoned her. I felt sort of silly doing it, yet I longed to talk shop with someone. How do you manage to write with kids around? Betty Friedan said she was too busy to talk to every suburban housewife who called her.

Christmas approached. I helped the children plan presents for their father. The hospital had given me a list of what not to bring: no shirts or pajamas with pins in them, no picture frames with glass, no jars or bottles that could be broken and used to attack an orderly, or slash a wrist. The day after Christmas, the three of us drove into Manhattan. The children had not seen John since he went into the hospital in October. They met him in a large room I had not seen before. No other patients were present, only a nurse. There was a fire burning in a French Provincial fireplace, chairs and couches arranged to face the hearth. Chintz curtains hung at the windows, partly obscuring the deep window seats that overlooked the East River. Everything possible had been done to give out the message that we were not in a mental hospital.

Lucy spread paper out on a strip of bare floor near the hearth and made good use of the crayons she had bought for John's Christmas present. John and Ian withdrew to a window seat. I sank into one of the couches, grateful for an hour off. Across the room, Ian showed his father the one hundred 3x5 cards he had painstakingly painted, little icons of scenes from Napoleonic battles. After a while John entered into a deep and earnest monologue; Ian listened attentively. Best to leave them alone, was my pious thought. A boy needs his father.

We had overstayed the hour, so I had to rush to get the children back home. Guests were coming for dinner, Lucy's former nursery-school teacher and her friend. I was ladling out the peas when Ian asked, "Is Daddy crazy?" The silver serving spoon banged against the dish. I saw the shocked embarrassment in the eyes of our guests. "Daddy is mentally ill," I said, carefully. "That's why he's in hospital." Ian was relentless. "Lucy was in hospital," he said. "I know about hospital. Where Daddy is, is that for crazy people? Is Daddy crazy?" Testing, testing. Like asking where do babies come from, while standing in the line at the A&P.

"Yes," I said, "Daddy is crazy," and went on doling out the peas.

Afterwards, when the guests were gone, I went up to Ian's room. *What was going on?* The story came out in chunks. Ian and his father had sat in the window seat overlooking the river. At first they had discussed the Christmas present, the soldier drawings. (Yes, yes, I had seen all that.) But afterwards talk turned to other things. *What kind of things?* John had explained that he was a prisoner of the CIA, KGB, FBI. They were going to try him, like Adolf Eichmann, in a glass box, then they would cut off his balls. If Ian would look very carefully, almost every day he would find jumped lines or typographical errors in the *Times* that were really a code. I, John's wife, was part of the conspiracy.

Damn, damn, damn. No one but myself to blame. I had been lulled by chintz and cheerfulness and French Provincial normal. I had put Ian in jeopardy and not had the guts to warn him ahead of time. Perhaps Ian's favorite story, "Childe Rowland," acted as his shield. Merlin had warned Childe Rowland not to buy into crazy talk, however disguised. *Once you near the Dark Tower in the Elf King's realm, you must cut off the heads of whomsoever you meet, however ordinary they may seem, else you will never get back to your own world. . . . Every head, even the dear old hen wife's.* "Even my own," I thought.

John came home from Payne-Whitney hospital in time for Easter. The psychiatrist had said that I must be strong but not act strong, not show that I was strong. *I must learn to lean on my husband.* Let him be the man of the family! I didn't want to be the man of the family. I didn't know how to be not-strong, given the circumstances. Someone had said that I was a ballsy woman. At first I had sort of liked that. Then, thinking about it, I felt like a circus freak.

In late May, Lucy's symptoms returned. Our Rockland County doctor arranged for her to be admitted to Columbia Presbyterian Hospital. Weeks went by. Tests were being made, benchmarks set. Visiting hours were very strict. I could go only three days a week to see Lucy, between the hours of one and three. I tried to think of ways to entertain her; tried to think of presents to bring her.

Late June and the cherries were ripe, red as heart's blood among the green leaves. I sawed two branches off the cherry tree and put them in the car, to take to the hospital. Lucy was sitting up in bed, her grin lopsided where the muscles failed, her hair shaved so she looked as though she were wearing a red-gold helmet. The scar from last year's surgery showed through, almost a perfect circle on the top of her skull. I stuck the cherry branches into the hollow posts of her metal bed. Leaves and cherries dangled over my child's head.

"Now you live in a bower."

"Like the princesses?"

There were two king's daughters lived in a bower, and then Sir William came to wed the elder of them, with glove and with ring, but then, after a

*while, his love turned to the younger daughter, she with her cherry cheeks
and her golden hair . . .*

Two days before, a nurse had stopped me in the hall. "I've something
for you," she said. "I usually don't do this but . . . it's such a glorious color.
After we cut Lucy's hair I couldn't bear to throw it away." I had been barely
civil to the woman. How dare she act as though she knew something I
didn't know! I took the bag home. Furious, I threw it in the trash. In the
night I woke. John, sedated, breathed and twitched by my side. When I got
up to go to the bathroom, I thought of going downstairs, out to the gate, to
dig through the garbage. Instead, I went back to bed. It seemed like a
betrayal – not to believe that there would be plenty more red gold for years,
a lifetime, to come. When I woke next, I heard the voices of the trash collectors, the scrape and grind of the truck. Too late, too late.

Lucy was waiting for more of the story, though she had heard it count-
less times. As ever, the elder sister waxed wroth, and plotted and planned
to kill the younger sister. *So hand in hand they went down to the river bank,
and the younger sister went to stand upon a stone, which lay half in, half
out of the water. The elder sister came behind her, slipped her arm around
her waist, and dashed her into the rushing mill stream of the Binnorie.*

"*'Oh sister, sister, reach me your hand!'* she cried. *'Oh sister, sister,
hold out your glove . . .'*" Lucy's hand was in mine, her head had drooped.
I was not sure if we shared a companionable silence, if Lucy were asleep,
or if she were drifting into deeper waters. In my own head, the story
went on:

*And the princess floated down the mill stream, sometimes swimming
and sometimes sinking, till she came near the mill . . .* The story reminded
me of that Pre-Raphaelite painting, the one with Ophelia floating among
the lilies, her crimped red hair spread out over the water. In "Binnorie," the
princess's hair *was caught up in a net of pearls.* And, when the princess
floated too near the mill dam, *the miller stopped the cruel mill wheel.* In my
own story, and in Lucy's, I didn't know how to do that.

Something warm was making my dress stick to the chair. I made myself
get up, turn around, squint at the red stain. Surely it wasn't time for my
period? A few days ago, a woman whose child was in the next bed to
Lucy's, a woman who had lost two other children, had said, quite casually,
"No one else will tell you this, but your womb will go crazy." I walked back
to the car through the hot streets. People who had watched me go by at

noon, holding the cherry boughs, now stared unblinking at the bloody show on my dress.

When the day of the second operation was set, John said that he couldn't get off work, could not sit through the long vigil with me. I knew that his excuse was lame, but secretly I felt relieved. Then I felt guilty for being relieved. Bette drove me into the city. Lucy had been sent upstairs, to Terminal Care. Bette would stay with me in the TC waiting room for a couple of hours. Evelyn Bromberg was driving in from Maplewood, to be with me for the rest of the day.

For the first few minutes after Bette left it was a relief to be alone, then I felt dizzy. I was falling into a void. *Someone went past with a stethoscope. Lucy had asked for a stethoscope, a real one. John bought one for her at a pharmaceutical supply house; an odd sort of Easter present, but it was what Lucy had asked for. A few days later, when I was washing dishes, I looked out into the yard and saw Lucy with her stethoscope pressed up against a tree. I left the dishes and hurried outside. "What are you listening to?"*

"The sap. I can hear the sap going up the tree." The tree was an old pin oak. I pressed the end device to grooved bark and was surprised to hear a roar equal to Niagara. Perhaps it was just the wind in the leaves, but it could be the sap. This was the month of May! "What else do you listen to?" I asked.

"Stones."

"Stones?"

"Yes. The stillness of stones."

Evelyn arrived in the waiting room, bringing tuna-fish sandwiches, fruit, and chocolate. We talked animatedly, in spurts, then sat in silence, pretending to read Penguins. They were old editions, with the green stripe that used to designate mysteries. My friend Helen Mitchell had contributed them to the cause: Josephine Tey, Ngaio Marsh, Dorothy Sayers. In medieval times "mystery plays," with scenes from the Bible, and of Heaven and Hell, were performed on cathedral steps and "pageant wagons." For years I could not see their connection with detective novels. Now I knew – in both of them, the meaning of life and death was being unraveled and explained. Unfair – to reveal the plot – but trust me! Ultimately (always), the Great Butler in the Sky did it.

I went out in the hall to talk to the nurses again. Word had not come down from the Operating Room. They would let me know as soon as they knew anything. I went back to the waiting room. An expensively dressed old woman had taken my chair, the only chair with a view into the corridor. Never mind. I took another place and called across to Evelyn that it would be at least another half hour until . . . I had to raise my voice over the clang of the elevator.

"Oh, my God!" said the old woman. "Did you see that?" She addressed the whole room. "The most beautiful child in the world just went by! Oh, my God! What have they done to her?" Scramble, scramble over legs and chairs (look out for the old woman's cane). I raced down the corridor to catch up with the orderlies.

Father, father, draw your mill dam. . . . So the miller hastened to the dam and stopped the heavy cruel mill wheels. And then they took out the princess and laid her on the bank. Fair and beautiful she looked as she lay there. Her golden hair was caught up in a net of pearls. Lucy's hair was bound in an intricacy of gauze. *But she was drowned, drowned.*

And as she lay there in her beauty, a famous harper passed, and saw her sweet pale face. Lucy's face was chiseled marble.

I turned back towards the waiting room. Evelyn also had sprung up and was standing by the door to put her arms around me. The old woman was chuckling, not unkindly. "What a mother! Did you see her? The moment I said 'The most beautiful child in the world' she was off like a shot. How did you know I wasn't talking about someone else?" She stopped suddenly, old and wise. "Oh, my dear," she said, her voice soft, and lapsed back into her own sorrows.

June slid into July. The weather grew worse. Air conditioning was not allowed in Terminal Care. Lucy emerged, though never all the way, out of her marble fastness: a touch of color in her lips; lopsided movement when she smiled. At home, piles of laundry grew, dishes drifted in the sink. I shopped, but couldn't remember what I had already bought. Lucy was in every drawer, behind every door. Her shape lurked in the shadows, her face was discovered in spoon and cup. *The glacier knocks in the cupboard . . .* Those lines from Auden hung about the edges of my consciousness. *The desert sighs in the bed . . .* John and Ian cooked for themselves or Ian fled to the Diver household. I found it was all I could do to make myself presentable enough to push out of the house by noon. *And the crack in the teacup opens . . .* I drove our old car in a state of heightened awareness. My mind photographed every blade of grass, every technicolored iris, every surreal rhododendron on Palisades Parkway. . . . *A lane to the land of the dead.*

Days went by. Lucy suffered a stroke, fell into a coma. Even so, visiting hours were strictly regulated from one to three. Bits of songs, nursery rhymes, stories, prayers, imprecations, memories, feelings – sometimes words, sometimes wordlessness – floated like weeds and flowers, to make Ophelia's funeral bier. I should have saved the bag full of her hair after all, I scolded myself. In "Binnorie" the famous harper, after years of journeying, returns to the grave by the mill dam. He takes the breast bone and a hank of hair, and makes them into a harp. There are a lot of stories where that happens. An innocent is murdered. Someone, not always the murderer, strings a harp, or makes a whistle, out of the bones. The bone tells the name of the murderer. The "singing-bone motif," folklorists call it. *I am so full of trivia.*

The whole Hudson Valley waited for thunder that never came. John talked incessantly, anxiously, wildly. One night, when he accused me of staging the whole incredible drama just to prove that he was crazy, I almost believed him. Surely what was happening could not be! I had made it up, I told myself. It was one of my stories. The psychiatrist prescribed new medicine. At least John slept at night; the price paid was his increased grogginess. Over and over the doctors instructed me to involve my husband every step of the way so he could be kept in touch with reality. I must let him be the man of the house. They gave me a mantra: *I must be strong, but not too strong.*

The telephone rang at four in the morning. One of the doctors, a young woman, said, "We suggest that you drive in immediately." I reached for my clothes. I felt detached, cool, dead. I shook John's shoulder, but not very hard; called his name, but not very loud. I had done my best, I explained to God. Dawn was breaking over Westchester. The Hudson was molten, the air stifling. I wondered at my lack of feeling. I must be a sort of monster. I should have yelled and shaken John into consciousness. Lucy was his child, too. He loved her as much as I did.

I drove down the Parkway, on the west bank. Westchester lay on the other side of the Hudson, then I was passing the Bronx. The towers of Manhattan loomed, sparkling and crystalline in the dawn. I could see the hospital, built like a castle, high above the river. When I reached the toll booth on George Washington Bridge the Charon at the gate leaned out to take my fifty cents. Usually there was a long line of cars but at this hour I was the only supplicant seeking passage across the Styx. I fancied my face was without expression yet the toll collector leaned down from his booth, peered into my face. "Sweet Christ, woman! What's the matter with you?"

"My little girl. Columbia Presbyterian. The doctors phoned me. Come right away."

"How old?" When I told him the man's eyes brimmed. He had probably been up all night, alone at his post. "I'll pray for you," he yelled, as I gunned the car. When I got to the hospital, Lucy was still alive. Go home, get some sleep, come back at visiting hours, they said. Maybe God was giving me a second chance, I told myself. Next time I would be sure to wake John, give him full opportunity to be husband and father.

Two in the morning. I had warned John that I might have to wake him. I was resolute in my shouting and shaking. I looked in on Ian. He was sound asleep, so pale and exhausted that I wondered at my neglect. I sniffed. The sweet smell of pot hung heavy in his room. I phoned Bette, told her that we were leaving. No, thank you, we would drive in by ourselves. I went out and started the car. "Don't rush," the young woman doctor had said. "Drive carefully." Then, with emphasis, "No *need* to rush."

An orderly was waiting for us in the empty lobby to take us up in the elevator. When we reached the Terminal Care floor I hung back, waiting for John to leave the elevator first. I would be a good wife. I would be the follower. There was a long pause. John stood like a dumb beast in its stall. The orderly waited patiently, holding the door open. I took a deep breath, remembering what the doctors had told me. I would not cajole nor coax nor push nor prod. Nor scream. I would not be, I promised God, a ballsy bitch. "Your floor, sir," said the orderly. John looked angrily at me. "We get out here," I said. Bossy! I could have bitten my tongue. The man rattled the metal lattice. I ran out of the elevator, John following.

The corridor glared under fluorescent lights. A phalanx of white-coated residents, all young, advanced towards us. A woman doctor (she must be the one who phoned, I thought) stepped forward, breaking formation. She looked like a scared little girl. "Lucy has passed on," she said.

Quick knee-jerk snobbery: not passed on! Dead, dammit! *Dead!* No, I had not said it aloud. Something else had come out of my throat. A wail. Part of me was looking down on what was happening. I thought I was going to faint. I wanted to lean on someone. John! I would lean on John! The dear-old-family-psychiatrist had told me to do just that. "You must learn to lean on your husband," he had said. Surely this was the moment.

I leaned.

As in the children's game, John took a Giant Step Sideways. In the moment before I fell I heard something crack. John stood on the other side of a chasm. The doctors were either too embarrassed or too dumbfounded to allow themselves to see, to know, that I had fallen. No one stepped forward to help me. Awkwardly, with much show of crotch, I picked myself up from my sprawl. I was standing all alone, on an ice floe. Everyone was whirling away from me as I whirled off in another direction. Someone opened the double doors to the ward; I was swept through on the current. As I moved towards Lucy's bed I heard the roar of dark waters, the remorseless clack of the cruel mill wheel.

CHAPTER 18
Among the Alien Corn

DR. HATTERER URGED ME TO TAKE John with me when we went to arrange for Lucy's burial. While I was trying to persuade the undertaker that all we wanted was a simple wooden casket (harder to do than you might imagine), John was yet again accusing me of staging the whole conversation as a test of his sanity. He protested to the undertaker that I was trying to prove that he was crazy, so I could put him back in the hospital, so I could carry on a lascivious affair with . . . He would not believe that Lucy was dead, and I could hardly blame him. I didn't want to believe it either.

A few weeks after the funeral, John and I drove down to Washington to take part in the great March on Washington for civil rights. We were so late in deciding to go that there was no room at the inn; all the hotels were full. I consulted with Sam Hyashi, our Episcopal minister. He said that, by pulling strings in both the New York and Washington diocese, he might be able to arrange for us to lodge in a private home.

John and I stayed in a large house in Georgetown. I don't know who our hostess was, but I do remember that she had a social secretary who informed me (I had the temerity to ask) that her employer would not be going on the march, nor would she permit anyone in the household to go. I now recognize that our hostess was taking risk enough, in her own world, to lend out several rooms to protestors who had come from afar to protest against something she might not even believe in. She had instructed the

Negro servants in the kitchen to pack each of us a lunch. I tried to talk to a woman who was making sandwiches for us, but soon realized that she knew better than to open her mouth under any circumstances, or to show any emotion whatsoever.

Everything had been carefully planned. We were escorted to the nearby church, where other marchers were gathered. Like us, most of them were not local parishioners, but everyone, either white or Negro, was obviously middle class. We sat next to an upper-crust family from Harlem; the father was a lawyer. In deference to the District of Columbia's notoriously humid weather, he had prudently dressed in Bermuda shorts and a knit shirt, high socks, and polished shoes. Very British. Very Anglican. Waiting for the action, he and I held a whispered conversation. He, too, had never done anything like this before. He and his wife, apprehensive though they might be for their teenage daughters, had decided that it was imperative that they all participate in whatever might happen on this historic day. Having risen before dawn to drive down to Washington, they had parked on the fringes of the city and walked miles to get to this particular church, recommended as being in a safe neighborhood.

The minister led a brief service, delivered a homily. We prayed together, sang hymns together, then came "The Peace," which our congregation back home had been discussing but had not yet adapted. Recently, after more than a thousand years of being almost forgotten, this ritual had been reintroduced into the Anglican-Episcopal service. In the first centuries of the Church, parishioners actually *kissed* one another. Now we just shake hands with everyone within reaching distance, and utter the word "Peace!" Even shaking hands is a big deal with Anglican-Episcopalians, of whatever race; we are not wont to touch or be touched, but on this particular day, when thousands and thousands of people would be marching in non-aggressive protest, the clasping of hands took on a meaning both intimate and powerful.

Time to march. A young man in a white alb led the way. Tall and strong, he held the cross high. Then came the minister, in embroidered robes, the rest of the clergy, in white stoles. The rest of us, several hundred, fell in behind, blasting forth a song most of us had known from childhood:

Onward, Christian soldiers,
Marching as to war,

With the cross of Jesus
Going on before!

The white people of Georgetown crowded to their windows, ran to the gates of their little Victorian gardens, to watch. Obviously unprepared to see history being made in their own neighborhood, they gaped as we went by in peaceful, purposeful procession – a runnel, a tributary, on the way to join an ocean of two hundred thousand. Revolution was lapping at their doorsteps! Some people smiled and nodded, but there was also fear and loathing in some faces. One well-dressed householder turned back toward where her servants were bunched, watching through the screen door behind her. "Bessie," she called, "come out here! Bring everyone with you!" Shyly, timidly, the servants came out of the house, down the steps, blinking in the light. The woman stepped away from the gate, pushed an elderly Negro woman into the place where she herself had been. "You should be standing here, not me. Look at all these white people marching past, marching for your colored people. This is *your* day." She was almost there, almost to the Promised Land, but I did not see her open the gate, did not hear her say to her servants, "Go! Join the march!" nor, "Let's *all* join the march." That was the march at which, standing by the reflection pool, facing the Lincoln Memorial, I would hear Martin Luther King's rich voice cry out, "*I have a dream . . .*"

When Lucy had been dead about six weeks, Dr. Hatterer insisted that John, Ian, and I go on a trip. A change of scene was a very old remedy for grief, he said. Too broke to go to Europe or to the South Seas, we headed north, and drove the little blue byways of New York State, rolling through old towns and farmland and the huge Montezuma wildlife refuge. Purple loosestrife and fields of goldenrod still bring balm and sorrow to my soul.

I stared out of the window hour after hour, wondering why I had come. We had brought with us the old *WPA Guide to New York State*, which, although published thirty years before, was helpful and a delight to read. I was thumbing through its pages when the word "Onondaga" leapt out. I knew that it was the name of an Indian tribe, part of the Iroquois Confederacy, but it was also the name of Father's first command – the United States Coast Guard Cutter *Onondaga*. Surely fate was directing our footsteps! I read aloud from the guide. What was left of the Iroquois-

Onondaga tribe lived on a small reservation north of Cooperstown. Once a year, in August, they held a corn festival. We looked at the map. The highway ran close to the boundaries of the reservation. We debated whether or not to make a detour. Then Ian shouted and pointed to a crudely lettered sign tacked to a telephone pole: "Corn Festival," with a date and an arrow. Out of the whole cycle of 365 days, we had arrived on the day we were supposed to.

We followed more signs down narrow roads, bumped into a field. A tent and a small sound stage with people milling about assured us we had come to the right place. Women with jet black hair were shucking corn, stripping off green leaves and sticky strands. Or they hovered over cast-iron cauldrons, dipping and stirring the bobbing cobs, hauling them out again, stacking them in regimented rows. I thought of the Cauldron of Ceridwen, into which Celtic heroes, slain in battle, were dipped, to emerge resurrected. The thought was only fleeting. Much better to keep my grip on the real world, where men were barbecuing chicken on ordinary store-bought barbecue equipment set about in the field, and children played at tag.

The menu consisted of corn chowder, corn on the cob, cornbread, barbecued chicken, and strawberry shortcake – the old-fashioned kind, with strawberries piled on buttered biscuits. (There must have been a Scottish connection: the Onondagas called them "bannocks.") Alas, although we were in the midst of dairy country, the whipping cream was squirted out of aerosol cans. We had no cash except traveler's checks. When we offered a twenty-dollar American Express check, the old men by the cash box summoned the chief. I had expected him to be an elder, someone who looked like the face on the buffalo nickel. Instead, a young man in blue jeans and with a GI haircut introduced himself. He was not long out of the army, he said, and had traveled abroad. He assured the old men (who *did* look like the nickel) that a piece of American Express paper was as good as U.S. green.

I would like to say that I sat and barely picked at my corn this and my corn that. I hated myself for eating too much and for not wanting to be where I was. I hated the heat and the flies and the smells and the disappointment of seeing my romantic notion of the last of the Onondagas reduced to banality. To *corniness*! I felt utterly alienated from the human race. *I was Ruth among the alien corn!*

The speakers on the sound stage began to squawk, and a voice tested, tested, tested. The dance was about to begin. Men and women left their pots and barbecues and, silent and serious, filed their way to an open place in front of the stage. The scene reminded me of Anglican communion, when those who have been instructed and confirmed make their way to the altar and those who have not been, or are unreconciled with God, stay sitting in the pews.

I was unreconciled with God, and I was appalled by the tackiness of the dancers. Some of the men were wearing plastic war bonnets with pink and blue dyed feathers, the kind sold in souvenir shops. I figured they were probably manufactured in Taiwan. The women left their steaming cauldrons. They had removed their aprons, revealing cotton-print house dresses that fell to just above their ankles. Most of the dancers were wearing moccasins; a few wore Indian headbands. The men had short haircuts. This was in the early sixties, before black was beautiful, before most Native Americans were actively reclaiming their special identity.

The dancers milled about, then they formed a line and began to shuffle in time to the drums. They looked embarrassed and I squirmed in embarrassment for them. Only the beat of the drum was worthy of respect, steady and melodic and sure of itself. The dancers took up the beat with a musical, insistent chant, at first hesitant, then confident. The shuffling had been premeditated, I realized; gradually it became a graceful, sure, slow step. "First the blade and then the ear and then the full corn doth appear," says the old Anglican hymn. Some of the dancers had their eyes closed and were swaying, swaying like tall stalks in the wind. I became aware that this was not a show put on for me and other visitors, nor was it moribund ritual. The dance was alive, a religious experience for each individual and for the tribe. This was the Corn Dance and the dancers *were* the corn, or the spirit of the corn. I was being made witness to an act not only of worship but of transubstantiation. The dancers were the bread of life! Tears pricked at my eyelids.

Lucy! Two years before, when Lucy was only five, I had been reading the *Primitive Mythology* volume of Joseph Campbell's *Masks of God* series. Lucy had crawled up on the couch beside me. "Read to me," she commanded, and I had flipped the pages to find an origin myth, translated from the Ojibwa in the 1820s. The translator, Henry R. Schoolcraft, was married to an Iroquois-Objibwa woman and had lived in upstate New York. He could speak her language fluently. As Campbell points out, he did not translate the story into the choppy argot favored by modern anthropologists, but used the most literary language at his command. Schoolcraft was a contemporary of the Brothers Grimm; their tales were first translated into English in 1823. Lucy was used to the flowery prose of the period, and she listened attentively. I remember, vaguely now, that this had happened at Easter time. I had told Lucy "this is sort of an Easter story." Lucy remembered what I had forgotten.

Two years later, when she was seven and knew she faced a second operation, she asked for "that Easter story." I reached for the Provençens beautifully illustrated *Stories from the New Testament*. Lucy listened politely, but that was not what she wanted. I tried *The Velveteen Rabbit, The Dead Bird*. Lucy was exasperated. She wanted "the one about the two friends who had a fight and one of them wore funny clothes." I was stumped. I had forgotten all about reading to her from Joseph Campbell. I failed her. We had unfinished business between us.

Campbell uses the Iroquois corn-god myth to illustrate a clan's transition from a hunting-gathering society to an agricultural one. I recognize this same green-gold god in the medieval poem *Sir Gawain and the Green Knight*. He is also John Barleycorn, the spirit who grows in the fields, and is captured (like wine) in a bottle. Dressed in straw, he is seen in the mummers' plays – and on pub signs, where he is also known as Jack Straw, the life force, as in "jacking off," as in "Jack and the Beanstalk." Lucy did not have to know all this; she had grasped the essential on her own: we were talking Conception and Birth, Death and Resurrection. The meaning is manifest in the Christ story, and in the Egyptian death of Osiris. In the Greek myth, of Demeter and Persephone, the spirit is embodied as a goddess, searching for her daughter. *Searching for her daughter!*

In the Iroquois myth, most of the familiar elements emerge. God comes down from heaven. Boy hero wrestles with Corn God. Corn God beats boy three times. On the fourth day, boy slays Corn God and follows his instructions: *"Tomorrow when you throw me you are to strip me of my garments, clean the earth of roots and weeds and bury me; then go away. But come back from time to time to see whether I have returned to life. Keep the grass and weeds from my grave and once a month lay on fresh earth . . ."*

Months go by, then one day the boy brings his father to the secluded grave *"to see a tall, graceful plant with brightly colored silken hair and golden clusters on each side. 'It is my friend,' he said. 'For this I fasted and the Great Spirit heard.'"*

I have read that children, provided with a wide choice, will eventually learn to choose the food that is healthy for them. So may they, given the chance, recognize spiritual nourishment when it is offered. I had read the Ojibwa corn-god myth to Lucy only once – before we knew she had a brain tumor, before her "brightly coloured silken hair and golden clusters" were shaved off. Two years later, when she demanded the story, she knew she was faced with a second brain operation. She knew which story she was supposed to hear.

After Lucy's death, I couldn't dream about her. I could remember her, but I couldn't *dream* her. When I did dream, Lucy was in the next room, but I couldn't wrench myself away from a garrulous hanger-on to go see her. Or I was standing on a railway platform, waiting for her to come in on the next train. Or I was in the kitchen, waiting for her to come home from school. The worst dream of all was that Lucy had died. I would struggle to wake myself, only to find that the reality was worse than the nightmare.

Four or five years would go by before, one night, I would have a dream that was so vivid, so lucid, that it was more than a dream. I not only dreamed about my child, I *saw* her. Dream, vision, or hallucination, I found myself walking across a moor. I came to a three-way crossroads where there was a huge standing stone. Several British schoolboys were playing there, 1930s village toughies, with short trousers, bare knees, thick boots. Their blue eyes were round and hard. I felt menaced, which seemed ridiculous. They were only little boys.

"Onion sauce! Onion sauce!" they jeered, like those rabbits in the opening scenes of *Wind in the Willows*. But I wasn't in *Wind in the Willows*. I was in the "Oisin" story, from Irish mythology. I knew where the three roads led. The broad road, straight ahead, was the Road to Hell. The steep and rocky path ascending the hillside was the Path of Righteousness. But the path on the left, almost lost, the one that disappeared from view as it ran along the cliff edge, was the Twisty-Turny Road to Tir-na n-Og, a sort of fairyland that lies beyond the Western Sea. *When we were living in a caravan in Cornwall, we used to walk along the under-cliff, on a path that hung above the sea. Looking down, we saw skeins of foam traced upon the green waters. "Mermaids' hair," we had told each other.* Lucy's hair, I thought.

I wanted to take the cliff path, but the boys were blocking my way. I was afraid they were going to rush me. I eyed their thick boots. "Sixpence for the private road!" they kept saying (just like those rabbits in *Wind in the Willows*). My fingers touched an American coin, a nickel. I drew it out and showed it to them – a buffalo head on one side, an Onondaga elder's head on the obverse. *A coin of alternate myth!* They let me by.

In the dream, I thought I traveled alone, but gradually I became aware of a rustle in the bushes, as though a small animal or a bird were near at hand. I sat down on a log and waited. I thought of the "Gingerbread Man" story: when Gingerbread Man could not cross the river, *he* sat down on a log and waited. A fox strolled out on to the path – a fox with red fur. Now, in my dream, Lucy stepped out. I, her mother, knew that she had red-gold hair, though it was covered. She was dressed in a hospital gown that came only to her knees. Or maybe she was wearing a clumsily constructed angel's costume, for the Christmas play. Her head was wrapped in white bandages. *She's so full of light, she doesn't need the glory of her hair*, I thought. I feasted my eyes on her. I wasn't dreaming. I was *seeing* her. I felt rather shy, as though Lucy were the grown-up, I the child. Our greetings were unexpectedly formal.

"Why have you come?" Lucy asked. (Like the man in the ghost story "The Golden Arm.")

"To *see* you," I said.

Her voice was actually stern. "Now you have seen me, don't ask again." Somehow I gathered there had been petitions, dispensations, requisitions, schedules changed, channels jumped, systems put at risk. Pother in Heaven! I've never *seen* Lucy again. Now I am free to dream about her – although not often. I remember her, of course, every day! But I've never *seen* her.

Perhaps I was allowed to see Lucy because all her life we had shared a rich archetypal world with one another. I stumbled into the Onondaga Corn Dance when I still had unfinished business with her. I discovered, not intellectually, but in the marrow of my bones, the universal currency of myth. When the right moment comes, American Express is as good as U.S. green, a buffalo nickel is as good as a silver sixpence, which is equal to fairy gold. Iroquois corn cobs become the Bread-of-Heaven, the body of Christ. An ordinary cast-iron cauldron may become the Cauldron of Ceridwen, a source of resurrection sometimes equated with the Holy Grail, and the sacred chalice. By accepting these myths as equally valid, I had bought my way into that Twisty-Turny private road, that Crack-in-the-Teacup lane, that leads to the Land of the Dead. I was allowed to see my child one more time. But I heed Lucy's warning. I will not go that way again. Not until I'm sent for.

THE SALMON
OF WISDOM

CHAPTER 19

Seeing Black

IN SEPTEMBER, THE MINISTER of our church, Sam Hyashi, insisted that I accompany him to a meeting that had been called by Carl Nordstrom, whom I remembered from Shanks Village. Carl now taught sociology at Brooklyn College. As an avocation, he had immersed himself in the history of the Negro population in Rockland County.

The purpose of the meeting was to address the reasons for the large number of Negro dropouts at Nyack High School, and the failure of Negro families to thrive economically. In the seventeenth and eighteenth centuries, slavery existed in the county; according to the 1790 census, there had also been a number of free Negroes. Their descendants were still living amongst us, some of them bearing familiar county names: white Conklins and black Conklins, white Swanns and black Swanns.

Rockland County is triangular, shaped like a wedge of pie: the Hudson Palisades, curving along the river, form the pie's crust. The sharp tip at the other end runs into the Ramapo Mountains, where live the mysterious and exotic Jackson Whites. Descendants of runaway slaves, Hessian deserters, and local Indians, they remain ever suspicious of government authority. (When John and other Shanks Villagers were training to take the 1950 census, their team leader told them: "If a Jackson White points a rifle at you, beat it!") In 1963, these people were still providing part of their livelihood by hunting and fishing, even though, on a clear day, they could climb the nearest ridge, look across the flatlands and swamps of New Jersey, and gaze upon the Empire State Building. However, most Rockland County Negroes lived in downtown Nyack.

At least one Negro had made his way into the history books. During the eighteenth century, Samuel Fraunces, free man, owned land on the west bank of the Hudson, although he was more renowned for owning and operating The Queen's Head (now the Fraunces Tavern) near Wall Street, in Manhattan. In 1783, the British command brought their ships up the Hudson, to formally relinquish occupied New York to General George Washington. They were invited ashore, to lunch with Washington at the Onderdonk House, a Dutch sandstone, with lawns running down to the river. Samuel Fraunces had catered that luncheon. A few nights later, De Witt Clinton hosted a gala celebration at the Queen's Head. Later in the year, General Washington would bid farewell to his troops from the steps of the tavern and announce his retirement to Mount Vernon.

Onderdonk House was just across the street from our house in Piermont. Inveterate reader of historical markers that I am, almost every day I stopped to read the bronze plaque set into a stone at the corner of our street. I knew that Fraunces was of African blood (John had told me that), but there was no clue on the marker to that effect, nor that he had owned considerable acreage hereabouts. Carl Nordstrom forced me to ask myself why someone as successful and well known as Samuel Fraunces did not still have descendants in the neighborhood – prosperous, well-educated, and influential. There must be other Negro families, less famous, less well connected, who had disappeared without a trace. Carl spoke of one family, who owned a farm in the early nineteenth century. All went well until the black property-owner ran for a minor local office. Mysteriously, a flaw was found in his tax payments, credit was cut off at every quarter, and the family sank into obscurity.

Carl Nordstrom had conducted part of his study by the simple expedient of looking at old high-school yearbooks. For a number of years no Negroes made it into high school. Then a few dark faces began to appear in the class pictures. After World War II, although there were a number of Negro students in the freshman and sophomore photographs, by junior and senior year the count had dwindled. Few Negroes actually graduated from Nyack high school. Carl had gathered us together to consider the reasons.

After Carl's lecture, we broke into committees. I gravitated immediately to a group that would discuss the situation in elementary, kindergarten, and preschool. I listened carefully while two kindergarten teachers told the rest of us what we did not want to hear: that on the day a Negro child walked through the school door, he or she was already far behind a white counterpart. Year after year these teachers had received children who were unfamiliar with the alphabet, did not know how to count to three, *did not know the names of colors*. A few children, that first crucial year, were obstreperous; most of them were scared and silent. They did not ask for help; they did not know how to accept help if it was given. As adults, most of these former pupils, many of them obviously intelligent, remained apart from the social and economic forces that empowered white students with whom they had gone through the same school system. The teachers were baffled and frustrated. They had been at the school long enough to see a second generation, and now the grandchildren, repeating the cycle.

In our ignorance and innocence, half a dozen of us decided to meet again, in a week's time, to discuss what we could do about starting a free nursery school in the neighborhood. Surely, if we administered a dose of what was good for our children, if we gave these Negro children a battery jump, a head start, they would soon thrive. I had been reading Jane Jacobs's *Life and Death of Great American Cities*, in which she described what she called "the ballet of street life." Geographically, the white people of our district were not isolated from the black population. I shopped in downtown Nyack (the malls had not yet been built); I walked its streets; I often drove along Broadway (east-west) and up Main Street (north-south). A woman from the neighborhood came once a week to clean for me. Yet I was embarrassingly ignorant about Negroes in Nyack. *Naomi's ghost was poking me in the ribs, whispering in my ear.* Pay attention!

A previously invisible world began to reveal itself to me. Main and Broadway were lined with Victorian brick buildings, with shops below and two or three storeys above. I had failed to notice that Negro families lived above those shops. Historic houses, with big lawns and well-kept gardens, lined the road that ran along the river, but toward the end, near the intersection with Main Street, things became rather muddled. Houses had been turned into multiple dwelling places; cheaper houses had been built where lawns used to be. The big surprise was Depew Avenue, one block away from Main Street and parallel to it, running up the hill, away from the river. Reversing figure against ground, I came to understand that Depew was the true main street of Nyack. Unlike Main, which led to the entrance of the

New York Thruway, Depew ended in a wooded glen, safe and a little coun-
trified. The houses there, neither old nor new, were mostly single-family
dwellings, with flower and vegetable gardens and, often, old cars rusting in
the yard.

I wanted to know more, but to go into a neighborhood just to mine information seemed rude; more than that, it was a sort of thievery. I must give
something in return. Money would have been nice, but the only thing I had
to give was spiritual – stories, and my ability to tell them.

On a Thursday afternoon early in September, I drove into Nyack along
the river road and stopped at the foot of Depew. I had targeted an old
church, now used by a Negro congregation. The porch had shallow steps
and Greek-revival pillars, which made a sort of proscenium arch and stage.
I planned to sit there every week – same day, same time – and wait for listeners, if they would come. Meanwhile, I would observe the neighborhood.
I had brought a stack of children's books, sent to me for review by the *New
York Times*. Now, as I sat on the steps, I thumbed through them, evaluating
them from a new perspective. Not one of them had pictures of Negroes, nor
did they show a neighborhood resembling the one where I was sitting, with
a street of stores, and families living above them. The books were irrelevant to what I wanted to do.

No one spoke to me. The few adults going by looked right through me,
as though I did not exist. Perhaps this is what happened to Negroes trespassing in white territory! What I was watching was Jane Jacobs's "street
ballet." Children, coming home from school, entered the set, then disappeared into houses, or went upstairs to apartments over the shops. The
ballet continued. The children, now dressed in after-school clothes, re-
emerged from the wings. Even the kids pretended that they did not see me,
but they were not as adept at that game as their grown-ups. I caught their
sideways glances as they played ball and hopscotch. Some of them edged
towards me, or clambered up to the porch, descending the church steps
behind me. If I moved hand or foot, they scattered like sparrows. Which
reminded me: I should have brought bread crumbs! Elaborately careless, I
stacked and spread and spilled the review books on the steps. At least they
had colorful illustrations! I stood up, stretched, walked over to the corner
store, bought a couple of dozen Tootsie Rolls. Silent children flitted around
me, at wary distance. I was paying for the candy when a nine-year-old girl,
obviously the neighborhood Miss Goody Two-Shoes, rushed in to tell me,

"Lady, the kids is stealing your books." Not fair, to tell her that was what I had hoped, what I had intended. No use giving the fire to Prometheus; he has to seize it! I went back to sit on the steps. I tore open the paper bag of Tootsie Rolls, let them fall and roll in glorious profusion past my feet. The kids edged closer. "Do you want some?" I asked. There was a scramble.

Now that I had already determined that none of the books was suitable for reading aloud (not even the pictures were worth showing), I wondered what stories I should choose, what would be meaningful? I decided to ask. Almost with one accord the kids shouted: "Little Black Sambo!" I was not only amazed, but horrified. I could be tarred and feathered; I could be hung, drawn, and quartered. Since the 1940s, both Negro intellectuals and the white liberal establishments had declared war against Helen Bannerman's little book, first published in 1899. For twenty-five years the book had been banned in schools and libraries. How did these kids even know that it existed?

In kindergarten I had loved the story about Sambo and his loving parents. Although I was a white child, I identified with him, and with his family's cozy home life. All five-year-olds must learn to venture forth alone. Little Black Sambo, creative and courageous, reassured me that I could make it in the scary world beyond my mother's knee. Faced by tigers, he kept his wits about him (exactly as I would have done, under the same circumstances), and remained the soul of courtesy (my manners were never better than when I sensed myself in danger, and was playing for time). Never a victim, more than a survivor, Little Black Sambo was a hero to be emulated.

Most of the objection to the book is focused on the pictures, which show characters with very black skin, prominent lips, and kinky hair. Some librarians, trying to defend the book, point out that Bannerman wrote and illustrated the book while she was living in India, ergo, the people she depicted were East Indians, not Africans. What a cop-out! Bannerman was not an artist. The drawings are hardly more than cartoons, with stick figures. Yet they have power. That power, I am convinced, comes from her unblinking honesty. Black is black! Less than two years after I began my encounters on the streets of Nyack, the new wisdom would become, *Black is beautiful!*

I was being asked to *tell* the story. There would be no illustrations, just each child's personal projection. I looked up and down the street. There were no Negro grown-ups around. There were no white liberals. I took the plunge: *Once upon a time there was a little boy called Little Black Sambo. His mother was called Black Mumbo and his daddy was called Black Jumbo. And Black Mumbo made him a pair of beautiful little blue trousers. And Black Jumbo went to the store, and bought him a beautiful green umbrella, and a lovely little pair of purple shoes with crimson linings . . .* Part of the objection has been to Sambo's colorful clothes – too colorful to be considered in good taste. The hero was deplored as a sartorial stereotype, a strutting Negro, dressed to the nines. But nowadays high fashion is plucked from the streets. New materials, new dyes, an avalanche of color are so much part of everyone's daily life that we no longer equate flamboyance with inferiority.

I had become friends with Arthur Bell, the public-relations director at Viking Press. Through him, I had met several children's writers and illustrators, including Ezra Jack Keats. Jack, an artist, later told me that he went through the same sort of struggles with art and social consciousness that I was experiencing, probably at the same time I was telling stories on the church steps. Keats lived on the Upper East Side, on the fringes of Harlem. From his window he could watch the neighborhood kids, who were mostly Negro. The thought crossed his mind that he would like them to have a book just for them, to see how beautiful they were. He was aware that there was a dearth of books for Negro children, that there was no place to see themselves reflected in art and literature. (Be aware that, in the early 1960s, few Negroes appeared in movies and television, none were to be seen in advertisements and commercials; they were rarely photographed for newspaper articles.)

Keats had started to experiment with a picture book, which Viking would eventually publish as *The Snowy Day*. He liked to work in collage. He cut out silhouettes of his characters, three-year-old Peter and his mother, then cut bits and pieces of patterned paper to make their clothes. (I wish I had asked him if he was aware that he had used the same pallette as Bannerman had used.) To create sky, he painted a blue expanse, stuck on a piece of surgical cotton to make a cloud. Then he photographed the whole thing. The result evokes both texture and dimension.

Once, when I was visiting Jack in his studio, he told me the story of how his consciousness had evolved over a period of trial and error. He had tried to cut out the silhouetted head of a particular little boy, but was horrified when he saw that he had created a "watermelon" head. He had heard the term used in a derogatory way. He certainly did not want to create a caricature, a stereotype! He tried again. He even sketched out what he thought Peter's head *should* be, but when he started to cut it out of paper, his hand took on a life of its own. "I was humbled," he said. "My artist's hand would not lie!" One of the most beautiful pages in the book shows a page-filling tribute to Peter's quintessential *African* skull.

October came. My bum and spine were chilled as I sat on the church steps. Kids were beginning to anticipate Thursday afternoons; they showed up to listen to me regularly. I was still ignored by their adults – except for a certain black policeman. I was nervously aware that, every time his police car went by, he slowed down to a crawl and stared at me through inscrutable dark glasses. I tried not to let it bother me, that I was under police surveillance. I had recently been encouraged by a small but significant incident. One cold afternoon, just before I began my stories, a window was flung open across the street and a woman leaned out: "Mrs. Bodger," she called. "Wait for Orville. Orville's looking for his jacket." Orville's tear-streaked face showed briefly at the window. I waved. "See? I told you Mrs. Bodger would wait for you." How did she know my name?

A few nights later I received a telephone call from Sergeant Blue, of the local constabulary. My heart raced. Perhaps they thought I was giving candy to small children with evil intent. Or they may have bugged one of the pillars, heard me whispering "Little Black Sambo." Mr. Blue proceeded blandly enough: besides being a policeman, he was secretary to the local chapter of the National Association for the Advancement of Colored People. Perhaps I had noticed that he had been observing me? He hoped my storytelling had not been disturbed, but he was interested in what I was doing. He and the NAACP board had been discussing my situation; they were afraid that I might stop telling stories because of cold weather. Would I mind if they negotiated with the local school, found a space where I could continue during the winter?

I would tell stories for a few months at the school, but several things were amiss. Little kids chose to stay of their own accord, but older kids, who had misbehaved, came under duress: they were sentenced to stay after school and listen to Mrs. Bodger. One of the tenets of story – telling and listening – is that it is a form of play; play, by definition, is entered into by choice (as Johan Huizinga points out, in his little book *Homo Ludens*). During play, the imagination soars, the listener becomes a partner in the creation of another world, a world contained within defined boundaries of space and time – a chessboard, a football field, the spell (magical time) that stretches between once-upon-a . . . and a story's ending. Gradually, I did induce most of the kids to play the game with me, but the population was never constant. No sooner did some kids begin to listen than their jail-sentence of so many minutes was up; they left in the middle of the story. The playing field became a battleground. I am grateful, though, for it taught me how to become a tough storyteller, a lesson I would carry with me. *"Listen, kid, I care about you and I care about this story. I will fight for this story . . ."*

I was still skittering about the edges of the racial issue. Only occasionally did lightning flash across the darkling plain. I was telling the story of "Tom Tit Tot," an English version of the German "Rumplestilzchen." (There are three or four spellings. This is from Julius Heuscher in his *Psychiatric Study of Myths and Fairy Tales*.) Both stories belong to that genre of folk tale known as "the hidden-name tale." In some obsolete German dialects, the word for penis is *rumplestilzchen* (still not considered a polite word to use, or even to know, in middle-class circles). The young woman in the story empowers herself when, at last, she gives a name to her husband's sexuality, and therefore claims her own. She gives a name to the life force. Similarly, the king's bride in "Tom Tit Tot" must verbally recognize that it takes a "tom" and a "teat" to make a "tot."

I had not thought through, ahead of time, what I was going to do about the imp in the story, that phallic-tailed, phallic-nosed *black* character. He is cast as a magical helper, who spins five skeins a day for the gatless girl (white) who doesn't know how to spin. He is also diabolical – which, I now realize, makes him godlike. He is the Great Spinner, the Creator, who can create a world from a filament, from almost nothing. *He makes the Cosmic Story happen.* He is the Anglo-Saxon version of the African spider-god, the trickster-hero, Anansi.

Just before I came up to the first mention of this creature, I thought fast, shifted gears, described the imp as being green. To my British heart and mind, *green* seemed like a good safe color, connected to fairyland, the Green Man, the Green Knight, Robin Hood, Puck, the Celtic god Llud. In the misty British Isles, *green* is the color of life, the Life Force. I was feeling quite proud of myself, when a hand shot up. "He was black," said a determined, outraged little boy. I did not know then how honored I was, that he would take the risk. In 1963, "black" was a taboo word among black kids, as powerful (more powerful) than any four-letter word for sex. It took courage, and trust, to speak the unspeakable, not only before the infidel (me) but in front of other black kids.

"You are absolutely right," I said. "I made a stupid mistake, and I apologize." I had been complaining that there were almost no stories about black people, but when a powerful black character emerged, I had almost deprived my listener of enjoying the most satisfying aspect of the tale – the black energy and black smarts that power the plot. Even more unforgivable, I did not immediately implement the lesson that the small boy set before me. Like Ezra Jack Keats, I betrayed my own senses.

During those weeks, when I was storytelling and observing, the planning group for the nursery school was meeting regularly at the house of Sonia Alland, on River Road. Sonia's husband was an anthropologist – as was her father-in-law – who specialized in African societies and taught at Columbia University. At our frequent meetings, as we struggled to define our goals, to plan and make decisions, we were surrounded by wonderful African art.

We agreed that the nursery school would be open four days a week. We wanted the school to be integrated. We had to find a rent-free place in the neighborhood, conducive to small children's play and art work (messy). We needed equipment and materials – paper, paints, crayons. We had to have a yard, and a sandbox. Most of all, we needed a director. Everyone turned and looked at me. I had taken graduate courses in child development at Teachers College, Columbia. I had worked in the Shanks Village nursery school and participated in co-op nursery schools in Berkeley, California, and East Orange, New Jersey. There was also the great unspoken: *now that Lucy was dead, I had time on my hands*. I was still working on the final editing of my book, *How the Heather Looks*. I was still in shock from Lucy's death. My husband was mentally ill. My thirteen-year-old son was drifting. I had every reason to refuse the job.

I knew that Ian was unhappy. How could he not be, given the circumstances? I knew he hated school. The truant officer called me almost every day. "I'll go look in the Divers' sail loft, then call you back," I would say.

The Divers' garage had once been a boat house. The storage space above it could be reached only by a steep, perpendicular ladder, daunting to grown-ups. Our kids and their friends used it as a meeting place; it was also a place to experience first cigarettes, first "grass," first sex.

To Ian, during weekdays, the loft became a solitary refuge. More often than not, I discovered, he repaired there to sleep the day away, instead of going to school. He had never been a good sleeper; in the last few years he had become an insomniac. He was exhausted most of the time, and no wonder. His sister's death, his father's illness, and his mother's insurmountable anger must have sapped the life out of him. When he was not in the loft, he was up on South Mountain, which reared almost straight up behind our houses on the riverbank. There were some World War I fortifications there, which Ian loved to explore as though they were archaeological ruins. Sometimes he hitchhiked up to High Tor, or as far as Bear Mountain State Park. He spoke of hidden waterfalls; he wrote a poem about watching fawns flit through the forest.

The truant officer, the school psychologist, and the principal called Katie Diver into the office to ask her about Ian. "Why me?" asked Katie.

"We see you talking to Ian Bodger in the halls. He spends a lot of time in your sail loft. It's not hard to figure out that he's your boyfriend."

"Boyfriend!" Katie laughed ("a scornful laugh," she told me). "You just don't understand. Ian can't be my boyfriend. That would be like incest!" As a matter of fact, Ian did have a girlfriend, Liz Orlando.

John and I thought a perfect solution was offered when a Summerhill-type school opened its doors about twenty miles north of us. Bob Bartlett, the founder and principal, had spent several years in England, at the A. S. Neill school, famed for its ability to engage and teach children who had difficulty in the usual educational setting. I had read Neill's book and thought his approach would be beneficial for Ian. We gladly enrolled him there. Outside of school, Ian was busy with his drawing, his friends, his soldiers, his moviemaking. Christopher Diver starred in the *All Quiet on the Western Front*, produced and directed by Ian Bodger. When snow lay deep on the ground, a cast of thousands (well, maybe a dozen) turned out for the retreat from Moscow, in his epic *War and Peace*.

I was not informed that Ian often wandered off from his new school. He spent most of his time at Haverstraw dump, among perpetual fires. He got high on drugs there, and practiced making pipe bombs. (In an article by Yale psychiatrist Kenneth Kenniston in *The New Yorker* magazine, I learned that this pattern – cutting school, hanging out in a smoldering dump, getting high, and making bombs – was well nigh epidemic among 1960s kids of the upper-middle class.)

In good faith, I daily packed Ian's peanut-butter sandwich, and got him on the bus that took him to Bartlett School. He did attend some of the classes some of the time. He told me how, when a cat was found dead on the road, his teacher had brought it into the classroom and dissected it. "I thought I'd be sick," said Ian, "but I was amazed how beautiful it was. The flesh lay like feathers." He spoke with awe and reverence: for the first time, he told us, he could get an idea of how the bones are held by the muscles around them. "I've been drawing all wrong," he said, and asked if we could find a life-studies class for him to attend. Because he was only fourteen, the law required that a parent sit in the class with him. John drove him into Manhattan once a week, to attend a night class at the Arts Students' League. Even if I stayed home, Ian was gone most of the time. I could not do any more for him than I was doing.

Right or wrong, I said yes to taking on the job of director of the Nyack nursery school. I knew it was a lifesaver, thrown just in time to preserve my sanity.

From the outset we involved Negro women from the Nyack community to sit on the committee with us, give us their advice and consent. These women were concerned that our idea was only a flash in the pan, that we would act like politicians – make promises, raise hopes, then disappear. Some of the white women on the committee were trained as elementary-school teachers. Some had worked as volunteers in the co-op nursery school that was descended from the one at Shanks Village. They were used to the idea of working in a classroom one or two days a week, with their own children and others. Not only would these women be willing to work as my assistants, but they would bring their own preschool-age children along. Mostly this came out of idealism, because they would like their children to have an interracial experience; partly it was because of the practicality of not paying a baby-sitter. Their husbands were fledgling professionals or businessmen, which meant they did not have much money left over after they had paid for groceries and the mortgage. We knew we needed a bank loan to buy equipment, but we were afraid to stick out our necks.

Priscilla Swann, a cleaning woman, mother of seven sons, pillar of the Seventh-Day Adventist Church, had joined the committee early. Her ancestors were named in the 1790 census. She told us that she preferred being called "colored." Some of her children had red hair. "I want to honor *all* of my ancestors," she said. "I have Irish, African, Jackson White, Indian, English, German blood in my veins. I have documents and family photographs to prove it." Priscilla cut through our procrastination. She would go to her own bank manager (Nyack had private banks then). She would explain to him about our plans, and ask for a five-hundred-dollar loan (nowadays the equivalent of several thousand). Thus challenged, four other women volunteered to sign with her. We'd think about how to pay the loan tomorrow. Tomorrow.

The next breakthrough came when the Seventh-Day Adventists offered us their old church on Depew, now used only for Sunday school. The offer was temporary, but it meant we could get the program started. The drawback was that there was only one room; it was large, but not large enough to be divided, so we could not have two classes with two age groups going on at the same time. We decided to run a program for three-year-olds and young fours on Monday and Tuesday mornings. Older fours and fives would attend Thursdays and Fridays. Wednesdays, I saw my psychiatrist.

Committee members went around the neighborhood, climbed dark, narrow stairs, knocked on doors, seeking children who might come to the program. They returned with reports of young single mothers in deep depression, sitting in rooms above the shops, shades half-drawn. They also discovered single mothers who had twelve or fourteen children by several different fathers. As late as the 1960s the Catholic lobby in the state of New York ensured that there were laws and regulations against disseminating birth-control information. True, the laws had been recently modified: a social worker could tell a woman about birth control, *if* the woman asked specifically. By the rules of the game, she was not allowed to tell the client to ask about something that the client didn't know there was anything to ask about. How could the client know that birth control existed? Even if she could read, the law, and the tenets of good taste, forbade magazines and newspapers to publish such information. Television and the movies were no help. In the movies, a married couple was not allowed to sleep in the same bed. Eventually, dancing on the cusp of the law, we would invite a Fifth Avenue obstetrician to come and lecture, with charts and plastic models, to show the workings of the womb and to discuss the several methods of birth control. The neighborhood women who attended were amazed, shocked, and enthralled. They were also angry when they discovered how not only doctors and social workers but we white women had been holding out on them. Virginia Dickerson (mother of eleven) took a pile of Planned Parenthood pamphlets with her as she left the meeting. Later, she told me, she made regular visits to the Nyack hospital maternity ward, to hand out information to women, almost as they came from the delivery room.

The Seventh-Day Adventists warned us that, come the end of June, they would be wanting their building back for summer Bible school. Unhappiness stirred the congregation: wear and tear on the building and its equipment was beginning to fray the initial impulse of generosity. Fair enough! Somehow we found another place to operate, a big old Victorian house on the corner of Depew and Broadway, rent free. The advantage was that we had more rooms, a bigger yard, and a place to call our own. Also, we could hold meetings there at night. The disadvantage was that there was no way to heat the building.

John and I were attending a cocktail party when a man who had been eavesdropping on my conversation murmured politely that he thought my work sounded fascinating. Was there anything he could do, anything we needed? Shamelessly I said, "Yes. We need a furnace." Our benefactor had one installed within the week. The actress Helen Hayes, who lived in Nyack, would sometimes drop by to hear me tell stories. She offered her house for a benefit tea; hundreds of people came and we made enough money to pay back the bank loan.

From the outset I had been adamant that we must accept no hand-me-down toys or equipment, no matter how good; no discarded merchandise, even if it was free. I would buy a very little of the very best equipment available, mostly from Creative Playthings, on West 23rd Street in Manhattan. This decision bought trust. When the neighborhood women came to our open house, they walked in and saw not one flimsy, cutesy thing. The playhouse furniture, rocking boat, climbing equipment, building blocks, all brand new and beautifully made from sturdy grained wood, announced their own integrity, and thus the integrity of our intention. Grace Radin, one of the young mothers and a former social worker, still talks about my decision to have everything new. She thought I was crazy not to accept contributions of good used toys, but when she saw those women's eyes as they looked upon what we had bought, fresh and virginal, for their children, she was convinced that the decision had been a stroke of genius.

Helen and Burroughs Mitchell invited me to dinner, to meet some friends of theirs. When the Mitchells guided the conversation to my work, the other guests said they would like to give some books to the project. Delicately (not so delicately), I turned them down, explaining my conviction that everything should be new, not so much for the children's sake as for the parents'. I spoke of the second-class schools in big cities and in the Deep South, where there were never enough books, and what books were handed out had been used beforehand by white kids. Silence. Then, gently, as I opened my mouth again, Burroughs said: "Joan, shut up. Just shut up!" I paused. "Evidently you didn't listen to the last name," he said. "These are the Brentanos." The Brentanos were some of the most prestigious bookstore owners, and art publishers, in Manhattan. In the world! They were prepared to donate almost a thousand dollars worth of children's books – my choice!

My first choice was *Mother Goose*. We did not have a lot of equipment, but we had woman-power and woman-hours in profusion, both white and Negro. Books and stories and words were important. So was touch. Epiphany came as I watched Betty Parry, a white volunteer, sitting on the floor with her own little girl. She took off the child's shoe and soon was playing "This Little Piggy" with her pink toes. I decreed that, as often as possible, the staff should play touching games, one-on-one, with every child in the school. To bolster my conviction, I read aloud from the preface to Iona and Peter Opie's *Oxford Nursery Rhyme Book*:

It will be found that the baby games and lullabies of the first section belong, for the most part, to the period before a child is old enough to be read to. It contains the verses which a mother croons to her infant in his cot, and the baby-play, knee rides, and sayings for undressing, washing, and going to bed, which, in truth, are not a joy to repeat with book in hand. Our feeling is that a mother may like to look at this section when on her own, perhaps even before the child is born, so that she may have a rhyme in her mind ready for the demands of the particular querulous, damp, or twilight moment.

With the more familiar nursery rhymes, I had the children act out, with their whole bodies, the drama contained: Humpty Dumpty *sat . . .* we bumped our bums up and down on the chair. Humpty Dumpty had a *great fall . . .* the kids deliberately fell off their chairs. *All the king's horses and all the king's men/Couldn't put Humpty Dumpty together again.* I waded into the mass of giggling bodies on the floor, picked up a flailing limb: "Hmmm. Wonder what this is. Looks like an arm . . . Maybe it belongs to Roland . . . No, it's Amanda's leg!" Another great success was "A is Apple Pie . . . B bit it, C cut it, D dug into it . . ." Children learn through aggression, through attack. (Even a university student will speak of "hitting" the books, "attacking" an exam.) "The Little Old Woman Whose Pig Would Not Go Over the Stile" had rhythm, action, repetition, anticipation, and *fierceness*, all of which proved captivating. "The House That Jack Built," also an accumulative tale, was another success. The only passive "character" in the whole story is the bag of malt.

Picture books, at first, were not as effective as stories and poetry, which could be listened to. Some children did not know how to look at pictures. They did not seem to have mastered dimension, which, if you think about it, is not true dimension, merely a code to indicate the reality. In Lois Lenski's gentle nursery-school classic, *The Little Auto*, Mr. Small's automobile is going downhill. There is a fence in the background. At least, that is what *I* saw. But the children we were trying to teach were unused to looking at pictures with a grown-up to guide them. Someone had to help them shift perception. To them, the fence was not in the background. It intersected with the car's front wheel. Mr. Small was running *into* the fence, about to wreck his car. The point of the story becomes a cruel joke. Boffo! *Wanna see a picture?* A picture was for dirty, or for cruel, flashed by an older kid. That stage was only fleeting, thank God, and not true for most of the children. But still, I was not sure what the children were actually *seeing*, much less what they *saw*.

Maurice Sendak's book *Where the Wild Things Are* had just been published. It was one of the few books, perhaps the only picture book, that so much as suggested that anger existed. Most of the children, along with me, gnashed their terrible teeth and roared their terrible roars with gusto. Some children were too shy and scared to let out so much as a peep. Remembering Robert Coles's praise of "justifiable anger," I would put my hand gently on a child's throat, and lend encouragement. "I can feel the roar inside there," I would tell the class. "Not today, maybe tomorrow." Great rejoicing when the sound erupted. Often it was like a cork out of a bottle. A child who had been afraid to say anything would suddenly spew four-letter words for a week, but after a few more weeks that child would find other ways to express him- or herself. As the child was given more words every day, from poetry, from stories told and books read, from conversations one-on-one with other children and with adults, the swear words would quickly evaporate. The child had something else to say – maybe, if we were lucky, "I feel angry!" The big message I proclaimed was, "It's all right to be angry. It's all right to say words, even bad ones. But you may not hit and you may not throw (blocks, chairs) . . ." Of course there was Popsy, our inevitable manipulator, who had never had any trouble talking, and who would blue the air, daring me to stop him. I stopped him. Who said I had to be consistent?

While this was going on with the kids (and mothers) of Negro Nyack, Dr. Hatterer, my Fifth Avenue psychiatrist, concentrated on my own enormous, but latent, hostility. At first, I did not know what he was talking about. *Who? Me? But I am such a nice girl!* Eventually I trained myself to become aware of when my hostility kicked in: I felt it, physically, as a prickle at the back of the neck, sometimes almost an hour after the provocation. Little by little, I was able to identify the emotion closer to the time it was triggered. I would stop everyone in mid-conversation: *Wait a moment! I am feeling hostile.* I was so primed for anger that, more times than I like to remember, it would turn out that I had not listened carefully, or had allowed myself to hear selectively. I had got it wrong! But sometimes my anger was justifiable, right on target. Either way, I was developing my own early-warning system and teaching the Nyack community to do the same. We became more and more *authentic* in our dealings. Virginia Dickerson told me that she had decided to trust me when I blew up at a black woman. "You treated her just like you do your white friends," she said. Her remark prompted me to put a sign over my desk quoting Mrs. Higgins in *Pygmalion*: "A true lady, Eliza, is equally rude to everyone."

My anger was like a force field around me. Virginia was not the only black woman to pick up on it; I was in their emotional ball-field. I was on the verge of craziness when I walked through a wall of teenagers on the street, found two of them circling each other. "Give me the razors," I said. And they did. I was as unpredictably dangerous as they were. I am not saying this was a good thing. *Now* I could not do what I did *then*. Nor could those kids capitulate now. Too much history has gone under the bridge! I am no longer that angry. Nor that crazy. I took risks, not because I did not care whether I lived or died, but because I was so numb, so *deadened*. I wanted to provoke, to look down and see my own blood, in order to know that I was alive.

Sylvia Ashton-Warner wrote two books about her work with Maori kids in New Zealand that I found of inestimable value when I was working with American kids in Nyack. One, a novel, was called *Spinster*. The other, non-fiction, was called *Teacher*. She discovered that what first inspired her pupils to read were words that were either scary or sexy. She helped each child to build up a file of his or her own "power" words, fraught with meaning and peculiar to his or her own experience: Fire . . . Whiskey. . . . Kiss . . .

I was still having a hard time teaching the children the names of colors and shapes, much less numbers and letters. I took small groups of kids for walks around the neighborhood, concentrating on just one color for that particular day. Red! We collected cigarette butts with lipstick, pieces of broken bottle with red whiskey labels, bits of plastic, discarded packaging, a boiled lobster claw from the fish store. Back at the school I stood by one little girl who was painting. She was Virginia Dickerson's daughter, Phoenecia, who was four. "Look," I said. "Red paint in the cup. Now red paint on your brush. Red paint on the paper. Look at your shoes. What color?" No answer. "Red," I said.

"Red," said Phoenecia. I was ecstatic.

"Now look at the stripe on your dress. What color is that?"

"Stripe?" she ventured timidly. Something was very wrong. My own children, most white children I knew, could name their colors, *tell* their colors, by the time they were Phoenecia's age. Phoenecia's mother was a vital and intelligent woman who came to our meetings regularly. I had taken to sharing the articles about black culture, black education, with the women connected to the nursery school. I explained that I was reading as much as I could, but I had no way to know if the article was helpful, or bullshit. Usually I did not get an opinion, only watchful silence, but after the meeting Virginia would come up to me and ask if she could borrow the magazine or journal. Later I learned that she and the other women went back to her house, put on a pot of coffee, and Virginia would read the article aloud a second time. "Sometimes it's two in the morning before we get done talking," Virginia told me. "We didn't know before that people would want to write about people like us." I had to tell her that, up until very recently, no one had been paying attention. Now she, and women like her, were hot stuff in academia. But that wasn't helping Phoenecia.

I decided to telephone Margaret Lawrence, a Negro, a woman, a psychiatrist, who lived in Rockland County. She had earned her M.D. in the 1930s, when few women, much less Negro women, were allowed to enter medical school. "What are you saying? What do you do when you talk about race with the children?" she asked. I was taken aback. We prided ourselves on not noticing that racial differences existed. She blew up at me. She almost crawled down the phone at me. "What! You've been in existence all these months and you never mention race? I thought that was what your school was all about. I should come down there and close the place. You are a fraud!"

I was chastened. I was humbled. I should have remembered my streetcorner adventures with "Little Black Sambo," should have remembered the boy who insisted that "Tom Tit Tot" was black, not green. I left my office and went out into the classroom. I sat down at a table, beside Jamie, a little boy who was looking at Ezra Jack Keats's *The Snowy Day*. Together we turned the pages. We came to a picture of Peter sitting at a table, bent forward, eating his breakfast. His mother hovered in the background. "Like my mommy," said Jamie, so softly, so tentatively, that I might have missed what was hardly more than a whisper – if I had not just been scolded by Margaret Lawrence. Ezra Jack Keats's rendering of Peter's mother was impressionistic, shadowy. She had no features; she was just a shape in the background. And the shape was not like Jamie's mother, who was slim as a model, not rounded like the mother in the book. *The only thing in common was skin color.*

"Yes," I said, "just like *your* mother. *Black*." In the picture, where Peter was leaning forward, he had exposed a triangle of black skin between his T-shirt and his pants. Jamie was sitting in the same position. Without thinking, I put my hand on the bare triangle of *his* skin. "And Peter is just like you," I said. "*Black!*" Jamie turned to me. It was as though I had stripped off a stocking mask from his face. He wore an expression I had never seen before. Relief! Joy! Then and there I realized that all this time he must have thought that I was too blind or stupid to see that he was black. One day I might open my eyes and see his blackness – and then I wouldn't love him any more. But now I had seen him and called him by his rightful name – and I obviously still loved him. I was hugging him, and tears were running down my cheeks.

From that day forward I incorporated a discussion about blackness at story time. I held up Ezra Jack Keats's book and pointed out that Peter was black. Who else was black, in this very room? The teachers listening were, at first, stunned into silence. The intellectual, liberal stance was that we saw no difference because there was no difference. Even their children, the white children, knew *without being told*, that a person's skin color was not to be mentioned.

"Who has an arm like Peter's?" I asked. Several children came up to me; we compared their arms to the one in the book. The arms were various shades of brown; no one, we agreed, was exactly, truly black. I held up my arm, asked for opinions. I expected the children to say that I was white, but no one spoke. Then a white child said that she thought I might be sort of pink, with brown spots. A black child, inspecting me gravely, ventured that I had a few hairs growing. Not very flattering. I confessed that I was tempted to wish that I could be brown like they were, but that would be not true. I liked being me! Not everybody is the same – that's the point. It's all right to be different, because everybody is different. It's all right to like your special, particular difference. It's all right to like yourself!

The most amazing outcome of all this was that, within a week, the children, including Phoenecia, suddenly began to name the colors and, soon afterwards, squares and circles and triangles. *Not until we gave ourselves permission to see their blackness – and to tell them that we saw – could these children give themselves permission to see themselves. Only when they could own their blackness without fear, could they allow themselves to see the rest of the world. Now they could begin to live their own stories, and to tell them.*

A few weeks later Dr. Jack Lukens came to visit the school. I knew him from my Shanks Village days. Now he was head psychologist at Saint Agatha Home for Children, a large Catholic orphanage nearby, filled mostly with children from Spanish Harlem. Word had gotten out about my

conversation with Margaret Lawrence, and my breakthrough with racial
perception. He wanted me to try an experiment that some psychologists
had tried in Boston. Did I know a book called *Two Is a Team?* Yes, I did, by
Harry Behn. Owned it, actually. It was one of the few books that had pictures of a black child. I had not had much success with it, perhaps because
it was too wordy and moralistic, even for an older age group than ours.
Nevertheless, Lukens wanted me to try something. *The book is about two
boys, Paul and David, who play together. Paul is white; David is Negro. To
make a scooter (a sort of skateboard with a box nailed to it), they gather
boards, boxes, wheels, and tools. While they are working together, Paul and
David have a quarrel, and make two scooters. Now they are rivals! They
have a race and do some damage – knock a bag of groceries from a lady's
arms, break a bottle of milk, snap a dog leash. They gather the two scooters' wreckage, make a wagon, get a delivery job at the corner store. With
the money earned, they pay for the damage. End of story.*

"What I want you to do," said Jack Lukens, "is to read the story, but
when you get to the place when the two boys are at the top of the hill, about
to start the race, ask, 'Which kid do you think is going to win?'" I dug out
the book and read it to the five-year-olds, following Lukens's instructions.
I was horrified by the results. When I asked the vital question, all but one
of my listeners answered: "The white kid's going to win." The one holdout
was a child whose father, a sergeant during the war and occupation, had
married a French woman. "I dunno," he said. "I think the black kid can win
sometimes." Before my startled gaze the other listeners leaped on him,
swarmed him, began to beat him up. Having restored order, I asked why
they thought the white kid would win. "That black motherfucker," said
Popsy. "He's too stupid to win."

This, from a five-year-old! I exploded, but not at the uncouth language.
I told Popsy that his opinion made me feel angry. I did some swearing
myself. I did not regard it as blasphemy when I said his opinion made me
goddamn angry! I was playing for keeps. "Popsy, you are just plain wrong,"
I said, breaking every rule in the book. I told him, and the rest of the class,
that I, personally, knew of some black motherfuckers who could win. I had
seen them on TV. Martin Luther King was a winner, and so was that man
who could float like a butterfly. Popsy could be a winner. Every kid in this
school could be a winner. Yes, that's right! Black kids! Winners!

The next morning I came into school a few minutes late. The doors were already open. The children were taking off boots and coats. Popsy had wandered into the story corner. He was sitting on my chair, book open. What was he doing? He was mimicking me – every tone, every gesture! A circle of kids had gathered around him. He had me down pat. He held up the book, *Two Is a Team*. He was pointing at the picture, at the black kid. "Do you see that black motherfucker?" His listeners, mesmerized, leaned forward to look. *"Today he's gonna win!"*

CHAPTER 20

Rafting the River

PRESIDENT KENNEDY WAS assassinated in November, 1963. We did not own a television set, so we watched the funeral with the Divers. Sometimes, crazily, I thought the huge public outpouring of grief must be for Lucy. The president's funeral was on a Monday; the entire population took the day off in order to watch. Louise Spenser, director of a nursery school that had evolved from the old Shanks Village original, confessed to me that, over the long weekend, each one on the staff had assumed that someone else was looking after the school hamster. When teachers and kids returned on Tuesday morning, they found the hamster dead in its cage. Obviously a funeral was in order.

The deceased was wrapped in newspapers, deposited in a shoebox, laid in state in the little red wagon. Meanwhile, a scuffle had broken out in the dress-up corner. Even the little boys wanted to wear a pair of the several pairs of high-heeled shoes stored there. Louise said she couldn't figure out what was going on until the funeral procession began. The kids in high heels walked "just like Jackie," Louise said. We surmised that, while older members of the family had sat crowded on chairs and couches, the youngest children had been relegated to the floor, at eye level with the bottom of the television set. They would remember for the rest of their lives the sight of Jackie Kennedy's shoes, carefully placed – one step at a time, one step at a time.

Which was how I was teaching myself to live. Driving in the car with John, I would tell myself, "I can last, I can endure, from here to the mailbox. I can last, I can endure, from the mailbox to the tree on the corner." Colors, shapes, shadows, even negative space, took on a surreal intensity. I lived from moment to moment, in sharp-edged technicolor awareness, in the here and now, screwed so tight that it is a wonder I did not implode, cave in on myself, disappear into a black hole. I thought I was clever to have reached that state, to will myself to live so, but our dear-old-family-psychiatrist was worried. "Only saints and mystics and crazy people live that way," Hatterer said. "And you're no saint."

What helped save me was my sense of story. I didn't have to know what would happen next, what was around the next bend, where I would end up. Let the story unfold! I would ride my story as I would ride a raft down a wild Western river, or a coracle on the Wye. I drifted along, rarely bothering to steer, sometimes bored by the flatness of the scenery, sometimes pushing off from steep canyon walls, sometimes paddling like hell. The roar of rapids in the distance did not frighten me. I was fully engaged with the present. No place could be more dangerous than where I was living now.

I also lived the metaphor. I was forever restless. I took the sailboat (we owned one-third of it, with neighbors) out on the Hudson. I had never learned to sail. Father scorned would-be Sunday sailors, and had refused to teach me, or pay for sailing lessons. Once, with a friend I had invited along, I got hung up on one of the enormous piers of the Tappan Zee bridge; ignominiously, we had to be towed back by strangers in a motorboat. Word of the escapade got around. I also was a restless driver. People refused to drive with me, much less sail with me. So, in my second-hand Volkswagen, I roamed by myself, hour after hour – north, past West Point, into the Catskill Mountains; east, into the Ramapos, even as far as the Poconos. Trapped in my sticky flypaper denial that my marriage was over, I rafted the river, using mobility like a drug.

In January 1965, when President Lyndon Johnson delivered his State of the Union speech, describing his vision of a Great Society, I could hardly believe my ears as he decreed that nursery schools would be set up throughout the country to give children ("poor children") a head start before they entered the regular school system. Not I, but dedicated others, plowed through forms and wrote the proposal needed in order to apply for newly available federal funds. Grace Radin, Ann Wellborn, and the rest of our board's finance committee worked on the nitty-gritty aspects of insuring our future existence and expansion.

Great was the disappointment and consternation when the proposal was turned down. What had we done wrong? The committee was informed that, because we were already flourishing, and doing exactly what the Head Start program would hope we would do, we were assumed to be already funded. The government would not give money to an organization that was up and running.

This time I *could* turn to John, and to his expertise in politics. John called Harriet Dow, a neighbor of ours, to ask how to get in touch with her husband. Quickly! John Dow had run for Congress on the Democratic ticket for so many years that people had lost count. When the Republican candidate died suddenly, John was unexpectedly elected. Too poor to set up a household in Washington, the Dows had decided that Harriet would stay on in their house on River Road and support herself by continuing to run her antique shop, while John found a place to live in Washington.

When we met with him, he was living in a basement room below a flight of steps leading up to an old brownstone. He had two chairs, a bed, a table, a typewriter, and a hotplate. He had never expected to be elected; he was convinced that he would not be elected again. He therefore decided to vote his conscience all the way. (He would become the first member of Congress to vote against the war in Vietnam!)

By the time we arrived he had already arranged an appointment for us with Sargent Shriver, an in-law to the Kennedys, who was in charge of the Peace Corps and, temporarily, the new Head Start program. I had written a letter, which I handed to him, and when he read it, he began to laugh. He called in other members of his staff, who crowded into his office while he read my letter aloud. I had written that the Nyack Community Nursery School had been doing exactly what it should have been doing for two years, with no legal sanction. But when Shriver and his colleagues were ready to make an official alliance, they had spurned us, "like a man who tells his girlfriend, 'Now that I am ready to be married, I can't marry you because I always planned to marry a virgin.'" Shriver asked me more questions (many more), then John and I drove home. The next night, on the Huntley-Brinkley television news show, David Brinkley mentioned the letter, saying that government circles rarely received correspondence as witty and interesting. A few weeks later, Shriver's office informed Nyack Community Nursery School officially: we would receive federal funds. We were the first Head Start project in New York State to be funded, and one of the first in the nation.

My book, *How the Heather Looks*, was published by Viking Press in the spring of 1965. I would receive no money to speak of, but book and publication opened new doors. Librarians and teachers asked me to speak at professional meetings, to act as consultant for several institutions. George Woods, editor of the Sunday *New York Times*'s children's-book page now began to send me regular assignments. Most important, I was offered a new job – to create and direct a therapeutic nursery school at a Catholic orphanage, Saint Agatha Home for Children. Although Saint Agatha had existed in Rockland County for almost a century, it was actually tied to the diocese of New York City and to the public-school system there. My new nursery school would be funded by the Head Start program, the monies funneled through the NYC public-school system. Administrative duties would be nil; the convent would take care of that. I was confident that Nyack Head Start would carry on without me. I am better at conceiving and creating a new idea than I am at maintaining and administering one. Looking for an escape from the instability of my marriage, the frailty of my psyche, my terrifying anger, I longed to launch my coracle again.

Over the years, Saint Agatha Home had cared for each new wave of Catholic immigration. Originally, there had been the Irish, then the Italians and the Middle Europeans. Now the children were mostly Puerto Rican; their parents lived in Spanish Harlem. The children in my nursery school would be from the rock-bottom, non-functioning poor. They might come from a single-parent situation where, although one parent was still alive, he or she had disappeared, or was not fit to take responsibility, and the other parent had died or been disabled. They might come from homes where one or both parents were on drugs, from homes where one or both parents were abusive, violent, neglectful. One child had been found in a garbage can! The kids were referred by the State Department of Welfare, and by the courts. Some of them had been institutionalized since birth; their first years were spent in the New York City Foundlings Hospital. At age two and a half, they were sent to Saint Agatha, where they would probably live until they were eighteen. Few Saint Agatha children were ever adopted. Most of them were not up for adoption.

The Mother Superior who interviewed me had recently come to her job. She held several degrees, was knowledgeable, powerful, intelligent, and worldly. What worried her most about Saint Agatha, she told me, was the high rate of familial recidivism. Parents and grandparents, who had spent all their young lives at Saint Agatha, would come to visit their children and grandchildren on Sundays, pleased to have them raised by the same methods, very often by the same nuns. More likely than not, these children would, in turn, go back into Harlem and the Bronx, enter into disastrous relationships, bear yet another generation of children to be referred to the orphanage. "We must be doing *something* wrong," said the Mother Superior. (I discovered later that she looked the other way when the younger nuns gave birth-control instruction, and birth-control pills, to the teenage girls in their care. Within a few more years she would close down the orphanage.)

In Nyack, I had been approached by Ann Eagle, who had recently come to work as a volunteer at the Nyack Head Start program. She was taking child-development courses at Sarah Lawrence College, in Bronxville, across the Hudson River. Her husband, Vernon Eagle, was director of the New World Foundation, an organization that contributed major funding to the work of such people as Martin Luther King and Robert Coles, as well as subsidizing various liberal publications. Ann had looked at all the educational programs that were happening in the New York–Westchester–Rockland area, and thought that what was happening at Nyack, under my direction, was the most exciting program around. Ann (whose maiden name was Sickle) lived in her family's seventeenth-century farmhouse on Sickletown Road, Sickletown, about three miles from Saint Agatha. I found out later that it was she who had suggested to the Mother Superior that I be hired away from Nyack, to start a Head Start program at the orphanage. If I went to Saint Agatha, Ann said, she wanted to be my assistant. I counted myself lucky to have her.

I approached the new project very much as I had the one in Nyack. I asked permission to spend a few weeks observing the children in their cottages and at play outside. I also wanted to size up the "neighborhood." Two dormitory cottages were involved. Each housed sixteen or eighteen children, ages two to seven. Although these kids were mostly Puerto Rican, plus some non-Hispanic blacks, the nuns in charge tended to be Irish; some of them actually had been born and brought up in Ireland. I had told the Mother Superior that I was not Catholic, nor did I have much idea of Catholic-American culture, but she had assured me that her aim was to hire by merit, not religion.

When I first walked into one of the cottages, I was mildly surprised. The furniture and decor were cheerful and comfortable. The children were dressed in colorful, individualized, brand-name clothes of good quality. There were toys and games to play with, a television set, puzzles, Lego – even books. But as soon as I entered the room, the children rushed to cling to me, stroking my legs, my hair, my breasts. They were both limp and aggressive. They called me "Mommy" and asked if I were going to take them home. They snatched at my pen, tried to write on my notes. One little girl, Yvette, persisted in fiddling with my clipboard. "Don't do that," I said. "That annoys me."

"What's annoy?"

"I think you know from the way I said it. When you grab at my clipboard, and keep me from writing, I feel angry." I rapped on the clipboard for emphasis. When I looked up, I noticed that the nun, the housemother, and several assistants were all staring at me. Disapproval floated in the air. When supper was announced, I followed the children into the dining room. When they were all seated, the housemother asked: "Who is happy today?"

The cook, who had come in from the kitchen, brandishing a spoon, cried out, "I am!" The children crowed in chorus: "I am, I am, I am!" All except Yvette, who said: "I'm not happy. I'm angry!" What on earth had given Yvette the idea that she was not happy? "I want my mother," she said. "My *real* mother." The housemother shot a baleful glance at me. She did not have to say it: *shit-stirrer!* The other adults rushed to fill the void. Yvette had made a mistake. Of course she was happy! How could anyone not be happy, living as she did at beautiful Saint Agatha in a lovely cottage, with so many people to love her . . . A few weeks later, when I opened the doors of the nursery school, Yvette was the first kid across the threshold. Hand on hip, tapping one foot, she said, "I'm still angry!"

"Then you've come to the right place," I said. "This school is going to be a place where you learn to be angry successfully." (The day would come when Yvette, helping while I swept the floor, would drop the dustpan, take my face between her two hands: "I'm not always angry," she said, looking

straight into my eyes. "I'm only angry sometimes. If I can't be angry sometimes, I can't . . . I can't . . . *be*.")

What characterized most of the children of Saint Agatha was their
lethargy, their inability to learn, their inability to make sense out of the
world. Even the preschoolers were waiting to be plugged in, turned on. I
remembered Jean Betz, my old professor at Columbia, saying that, in order
to create, one had to be able to have the right to change and destroy, the
right to make false starts and mistakes. This right implied ownership.
During the time when I was waiting to open the nursery school, I had gone
for a walk through the woods and found the Saint Agatha dump for broken
toys, lamps, and furniture. I took the children there, to that place of bicy-
cles and tricycles without wheels, games and gadgets without batteries,
broken pots and baseball bats, a smashed plaster saint. That dump, a place
for discarded toys, was a metaphor for Saint Agatha, a place for thrown-
away children.

Back at the cottage, if there was a flaw in anything, these same kids
would go into a tantrum, a sort of hysteria. Here, in the dump, there was
nothing else to do but break everything down – or to pull order out of chaos.
Little girls bashed armless dolls, then reclaimed those same dolls, set up
housekeeping, filled broken cups and pots with dandelions. Little boys
stamped and kicked, chucked bits of broken plastic until they were tired,
then set about the business of trying to thread wheels onto axles, make
strange assemblages that would have won a nod from Calder or Duchamp.
Part of the charm was in the ephemeral nature of the objects: they could be
discarded and transmogrified at will – yet, strangely, they were *owned*.
Once in a while a child insisted on taking an object back to civilization. I
would allow that, as long as they lugged, dragged, tugged, their prize by
their own strength and determination. If they were successful, I was willing
enough to put the child's name on what had been so hard-won, and lock it
in the shed, from whence it could be resurrected, painted, augmented,
destroyed, *transformed!* Out of their experiences with cast-offs came an
increased ability, an eagerness, to explore the possibilities of the toys and
materials the nursery school provided. In order to create, you must change
something; in the process of changing you will change yourself, and you
will enter into ownership – not only of the object, but of your own soul,
your own identity.

One of the advantages of working within a large budget was that we could allow every child to paint as many pictures as he or she wanted, every day, on full-size sheets of newsprint. As a child painted (created), the paintings became a way to discharge emotion, and a means to match emotion with words. The paintings were also a record. Every picture was labeled with the name of the child, the date he or she painted it, and the words they gave to explain it. These explanations, expressions of the child's deepest fears and concerns, grew more elaborate and detailed as the children's vocabularies, and their trust in us – in themselves – increased.

We sorted out the paintings by name and date and stored them in an attic space. It was Ann Eagle's idea that, from time to time, we invite a child to go through his entire collection, while Ann or I read back the words that had accompanied the experience and recalled the circumstance when it had all happened. These children's lives were writ on water. There was no one to care deeply enough to be able to tell and retell the story of a short life to the one who was living that life. There was no one to recall a certain incident, to say "you used to spit up orange juice." An artist is immortalized by his or her creation! These retrospectives gave us a way to talk about a continuum of shared past experience, to let the child know that he existed in time and space, *and* that he was a part of our memories as well. *At Saint Agatha, the most hateful, hurtful thing one orphan child could say to another was, "I'll forgetchya!"*

During the first few weeks, I was appalled by the children's reaction at story time. There was not only lack of attention, but an outbreak of anger, even violence, that accompanied the mere suggestion that they sit down to listen. As an experiment, I decided to let them choose between listening, or playing in the next room. All hell broke loose! I rescued Ann just in time from being injured by flying wooden blocks. I faced the dilemma squarely: I could either give up books and stories altogether, or I would make the kids listen. Spanking was allowed at Saint Agatha, if a child hurt someone else or broke something valuable. To me, nothing is more valuable than story! I told the kids that I would *fight* for the story. Once again I heard my voice saying, "I care about you, and I care about this story. I'll hit anybody who tries to break it up." Yes! I know the arguments against physical punishment. But there are worse things that can happen – never learning to listen; never learning to make images in the mind, or being touched by the magic and beauty of literature; never absorbing a sense of form. *Never becoming not-bored.*

Boredom comes from repression of emotion, of anger, sadness, fear, and joy. These children rejected stories not because they didn't care, but because they cared too much. They were afraid to be touched, to be opened, to be made vulnerable. Young as they were, they deadened themselves against feeling. I was determined to enter their scary places, to go through the woods with them, be there when they faced up to what frightened them most. Only then could they shake off their evil enchantment, learn how to be alive. *Once there was a man who had two children, Hansel and Gretel. When his wife went off somewhere, he took up with another woman, a mean woman.* (Every head turned. The children of Saint Agatha were hearing their own story!) *"Tell your kids to get lost," she said, so they took Hansel and Gretel into the woods . . .*

These children would become addicted to stories, but that did not happen until after we developed a curious ritual. Every day I would announce: "I will fight for my story." The kids would rush me, giggling and pummeling and pushing. I, the storyteller, would push back – hard. As the battle swayed, my listeners and I acted act our very real resistance, reluctance, and hostility to each other; we broke down a wall of apathy, cleared a space, created a new kind of energy, where anything was possible, including honest expression of feeling and emotion.

I discovered that the children were telling stories to the older children in their cottages, who were telling versions to their therapists. Through telling and retelling, the stories often underwent a sea change. The head psychiatrist came to me. "I have been hearing variations of a story called 'Wolf Man,'" he said. *There's this monster. He does a sort of break-and-entry, where Wolf Man lives with his gang, and several of his guys are killed. Wolf Man fights the monster and tears his arm off. The monster hurts so bad that he goes to see his mother. The most important point of this story is that the monster's mother is a good mother! Although she has not been out of her apartment for years, she heaves herself out of the mud . . . off the couch . . . and goes looking for Wolf Man . . .* "Do you have any idea," the head psychiatrist asked, "with how much glee scholars are going to pounce on an Hispanic *Beowulf*, found twenty years from now, alive and well in Spanish Harlem?"

Blood feuds were alive and well in Saint Agatha nursery school. Awful threats were not only made, but carried out. I decreed that you may *say* angry things, but you may not throw chairs – or hurt anyone, or break something. For the usual *motherfucker* category of oath (which did not shock me into reprimand) I substituted some mouth-filling words which seemed to be just as satisfying. I introduced Lucy's teeth-wrenching *igneous rock*, by saying it myself, then clapping my hand over my mouth. I also took to Latin declensions, *hic haec hoc, hujus, hujus, hujus*, and, from English folklore, *fee-fi-fo-fum.*

Violent obscenities I found tedious. Violent actions, repeated over and over, wearied me – but they also interested me. When Billy cried out, yet again: "Teacher! Teacher! Tommy took my car!" Tommy would rejoin with, "I had it first." The theft (if it was a theft) always happened just as I blinked or turned my head away. I could not say for sure who was lying, who was telling the truth. I might as well save my breath to cool my porridge, rather than lecture about sharing. To pry Tommy's fingers off the truck seemed undignified for both of us, and useless besides. I came to observe that, although the Tommys may snatch, the Billys of this world are the more angry, the more manipulative. I have seen a Billy go slack, almost let the toy fall from his grasp, so he could once again play victim.

Gradually we developed an existentialist approach. "Tommy has the car," I would say. "Right now, he *owns* it." This would be news to Tommy. He might stop dancing away, actually draw nearer, to hear what I would say next. "Billy, if you want that car, you have to ask for it. I won't do the asking for you. I'm not the one who wants the car – *you* are. Ask Tommy if you can have the car *after a while*. He's not ready to give it to you yet, but I don't know what's going to happen. Things change! Maybe Tommy will give it to you. Maybe he won't. It will be interesting to see what happens." Tommy, listening, as often as not became as curious as any of us to see how the plot would evolve, the story unfold. He might become the hero of the tale!

The more angry Billy was, the more helpless and passive he was. He might not open his mouth, or only whisper if he did. As weeks went by, the children began to understand the process. They would form a ring around the protagonists. This was theater, and they the critics. "Ask louder," they would say to Billy. Or (quoting me), "Put more guts into it." Or (nodding sagely among themselves), "That was good asking!" I was always amazed at how soon the Tommy character would hand over the toy, usually within less than five minutes. I think the stasis shifted whenever a Tommy heard me confirm his ownership. *He could not give until he knew he owned.* Once blessed and anointed with the power of ownership, he could make princely choices, create meaningful change.

Ann Eagle was so enthusiastic about our work that she persuaded Dr. Maria Piers, the director of the Erik Eriksen Institute in Chicago, to observe us. Dr. Piers and her husband, along with Eriksen, Peter Blos, and a few others, had belonged to that little circle that surrounded Anna Freud in pre-war Vienna. Although Maria was not Jewish, she had married her fiancé so as to share his fate in a concentration camp, whatever that might be. At the last possible moment, Anna Freud, having escaped to England, was able to intervene on the Pierses' behalf, and save them from being transported to Auschwitz.

After the war, Anna Freud dedicated herself to working with six children who had lived in the concentration camps and somehow survived. Maria Piers was writing a book (with Robert Coles) about the abandoned and neglected children of poverty. The book would be called *Wages of Neglect*. Piers felt that our work at Saint Agatha, with the neglected children of the rock-bottom poor, had similarities to the work that Anna Freud was doing. A description of our work would eventually be contained in Chapter Four, "Feeling, Speaking, Learning." Anna Freud's work is described in Chapter Five: "Six Hitler Orphans."

I still had a family life, although every day (and night) my life with John was becoming more difficult. All the years of our marriage, I had refused to let a television set come into the house. We were a reading family, I said. We got our news from the *New York Times*, and from Huntley and Brinkley on NBC radio. *A happy family does not need a television set*, was my smug mantra. Then one day I woke up, said to myself: *My daughter has died; my husband goes in and out of mental hospital; my son is on drugs. We are not a happy family!* I went out and bought a television set. That night, at dinner time, we did not sit around the dining-room table, staring at Lucy's empty chair, listening to John's long harangues, to my sharp tongue, to Ian's foggy silences. The numbing, neutral act of watching television kept our family together for another few years.

When we finally learned that a teacher at Bartlett School was supplying Ian with drugs, we pulled him out and enrolled him at Rockland Country Day, a blazer-shirt-necktie sort of place. Ian did not last long. Meanwhile, a new divorce law had been passed, permitting residents of

New York State to obtain an immediate legal divorce in Mexico. Before that, a divorce would have taken two years. If John went back into the hospital during that time, I might not be able to get a divorce for another seven. Hatterer advised me that, if I left, I should tell John to meet me at his office, in case John should break down, or become violent.

When I could no longer endure, not even to the birch tree on the corner, I packed my suitcase and withdrew my entire fortune from the bank: $308.23. I had told John to meet me at Hatterer's office, and he did; the meeting passed without particular incident. From Hatterer's office, I drove back to Rockland County and checked into a motel. A few days later, when I went to the post office to pick up my mail, there was a note-sized envelope from Evelyn Bromberg. "To maintain your dignity," was all she wrote. She had enclosed a check for a thousand dollars. In 1966, a thousand dollars was a lot of money! It kept me afloat. It maintained my dignity.

Tolstoy has said that all happy families are the same. I maintain that all divorces are, too. I will keep all mention of mine to a minimum, mere guidelines to orientation and explanation. In May 1966, I flew down to Juarez, Mexico, and obtained a divorce. John moved out of the house and took a flat three miles away, in an old house closer to Nyack. Through our lawyers we agreed that Ian and I would stay in the house in Piermont until Ian graduated from high school, or until he reached nineteen. Ian would spend every other weekend with John. A lot of money had been eaten up by illnesses, joblessness, frequent moves, houses, special schools. I would receive a sensible monthly allowance to maintain a home for Ian. It was up to me to earn money for myself. If I wanted Ian to continue to live with me, I would not be allowed to move out of Rockland County. *I felt canyon walls closing in on me. I felt the quickening current.*

Our family doctor, Norman Rubinstein, had recommended a psychiatrist for Ian. Dr. John MacCallister had recently moved to Rockland County, to work with teenage kids (this was a new specialty). MacCallister refused to take a patient unless he could work with both parents. Although this might seem reasonable, I said I was too exhausted, after years of trying, to sit in another psychiatrist's office with John. Rubinstein called MacCallister on my behalf. So did Hatterer. I consented to a compromise: I would meet just once, with John present. Years later, MacCallister confessed that he had learned something from me: the folly of his own rigidity. John was too far removed from reality to be able to contribute to family therapy.

MacCallister recommended that we send Ian to a school in Manhattan. Robert Louis Stevenson High School had been founded early in the century, but had recently been converted to a therapeutic institution. Ian saw the irony, the humor, of his going to a school named for a saint of his early childhood. I had read to him from *A Child's Garden of Verses* almost from the day he was born; he had been to Stevenson's grandparents' home (where the famous garden was) on the outskirts of Edinburgh. John and he had read *Treasure Island* and several other Stevenson novels together, as well as *Travels with a Donkey*. RLS had never fitted into any school situation, and had disappointed his father and uncles when he withdrew from the family trade and tradition of building lighthouses. He had gone off to San Francisco ("to Haight-Ashbury," Ian claimed, "and might never have been heard of again, except . . .")

Ian's favorite class was built around reading a variety of daily newspapers. Half a dozen students, plus the teacher, would sit around a coffee table, feet up, drinking coffee and smoking cigarettes. (The dangers of smoking tobacco were not yet viewed as so alarming as to seem to equal the dangers of pot. Having gone through the experience with drugs at Bartlett School, I was not about to object to the lesser evil.) Every morning the class chose a subject in the news, then the kids took turns reading aloud from the *New York Times*, the *Amsterdam News*, the *Wall Street Journal*, the New York *Daily News*, the *New York Post*, the *Washington Post*, the *Chicago Tribune*, and a few foreign newspapers. The teacher would then attempt to place the issues in historical, legal, and political perspective, and the kids would argue from different points of view. Ian thought this was the best class he had ever had in any school.

Every student in Ian's new school was an upper-middle-class kid on drugs, which made Robert Louis Stevenson not much different from other middle-class private schools in the sixties. An important difference was that this school admitted to the situation. Every student was required to have his own psychiatrist. When Ian stayed after school to be with his friends, he often found himself in a waiting room, reading magazines. He claimed that, just as dog-owners tend to look like their dogs, clients tend to look like their shrinks. (Ian and MacCallister could have been cousins.) After a while Ian stopped coming home from Manhattan every night; instead he crashed at friends' apartments.

I was still director of the nursery school at Saint Agatha; in order to earn more money, I also worked one-to-one with some of the children, using a method of play therapy that Virginia Axline had developed in the 1930s. I was asked to speak at Sarah Lawrence College, and to serve as a consultant to the laboratory nursery school for a day. I was also invited to speak to the staff of the Bird S. Coler Hospital, on Welfare Island, in the Harlem River. The wards were full of children, mostly black. They suffered from birth deformities, horrific injuries, burns, and truncated limbs induced by thalidomide poisoning. After my talk, several black nurses approached me. They said that what I had to say about the learning patterns of poor black children struck closer to the mark than anything they had heard. I was offered a job there. I told myself that I did not pursue it because I wanted to be home for Ian, but the true reason was that I was too overwhelmed by the misery and suffering I saw. I ran away.

By now, Ian had dropped out of high school and I saw him less and less. When he did come home, he was stoned. I developed a racking cough which seemed about to tear my body apart. Only later did I discover that I was suffering from the effects of secondary hash smoke. *Now I could hear the rapids up ahead. I was paddling like hell.*

I applied for and received a scholarship at Yeshiva University, on Fourteenth Street, in Manhattan. The university was close to Bank Street College, where I would be teaching a course in storytelling. I had decided to work for a master's degree in human relationships (a new discipline). I spent several days going into the city, to look for a pied-à-terre, in case I had to stay late at class or study at the library, but I was appalled by the price of space. Then I came home unexpectedly and found Ian hiding under the bed; he was so demoralized that I decided to stay home and look after him. I took jobs which did not require that I be gone for a full working day or overnight: one evening session a week at Bank Street College, two mornings at Brooklyn College (where I taught Children's Literature). At home, I wrote for the Field Textbook Company in Chicago, and wrote reviews, mostly for the *Times*. I was falling behind in my finances, and Ian was drifting even further away from me. He was eighteen years old and six foot two. I found myself considering whether I could fetter him in irons, chain him to the stone wall in the basement. I told him that he was not playing fair. Lucy had died; I suffered agonies, not knowing what had happened to him. "I don't care what you are doing, who you are with, or where. Phone me." A television show sported a running gag, a streamer on the bottom of the screen: "Oedipus, call your mother." I was not amused, although there was some small comfort in knowing that what I was suffering was part of a national epidemic. One of the few times I did get a phone call, Ian told me he was in the East Village, in bed with two people (male and female). They had asked him to get up, to fetch their stash from a shelf in the kitchen. "That's why I'm calling you," he said. "They keep their grass in a tin biscuit box with a picture of Elizabeth and Margaret Rose on the cover, like the one Nana has. I just wanted you to know that I'm in bed with nice WASP kids you would approve of."

He was not being disingenuous. And he was not usually so cruel. There were moments of gentleness and insight. When his father remarried, he said that he wished that I had someone to love, too. Then: "I've been trying to say this important thing to you. I'm trying to get it right. I want you to get married again, but I don't want to have to like the person you marry. But I don't want you *not* to marry someone just because I don't like him . . ." Sometimes Ian's behavior was so bizarre, even hallucinatory, that his doctors began to consider that the cause was not just drugs. Drugs confused any diagnosis, but there was reason to believe that Ian was exhibiting signs of schizophrenia.

During this time, a young woman attending graduate school at Bank Street College of Education had heard about my being a freelance storyteller. She telephoned me and said she would be willing to come out to Piermont, by bus, in order to talk with me. Diane Wolkstein was a storyteller – of a new breed, as I was. She did not belong to the Libraryland coterie of storytellers, but was an independent, aching to break the old rigidities, strike out in new directions. After majoring in French and drama at Smith College, she had gone to live in Paris. She made her living by selling the *International Herald Tribune* on the streets, telling stories in a synagogue, and acting as reader-companion-storyteller to an old lady. She had converted an African-American folk song into a children's book, which was about to be published, and she was in correspondence with one of my favorite collectors, Harold Courlander. He was an authority on African and Haitian folklore. Her ambition was to go to Haiti and collect Creole stories, in the field. (Eventually she would produce a classic collection, *The Magic Orange Tree*.) She was erudite, funny, outrageous, and ambitious. She was my first real colleague, someone with whom I could talk shop. Although she was twenty years younger than I, we would become life-long friends.

Unexpectedly, I heard from my old acquaintance, Leona Garvey, who had been the children's librarian in Berkeley when John was going to library school. She was now head of children's libraries in St. Louis, Missouri. She was inviting me to speak to the Missouri Library Association (MLA).

In October 1967, I flew out to St. Louis. Before I gave my address, I was introduced to Charles O'Halloran, State Librarian, a tall, personable man probably in his early forties, and to Susanne Alexander, his assistant. They, in turn, introduced me to a blue-haired lady who spent most of her time knitting a strip of baby-blue wool, about three inches wide and several miles long. I learned that the lady was director of children's services at the State Library. When, overcome with curiosity, I asked her what she was knitting, and for whom it was intended, she told me: "Bandages for lepers." Her mother, grandmother, great-grandmother, and all the aunts had pledged to keep a certain hospital in the Congo supplied, as long as they had breath in their bodies.

Leona Garvey had expected me to talk about my book, *How the Heather Looks: A Joyous Journey to the British Sources of Children's Books*. Instead, I disappointed and upset her by talking about my work with the children in Nyack, and at Saint Agatha. This was to be the first of my many misunderstandings with the State of Missouri! Charles O'Halloran, however, clasped my hand warmly and said he thought my work was on the cutting edge of what he thought library work with children should be. I also met A. P. Marshall, head librarian at Lincoln University, an institution that had been founded for free men and former slaves just after the Civil War. Mr. Marshall (everyone called him "A.P.") explained to me that both the State Library and Lincoln University were in Jefferson City, the state capital of Missouri. He told me that he had been so impressed by what I had to say about black learning patterns that he was determined to have me to speak to the students at his university. He was going to try to get a grant to pay for me to act as a consultant. At the end of the conference, when I was standing in the receiving line, A.P. shook my hand firmly, looked me in the eye, and said, "You will be hearing from me."

In November 1967, in protest against the Vietnam war, I went down to Washington, to march on the Pentagon. The weather promised foul, so I wore my old yellow raincoat. I knew that a contingent of Rockland County people had preceded me. When I arrived, I looked for them, but the crowd was so enormous that I abandoned the hope. I saw an old army buddy, I saw someone from Astoria high-school days, I saw a man whom I thought I knew, under a sign that said VETERANS AGAINST VIETNAM. Nagged by his familiar features, I fell in with him and his fellow marchers. I asked him if he had ever lived in Shanks Village? Almost as good! He turned out to be Norman Mailer.

As we crossed the Lincoln Memorial Bridge I looked down, saw cobblestones beneath my feet. Same bridge, same cobblestones I had marched over before, on the way to Franklin D. Roosevelt's funeral. *One foot in front of the other.* Something was happening up ahead. We had to sit down and wait. Someone had a radio. A tinny voice was saying that the marchers were rioting on Lincoln Memorial Bridge. We old soldiers turned to each other. *I'm not rioting. Are you rioting? No, I'm not rioting. I'm sitting on my ass.* Typical SNAFU, we old soldiers agreed. We began marching again. Mailer and I were marching along together when we came to an overpass. One kid, with less sense than enthusiasm, had allowed himself to be lowered by his ankles, head-first, while he waved a banner almost in our faces.

When we got to the Pentagon, Mailer disappeared into the crowd. I wandered about on the huge lawn, talked to people of all ages, kinds, conditions. The middle-aged and elderly were neatly, sensibly dressed, as though they were going for a Sunday-afternoon stroll. A young man, perched in a tree, saw an old classmate from Dartmouth down below. Each had found a job, teaching college English 101. An earnest discussion ensued, concerning the best text to use. Some people were smart enough to have brought sandwiches in brown paper bags. Lots of people had brought toothbrushes and a change of underwear, in case they landed up in jail or could not get transportation home. I cursed myself for not having had as much foresight. Now, gazing up at the Pentagon, I contrasted the past (when I had worked in the War Department code room) with the present (when I stood outside its walls, laying siege). I looked up. Soldiers were standing on top of the Pentagon, their guns aimed at us. Surely Lyndon Johnson, patron saint of the Great Society, purveyor of funds for Head Start, would not want to shoot me! But he was several miles away, across the Potomac, in the White House.

More soldiers formed a ring around the five-storied, five-sided ziggurat. I surmised that they had come from Fort Meyers, perhaps from the very barracks where I used to live. They were hardly more than kids. Some demonstrators, youths and maidens their age, had walked right up to them, as they stood in rank. Eye-to-eye, nose-to-nose, the flower children were threading chrysanthemum stems into rifle barrels, smiling and talking all the while. They were trying to convince the soldiers to step forward, to leave their place in rank and join the protestors. I was furious at the irresponsibility and cruelty of the flower children. A soldier, a kid their own age, could be shot as a deserter, or spend years in Leavenworth. Kids in uniform were not the ones to persuade. The generals, the secretaries, and, yes, Lyndon Baines Johnson, were who we should be talking to. Where were they?

November clouds hung to the ground, like dirty sheets. Cold crept into my bones. I wanted to pee. I heard a voice shouting military orders, orders I couldn't make out. I shinnied halfway up a small tree, the better to see and hear. More soldiers, marching down from Arlington, had come to a halt on the west lawn. At last the lowering sun was breaking through, shooting beams of light from beneath the clouds, just as a voice barked, "Unsheathe bayonets!" For the first and last time (I hope) I saw sunlight glint and ripple along a line of steel, as bayonets were being bared. Now I knew what fear was! I thought of the Boston Massacre! Thought of Peterloo! We ran. I read in a newspaper the next day that the field was littered with discarded brassieres and panties, further proof of the immoral and (therefore) unpatriotic tendencies of the rioting crowd. Believe instead: the rioting crowd was made up of ordinary middle-class American citizens who could not conceive of going even one day without clean underwear.

In the early months of 1968, as he had promised, I received a letter from A. P. Marshall, the librarian from Lincoln University. He was inviting me to come to Jefferson City for three days. He wanted me to talk to the faculty and students there. In conjunction with Charles O'Halloran at the State Library, he had been able to get a grant to pay my fare and expenses, plus honorarium. O'Halloran's letter followed. He would like me to spend a day at the State Library, where he would be eager to hear my opinions on the children's collection, and on the role the library should play now and in the next decade. Moreover, he had arranged for me to tell stories at the governor's mansion. Children from all over Missouri would be brought to hear me. I accepted the invitation.

On April 4, 1968, a week before I left for Missouri, Martin Luther King was assassinated. In June, Robert Kennedy would be assassinated. In July, when he turned eighteen, Ian would go before the draft board. Despite his obsession with soldiers, he never went to war. He frightened his draft board, he frightened *me*, by declaring that, if he had been at the My Lai massacre, he would have shot Lieutenant Calley, and, furthermore, he would shoot any officer who ordered him to shoot a civilian. This, plus a letter from his psychiatrist, decided the members of the draft board that he was too crazy to be sent to Vietnam.

By now, Ian definitely spent more time in Greenwich Village than he did in Piermont. In less than a year, when he turned nineteen, I would no longer receive money to keep a home for the two of us. The time was fast approaching for John and me to sell the house on Ritie Street. My coracle tugged at its moorings. I would soon be adrift, not knowing what lay around the next bend in the river.

CHAPTER 21

Hulla's Well

THERE EXISTS A GENRE of fairy tale in which the hero or heroine must go through a door, or run through a forest, or face a dragon, or jump down a hole, not knowing the outcome. The only weapon that will counteract the risk must be tempered in spontaneity.

Lincoln Institute, now Lincoln University, had been established in 1866, just after the Civil War. The Student Union building was brand new, paid for out of LBJ's New Society programs. In the classroom, when I talked about my observations and experiences with black children, these black students lolled back, eyes hooded. Kids don't like to show excitement or emotion, especially when hit with something that is disturbing to them. I could not figure whether the students were resisting me because I was an over-thirty-not-to-be-trusted adult, because I was white, or because I was boring. Some kids were nodding off. (Ian had taught me more than I wanted to know about recognizing the symptoms.) Here and there I caught a gleam, a telltale hint of intelligent life on Mars. Maybe they were just putting me on.

On the day that I spent with Charles O'Halloran and Susanne Alexander, they took me on a tour of the State Library. The State Library was for reference purposes only. The children's collection was not meant for children, but for the use of teachers and librarians. Most of the books were *about* children and children's books. The choice struck me as being very safe, very outdated, and I said so. I had expected to meet the leper-bandage lady, but she was not even mentioned. Only later did O'Halloran break the news to me: she had been killed while driving between Jefferson City and the city of Columbia, Missouri, where the state university was. Her position had not been filled.

After lunch, I took a walk before going back to my hotel to rest and to prepare for the storytelling session at the governor's mansion. Jefferson City is not very big. The Capitol and other government buildings, including the State Library, are set on a ridge above the Missouri River. The Capitol dome dominates the city. What I was not prepared for was the governor's mansion. So elegant, so French! I had forgotten that New France, stretching from Quebec to New Orleans, had once governed this territory. I had not thought to connect the name of the city with the Louisiana Purchase, with Thomas Jefferson's role in removing the curb to Anglo-America's westward expansion. But the French connection had not been forgotten by the Victorian architect. He had designed a *faux château*, made of wood. Perfectly proportioned, it had a mansard roof, delicate carvings, and was painted in shades of pale pink, green, and cream. All gaiety and charm, it stood in stark contrast to the high, bleak wall of the state prison, just across the street.

A.P. came to the hotel, to escort me to the storytelling session. As we ascended the steps of the mansion, I felt like Shirley Temple in *The Little Colonel*, dancing up those movie-set steps with Bojangles, for on either side of each broad step stood a black man, each dressed in a spiffy white uniform. As in a chorus, they grinned and grinned; they capered and shuffled, and grinned again, waving us on, bowing elaborate welcomes. I was embarrassed, and also bewildered. Only later, much later, did A.P. tell me that these men were from the prison across the street, trustys detailed to serve the governor and his family as personal servants. The reason they were grinning so was because this was an historic moment. Forbidden to speak, each white-clad black American was trying, with every gesture, to convey his awareness of the significance of the occasion: Albert P. Marshall was the first black man ever to enter through the front door of the governor's mansion – as an invited guest.

Children, teachers and librarians were waiting for us in the entrance hall, just inside the door. Actually, it was a rotunda, with a cantilevered staircase that seemed to float in space. From the dome of the rotunda, suspended on a long chain, hung a crystal chandelier. I knew at once what story I would begin with! When Childe Rowland entered the Elf King's hall, he saw that . . . *The roof was supported by fine pillars, all of gold and silver, with fretted work, and between them, and around them, wreaths of flowers, composed of what do you think? Why, of diamonds, and emeralds, and all manner of precious stones. And the very keystones of the arches met in the middle of the roof, and just there, hung by a gold chain, an immense pearl was hollowed out, all pearly and transparent, like a lamp. And in the middle of this was an enormous ruby, which kept spinning round and round, so that crimson light shivered and shimmered throughout the hall . . .* This was an image that Lucy had used, after her first operation, to let me know that she knew that she might be going to die. *But don't think about that now, not now!*

Only one black child, a boy, was in the audience. For him I told "The Cowtail Switch," emphasizing ahead of time that the story came from west Africa, where the Ashanti people are very tall, handsome, and intelligent. "In the middle of the story there will be a sort of trial. The listeners move right into the story and start to argue, to take sides, over which son should own the cowtail switch. The Ashanti people love argument, love to talk about ideas. They are very smart."

Afterwards, the boy edged up to me, whispered shyly that he had liked the story about "the Indians." I had to stop and think. "No," I said. "Those people were not Indians. They were *black* people – tall, handsome, and intelligent. Not Indians. Africans. Black, like you. Smart, like you." The kid looked scared to death. He had one arm shorter than the other. Withered. Shriveled. Probably a birth defect. Maybe that's why he was allowed to come to this auspicious event: no need to fear a Negro male – if he's a little boy, one-armed, and small for his age.

Tea and cookies afterwards. O'Halloran politely fetched me a cup and invited me to come sit in a velvet-draped window seat with him. He wanted to talk to me, he said. I was tired, looking forward to catching my plane in another hour. He told me that he had not replaced the leper-bandage lady. Her job, director of children's services, State Library of Missouri, was still open. He was offering it to me. Yes, he knew that I was not a librarian. My mandate would be to wake up the children's librarians of Missouri. He wanted me to make them aware of what was happening in the 1960s, and to lead them, eyes wide open, into the 1970s. He wanted me to move to Jefferson City as soon as possible.

In the "Mother Hulla" story, there are two sisters. When the first sister drops her spindle (her own story, so far) down the well, her stepmother tells her she must go fetch it. The girl does what has to be done: *she jumps down the well, not knowing what will happen to her. She wanders through a meadow (a cosmic, once-upon-a-time place) and, again,* does what has to be done, *however mundane, however cosmic. She responds spontaneously – plucks the paleolithic apples, milks the neolithic cow, rescues the baked (manufactured) bread. When she comes to a little house, she is frightened by the old woman who peers through the window, but* she does what has to be done. *She knocks on the door, asks for help, and takes a job – to keep house for the old woman, for a year and a day.*

At the end of the time, she asks to be returned to her own world. The old woman tells her to stand in a doorway, and to hold out her apron. She is rewarded by a shower of gold. When she returns home, every time she speaks, gold coins come out of her mouth.

The second sister (my prudent, cautious side) wants the same thing to happen to her. With the approval of authority (the overprotective witch mother), she sets out to live her sister's story. Dressed in warm clothes, supplied with a good lunch, using her sister's map, she believes she is taking no risks. All she has to do is follow directions, do what has been done before. Scornful, she fails to respond to the blandishments of the menial-cosmic tasks. She rushes towards the house and the old woman, whom she sees as an easy touch, rather than someone to be viewed with holy awe. (Frau Hulla is really the great goddess in disguise.) She sees no reason to honor her contract. Long before time is up, she demands her payoff. Confidently, smugly, she goes to stand in the doorway, expecting a shower of gold. Instead, she is covered with pitch and soot (in some versions, shit). When she speaks, toads hop out of her mouth.

Back home, I talked over the job offer with Ian, with Bette, with Eugene and Trish DuBow, who were Bette's lodgers at the time. I even talked it over with John. Eventually, I would have to give up the house where Ian and I were living. Ian still spent more time in the city than he did in Rockland County. I was not leaving Ian; he had already elected to leave me. If I didn't let go, take a risk, I would lose the chance to take on an important job, a whole new life.

Ian was concerned for my welfare: "Do they know what they're getting?" he asked. As for advice on the interview, he said: "Do something big. Suggest they knock down a wall, or something!" Eugene DuBow, social worker and a New York City parole officer, was a level-headed male friend to whom I turned. He advised me to ask O'Halloran for the chance to revisit Jefferson City before I made up my mind. He pointed out that the offer had been sprung on me at the last minute, after an exhausting three-day consultancy. I should value myself enough to ask the State of Missouri to pay my way out there, so I could look the place over in a new light.

I did what had to be done. I flew out to St. Louis a few days later, and caught the little seven-seater that flew to Jefferson City. I was shown around the library, shown the desk I would occupy if I took the job. I thought about what Ian had said, about knocking down a wall. My predecessor had created a collection and environment of unmitigated blandness. No one would guess that the sixties were in full swing. Ian was right. The wall must go! O'Halloran impressed upon me that what he wanted was to bring the children's librarians of the state into the turbulent present. Susanne Alexander showed me a film, about the library, and about O'Halloran's great works there, of which she was touchingly proud. In 1968, the electronic revolution lay in the future, but O'Halloran quite rightly saw the importance of keeping abreast of ways to communicate. If I took the job, he would want me to act as a model for the children's librarians of Missouri, show them, by example, how to implement films from the new federal film deposit in Nebraska. My other mandate was to haul these same people, maybeit kicking and screaming, into the new era of the 1960s and 1970s. The State Library of Missouri had been a backwater. Youthful, handsome, intelligent, ambitious, charming, O'Halloran yearned for greatness. Like Parsifal, he had been living in the backwoods too long. He wanted out. I was to be part of the plan.

Once again, I explored the town. This time I walked along the main street. I did not know then, but some of the non-professional staff were watching me from a window. They said later that they knew right away that I would be trouble – because of the way I walked. (I still wore flat shoes, still took thirty-inch strides.) I noticed a tiny clapboard synagogue on a side street. I dropped into Levy's shoe store, the only Jewish establishment in town. The Brothers Levy were in their early forties. They wore hats indoors, and looked like the people on the Lower East Side of Manhattan, but when they opened their mouths, pure Missouri issued forth. Were there other Jewish families who lived in town, I asked? Thirty-two families, I was told. The little wooden synagogue was the oldest one west of the Mississippi. What was it like, living in Jefferson City? Could I survive? One of the brothers had gone to Columbia University in New York, but had returned home after two years, to help run the shoe store. In retrospect, he was grateful for the experience, he said. He and his brother took me seriously. We must have talked for an hour. We came to the conclusion that it might be possible for me to live in Jefferson City. We came to the conclusion that, yes, I could do it, but that the doing would be difficult.

Now that Robert Kennedy had been assassinated, Hubert Humphrey and Eugene McCarthy were the only contenders for the Democratic nomination. In July, Bette and I, with our kids, watched the Chicago convention on television. In the parks outside the convention hall, Mayor Richard Daley's policemen were beating up demonstrators, non-demonstrating bystanders, even journalists. The police seemed to single out those who were young; they beat heads savagely. Ian, Katie, and Christopher went off to bed; Bette and I were still watching at two o'clock in the morning. Survivors, bloodied and disoriented, were wandering on the battlefield, trying to find a way to safety. Camera crews, recording the events, were constantly waved off or menaced by the police. Ordinary Chicago citizens, who, like us, had probably been watching television, began to show up, cruising in cars, engaged in a spontaneous rescue mission. We saw a woman, about our age, drive across the grass. (She looked like the kind of person who did not usually *walk* on grass.) She opened her car door, called, "Get in, kids!" The police turned towards her, clubs raised. Brave – and dignified – she outfaced them, while a clutch of kids clambered into her car, pulled their friends in after them. She sped off quickly, car door flapping. Bette and I turned to each other: *Dunkirk!*

In August, Ann Eagle invited me to spend two weeks at the Eagles' summer home on Martha's Vineyard. Ann's husband, Vernon, was three-quarter Sioux, raised in a Jesuit orphanage. Too young to go to Spain, he got himself over to England as soon as he was eighteen, to be trained as a commando. He was assigned to the French resistance; wounded, he had to have his left leg sawed off at the hip, under primitive conditions. When he returned to the States, he was accepted at Harvard. Brilliant, bitter, manifestly heroic, he was welcomed into an inner circle of powerful intellectuals and wealthy radicals.

On Martha's Vineyard, there was a tacit truce, an understanding, that for the month of August a person was safe on the Vineyard, no matter what was going on in Washington, whatever was happening on the stock exchange, in academe, in the press and other media. Every year, an inner circle (all male) participated in a sort of paleolithic ritual – picking beach plums together, making jam together – presumably as they decided the fate of the nation. A gift of a little jar of Vineyard beach-plum jam, picked and potted by the priesthood, served to confer instant status on the receiver.

One morning, Vernon casually informed Ann that he had invited a score or so of people to a little dinner party, so, the appointed day, we all rose early to clean the house from attic to root cellar. We got the kids to help us lug in a picnic table from the yard, to take care of the overflow guests. Although I had not met any of the people who were coming, I felt I already knew some of them. I had read what they had been writing for years, seen their pictures in the newspaper or on TV. Adam Yarmolinsky was there, along with several other knights from John Kennedy's Camelot. John Oakes, Scotty Reston, Anthony Lewis (from the *New York Times*) came with their wives. Michael Straight, who was publisher of the *New Republic*, sat across from me. His wife sat on Vernon's right; I sat next to her. Nicholas Katzenbach, undersecretary of state, sat on the other side of me.

Belinda ("Bin") Straight was willowy, blonde, aristocratic. On that hot and humid August evening she wore a yellow chiffon dress, pleated like a Greek chiton; it floated from her shoulders, making a little breeze wherever she went. Vernon leaned over to introduce her to me. Patting her hand paternally, he spoke over her head, as though she were a child: "You would never dream that this little lady has five children, holds a degree from Cambridge, and an M.D. besides." Then, to her, "How do you do it, my dear?"

She withdrew her hand. "Because I'm twice as smart as you, and because I work ten times as hard." In her place (in 1968), I would have blushed, felt angry (not knowing why), stammered out some sort of "*'Tain't nothing.*" I was stunned by her coolness and self-assurance. Grim salvos echoed in her tone: Fort Sumter was being fired upon.

Conversation turned to the war in Vietnam. Katzenbach's wife was visibly upset, because people were hammering at her husband, Nick. "You sit here and say all the right things when you are with us," Reston accused, "but you continue to sit in Johnson's cabinet."

"Resign! Resign!" came the cries. Katzenbach defended himself, his loyalty: "The President's job is such a lonely one . . . Johnson is surrounded by hawks . . . at least I have Johnson's ear . . ." Someone else cut in: "We have reached a period that must be like pre-war Germany. Brother against brother, friend against friend. We can't go on pretending, as though nothing is happening . . ."

"Can't go on picking beach plums together," Vernon interjected.

"This dinner party may be our last," Reston said.

"However much pain that costs?" asked Anthony Lewis.

"The time for mere politeness is past," said Reston. "Each of us must take a position, according to his conscience. It's not good enough, Nick, to say you disagree with your boss – in private, among friends. *You have to speak out in your public capacity, or we cannot continue to be friends.* Tomorrow I'm going to put a full-page ad in the *Vineyard Gazette*, asking Nicholas Katzenbach to fish or cut bait. Anyone else who wants to sign, you're welcome to join me."

"How can you do that to us?" asked Mrs. Katzenbach. "Nick is doing his best to change things. He's under terrible strain. We came to the Vineyard so my husband can get a rest. I thought the rule here is that we are all friends, no matter what." She burst into tears. Nicholas Katzenbach suddenly turned to me. "I want you to change the subject," he said. "I understand that you are an authority on children's literature. Let's talk about kids' books. But let me warn you: there's a lot of children's literature I don't like."

"There *is* a lot of schlock," I agreed. He said he wasn't talking about schlock. He was talking about books recommended by librarians and children's book experts. Take, for instance, that awful woman who lived in the Lake District. "Beatrix Potter?" I asked. Yes, that's the one he meant. When he was little, and now, when he read to his kids, he could hardly stand the anxiety of that moment when the mouse is running to and fro under the gate, carrying peas to her children in the wood. And Peter is too fat to escape, and Mr. McGregor is after him . . . But even worse was the story about the squirrel . . .

"*The Tale of Squirrel Nutkin!*" I exclaimed. Yes, that was the one. How could anyone say that it was good for a child, to hear about a squirrel having his tail snapped off – by an owl? "But Squirrel Nutkin was trespassing on Mr. Brown's territory," I countered. Despite all warning, he kept pestering Mr. Brown – saying rude things, bombarding him with nuts. "He was just getting his comeuppance," I argued. "Children are very moral. They like knowing that there are consequences for doing something bad, for going too far." Then, struck full force with the idea, I rose from my chair, extended my arm, pointed a finger at my hapless dinner companion: "*Nicholas Katzenbach,*" I thundered. "*If the United States goes on bombing North Vietnam, we are going to get our tails snapped off.*"

After Labor Day, I drove out to Missouri in my VW Beetle. It was in a frail state. So was I. A chronic infection was making me tired all the time. Our house in Piermont had been sold, but the money (no fault of John's) was slow in manifesting itself in my bank account. I had never owned a credit card, nor did it occur to me to avail myself of one. (I have been told since that, in 1968, the bank would probably have refused such to a divorced woman.) I had barely enough cash to drive across the country. I learned to pull my Volkswagen bug into truck stops, park it among the big rigs. I slept diagonally, in the back seat – head in one corner, feet propped on suitcases and the back of the tilted driver's seat. I figured that there was safety among numbers: if someone tried to attack me, I would yell bloody murder for others to rescue me.

Susanne Alexander invited me to use the separate apartment suite in her house, until I could find permanent quarters. Emotionally and physically exhausted, I was not a good houseguest. I must have seemed insufferably lazy, and I was flat broke. Eventually, probably in desperation, she found me an apartment in an old mansion that looked down on the river and the bridge that spanned it. Meanwhile, urged on by O'Halloran, I was arranging workshops for children's librarians, inviting them to come to the State Library to meet me, to look at films, to become aware of what was going on in the country and the world, and to do what we could, through books, films, and periodicals, to interpret those events to the children and young people of Missouri (or catch up with them). I also talked about the importance of storytelling, and announced that there would be a conference on storytelling, to be held in the spring of 1969.

I looked over the list of films housed in the federal film repository. I wanted to show what films were available, and I also wanted to spark discussion about what was going on among the young people who were demonstrating and rioting throughout the United States. I chose a film

about the 1930s and the events leading up to World War II, and another
film, about the Nazi persecution of the Jews in Germany and the horrific
revelations when the Allied forces liberated the survivors in the concentration camps. I had seen both of these films several times before. I also
glanced over a list of new films, and chose one that showed the November
1967 march on the Pentagon.

In my first meeting, with about twenty librarians from all over the state,
I tried to make the point that the young people who were rioting thought
honestly that the treatment of black Americans was to be equated with the
treatment of Jews in Germany, and that the war in Vietnam was unjust,
equivalent to the Germans' invasion of Poland and Czechoslovakia. (My
experience at the dinner party on Martha's Vineyard emboldened me to
take this tack.) I led off with the film about the Pentagon march. It was
called *This Is the Enemy* and, according to the credits, had been prepared
by the FBI, as a training film for U.S. marshals. I should have run through
it beforehand, but it had come later than the other films. Hippies and flower
children (always good footage) were singled out at the beginning, but the
film concentrated on the middle-aged, middle-class marchers, wolves in
sheep's clothing. "*This* is the enemy!" said a voice-over. Then there was
a shot of a group of marchers coming up to an overpass. At first I did not
grasp the significance of what I was seeing – a boy, suspended by his
heels, waving a banner? The cameraman must have, next, run ahead of
the marchers, for there was the same group, approaching once again.
They were displaying their own banner, which said: VETERANS AGAINST
VIETNAM. And here came Norman Mailer! And, wearing a ragged yellow
raincoat, there was a rather stout middle-aged woman, marching beside
him. Startled, I cried out, "That's me!"

When the lights came on again I talked about what we had just seen. I
told about my own experience at the Pentagon march and at the march
when I heard Martin Luther King. I emphasized that it was not just hippies,
not just young people, who were dissenting from the government's policy
in Vietnam. Ordinary middle-aged people, like me, like *you*, felt called
upon to stand up and be counted. I was met with blank stares. My audience
was hard to read.

I ran the other films, about the Nazi camps. When the lights came up
again there was a long silence. Someone said, "Now show us the other
side. Show us the German side." I was so stunned that at first I could not

comprehend what was being said to me. I must have stammered something; then someone, in a kindly voice, as though to an ignorant child, explained: "You have to understand that those pictures in the camp are faked. What you call the 'holocaust' never happened. Those are just actors . . ." I felt physically ill. I said, "I hear what you are saying, but I disagree." I knew they were wrong, but how could I prove it? I thought the film was proof enough, not to say all the historical data. Someone asked me if I were Jewish. I opened my mouth, thought of my friend Evelyn Bromberg, and all my other Jewish friends. "I refuse to answer that question," I said. Then I told them about how, when the Nazis proclaimed that all the Jews in Denmark must wear a yellow star, the king of Denmark had insisted on wearing a yellow star, too. "Whether or not I am Jewish has nothing to do with what we are talking about," I said. Someone, still maddeningly kind, said not to worry. Even though I did not want to admit it, everyone already knew I was Jewish. I was from New York.

I do not want to imply that every librarian there was of the same persuasion. But they were not dumbfounded, as I was; they must have heard it all before. Perhaps they had become desensitized. They listened politely to the exchange between me and my critics. Only later did a few people come up, to say that they believed the films were telling the truth. When I reported the experience, O'Halloran said that this was why he had hired me – because I was an outsider, not only to Missouri but to Libraryland. I was not programmed to react in an expected way; my reactions were spontaneous. *I was to be Sir Gawain, at King Arthur's court, the most impetuous of all the knights. My spontaneity was meant to break the frozen grip of winter, to restore the Wasteland to fruitfulness.*

I actually longed for my ex-husband, John, to discuss with him the historical and political ramifications of what I was seeing, hearing, experiencing. I tried to remember some of the lectures about his thesis on immigrant loyalties, delivered to me over the dinner table. After the Reformation, German Catholics tended to migrate to Russia and Poland. Knowing that backwoods America was dangerously anti-Catholic, they did not come to America until the way had been paved for them by German Protestants and Jews. In the 1840s, bypassing the already-settled Atlantic states, congregations of German Catholics made their way westward, to Missouri, Ohio, and Texas. There had been some vague scheme of making part of North America a German-speaking entity, a new Germania, but that idea had fallen through. Most Germans assimilated quickly and adopted the English language. However, in Missouri and Texas, the ideal of isolation had lingered. Until World War II, in some towns and villages, German was the accepted language. Local priests, hired directly from Germany, projected an atmosphere of medieval paranoia and suspicion of all outsiders.

In October, almost a year to the day when I had first come to give my speech, I attended the 1968 Missouri Library Association's annual convention. The meeting was held at a hotel in the Ozarks, in the southern part of the state. When A. P. Marshall offered me a lift back to Jefferson City, I took him up on it. Before leaving for the conference, I had gone into the tourist bureau on High Street and found a guidebook, which included a list of good restaurants. Now that I had received my first paycheck, I thought it about time I repay Mr. Marshall's frequent kindnesses, so I suggested that we stop in the next town, Westphalia, where I would treat him to an early dinner at the highly recommended restaurant there. However, when we rolled into the parking lot, it was empty. Almost before the motor stopped, I was out of the car, peering at the sign on the front door: "Closed on Mondays." When I gave him the news, A.P. began to laugh. Only then did he tell me that Negroes were not allowed to stop in Westphalia, much less eat in its famous restaurant. Ever since I had suggested dinner, he had been in an agony of mixed emotions, chief among them, terror. His daughter Satia, a student at Howard, had scolded him: he must ignore the past and march into the future, taking for granted that he had a right to go anywhere. He choked on his laughter and said, "I was *sweating*, I was so scared. Westphalia is the worst town of them all. A Negro's not even supposed to drive through here." He started up the motor; we drove off. "Still," he said, "it would have been interesting. Something to tell Satia . . ."

When I paid my visit to the tourist bureau, I had met Nell Culver, who worked there. Later, we went out for coffee several times; eventually, she asked me home to dinner. She and her husband had both been married before. Nell had two sons, in their early teens, and a younger sister, who had left university and, like my own kid, was dabbling in drugs. Nell's father owned a farm, but occasionally he (actually and metaphorically) left the plow standing in the field while he served in the state legislature, living out Jeffersonian democracy in its purest form. Her husband's grandfather had been governor of the state at the same time that Nell's grandfather had been chief justice. Her brother worked in the state attorney-general's office, Nell and Jack both worked for governmental departments. Churchmouse poor, they nevertheless knew everybody, and everything that was going on – not only in Missouri, but out there in the big world. They read voraciously, more or less the same books, same magazines, that I did, plus the Sunday *New York Times*. They were funny and witty and spoke my language. They became my alternative family.

For the next few months my job took me to every corner of the state. I delighted in its beauty and variety. I was amazed by the richness of its history: mound builders; Osages, Apaches, and Jesuit missionaries; slaves, slave owners, and abolitionists; Spanish explorers, French fur-traders, English-American farmers; mountain men, Lewis and Clark, and the pioneers who followed; coal mines, cotton, and steamboats; Mark Twain and Huck Finn; Civil War skirmishes, cattle drives, and cowboys; German immigrants and Pulitzer's esteemed *Post Dispatch*, in St. Louis; stockyards and steamy politics in Kansas City. I fell in love with Missouri!

I had started preparing for the conference on storytelling from the first day I arrived. It was to be held in April 1969, and I planned to invite my friend, Diane Wolkstein. I also had invited Dr. Julius Heuscher, a Swiss psychiatrist who lived in Los Gatos, California. I had read and admired his book, *A Psychiatric Study of Myths and Fairy Tales*, and was looking forward to meeting him.

My job also involved traveling throughout the state, acting as consultant to libraries and holding meetings with librarians. I had recently been invited to speak at a conference being held by the School of Journalism at the University of Missouri, in Columbia, Missouri, thirty-two miles away from Jefferson City. The conference would be held under the shared auspices of the American Library Association's brand new Intellectual Freedom Committee. I had not yet given much thought to what I would say about children and censorship. I would be just one more member of a rather large panel of experts, most of whom were coming from New York and Chicago. I figured that, by the time the conference got down to the last few local people, I'd have about five minutes to make my pitch. Since I was not a trained librarian, however, I decided I had better bone up on the

Library Bill of Rights, which was posted on a wall at the State Library. I had read it several times already (I didn't know that most librarians had never read it, or if they had, not since Library School).

As I remember, I started out at the conference by talking about *Where the Wild Things Are*, the picture book by Maurice Sendak that explores a child's feelings of anger. I told how I had used it with preschool children at Nyack and at Saint Agatha's. I talked about the consternation it had caused among some parents, teachers, and librarians. I also talked about how useful *Wild Things* had been when I was teaching abandoned children in the orphanage nursery school. I talked about Robert Coles's remarks on "justifiable anger." From there, I jumped into a discussion of young people who were showing their rage and frustration about the war, and about the race question, on campuses all over the United States. As advocate for children and young people at the Missouri State Library, I was interested in collecting archival materials, produced not just *for* young people, but *by* them, much of it ephemeral. If libraries ignored what was being said and produced by these angry kids, we were practicing censorship, obliterating history. I suggested that we keep some shelves empty, so as to collect and display not only books, but newspapers and pamphlets being produced by the dissidents, actual demonstration signs, bits of tie-dye clothing, embroidered blue jeans, photographs of flower-painted cars and motorcycles, advertisements for waterbeds and hot tubs. The medium is the message! We should not be afraid of the messenger.

People clapped politely when I was done. All during the conference students and reporters – from the Library School, the School of Journalism, the campus newspaper, the city newspaper – were industriously taking notes. Others, with self-important bustle, were taping and filming every word. You would think we were the United Nations Security Council! I am not sure if I paused to consider where all this information was going, what was going to happen to it. Published in newspapers? Discussed in class? Warehoused for posterity? *Implemented?* (The date was February 7, 1969. Thirty years later I have been unable to find, anywhere in Missouri, a record of what was said that day, by me or any of the other invited speakers.)

Other forces were sweeping the campus. On February 12, members of Students for a Democratic Society set up a booth in the Student Union (the very building where the Intellectual Freedom Conference had been held) and started selling copies of *New Left Notes* and *The Movement*, alternative newspapers that were circulating on other campuses throughout the country. At M.U., the papers were immediately banned, the students ordered out of their booths. A week later, students issued a paper of their own, the *Free Press Underground*.

Because the paper was banned, not even the State Library could get a copy of it, despite my best efforts. Nor could members of the State Legislature, or the library staff, or the members of the State Library commission. The police had destroyed the evidence! Finally, a reluctant student let me have a peek. Most of the front page of the *Free Press Underground* was taken up by a cartoon, reproduced from the previously banned *Movement*; it also reprinted an article from there. The cartoon showed the Statue of Liberty, lying on its (her?) back. A line of Mayor Daley's policemen, trousers dropped, were waiting in line to rape her. The cartoon was shocking, well drawn, obviously professional.

The article inside, which would cause so much sensation, was sophomoric and consisted of little more than its headline: MOTHER FUCKERS PARDONED IN BOSTON. Members of a Boston street gang, using the above appellation, had been pardoned – not for fucking their mothers, which was not the charge, but for petty theft, which could not be proved. Gotcha! I was annoyed by the silliness of the trick. The only article worth reading in the whole paper was about how to get to Canada in order to avoid the draft.

This time, when the students selling the paper were ordered out of the Union building, four students were arrested on the sidewalk. Violence was narrowly averted when other students gathered. On February 24, when a student discipline committee was meeting, twenty-five hundred students rallied. The student committee dismissed the charges, but the university chancellor decided to take action anyway.

Saturday night, I drove over to Columbia to see a play produced by the university drama department. The play was about Galileo's famous trial, in which he was condemned by the Inquisition for agreeing with Copernicus that the earth moves around the sun. Over the weekend, I decided to write a letter, not to the official campus newspaper, but to the editor of the Columbia *Tribune*. On Monday morning, I was disappointed to find that O'Halloran had gone to Kansas City, so I could not discuss my letter with him. I told Susanne Alexander what I was doing. She said she had a noon telephone appointment with Charles, and would be glad to read the letter

to him over the phone. I remember leaving my desk, walking over to the
wall to re-read the framed copy of the Library Bill of Rights:

III. Libraries should challenge censorship in the
    fulfillment of their responsibility to provide
    information and enlightenment.

IV. Libraries should cooperate with all persons
    and groups concerned with resisting
    abridgement of free expression and free access
    to ideas.

*Pick the apples, milk the cow, save the bread from burning. I did what had
to be done.* I wrote the letter, first by hand, then did a draft on my typewriter. Alexander read the letter, said she liked it. Early in the afternoon
she came into my office to tell me that she had read it to O'Halloran. "He
said to tell you he's proud of you," she reported. When I typed the final
draft, I used official State Library stationery and signed my name officially:
Joan Bodger, Consultant to Services for Children and Young People, State
Library, Missouri. I did so with no intention of deceit. If I had been writing
a private letter, I would have seen no reason to run it by my boss. I took it
for granted O'Halloran understood that. I was remembering what Scotty
Reston had said at the dinner party on Martha's Vineyard – about how
important it was to protest in one's official capacity. I also remembered
Hannah Arendt's book, *The Banality of Evil*, which was about Adolf
Eichmann, the Nazi bureaucrat who made the trains run on time – to the
concentration camps. Arendt had pointed out that, although they may have
done so in private, no German bureaucrat had ever questioned or deplored
the purpose of those trains *in official capacity*. And I remembered what my
old professor, Dr. Pitman, had said about his elderly counterparts in Nazi
Germany: with nothing much to lose, they chose, even so, not to risk
voicing their dissent.

My letter was published in the Columbia *Tribune* on March 26, 1969,
under the heading "Stargazers Banned." My short message touched on the
irony of the State University allowing its drama department to produce a
play about the Inquisition, while at the same time the administration was
arresting and threatening to expel students for speaking what they believed

to be the truth. The First Amendment assures that everyone has the right to publish and distribute a newspaper, however upsetting its contents. The recent conference, scheduled to be held at the university's recently established Intellectual Freedom Center, had spelled this out. When I had spoken at that conference, saying almost the same thing as I was saying in the letter, no one had disapproved. In my own mind, I equated the act of *writing* in my official capacity with the act of *speaking* in my official capacity.

Across the street from the Capitol building there was a restaurant, famous for its eggs and ham, red-eye gravy, grits, and biscuits. On the next Sunday morning I decided to treat myself to breakfast there, but first I stopped at the drugstore, the only place in town that carried the *New York Times*. Browsing, I spotted a banner headline in the *Jefferson City Post-Tribune*: COMMUNIST PORNOGRAPHER IN STATE LIBRARY? Naturally I was interested. I worked in the State Library! I paid my money and bought a copy of the newspaper. I discovered that a woman named Joan Bodger was the Communist pornographer in question.

CHAPTER 22

The Loathly Lady

THE WOMEN IN THE staff room, eating their bag lunches, had asked me what kind of gun I carried in the glove compartment of my car. When I said I had no gun and did not intend to buy one, they had exchanged meaningful glances. I came to understand that they had marked me as a woman who did not care what happened to her, a woman who would be asking for it. After the news broke in the Jefferson City paper, the brown-baggers in the lunch room would quiz me about Communism. One woman in particular pursued me with untoward zest. Eyes glittering, she wore an enameled look – the same look she wore when she talked about her hot flashes. I worked out a syllogism, applicable to her thinking process: sex is a forbidden evil; Communism is a forbidden evil; sex is therefore Communism and Communism is therefore sex. Ergo: Joan Bodger, defender of a dirty Communist newspaper, is a walking embodiment of Communist pornography. Just talking to me gave her an orgasmic thrill!

In the midst of all this, *I did what I had to do.* I continued to visit libraries throughout the state, and worked on my plans for the conference on storytelling, to be held April 12. The publicity had gone out, the hall was rented, the guest speakers had been hired, their plane tickets paid for. Julius Heuscher, the Swiss psychiatrist, arrived from California – a gift from heaven. We discussed his book, *A Psychiatric Study of Myths and Fairy Tales.* He listened to me, let me listen to myself, as I told my own story of recent events. He talked about the Grail legends, likening my predicament to that of a knight, a warrior, who faces danger, not knowing what the outcome will be. I acknowledge my warrior, but the parallel story, more meaningful to me, was still "Mother Hulla" – both cosmic and domestic.

I did what had to be done. With no guarantees, not knowing what was going to happen, *I jumped down the well.* Newspapers throughout the state attacked me, attacked Charles O'Halloran, attacked the State Library. O'Halloran was humiliated and reprimanded by the board. In an agony of *mea culpa*, he volunteered that he had been "imprudent, impulsive, and impertinent" – as if those were bad qualities to have, when fascism was knocking at the door. The governor wrote a letter to O'Halloran, telling him he wished his daughters to be kept out of the State Library as long as Joan Bodger worked there.

Diane Wolkstein arrived with her fiancé, Bernard Zucker. I was glad to have them as moral support, although much was being made about their sharing a hotel room. Diane went with me while I bought a new dress. I was in the fitting booth, expecting to have a hemline shortened, when the salesgirl, pale and trembling, rushed out. She did not notice Diane, sitting in a chair nearby, when she implored her supervisor to take her place. "It's *her*," she said. "That woman! The Communist!" By coincidence, ex-president Eisenhower died. O'Halloran wanted to call off the storytelling conference "out of respect." I refused to do that. The two days passed without incident and seemed to be, somewhat surprisingly, a success. The guests departed.

Here and there I did receive some support. A woman telephoned me from Joplin, Missouri. Two schoolteachers from Boston, about to embark on a Mississippi River cruise, read between the lines of an article in a newspaper and telephoned to say they wished to commend me for my courage. When I checked into a motel, in a town where I had promised to visit the local library, the woman at the desk watched carefully as I signed my name. "You write big," she commented. Then, hesitatingly, admiringly, "You aren't one to be afraid, are you?" Me and John Hancock.

Maybe I didn't have the wit to be afraid. From his vantage point in Greenwich Village, Ian offered to come out and stay with me. He was worried for my physical safety. The liberal writer for *Esquire* magazine, Nat Hentoff, called to offer encouragement. My Jefferson City friend Nell Culver warned me I should watch my back. I didn't know what she was talking about. A man from Kansas City called me. He said he had had an

experience, something like mine, happen to him a few years ago. He knew
how it felt to be in such a lonely position. Perhaps we could have coffee?

We met, we talked. He had lost his job over the incident; his marriage
had fallen apart. I told him about my marriage, about Lucy, about Ian. We
met again, had dinner. He came up to my apartment. We went to bed
together. I didn't want sex so much as to have someone – a man – put his
arms around me! Neither of us ever completely undressed; sex was not
happening. After about an hour, the would-be lover said he had to leave –
he had an appointment somewhere else. "You haven't asked very much
about me," he said. "I could be anybody. Has it occurred to you that I could
be a member of the MBI?" Again, I didn't know what he was talking about.
I am embarrassed to confess that my focus was on being rejected – sexually rejected – yet again. I didn't ask what he meant, and he left without
telling me.

The next day Nell Culver told me we must meet for coffee. "My brother
(in the attorney-general's office) says to be careful. They're going to try
to frame you; they'll find something on your expense account, or set you
up sexually."

"Who's they?" I asked.

"The MBI. The Missouri Bureau of Investigation," she said. I began to
laugh. I could not believe that anything so silly could exist. Like the Swiss
Navy! I suppose I was laughing hysterically. I was too ashamed to tell Nell
(glamorous, experienced Nell) what had happened. I was ashamed for
(almost) having sex with a stranger. I was ashamed for *not* having sex, for
being rejected. I was ashamed for being ashamed. Years went by before I
could tell anyone what had happened (not happened) to me. True or not, I
believed (still believe) a spy had been sent to seduce me – and found me
to be a lady too loathly for seduction. Or maybe he was not professional
enough to go through with it.

One good thing did occur, to restore my faith in human nature. My old
friends, the Brothers Levy, waylaid me on High Street and told me that
their mother had invited me to dinner. We had sorrel soup. And lamb. I had
not been able to buy lamb, either at the butcher's or at the A&P supermarket. Missouri was cattle country, the A&P manager had explained to me.
Sheep nibble grass down to the root, leaving nothing for free-ranging
cattle. In the old days there had been wars; sheep farmers were killed or
driven out. He said he used to order lamb for the few Jewish families in

town, but for the past few years lamb-eaters had had to drive all the way to St. Louis, almost two hundred miles away. That's what one of the Levy brothers had done, as an ultimate gesture of hospitality.

Mrs. Levy was tiny, hardly more than four feet tall. She had been a mail-order bride, coming all the way from Russia to Jefferson City, Missouri, in 1904, to meet and marry her husband, who was a shoemaker. She had gone hardly anywhere since. She rose suddenly from the table, went over to the window, to lower the shades. "Just as well that people don't see who we are having to dinner. I have not thought about such things for many years," she said. "Quite like living in pogrom times, isn't it?"

Now, wherever I went, I was greeted with stares – as though I were a freak – and sometimes with insults. When I gave a pre-arranged talk in St. Charles, Missouri (on playing, pretending, creativity, and their relevance to poetry, stories, books), a band of mothers and children picketed the library, which was housed in a storefront in a shopping mall. The women in the group, organized by the John Birch Society, carried buckets and mops. "Wash away Joan Bodger's filth," the signs said. Also, "Jesus Christ, Save Our Children."

An elderly reporter, sent by the local newspaper, having settled his considerable bulk onto a child-size chair, had fallen asleep. He snored audibly. I was facing the audience of parents and librarians; their backs were to the storefront's huge plate-glass window. As I spoke, the demonstrators outside grew louder and more frenzied in their protestations. They pushed towards the window, mouthing words I could not hear, shaking their fists – and their mops. They were not paying attention to their children, who were being pressed against the large expanse of glass so hard that I feared it would break and they would fall through, on jagged shards. *Jesus Christ, where are you?* I tried to warn the women that their children were in danger by waving my arms; they interpreted my motions as defiance (or lewdness), and only became more excited.

The audience inside the library was looking at me askance, wondering if they did indeed have a loony on their hands, as I danced up and down, gestured. All of this took place within seconds. At last some police cars arrived behind the crowd, pulled the women back a few feet; their children fell back, too. No one else had seen what I had seen, that children had been placed in jeopardy. Afterwards the reporter lumbered forward to question me. He had not seen any of the drama, nor listened to the talk on play and creativity. From his pocket he produced a little notebook, a set list of questions. What did I think of the cartoon on the front page of the *Free Press Underground*? Did I think it was obscene or did I think it was political? If I thought the cartoon was political, then I did not think the subject was obscene, which meant that I was so degraded that I could not recognize obscenity. Or, if I did think the subject was obscene, then I was protecting the right to print pornography. I must have a mind that reveled in it. What did I *feel* as I looked at the cartoon? The old man almost licked his lips.

O'Halloran had only "suggested" that I not go to St. Charles; if I did insist on going, he "suggested" that I not to speak to the press. He prided himself on never giving a direct order. I kept telling the reporter that I had nothing to say. I would say nothing. No comment. Finally, as he persisted, I said, "You are boring me." Fatal answer. Next day, in the press: "Joan Bodger bored by events in Missouri . . ." I had walked right into the trap.

Easter weekend, I realized that my situation was untenable. If I carried out my job description, to travel about Missouri, visit libraries, give talks, I would be fired. If I did not follow my job description, I could be fired for not doing my job. Over the weekend I worked on my letter of resignation. I tried to reach O'Halloran by telephone several times. He was not at home, not in his office. His wife, whom I liked and respected, did not know where he was. I believed she was telling me the truth. She sounded worried. I asked her if she thought he was at Susanne Alexander's house? I called there. No answer. I kept calling all day and into the night. After a while I realized that Alexander's phone had been taken off the hook.

On Monday morning, I went to the library before eight o'clock, so early I had to let myself in with a key. O'Halloran was already in his office. I told him I was resigning, and showed him the letter, which was a declaration of my beliefs concerning free speech. O'Halloran read my statement through, said that I had obviously written it for publication. He asked me not to publish it, or to wait at least until he could notify all the people on the board. I agreed, out of courtesy. I waited all day. Again, my boss had disappeared. Again, his wife did not know where he was.

Again, on Tuesday morning, I went to the library early, and O'Halloran was in his office. He handed me a piece of paper: I had been fired. I crumpled it up, threw it on the floor. Tears jetted from my eyes. Dammit! They couldn't fire me. I had already resigned! He said that all the members of the board had agreed, unanimously, to fire me. (This later turned out to be untrue. Several members, were not reachable, perhaps because of the Easter holiday. Most important, ninety-year-old Rabbi Ferdinand Isserman, from St. Louis, had already told the board that he did not like what was going on. He had consulted with several prominent lawyers, who had said that the arrest of the students was probably unconstitutional. Firing me might be illegal; either way, what the board was doing to Joan Bodger was unethical. He hereby resigned. He died a few weeks later.)

I demanded to speak to Mrs. Jerome Duggan, chairman of the board. O'Halloran lifted the receiver from his desk phone, dialed, handed me the receiver. I got Mrs. Duggan on the first bounce. I told her that she couldn't fire me, because I had resigned the day before. Silence. Silence. I repeated what I had just said. Silence. Silence. Finally, I handed the phone back to O'Halloran, saying, "She doesn't have the guts to answer me." I went back to my own desk, and phoned the *St. Louis Post Dispatch*. The sun was barely up.

I prefaced my remarks by saying that I was saddened and disappointed that Joseph Pulitzer's original newspaper had not come to my defense; neither had the renowned school of journalism which he had founded. I mentioned that I reviewed children's books for the *New York Times*. Maybe I had reached the night editor, just going off duty, or the editor-in-chief, just coming on. Whomever, I sensed that at last I had the ear of someone important, partly because he was typing with one finger as he took down my statement. Next day (Wednesday, April 9, 1969) my statement was printed in full, in the *St. Louis Post Dispatch*.

Months later, during an official investigation by the ALA's Intellectual Freedom Committee, Duggan would say that I was fired because I had spoken obscenities to her over the telephone. O'Halloran, brave at last, acted as my witness. What Duggan had said about the sequence of events, and about Joan Bodger's remarks, he told the investigators, simply wasn't true. But he was too late. *What I had dictated to the* St. Louis Post Dispatch *may have been pure gold, but I felt covered with shit.*

Before he left the storytelling conference in Jefferson City, Julius Heuscher had strongly recommended that I register for a seminar in Gestalt therapy at the Esalen Institute, situated at Big Sur, on a remote stretch of the Pacific Coast Highway, north of Santa Barbara, south of Monterey. Esalen was famous for more than its hot springs. It had become a notorious seedbed of New Age culture, and a place reputed for sexual orgies. I was rather surprised that Dr. Heuscher, so Swiss and proper, would recommend such a place to me. But Esalen was also a spiritual center, a training ground for new methods of healing and psychotherapy. Fritz Perls, one of the pioneers of Gestalt psychotherapy, held sway there, as a sort of chief guru.

In the late 1930s, Fritz Perls and his wife, Laura, had fled Nazi Germany for South Africa, then went on to New York City. A colleague of Freud and Jung, Perls had broken with their approach to analysis. Together, he and Laura worked with Max Reinhardt's acting studio; they borrowed from theater techniques, from art, from Sufi mysticism, to devise methods by which they could apply the tenets of Gestalt psychology (a theory of perception, concerning figure against ground), to living a life. They sought to devise a new discipline, *Gestalt psychotherapy*, which would heighten awareness of the body, as well as mind, and offer existential models for behavior. Fritz was a famous womanizer. When the marriage fell apart, he moved to Esalen. He had been there for almost a decade but, a few days before I arrived, he suddenly uprooted himself and moved to Saltspring Island, in British Columbia, Canada.

I headed west. By coincidence, I had two speaking engagements scheduled, one in Nebraska, one in Kansas; in both places I had been asked to speak to children's librarians on subjects literary. The agreements had been made when Joan Bodger was regarded not as a troublemaker, but merely as the harmless author of *How the Heather Looks*, director of children's services, in Missouri. O'Halloran had been gratified to have me invited to neighboring states; he saw it as yet another feather in his cap. I was determined to keep the engagements. I could use the hundred-dollar honoraria for gasoline.

I love driving across North America. Even the uninteresting parts are interesting. Driving across the prairie, I half remembered a line from Somerset Maugham, comparing the undulating landscape of Nebraska to women's breasts. I felt like my body was becoming part of the landscape, that the landscape was part of my body. The notion was healing. In Kansas, I spent half a day clambering around a place called "Spanish Fort." It had been fortified by early Spanish explorers, but there was little doubt that they built on what remained of an earlier civilization, which had disappeared before the Spanish arrived. I also took note of the new and current migration: half of young America must have taken to the road! From time to time I picked up a hitchhiker – male or female. I usually picked up two or three separately, reasoning that passengers picked at random did not know each other, and therefore would protect me, one against the other. A couple of times, when I did not like the "feel" of someone in my car, I drove into a gas station, where there were other people about. I was completely open: "I don't know how to explain it, but the vibes are wrong." The decision, each time, was philosophically accepted.

When my motor conked out in the middle of the Arizona desert, I phoned my parents for money. I sat all day in the public library of a little town (I can't remember the name) and waited for the money to come by telegraph. I sat for a few more days, waiting for auto parts. In order to keep my new motor cool, I crossed Death Valley in the moonlight. My Volkswagen climbed from desert floor through the varied climate zones of the San Diego mountains – from cactus to cottonwood, to lemon groves, to apple groves, through deciduous hardwoods, to pine. When morning came, I found myself standing in snow, looking down on the beaches of San Diego.

My parents still lived in San Pedro. Their apartment overlooked the harbor. Father had an enormous pair of binoculars, mounted on a stand, through which he could watch the comings and goings of ships. My mother was not well; she spent a lot of time alone. Father was retired, but he might as well have had a full working day. He toured the harbor, spent time at the gym, went to various luncheons with members of the Harbor Department, or at the officers' club at the navy base on Terminal Island. Or he simply disappeared for hours. When I told my mother I was bound for Esalen, she blanched. Even she had heard of that place! I was over forty years old, but she worried about my becoming involved in something "unsavory" – namely, sex orgies. In vain I tried to calm her apprehensions by telling her I had simply signed up for a course in psychology. As a matter of fact, I was not quite sure myself what I was getting myself in for.

From San Pedro, I headed north, to Mountain View, near San Jose. I wanted to see my friends, Anita and Leonard Winston, who used to live across the street from us in Shanks Village. The Winston kids were my godchildren. (They referred to me as "the goddess," as in: "Hey, Mom, the goddess is on the phone.") Julius Heuscher lived nearby, in Los Gatos. I had already made arrangements to call on him, and now I wanted some advice on what course I should take. Over tea and biscuits we consulted the

Esalen catalogue. He suggested that I register for a two-week course in psychodrama. He assured me that it was a close cousin to Gestalt therapy.

At the beginning of the week, I did not have a glimmer of what people were talking about. I didn't understand the jargon: *letting go, a new way to be, lose your head, come to your senses, living in the here-and-now.* I felt stupid and uncomfortable. It was easy to be scornful. But the play-acting took me back to that glorious year in England, when, after our lessons, my cousins, sisters, and I produced a play.

During the week, as each of us delved into his or her unconscious, images from our lives emerged, and were acted out, with help from other members of the group. The very act of acting, accompanied by guided visualization of the past, triggered submerged experience and feeling. Dimly, I perceived that we were drawing from the same source, the same magic cauldron, from which come imagery, dreams, plots, characters, poetry, art, music, memories – and folk tales! In a flash of revelation, I knew I had been here before. When I enter fully into the state of story-telling, when I see a story afresh, no matter how many times I have told it, I somehow blunder into that secret country, into a place that verges on (but is *not*) insanity. I was already hooked on storytelling. Now, at Esalen, without benefit of drugs, I was hooked again: I was tripping out! The Doors of Perception creaked invitingly. To be stuck outside those doors is to live a life without magic, or spirituality, or fun. To be stuck inside is to live a life of delirium, illusion, craziness. By very definition, play is defined by the element of choice. I wanted to learn how to travel back and forth through those doors – at will, when I wanted to, by choice.

In 1928, when the famous anthropologist Leo Frobenius gave a paper on the force of the demonic in childhood, he recited an incident about a professor (himself, perhaps?) who was told to keep an eye on a five-year-old. *Trying to keep his child from bothering him, he gives her three burnt matches to play with. Immediately she dubs them: Hansel, Gretel, witch. Time elapses, then a shrill scream makes the father jump. His little girl is shrieking: "Take the witch away!" She cannot touch the "witch." The match is not a witch, nor was it when the child began to play. It became so, through the process of play. "The shift from sentiment"* (does Frobenius here mean "feeling"?) *"to the plane of consciousness occurs without conscious effort. The process is creative in the highest sense of the word. . . ."*

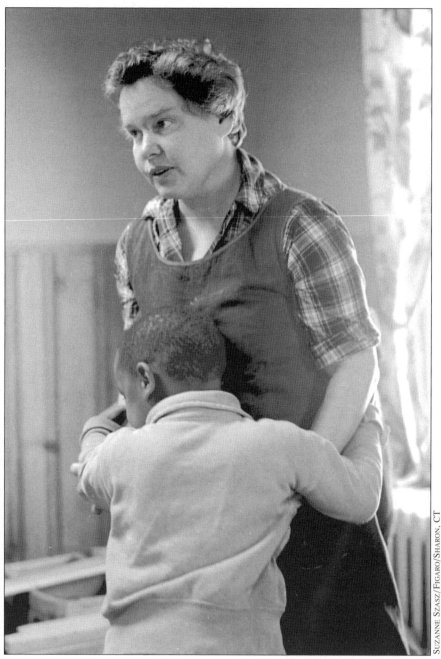

With Popsy at the Nyack nursery school, 1965. The grief of recent events is still evident.

Bette Diver, 1997, a few months before her death. Quizzical and elegant.

Evelyn Bromberg in downtown Maplewood, New Jersey. Scholarly, gentle, generous.

Joyce, with her omnipresent cigarettes, 1971.

Storyteller Diane Wolkstein and Ian, on the A train, 1971.

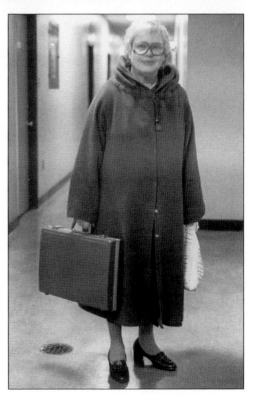
The Random House editor.

Alan Mercer, 1975.

Father and Alan on an official tour of Toronto harbor, 1973.

What do I believe in?

Chess and
Infinity,
Insects and
the Stars ...

AL

Alan B. Mercer
b. August 13, 1921
d. June 25, 1985

Alan and his telescopes on our apartment balcony in downtown Toronto. This card was sent out after he died.

Ian Bodger, 1992. "I once was lost, but now am found."

Ian. A detail from a self-portrait, 1994.

(Above left) Joan Amphlett Corfield Higbee. A happy moment in her eighties.
(Above right) Frank D. Higbee, age ninety.

Joan with Joyce, at one of their last meetings, 1983.

A Winter's Journey to King Arthur's Britain. With fellow tour-leader, Ken Setterington, climbing Glastonbury Tor, December 30, 1996.

The same sort of experience can happen when I am telling a story. Godlike, I set a whole world a-wagging – for me, *and* for my listeners. Similarly, the "force of the demonic" can seize me when I am deep into the process of experiential (acting out) therapy – which is a form of play. Esalen was the place where, for the first time, all these elements came together for me, made sense for me.

The other important thing that happened to me at Esalen was the beginning of a reconciliation with my body. In the evening session on the first day, our leader-teacher announced to us that our group would have access to one of the hot tubs between the hours of eleven o'clock and midnight. The tubs were fed by hot springs, further down the cliff from where we were meeting; they issued from a cave overlooking the sea. When the hour came, I hung back: I had not brought a bathing suit with me. Laughter – no one would be wearing a bathing suit! Indeed, they were forbidden. I tagged along, figuring that the night was dark; I would stay in the pool up to my neck. I had not counted on the richness of the minerals in the water, nor the buoyancy of my avoirdupois. No sooner did I lower myself to my chin, than I shot up again – like a damn dandled tea bag.

Visits to the baths were unscheduled between dawn and the beginning of morning sessions. Anyone could go, to bathe or just to mingle and enjoy the view of unlimited sea and sky, waves breaking on rocks, and bewhiskered seals slurping down oysters as they floated on their backs below. The only rule was that no one was allowed to wear anything. After another day of therapy, and another scheduled sharing of the hot tub, I found that I no longer cringed quite so much when I "wore" my nakedness. Accordingly, I went down to the baths, took off my clothes, and ventured out on the balcony, a sort of esplanade where people paraded, chatted, enjoyed the view.

When I tell this story, some people say to me, "I wouldn't know where to look." I knew exactly where I wanted to look: at breasts and cocks and Venus mounds. I was amazed by the variety of size and shape. One was not better than the other, only different – old, young, middle-aged, fat, thin, pregnant, crippled, scarred, firm, sagging, tall, short, dark, fair, hirsute, hairless. The words "well endowed" had no meaning. We are all endowed, all blessed. Usually we see only each other's hands and faces; in summer, a little more. But we rarely see each other as a seamless piece of work. I was struck by the beauty of ordinary people. No one – naked – is unbeautiful! For once I ceased to loathe myself. The miracle did not last for long; the insight was barely more than a flash, but I had glimpsed (I had *felt*) how it would be to inhabit my body in a new way.

When the course ended, in June, my eighteen-year-old god-daughter, Mia Winston, and I, set out for the east coast together. I had the promise of a place on the Upper West Side of Manhattan, where I would apartment-sit for the month. At least I had a roof over my head! I also had a summer job at Bank Street, for the month of July. In the month of August, I was invited to become part of a federal task force, led by Pauline Winnick, a former librarian, now a consultant in Washington, for the department of education. I would become part of a group of children's librarians, writers, illustrators, and editors who would travel throughout the Middle West. We would be lecturing to children's librarians, and taking part in human-relations seminars, which were designed to open up discussion on new currents in children's literature: books about black children, about single-parent families, about mental illness, alcoholism, illegitimacy. Also, a new criterion had emerged from the women's movement: how to evaluate books about girls – and books that ignored girls. The goals were similar to what I had been trying to accomplish in Missouri, but now I was not alone.

In early fall, Bette Diver (fortuitously for me, if not for her) fell down the stairs in her house and broke her arm. I was flat broke and glad to move back to Piermont, to shop, cook, and clean for her, to be her chauffeur, drive her to work. The relationship was understandably strained. In the last few years of her marriage, Bette had prudently gone to Columbia, to earn a master's degree in Library Science. She had disapproved of the State Library of Missouri's decision to hire me – without a degree – and she thought the way I had behaved there proved her point. If I had been a professional, she told me more than once, I would have known better than to use official stationery! Now she was stuck with me, the penniless prodigal, with no job in sight. She was also a little paranoid about being associated with me; it might even affect her job. Bette and I were like sisters. We bickered.

When I was teaching at Bank Street during July, one of my students had approached me, to ask if I could possibly be the Joan Bodger who had been fired from the Missouri State Library. The man she lived with was John Barry, who was editor of the *American Library Journal*. He was eager for an interview with me about the mess in Missouri. I was almost out the door, on my way to join Pauline Winnick's task force, so we postponed the interview until September. By that time I was living with Bette, in Piermont. Bette was thrilled. She invited Barry and several of his associates to one of her elegant little lunches (which I prepared under her direction). She was both reassured and irritated by the reverence with which they treated me. After all, she was the one who was feeding me, giving me a roof over my head!

My one hope for a job was at Random House. While I was in Missouri, my friend, Arthur Bell, had been lured away from Viking Press to Random House–Pantheon–Knopf. He was certain that, if I would be patient, a job was going to open up for me there, a job for which I would be eminently suitable. I made feints at finding other jobs, but I was exhausted. I had run out of gas. I wasn't trained for anything specific; I had no piece of paper or certificate, and my luck had run out – no prospects, no place to live. Keeping house and chauffeuring for Bette had given me a couple of months respite, but she was understandably fed up with my presence. I was running out of ways to keep myself from knowing how scared I was. I did not know where Ian was. (Later, I found out that he was wandering through the Deep South, on his way to Haight-Ashbury.)

Events turned, pieces fell into place. Diane Wolkstein married Bernard Zucker. They moved to an eighteenth-century mews in Greenwich Village. I inherited Diane's studio apartment, just around the corner from her new place. And I could pay for it! The job at Random House came through at last. Bennett Cerf, the most prominent figure in publishing at the time, and president of Random House, made the decision in my favor. According to Arthur Bell, he closed the meeting that decided my appointment, with "There must be some good in a woman fired as a Communist pornographer."

A new title, liaison editor of children's books, was invented for me, and I was given a blue-and-white coffee mug with the Random House logo on it, to prove I was of editorial status – rather than the brown-and-white mug, which would prove that I was a lesser breed. I was to be a sort of roving ambassador – not quite an editor, not quite a salesman. My task was to talk about children's books in general (not just about Random House books) to librarians situated all over the United States. I was also supposed to *listen* – to the attitudes, needs and expressed opinion of librarians and the general public – then write reports for the benefit of editors and the sales force in-house. Children's literature, like everything else in the United States, was undergoing a revolution. I was to keep abreast of the times and, perhaps, help shape them. The unspoken wish of those who hired me was that my notoriety would open doors to the curious and powerful, and that my credentials, as author of *How the Heather Looks*, would be well received, demonstrating a serious commitment to children's books.

While I was working for Random House part of my job was to attend the American Library Association convention, which that year would be held in Detroit. I looked at the map and persuaded myself that it was my duty to visit Toronto's Osborne Collection of Early Children's Books, on the way. In a letter to Miss Judith Saint John, then director of the large and prestigious collection, I asked her to recommend a hotel in Toronto, and she suggested the Westbury, about a thirty-minute walk from 40 St. George Street, where the collection was then housed, practically on the campus of the University of Toronto. Miss Saint John said that she felt she already knew me through the pages of *How the Heather Looks*. She invited me to lunch.

Aside from my own pleasure and edification, the reason I wanted to visit the Osborne was so that I could share my experience with U.S. librarians, reassure them that my interest in children's literature was high-minded and ever-evolving. Although I had never been a librarian, I wanted them to view me as a serious colleague. The Osborne Collection was superb, the librarians knowledgeable and gratifyingly appreciative about the research I had done for *Heather*. The ladies of the Osborne never mentioned that unpleasantness in Missouri. I surmised it was because they were so excruciatingly polite. They never mentioned it, I later came to know, because interest in the seething politics of U.S. Libraryland stopped at the Canadian border.

After a satisfying day I returned to my hotel, took a nap (as had become my habit), and wondered what to do next. Time, when I wasn't actually working, moved so slowly that sometimes I longed, if not for the grave, at least for a disaster. During the past five years, John had suffered bouts of mental illness, Lucy had died, Ian had gravitated toward drug culture, I had become adept at being brave and decisive in the face of tragedy. It was my schtick. Now I was drowning in nothingness.

I knew the signs of medical depression. I didn't want to mope in my room, I told myself, nor read yet another book in yet another hotel dining room. *Play it safe, take it easy*, the Devil countered in my ear. *Stay in your room, order up room service.* Just a few short years before, I had had a husband, two children, a house on the Hudson River. Wave a magic wand and I'm spending half my life in a one-room apartment in Greenwich Village, complete with cockroaches in the fridge and drug addicts on the stairs; the other half, in posh hotel rooms, every few nights in a different city. A better woman than I could use that circumstance to her advantage, I scolded myself. She would figure out how to meet a man, how to get laid. *No*, said the Devil, *she would avail herself of the opportunity to explore the intellectual and cultural aspects of an unfamiliar city, in a different country.* I wished that I had lost that fifty pounds. I wished that I liked to drink. I wished that I knew how to hang out in singles bars.

I took the elevator down to the lobby and issued through the hotel's revolving door just as the heavens opened in a dramatic downpour. The date was June 18, 1970. Every year since then I have noted that on June 18, or very close to it, the same phenomenon occurs in Toronto. Warm rainwater spouts from the sky – not in discrete drops, not in pencil-stroke lines, but in chutes and sheets and gushes. It's very sexy, like in that old Somerset Maugham story, "Rain."

Instead of retreating to the lobby, where I was afraid I would be sucked upstairs again, I stood under the covered space where taxis and cars drove up. People walking along the sidewalk ran there for shelter; soon a small crowd had gathered. The very intensity of the downpour, backlit by a flickering chartreuse glow from a sickly sun, gave false promise that the rain would soon exhaust itself. At first I amused myself by people-watching; after a while I took out a book. Years of practise: even while standing in a crowd I can isolate myself. I began to read and mark the pages. I was only vaguely aware that someone else was standing next to me, a tweedy-looking man with a camera hanging from his neck. If I thought about him at all, I surmised he was a tourist, possibly British, and went back to my book. I couldn't help noticing, however, that he had the bad habit of reading over people's shoulders, a fault that I could understand too well.

"Are you an editor?" he asked finally.

"I work for Random House," I said. "How did you know?"

"Saw the proofreader's marks," he said. "I work in publishing, too, for Maclean Hunter." I gazed at him, baffled. "Canadian publishing company. Magazines," he explained. I didn't know what to say, so I returned to my

book. (Even when God handed me a man on an hors d'oeuvre tray . . .)
Silence. Except for the sound of rain.

*I could have told him that I had learned proofreader's marks when I was
editor of my high-school paper. I could have told him that, back in 1939, I
had fought tooth-and-nail to take Linotype printing instead of sewing. I
could have told him that I took printing not only because I wanted to write
books and get them printed, but because I figured that I would be the only
girl in a class full of boys, like shooting fish in a barrel. I could have told
him that even then I didn't snag one damned date.*

"Is that the E. B. White who writes for *The New Yorker*?" he asked after
a few minutes. I returned a non-committal yes, and kept on reading.
"Funny," he mused. "I thought I had read all his books, or was aware of
them." I explained that *Stuart Little* was meant for children. Perhaps that
was how he had missed it. "Why are you editing it?" he asked.

I told him that I was not actually editing. I was only marking one of
the chapters for my personal convenience. The one about the time Stuart,
an upper-middle-class mouse who lives in Manhattan, captains a racing
sloop on the model-boat pond in Central Park. *I felt that I was making
myself perfectly clear.* Two weeks hence, I continued, I would be standing beside that very pond (near the 72nd Street entrance to the Park)
telling a group of children and adults the story of the famous boat race.
Not reading. *Telling!* This year marked the twenty-fifth anniversary of the
publication of *Stuart Little*. I would, in my particular and peculiar way,
be showing homage to its author. That was why I was making notes and
marks – to transpose White's literary rendition to a state more suitable
for the oral tradition.

"Anyone who would change one jot or tittle of E. B. White's prose, I
could have nothing to do with," said the man.

"You've been reading too much Strunk and White," I snapped. *Why do
I always have to be so smart?*

"I think this matter calls for further discussion," said the man. "Would
you care to go into the hotel for a drink?"

We talked. We talked as though we had always known each other. His
name was Alan Mercer. He was obviously comfortable with women. Most
of the men in the children's book field are either gay or married. He wasn't
gay and he didn't come on to me, so I took it for granted that later he would
go home and tell his wife about the interesting conversation he had had

with a woman from Random House. He did not come on to me, I surmised, because I was busily giving out my usual message: *You have nothing to fear from me. I am not after your body and I know you could not possibly be after mine. You just admire my fine mind.*

One thing led to another. He had been a navigator in the Royal Canadian Air Force during the war, stationed in Britain. He had been married twice: divorced the first time, widowed the second. (So I was right about his being comfortable around women, wrong about his marital status.) He was a professional photographer, as well as a copywriter. Hence the camera. I told him, briefly, about Missouri. He asked good questions, the kind a journalist asks. He listened to my answers gravely, with patience and interest. We talked about other things. Laughed. *One thing led to another.*

We went somewhere to dance. I am a terrible dancer. He was very good. He did not, as in the movies, transform me into Ginger Rogers, with a few swoops over the dance floor. Instead, with no show of rancor, he allowed me to escape from my misery, simply led me back to our table. Later, much later, we walked back to the hotel. *One thing led to another.* I amazed myself by asking him to come up to my room. I knew perfectly well that we were going to bed together. We went to bed together. *One thing led to another.* He said later, in answer to my query, that he figured I was ignorant but educable. He knew I would get better. And better. And he found it sort of kinky, to go to bed with a Communist pornographer. (In 1973, when my name was finally cleared by the American Library Intellectual Freedom Committee and, indirectly, by the U.S. Supreme Court, Alan would complain about false advertising.)

The next morning he escorted me to Union Station and saw me off on the train to Windsor, the Canadian station nearest to Detroit. We had already exchanged addresses and phone numbers, but at the last moment he asked for the name of the hotel where I would be staying in Detroit. Flustered, I gave him the wrong one. I didn't discover my mistake until, toward the end of my train ride, I checked my reservation. When I arrived at the hotel in a taxi, the first person I saw was John Neumann, a colleague, friend (gay), author of two good books for children, and an editor at Golden Books Press. He, too, had been a member of Pauline Winnick's federal task force, so we knew each other well. He came to greet me, took my suitcase, peered into my face, and said, "You look different. What's happened?"

"I just met the man I'm going to marry," I said.

"I believe you," he said.

At two in the morning my telephone rang. It was Alan, the professional investigative reporter. He had worked his way methodically through a list of big hotels in Detroit, and finally found me. I had barely settled down to sleep when he called again. He said he took it for granted that I knew that we were going to be married. In case I had any doubts about that, he was asking me now. He would be coming down to New York in two weeks' time so he could hear me tell stories by the model-boat pond in Central Park. So he could listen to some good jazz. So I could give him an answer to his proposal.

During the next two weeks I learned (because of when he telephoned me) that Alan was a night person. I am a day person. I already suspected that he drank too much. I hardly drink at all. It is not a matter of willpower. A gate closes across my throat when my first drink is only half-finished. During the two weeks while I waited for Alan to come down to New York I tried, frantically and euphorically, to diet off fifty pounds. I was afraid that he would take one look at me, turn around, and go home to Canada. *I had forgotten that flash of enlightenment, experienced at the baths at Esalen.* I was forty-seven years old and I was acting like a thirteen-year-old. I was miserable. And scared. And ecstatic. And disgusted with myself. Love was not worth the trouble.

My apartment in Greenwich Village was a fifth-floor walk-up studio apartment with standard cockroaches. There was a bathroom with a skylight that let soot fall into the tub; the rest of the apartment – kitchen, bedroom, dining, and living – was all in the same room. The windows (both barred) were the only redemption; they looked down on the gardens belonging to old townhouses on 11th Street. Diane Wolkstein and Bernard Zucker, who now lived around the corner, were still in honeymoon mode, incurably romantic about my love affair. They joked with me and teased me, helped buoy my expectations by being a little more insane than I was.

My friends Jules and Evelyn Bromberg, still in Maplewood, remained dubious. They suggested that I hire some sort of investigative agency (or they would, if I couldn't afford it) to check out this person, Alan Mercer. He might be the sort of man who seduced women and buried them at the bottom of the garden. I knew that they were being sensible for my own good. I also knew that no private investigator would possess measuring devices delicate enough to evaluate the worth of a man who so passionately defended the integrity of E. B. White's prose.

On the appointed day, I heard Alan's steps on the stairs and rushed to open the three locks on the door: upper, lower, and fox lock. This last was a medieval-looking device that involved a brass bar that slid along a brass groove in the floor. Standard equipment for Village apartments, it worked on the same principle as a broom wedged under the door handle. Alan was both amused and infuriated by the delay. "What the hell is going on in there?" he bellowed through the door. When at last I flung it open, he dropped his suitcases and we rushed into each other's arms. Then we backed off and took a good look at each other. I saw a man a little less than six feet tall, with brown hair and bushy eyebrows, one bushier than the other. He had beautiful brown eyes that shone with wonder and curiosity and – could that be – love? I saw that his nose was too big and that it had veins in it.

I was not sure what he saw in me.

Alan wanted to explore the neighborhood. We went for a walk around the block and stopped at the place on 11th Street where, a few weeks before, the Weathermen had blown up a beautiful old townhouse while engaged in making bombs. One of the terrorists had been the daughter of the people who owned the house. Something had gone horribly wrong. I was uptown, at work, when it happened, but Maurice Sendak, who lived over on Eighth Street, told me that he had been meticulously cross-hatching an illustration when the blast struck. Ink all over the place! Alan, as a draftsman, was appalled by the ruination, but the name-dropping was wasted on him. I found it refreshing that he had no idea who Sendak was.

The front of the house and the floors had been blown away. Alan took some pictures of the only wall left intact. Above our heads, on what had once been the second floor, was a tier of bookcases still bolted to the wall. The book spines were curiously vitrified, which only served to make the titles brighter. I recognized a huge coffee-table book, *The Etruscans*, propped face-out in the bookcase. I had mooned over copies of that same volume in a bookstore. A photograph of an Etruscan tomb gleamed on the cover. The Etruscans were a highly evolved civilization who decorated their tombs with sculpture taken from what was apparently a favorite scene in daily life. Their idea of heaven was for a man and a woman to be lying on a scroll-end couch, facing each other, knees touching, talking and laughing and drinking wine through all eternity. If Alan and I were married, I thought, we could spend the rest of our lives in Etruscan heaven.

In the afternoon we went up to Central Park. I told the story of Stuart Little at the boat pond, as promised. Then I stood by the statue of Hans Christian Andersen, just a stone's throw away, where Saturday storytelling usually took place. Diane Wolkstein, who had been appointed as official storyteller for the City of New York, told a few stories, then she asked me to tell one. I chose "The Marriage of Sir Gawain."

On the day after Christmas, King Arthur goes out on a quest and meets with a giant knight who asks him a riddle: What does a woman really want? The knight is brother to the Loathly Lady (the Winter Hag) whom Arthur encounters in the wood. Seated on a log 'twixt oak and holly, she tells King Arthur that she will reveal the answer to the riddle if he will promise, in return, the hand of his nephew, Sir Gawain, in marriage. Arthur is aghast, for the lady is the most ugly he ever saw, but he leans down from his horse and listens to the words the lady whispers into his ear, although I must admit he closed his eyes. That night, back at the castle, Gawain, the most impetuous knight in the court, says he would see this lady. Next morning, in the snow, he falls on his knees and proposes to her. (You know Sir Gawain!) On their wedding night he kisses her of his own free will but, because she is so loathly, he closes his eyes. When he opens them he finds, encircled in his arms, a lady fair of form and face. But alas, because he closed his eyes, she can only be this way half the time . . .

About ten o'clock we left Greenwich Village to go uptown to Jimmy Ryan's jazz place on West 54th. Alan, as usual, had a camera slung around his neck. He told me that Toronto was a great jazz town and that for years he had taken photographs of musicians who played there. Partway through the evening, one of the trumpet players came down from the stand and said to him, "Hey, man, I thought you were in Toronto. What you doin' here?" Alan was having a wonderful time. By two o'clock in the morning my head was on the table – from sleepiness, not drink. Thank God I was forty-seven, not thirteen. I gave Alan the keys to my apartment and asked him to get me a taxi. I didn't care what he thought of me, whether I would ever see him again. I just wanted to go home to bed. He told me he thought I was wonderful. Most women, he said admiringly, would have (a) stayed, and suffered in silence; (b) stayed and nagged; (c) nagged and dragged him back to their apartment. He thought it boded well that, with good grace, I was willing to do my own thing and let him do his.

The next morning I woke to find hot bright sun streaming into my stuffy backroom studio. Alan was asleep, snoring gently. I lay against him, grateful for his presence, but he was oblivious. No cuddles. No nothing. After a while I was not only uncomfortable but bored. I wanted a good cup of coffee. Finally I decided to get up, get dressed, go out for the Sunday *New York Times*. I would stop at Sutter's, on the corner of Greenwich and Tenth, buy some croissants to bring back with me. Stealthily I climbed out of bed, and reached for my brassiere. I had left it hanging over a chair the night before.

There are two ways of putting on a brassiere. A slim woman puts the straps over her shoulders, the cups over her breasts, then reaches round to the back to fasten hooks and eyes. A fat woman places hooks and eyes on her stomach, fastens them, inches the brassiere round her circumference until the cups are in front. Then she leans over, bridles her breasts, and hauls the straps up over her shoulders. I crept into a corner, behind the chair, and with my face to the wall engaged myself in the process more suitable. Despite my stealth Alan woke up.

"What are you doing?" he boomed.

"Putting on my bra," I replied, my voice slightly muffled.

"Why are you doing it *that* way?"

The Devil made me speak. "Because I am fat," I said.

"What does that have to do with it? Why are you over there in a corner, with your face to the wall?"

"Because I am fat," I said. Barely whispering. And then (I am convinced it was because of that flash of insight at Esalen), I allowed myself to hear what my lover had to say: "*Stop whispering*," said Alan. "Listen to me. I am your lover. I have come all the way from Toronto to see you. Turn around! Don't you understand? I love every fold and crease of you!"

Slowly I turned, my bra dangling from one hand. Oh my impetuous lover! Braver than Arthur! Braver than Gawain! *When Alan Mercer kissed the Loathly Lady, he did not close his eyes.*

CHAPTER 23
Viewing the Moon

WE CALLED MY PARENTS to say that we were getting married. Father's deep voice boomed out of the telephone: "What makes you think you are good enough to marry my daughter?" (His daughter was pushing fifty!) I was chagrined, but Alan said he knew right then and there that he was marrying into a good family. His answer: "Because I love her. Because we are both intelligent. Because we have much in common." Father's next question, "What did you do in the War?" was answered with: "I was a navigator in the Royal Canadian Air Force. I flew thirty-two missions over Germany." There was a long pause at the other end of the line.

"I am abashed," said Father.

We had met in June 1970; we were married in September, but I did not officially move to Toronto until March of the following year. As Alan said, it would have been nice if one of us had been rich. Alan lived in a one-bedroom apartment in downtown Toronto. His walls were lined with bookshelves, which held (horizontally) rows of books. Books on the floor were piled (vertically) almost to the ceiling. There was almost no place for me to put my things; no place to call my own. I was used to a whole house, and found the lack of privacy almost frightening.

Alan had not been to university, nor had he finished high school. In the depths of the Depression, his father had delivered a sudden ultimatum: Alan must quit school and go to work. Alan asked for two more weeks.

During that time, he stopped going to all his classes and showed up in the all-girls typing class every day, from first period in the morning to the last one in the afternoon. He was president of his school and head boy in his class. He knew he would one day be a writer. He defied his teachers and the principal by refusing to move out of the typing class. Finally, they left him alone so he could give himself a crash course in typing before he left school forever. Alan's father worked in construction. He was an intelligent man, but he could not read. His wife and children read the newspaper to him, and he listened to the radio. In later years, Alan came to assume that his father had been dyslexic. Alan's maternal grandfather lived with them; it was he who introduced Alan to the library, by sending Alan to get books for him. After he left school, Alan set out to read everything he assumed a university student would have read.

Meanwhile, he worked in a grocery store and became middle-weight champion of Ontario – for a week. He quit while he was winning. "The only thing I had going for me was my brain," he said. "I didn't want to scramble it."

Very soon he applied for a job at the old Toronto *Telegram*, where he worked in the commercial advertisements department. He wrote a few sports articles, learned about layout, tried his hand at cartooning. When Britain entered the war, he applied to the RCAF and was sent off to officer training school. When he returned from the war, he became art editor at *Saturday Night* magazine. His first wife, an Australian WAC, whom he had met in London, arrived with her parents. And her brother. Alan drifted out of the marriage, drifted through the solar universe of Canadian advertising and publishing, and finally docked at Maclean Hunter, the biggest media complex in Canada. I cannot help wondering how different his life would have been if he had allowed himself to attend a good university, on the Canadian equivalent of the G.I. Bill. Instead, he taught himself photography. He never went anywhere without his camera slung around his neck. At home in our apartment, he took the pictures for a book catalogue that Maclean Hunter sent out to the Northwest Territories, and to Australia, twice a year. He loved the job because he had to read all the books and write a one-liner précis to go under the picture. Best of all, he got to keep the books. He had married a second time, someone whom he met at the office, and who was one of his boon companions at the pub. After fifteen years, his second wife died of cancer.

I had sold or given away most of my household effects. I left my collection of rare children's books in a friend's attic in Piermont, and hired a U-Haul van to bring bits and pieces of furniture (my marble-topped table, a rocking chair, a few rugs and keepsakes) to Canada. I arranged them in a ring, inside the ring of furniture already owned by Alan. We shoehorned ourselves into our new life. Alan saw an advertisement for a job with Mini-Skools, a private daycare company, with headquarters in Winnipeg and plans to expand to the United States. I applied, and was hired as program director for the Canadian operation. The inspectors in Queen's Park were dubious about me from the start. I was an outsider and, worse, an American. Somehow, they projected that I had been a secretary in my former life. Although that misapprehension was corrected, the prejudice never dissipated. Part of the reason was their strong opposition to a large private company entering the field. Even worse, I was unpredictable. One day, during a hot spell, when no one felt like eating, I ordered that all the schools serve dessert (tinned pears) before the meat and vegetables. At least the children would have something in their stomachs! Furious calls to and from Queen's Park. The moral fabric of a nation is threatened if you can't say to a child, "No dessert unless . . ."

Alan was a drinker; I am not. Alan did not come home for dinner; I was raised to think that having dinner together was the be-all of a marriage. I found myself without friends, and no way of making friends – except among my employees, which was risky. However, out of the blue, a young woman called me. Deanna Kamiel-White, who lived in Toronto, was writing a book (*The Lace Ghetto*), and wanted to include a section on girls and women in children's literature. She had called Gloria Steinem (whom she had interviewed once, for television) to ask for a name to call in the States, and Steinem suggested Pat Ross, an editor at Pantheon–Random House–Knopf. When Pat Ross was reached, she said, "But the person who knows most about that is Joan Bodger, and she has just moved to Toronto." Although there was a twenty-year difference between us, Deanna Kamiel (now divorced) and I became fast friends. I needed only one good friend to fill the hole. (Later on, Deanna would move to PBS Minneapolis–Saint Paul, to make eight-minute documentaries. Eventually, she won a Guggenheim fellowship, and moved to New York City. In 1988 a retrospective of her films was shown at the Museum of Modern Art.)

Alan worked at home most of the time, on his ancient Underwood, but

every afternoon, hours after I had left the apartment, he took his work in to
Maclean Hunter, where he submitted his copy and did layouts (this was just
before the computer era). Afterwards, he went to a pub with a little band of
friends and their wives. He came home about eight or nine o'clock,
watched television with me or read a book, and then got to work. I went to
the pub with him several times, but since I didn't drink and I did not share
a past – or any present interests – with his pub friends, I found myself both
bored and angry. Alan never tried to make me drink, and he understood that
I resented wasting my time with people with whom I had nothing in
common. I did not expect to change his ways; he did not try to change
mine. When we were in our own little world together, we were content and
compatible. After I went to bed, Alan spread out the work he did for
Maclean Hunter. He worked until about three o'clock in the morning, then
came to bed, often leaving his set-ups for photography. (They could stay
there for days. I learned to live around them.) He did not get up until noon;
he went to his office around one o'clock. Weekends, we spent most of the
time together.

Our marriage was not perfect, but it was good enough. Despite our auspicious first encounter, sex was erratic and problematical, partly because
of Alan's drinking. I like the idea of being a person who enjoys sex. I like
to know that someone finds me desirable. But I am no Aphrodite. Intellectual and emotional companionship with someone who is affectionate, plus
sex sometimes, keeps me happy. And there is another essential ingredient.
Once someone asked me and some other women what we found most sexy
in a man. Various anatomical parts were nominated, but the first word that
popped into my head was "Integrity!" Both my husbands have had it. So
did my father.

The marriage suited both of us. I flew to Winnipeg about once a month.
As the company expanded, I travelled to Atlanta, Denver, and San Diego to
act as a consultant and to help design programs for infants and preschool
children. Alan did not resent my travelling; he missed me, but he was able
to fend for himself. When I was in Toronto, I did not have to rush home and
put dinner on the table. I could stay late at the office if I wanted to, then
drive home in my company car, with a chance to eat supper – and to unwind
– before Alan came home. I told Alan, when I took the job, that I figured it
would last three years. Mini-Skools would pick my brains, exploit my creativity, make me codify what I had done and write a manual, then – when

everything was humming – hand over the administration to someone better at that game than I was. And pay them twice what I was getting! As a matter of fact, I lasted five years.

Alan had no family: his parents were both dead; his younger brother had been killed in the war. Most of his pub friends did not have children. He was justifiably puzzled by the young people who drifted through Toronto to see me, or who corresponded with me. I seemed to attract a certain category of my son's friends, my friend's sons – and daughters. Perhaps because I had left our social and academic ghetto, because I had leapt over the wall, these wandering souls felt a compulsion to see how I was surviving after a decade of multiple disasters. Drop-outs, draft-dodgers, drug-users came to see me. A niece had had an abortion, a nephew was HIV positive, two kids later committed suicide. My Canadian husband was appalled. "I don't understand," he said. "You and your friends are intelligent, well-educated, most of them are well-off. Your kids are well-fed, well-read, well-traveled. They've gone to museums and art galleries, they're bright and articulate on every subject. Hell! They aren't even kids any more. They're getting on for thirty. How could they turn out to be such a bloody mess?" I agreed with him. Damned if *I* knew!

"What were you doing when you were twenty-eight years old?" I asked. The question was not rhetorical. It dated back to my family's tumbleweed existence, and my lack of experience in watching someone grow up. I needed a benchmark, some sense of what was right and meet to expect of a boy grown to manhood. There was a long silence.

"I was bombing Dresden," said Alan.

Ian came to see us only once. I thought he was stoned, but now I am not so sure. Whether or not he was taking drugs, the chemical imbalance in his brain was beginning to win the upper hand. After that, he appeared sporadically – in my life, and in his father's. Garbed in campaign hat, camouflage fatigues, and combat boots, he became a parody of the soldier he was not. Gradually he disappeared altogether, wrapped in his Cloak of Darkness, like in the fairy tales. Neither John nor I knew his whereabouts, although he had been sighted in San Francisco. John had remarried and moved to another state. I knew where *he* was. I had remarried and moved to Canada. I knew where *I* was. Lucy had died, and was buried in a graveyard overlooking the Hudson. I knew where *she* was. But I didn't know whether my son was alive or dead. A hard thing, to know that your child has died. Harder still *not* to know.

One night in 1973, Chris Diver phoned his mother to report that he had run into Ian at the San Francisco Public Library, main branch. I was bound for California, on Mini-Skools business, so I decided to take a few extra days and seek out Ian; I was utterly confident that I would find him. I took a hotel room near the library, and I spent three days in the history department, hoping Ian would show up. Despite my intuition, by the end of the third day I was ready to acknowledge defeat. As I was walking along one side of the mezzanine, bound for an exit, I saw two enormous feet sticking out from under a display case: no socks; holes in shoes – but somehow the ankles looked familiar. I bent down. "Ian?" He wriggled out from his lair, stood up. He was thin, bearded, incredibly dirty. I took him to a nearby diner, but he could not eat. I took him back to the hotel. The concierge looked askance, but I said, "This is my son. He was lost and now he's found." I asked for my key; we sailed towards the elevator.

Ian took a bath, then he took another bath, but dirt was still ingrained in his skin. I ordered a roast-beef dinner for two, through room service. Again, he could not eat. When he tried, he vomited. He said he was not used to eating. He lived by panhandling and by selling his blood. My room had two beds, but he would not stay the night there. He said he would meet me next day. "Where?" I asked.

"Near the Reader's Guide, in the main reference room."

"Don't stand me up," I said. "I spent three days in the history collection, hours and hours. Looking for you, waiting for you."

His reply was sympathetic: "The collection *is* rather thin."

He was there, where he was supposed to be, when he was supposed to be. I led him to my rented car. "Maybe there is some place you would like to go, that you can't usually get to," I said. "Tell me where you'd like me to drive you." He was not up to making decisions. I decided for him, to go out to the Palace of the Legion of Honor, overlooking the Golden Gate. We drove through the grounds at the Presidio, and along Lincoln Boulevard, parked the car, and walked along a path above the cliffs. Ian was so weak that we stopped after a quarter of a mile and sat down under a pine tree. He became very agitated. "I am scared you are going to kidnap me and take me to a mental hospital," he said. "I am afraid I will do something crazy and hurt you. I think we should go back to the car." I was touched by his concern to protect me, *and* I respected his paranoia. We went back to the car. "Take me into the city," he said. He began to shake. I concentrated on my driving. When we came to a red light, I had to stop, in the center lane. He opened the car door and stepped out. The car behind me honked. I watched him as he blundered across the lines of traffic. I did not know then that I would not see him for another thirteen years.

Innocent and arrogant, our family was convinced that we owned the best recipe for everything in the world, including mint sauce. That, and bringing up children. Wherever we moved, and we moved often, Mother planted a patch of mint by the kitchen door. A leaf to pluck as we went by, a sprig to cook with new green peas. The exile did her best to impart the sacred tribal lore: tear, never cut, leaves from stalk. Bruise the leaves with your bare hands and work in the sugar. Add the vinegar drop by drop. Infuse the whole with tales of an Edwardian girlhood spent in a house by the banks of the River Wye. (She often said things in this backwards way: The River Wye, the Brothers Grimm.)

Sweet and sour, that elixir made to enhance roast lamb. I liked it best when, mixed with sacrificial juices, it seeped into everything else on the plate. Just so did my mother's stories, taken from life, blend with those she read to us from a book. Her brothers had been young and handsome and full of laughter. Mixed with mint sauce, myth, and story, those Brothers Merry rose again in my consciousness, as Brothers Grim, cohabiting with characters in my fairy-tale books, laying long shadows on my childhood. The tall young men, who should have been our uncles, lived underground in a brightly lit palace in a land called "No Man's." Slightly sinister, they danced the night away with the Twelve Dancing Princesses. All except Uncle Harry, missing in action. He was the old soldier, wrapped in a Cloak of Darkness.

In 1951, when Ian was not quite a year old, we moved to California. We lived with my parents while we looked for a house. *In my father's walled garden I sit on the teak bench (salvaged from the stern of the old Terminal Island ferry), underneath the orange tree. Flowers fill the confined space, vivid as a page from a medieval manuscript. I, as Madonna, sit in golden light in the Garden of Paradise and watch my golden child – naked – chase the oranges that plop to the green, green grass and roll down towards the house.* I know (now) a golden ball represents the perfect sphere of childhood.

So, the ball in "The Frog Prince." So, the ball in "Childe Rowland." So, those apples in the Garden of the Hesperides, and that other apple, in the Garden of Eden, and the musical apples on a silver branch, in Irish mythology. In my personal myth, myriads of oranges bob just beyond the breakers, at Cabrillo. One of them is miraculously transported to hang over the head of poor little Bertie (drowned at sea), memorialized in the stained-glass window at Abbey Dore. Others, shape-shifted into hazel haws, dangle over the Pool of Knowledge, wherein the Salmon of Wisdom swims. Sooner or later they fall, are lost, or bitten into.

Ian has learned to push his stroller up the incline of the lawn, turn it around, jump on the platform at its base and, holding on to the seat bar, shove off. Away he goes, squealing and laughing, heading straight for the mint bed. Deliberately, he rolls himself in the mint. I run to pick him up, my saucy, scented, sacred lamb, and set him on his feet again. Once more he trudges, pushing his phaeton, pausing now and then to kick an orange with his foot, kick-starting the sun.

1973. Ian was missing – missing in action. With nothing to go on, it was easy for me, and everyone who had ever known him, to project. I made up a hundred stories about my son, what had happened to him. People were only too eager to recite their scripts: Ian is a mathematical genius, doing his thing in Silicon Valley. He is a very rich drug lord, a member of the Mafia. He is married, has kids and works in a factory. The only real thing I could rely on was the weather report from San Francisco. "Cold and rainy" – does he own a pair of socks? "Warm and sunny" – does he love and have someone to love him? Oh, God, what if there's an earthquake, the Big One, and I *never* know what's happened to him?

Several years go by. I am walking through College Park mall in Toronto, very early in the morning. A man is sitting at a table in the galleria, although none of the coffee shops is open yet. He is dirty, scruffy, hunched, hirsute. In the month of May, he wears two coats and three hats. His hair is filthy, his beard unkempt. Hard to guess, but he's probably around Ian's age.

There is a story in the Brothers Grimm, about an old soldier who makes a bargain with the Devil. The Devil will give him his due if, for seven years, he wears a smelly bearskin. *In all that time, he must not wash nor comb nor trim, nor pare his nails, nor wipe the tears from his eyes.* I slow down and take a good look at Bearskin. Just as in the story, *you could have grown cress on his face.* A businessman, about my own age, has come up alongside of me; he slows down, too. I brace myself. I know the script: "At least he could wash" or "Why doesn't he get a job?" Instead, this man – this man in a Bay Street suit – clutching a briefcase, says: "I have a son like that."

"I do, too."

"Tomorrow is his birthday," he says. He hurries off. "What a waste! What a waste!" His voice echoes in the empty arcade.

Always in the background was the concern about my mother. For twenty years, whenever I went out to California, on business, or specifically to visit her, I feared this would be the last time, half hoping it *would* be. She had given up. Her mind was clear, but more and more she slept her life away. She was often in pain. *My mother dozes. I take her hand, gnarled and dappled. The veins stand out, roots on a bonsai. I stroke her arm. The skin is transparent. How I love her, love the very skin hanging from her bones. I could pleat it. It's already pleated! I acknowledge intricate intersection, wrinkled as old linen long folded away, lifted out, hung on a rod.* I split, in a split second: I don't want to be here! *I could be at Cabrillo Beach, I tell myself, letting waves roll over me – roll in, envelope, and recede. Instead, I sit with this old woman, my dying mother, not fighting, not denying, whatever thought or feeling comes to me: ebb and flow; high tide or low. One moment I hate her – hate her for dying, for dribbling, for smelling of sickness. She, who had always been so fastidious!* I am flooded with remorse. *No I don't! I love you . . . don't die, please don't die, I love you so. I wish I could tell you how wonderful you are. How you used to make us laugh, how you used to laugh! And your courage! My God, you were brave. You used to stand up to anyone, including Father. Especially Father!*

The wave recedes. *What a bitch you are. You hold Father on a short leash. If he goes away for more than an hour you call him an old fool, accuse him of infidelity (forgetting that both of you are almost ninety).* A runnel, foaming at my feet . . . *But no fool you! Even now, he's probably bedded down with the prettiest seventy-year-old in town.*

Back in Toronto, on Sunday mornings, I went out to breakfast, leaving Alan to sleep. I took the Sunday *New York Times* with me, as old friend and companion. I had become a regular at a place called The Underground Railroad Soul Food Restaurant. Friends and acquaintances relied on my being there, and took to dropping by. Sometimes I even met salesmen there, rather than have them trek way out to my Mini-Skools office, almost an hour from downtown. They would bring books and toys to display to me, which added to the fun and conversation. Even the waiters got into the act. John Henry, one of the principal owners, was a retired football player from the state of Georgia. He was interested that I worked with children, and especially interested when I talked to him about my work with black children. When he learned that I was a storyteller, he told me that he was going to work on a plan for me to tell stories at his restaurant. He made it plain that he did not want me to limit my stories to African tales and black folklore; he wanted his restaurant to be a home to stories told by people from every place and culture.

Christmas 1974, I told stories at the Underground for the first time. A small group of friends came to listen to me. So did Alan! He struggled out of bed, in absolute anguish at being up so early. Once at the restaurant, he sat nursing a cup of coffee, morose but listening. For nine years, every third Sunday of the month, I would tell stories at the Underground Railroad. People planned their calendars around the event. Whole families came. People without families invited friends to share a table. Regulars got to know each other. They got to know Alan. Alan's attendance never failed to amaze me. He looked as though he were undergoing work on a root canal, but he came. He was there for me.

In 1971, Fritz Perls died, and in 1972 the Gestalt Institute of Toronto opened its doors to train Gestalt therapists. There was a back-up of people with degrees in medicine, psychiatry, and psychology, with a sprinkling of other academics (Tony Key, for instance, had a Ph.D. from Oxford, in physics). They had been waiting for several years for the day to apply, and I applied immediately, eager to be in the first class. During the time when I was waiting to know if I would be accepted, Alan asked me out to dinner at our favorite restaurant. He was very grave. "I am afraid," he said, "that if these Gestalt people decide to accept you, and if you decide to enter into training with them, it might prove to be the fulcrum on which our marriage breaks." I surprised myself with the alacrity of my reply: "If they accept me, and if I decide not to take the training just to please you, our marriage will break anyway." He heard me.

The Gestalt Institute accepted my application, although I had only a bachelor's degree and I was ten or fifteen years older than anyone else on the list. Our two leaders had trained with Fritz Perls at Esalen. They were an odd couple: one of them (whom I'll call Harry) was an esteemed psychiatrist; the other (Jay) was a sort of gifted charlatan-genius, charismatic and narcissistic. He was originally from Brooklyn, but his Semitic ancestors were sprung from the deserts of the East. He was tall, hawk-nosed, handsome, and of noble bearing. He wore beautiful antique buckskins and was loaded down with turquoise jewelry. I enjoyed *his* enjoyment in playing the role of a Spanish-Indian mystic, sprung from the deserts of the Southwest United States. I saw his act as a running gag. I was willing to share the joke with him, and laughed appreciatively. It did not immediately occur to me that he took his own hoax seriously, as did some of the people in the class. This was especially true of the British-born and Europeans in our group who, to my astonishment, believed him. It was especially true of the men, who held Jay in awe and reverence. By example, he gave them license to act out their boyish fantasies concerning women. And he persuaded some of the women that sex with him was part of the learning experience. He did some good, and he did some harm. In historical retrospect, I realize what was going on at the Gestalt Institute of Toronto was not much different from what was going on in every graduate-level learning institution in North America.

One of the reasons I was accepted by the Institute was because I was a storyteller. During the interview, my teachers-to-be told me they hoped I would find a way to tap into stories and storytelling, release their power through Gestalt techniques. I had observed, at Esalen, that Psychodrama uses the client's personal story, ignores the body of folk tale and myth. Jungian therapy uses story and myth intellectually, to analyze. But, unlike Gestalt and Psychodrama, it is not playful and experiential.

The class met one evening a week, one weekend a month. Jay soon made it clear to me that I had been admitted on sufferance. During the second weekend, at a remote farmhouse somewhere in the wilds of Ontario, he told me to pack my baggage and leave the class. In front of the whole group, he told me that he did not like fat, middle-aged women. I stood eyeball-to-eyeball, toe-to-toe, and refused to go. (After all, I had had hours and hours of expensive Fifth Avenue psychiatry!) I did not want my money refunded, I said. I wanted to become a Gestalt therapist, and I knew I could be a good one, given the training. Afterwards, Harry drew me aside. He told me that I had won the war. I could stay. But he advised me not to discuss the incident any further. I believe he gave me good advice. I did not want to waste my valuable time by bickering with Jay: *Did. Didn't. You are. You're another!* I did not tell Alan what had happened. He would have told me to quit. Paradoxically, it was because of Alan's affirmation that my body was lovable, that I did not have to quit. I knew I was right and that, in this particular instance, the two men who ran the Institute were wrong. I also knew that I could learn a lot from them.

At the end of the second year, we were each given homework to do over the summer. Jay told me to stop whining about not having any breathing space in Alan's apartment. "By next September, I want you to have found a space of your own," he said. "Or don't come back to the Institute." Over the summer, I re-read Virginia Woolf's *A Room of One's Own*, and was overcome with a great longing. I visualized what I wanted: a large and light-filled room, with space for my marble-topped table (which I had used as a desk to write *How the Heather Looks*), and space for my books. I wanted a straight chair to sit on while I typed, and I wanted two or three other chairs – one for comfort, and two to use while conducting therapy. When I went looking, I found that most of the rooms advertised were already furnished. Landlords were suspicious – especially when I said I did not plan to sleep in the room I was renting. Was I married? Did my husband know what I was doing? What, exactly, *was* I going to do? Would I be having visitors? *No men!* Eventually, Deanna Kamiel helped me find just what I was looking for, in a narrow Victorian townhouse in the Cabbagetown area of Toronto. The house was owned by an artist friend of hers: he lived on the second and third floors, and was delighted to rent out the two rooms on the first floor. He did not care a fig about my morals, as long as I was quiet and took out my own garbage.

Alan was perfectly amenable to the idea. Actually, he did not find things were much different. I had become wonderfully clever and inventive about finding hotel lobbies where I could read and coffee houses where I could write while he was spreading out his work all over the apartment and developing his pictures in the kitchen and bathroom. I owned half the bed, half the couch and half the kitchen table – to use for cooking. But now I would have a whole room to call my own. I had had several nebulous ideas about writing another book – or books. Now I could write in earnest. And I could, in good conscience, invite friends for conversation and a cup of tea without interfering with Alan's work. But best of all, I could be alone. I could revel in solitude. Which was different to being alone in our ridiculously overcrowded, messy apartment.

In 1975, I graduated from the Gestalt Institute, and began taking clients sent to me by the Women's Referral Service. I charged almost nothing, since most of the women who came to me were on welfare. However, when I asked for three dollars from one woman, she told me I was a disgrace to my sex, and insisted on paying me ten! A few weeks later, I received word from Mini-Skools that they had merged with another company, and that my services were no longer needed. Almost the same week, we learned that Alan had cancer of the esophagus.

I continued to make frequent trips to California, to see my mother. She was breaking my heart – her skiff had loosed it's moorings, she yearned towards the tide. Every time her shallop drifted, Father made family headlines: ADMIRAL DIRECTS HEROIC RESCUE. The YMCA's oldest member, he lifted weights, swam his half-mile, checked the scales, measured his girth (his Plimsoll mark), proofs of his buoyancy. As long as my mother lived, he was convinced of his own immortality. I longed to shout at her: *Listen, I learned this from you. Abundance lies just beyond the breakers, plentitude issues from the wreck. Embrace the tide! Trust the deep waters!*

In the 1970s there was an explosion of interest in things exotic and esoteric. Books proliferated on subjects that, hitherto, I had known a little bit about – because of my dovetailed interests in fairy tales, anthropology, archaeology, psychology – but rarely found reflected in popular culture. Now whole bookstores devoted themselves to selling volumes on Celtic lore, shamanism, feng shui (which I had touched upon in 1958, in *How the Heather Looks*), ley lines, fairy mounds, flying saucers, Atlantis, the Sphinx, the *Book of the Dead*, the *I Ching*, Carl Jung, the Goddess, goddesses, the Green Man, Druids, the Holy Grail, chariots of the gods, standing stones, stone rings, the Tarot pack, ancient trade routes, ancient ritual, origins, prophecies – all things that were meat and drink to me. Even if I did not believe half of what I was reading, I found myself amused and fascinated. I haunted the bookshops on Harbord Street in Toronto, especially one called the Fifth Kingdom – now, alas, defunct. It was there I found two books by Michael Dames that have influenced my life ever since: *The Silbury Treasure* and *The Avebury Cycle*. Thanks to Dames, I have come to view my body as a glorious landscape.

The idea for a children's book was beginning to form. Eventually it would be published under the title *Clever-Lazy, the Girl Who Invented Herself* – by a woman who was in the process of inventing herself! I started to write while Alan was in the hospital. Writing is a lonely business. When I tried to settle down to my work, the specter of Alan's death leered at me, mocked me, no matter how I tried to forget or avoid it. I finally decided to use a technique I had learned in Gestalt. I looked what-I-fear-most square in the face. I visualized it as a Sioux medicine bundle – a skull, a hank of hair, a clutch of bones, wrapped in a buffalo hide. In the mornings, before I began work, I took a good look at it in my imagination, then (metaphorically) stood the whole macabre contraption in a shadowy corner of the room. I could still see it from the corner of my left eye as I sat at my typewriter, but as I immersed myself in my work, it gradually dwindled. Only to re-emerge the next morning!

Clever-Lazy was about a girl inventor who lived in mythic Xanadu. In order to understand her inventions, I had to spend hours at the Royal Ontario Museum, reading about the history of Chinese civilization, boning up on the attributes of Sung dynasty teapots, water wheels, lenses, magnets, the manufacture of fireworks, and (incidentally) gunpowder. I also read a great deal about goddesses, for the girl's mother and grandmother had been priestesses of the Goddess.

I don't believe in goddesses or in *a* Goddess, but I believe that there were people who believed. (I attend the Anglican church regularly, but I am not even sure I believe in God! My faith is far from constant.) I do know that *thinking* about the possibility of female deities has led me all the way from being empowered by the idea, to another idea – that the notion of goddesses rose with the invention of agriculture and has, in the long run, led to the loss of women's liberty. Hunter-gatherers ate better, had more freedom, and fewer children (widely spaced) than Neolithic women who scratched the soil, planted seeds. Farming takes many hands to do the work. Woman becomes a symbol of fecundity and wealth; she becomes a sort of plowed field, herself, to supply a labor force. A gathered harvest needs a pot to put it in, a pit, a bin, a barn. Trade ensues. People congregate, make a town, which needs a wall around it, so the dreaded Others can't get in and steal the grain – and the women. Wars ensue. Men take charge, and establish hierarchies. To vindicate what they are doing, they put woman on a pedestal, worship her as a goddess. A pedestal is a precarious position on which to maintain balance. You lose your power, standing on a pedestal – the power you used to have when you went striding over the landscape. A pedestal is a prison. Beware!

In 1979, I used the money from *Clever-Lazy* to go to Glastonbury, in Somerset, England. That part of Somerset was once a tidal marsh, extending from the Bristol Channel. The land has since been reclaimed for agriculture and grazing. Low hills, once islands, rise out of the flat green landscape. Some people believe that they have been shaped and nudged into gigantic earth sculptures, figures in an ancient zodiac, reflecting the patterns in the heavens. *As above, so below.* The credit for contriving and executing such a giant undertaking is up for grabs – men from Atlantis, visitors from another planet, Neolithic tribesmen, Sumerians? I went to Glastonbury, to walk and hitchhike about the countryside, in order to find out for myself if there was any substance to the idea of the Glastonbury Zodiac. (Certainly, some of the shapes exist, most notably that of Virgo, by the village of Babcary.) But that is not Somerset's (Sumer-set's?) only claim to mystic fame. Many people there are firmly convinced that Jesus came there as a young boy, soon after he had astounded the elders in the Temple. They claim he was brought all the way from Jerusalem by his maternal uncle, Joseph of Arimathea, a wealthy merchant, said to have held interest in the tin and silver mines nearby. (This Joseph was the same rich man who owned the tomb where Jesus was buried, after the crucifixion.) William Blake believed this, as did the Elizabethan alchemist John Dee. Glastonbury is also noted for its connection to the Arthurian legends: it is supposed to be the Isle of Avalon.

The next year, Robert Wilhelm, Catholic theologian and storyteller, invited me to tell "Tristan and Iseult" to a group of Arthurian scholars gathered at Cambridge University. Afterwards, I joined a group, to go on a nine-day walking tour along the Offa's Dike trail, on the Welsh border. It goes through a landscape described in the *Mabinogion*, that fragmentary hodgepodge that is all that is left of Welsh bardic myth.

Meanwhile, in Toronto, a young man named Dan Yashinsky had phoned me. He wanted to talk about storytelling. I invited him to my studio. He was an American; his parents had moved to Canada so their only son could escape the draft. He had grown up in Detroit, gone to college at the University of California in Santa Barbara, where he had majored in English. Also, he had studied with Jacob L. Marino, the "inventor" of Psychodrama, in New York. He agreed with me about stories coming out of the same stockpot as Psychodrama, but he was not interested in becoming a therapist. He wanted to be a storyteller, and to write about storytelling. He had already been talking to some of the older children's librarians in Toronto, Alice Kane and Rita Cox, who were trained in the tradition of the New York Public Library. He had done his homework!

Partly inspired by my gig at the Underground, Dan was telling stories at a little restaurant in the old Kensington Market district. The place was named Gaffers. Dan had originally talked the owners into allowing him to tell on Friday nights, between the musicians' acts, but one night the musicians failed to show up, and Dan was shoved on stage to cover the entire evening. Even so, his performance was so successful that the owners decided to keep him, and dispense with the music. He was only a beginning storyteller, and he knew very few stories, so he was asking other storytellers in the city to rally round. We came crawling out of the woodwork. But the evenings were not limited to those of us who were trained; *anyone* was allowed to come up to the stage!

Gaffers restaurant was very small. On Friday nights, even in the bitter cold of a Toronto winter, a line of would-be listeners formed outside on the steps. Word-of-mouth had spread the news that stories were being told here; people were waiting for a chance to get in. One night a taxi driver, pulling up to the address, asked his customers what the line was for; when they explained about the chance to tell and listen to stories, he followed them into the restaurant and entertained us all with taxi-cab lore.

When Gaffers closed (due to marital strife between the owners), we floated around the city, from the Amsterdam Café, in the gay ghetto, to an old synagogue–cum–art-school in the university district, to a church near bohemian Queen Street. Dan dubbed the enterprise "One Thousand and One Nights of Storytelling in Toronto," a name that has stuck for almost twenty-five years. During that time we have listened to Carol McGirr tell the Icelandic sagas, Bob Barton tell modern literary tales, Dan Yashinsky regale us with tales from Turkey, and a thousand other storytellers tell thousands of tales.

After our first annual storytelling festival (attended by 450 people), our listeners asked us how they could learn to tell stories, too. Dan, our trickster hero, responded to the demand. He called a meeting of half a dozen old hands. All of us were so busy that it was difficult to find a time to get together, but we finally hit on a breakfast meeting, seven-thirty A.M., at the Chelsea Hotel. And so it was that the Storytellers School of Toronto was launched. Nowadays, thousands of people show up for the annual festival and thousands have taken courses at the school. Not all of them are tellers. As an added bonus, we have developed a rich lode of educated, experienced listeners, critical and appreciative as any concertgoers.

One of the many fallouts from the School was a project sponsored and funded by the Children's Aid Society Foundation of Toronto. Barry Dickson, a social worker who attended one of my classes, was fascinated by my tales about storytelling at Nyack and Saint Agatha. A quiet man, but also powerful, he nursed the knowledge for several years before approaching me, and then approaching the CAS Foundation. He persuaded them to put up the funds to hire me, to hire assistants and a trained researcher. We set up a course for "mothers at risk." These were women who had previously abused their children and had them taken away, at least for a while. Now, reunited, and with younger children in the single-parent family, they sought a second chance. These women were interviewed at length, for the purpose of a formal study. During the interview, when the researcher asked if and when a mother talked to her baby, what she said to her baby, she was often met with indignation. Why would anyone want to talk to a baby? By teaching them to teach their children Mother Goose rhymes (often before the child could speak), we sought to build up an arc of anticipation between mother and child. The mother, bending over a child to change a diaper, or feeding a child, might say a rhyme. The child might respond to being touched and held, to being paid attention to, to the mother's expression and the sound of her voice chanting a rhythmical chant. The child might smile; the mother, rewarded, might respond. Or, in time, the child, growing accustomed to rhythm, and learning to anticipate rhyme, might instigate the exchange. We called the program "Mother Goose Comes to the Children's Aid."

Remembering my experiences at Saint Agatha, I realized that these mothers were very like a grown-up version of those children I had known and observed more than ten years before. Although they were adult women, they were often so needy as to enter into infantile competition with their own offspring. We cherished them, even as they were being taught to cherish their infants. I wanted to *nourish* them. Dinny Dickson, also a CAS social worker (and Barry Dickson's wife), had the genius to take this idea literally. She requisitioned an electric oven, so that, when the women arrived for each session, they could smell baking bread or muffins as they came along the corridor. We were shameless in our seduction! But most of all, I wanted these women to learn how to listen to stories, too, so that they would have some sense of what their children were experiencing as they learned to hear and respond. Each offering in Mother Goose is a tiny, perfect story, comprised of jewel-like images, arranged in patterns that rhyme. The stories are often aggressive, even violent. Certainly, they are full of action. To the mothers, my assistants and I told earthy, textured folk tales, also full of imagery and action – and sex, explicit or implied. I aimed to jolt these neglected women out of their lethargy, the boredom that, alas, had become so familiar to me. The program was so successful that we were given funds to do it again; then we were given funds a third time, to work with abusive fathers. One of them was brought from jail, under guard, to learn how to play and talk to his child.

In my own life, losses threatened and proliferated. When Alan had discovered that he had cancer, the doctor had asked him how much he drank. Alan said X, I said Y. "But I never drink before noon," Alan said. I pointed out that he worked until three A.M., didn't get up until one P.M. Alan was furious. To prove to me that he was not addicted, he stopped drinking and smoking from that moment on. He was hell to live with for the first two years, but as result of his anger he would live much longer than had been expected. His cancer went into remission for seven years.

My mother died three days short of her ninety-first birthday. Anne had come to stay in the house permanently, and Joyce (studying for her law degree) made day trips from Pasadena. A few days before Mother died, Joyce was standing by her bed. "All of a sudden," Joyce told me, "I heard the voice of a small child, maybe three years old, crying out, 'Mother! Mother!' I actually looked around, thinking there *was* a child present, a child lost or hurt. Then it came to me – she was crying out for our grandmother! When Mother was dying, that's the person she called for, that's the one she turned to – her own mother!" (Joyce died four years later. I like to think that she was able to walk through the black wall, to be reunited with the *real* mother, the one she lost on the beach, when she was three.)

When Alan's cancer returned, people pulled me aside, sang siren songs into my ear: "Take him to that place in Texas . . . Sweden . . . Tokyo. Take him to Mexico." They could not bear to acknowledge what the doctors had told us: my husband probably had only two more weeks to live. When weeks turned into months, months turned into years, they spoke conspiratorially to me of mega-vitamins and evening primrose oil. They inferred that I must be whipping up a little something in a test tube. Or in a cauldron. I did take out my mother's recipe for *crème anglaise*, dusted it off, hoped that the results would slip down the afflicted throat. Boiled custard, under any name, curdles as it cooks if you don't watch out. I cheated, bought yogurt.

"How many times have I told you," said Alan, "I do not eat yogurt!"

"But I thought that now, when you're so sick . . ."

"How many times do I have to tell you," said Alan. "*I am not sick. I am merely dying of cancer.*"

This new-hatched, non-alcoholic Alan craved sweets. He lived on jelly beans, cheap chocolate bars, cookies, supermarket-shelf cakes. In revenge, I became a serious soup maker. He counterattacked by bringing home six-packs of little tins of Laura Secord puddings, adorned with her picture. I hated her pink-faced smugness. Hussy! But even the puddings were eventually rejected. Alan told me that it was texture that betrayed him. What he could eat one day he couldn't eat another. Eventually, even a drink of water would become a hazard. *Eventually, a drink of water would drown him.* But in those halcyon days, when we were still together, our Sunday-night sin was to sit in front of television while we ate Pepperidge Farm vanilla cake. Not nature, but films *about* nature, Alan enjoyed, especially those PBS ones about termites and bees and ants. And that awful one about body mites.

Sometimes we talked about his dying. He said he did not want to be buried in the family plot out in Scarborough. He wanted his ashes scattered in downtown Toronto, somewhere south of Bloor, between Church (where we lived) and University (where his office used to be), preferably under a library. Maybe under the new opera house, which I would be able to see from our balcony. Once, I remember, we played a sort of game: write your own epitaph. He said that what he wanted on his tombstone, if he wanted a tombstone, which he didn't, was *He could write a good sentence.* But mostly we just read. "Happiness," said Alan, "is sitting in the same room with someone you love, not talking for hours. Both reading." I thought of those happy couples on the Etruscan tombs.

When Alan made it into our fifteenth year of marriage, a new contingent of people told me it must be because of his supreme and steadfast faith in God. Hell! Alan was an atheist and remained one to the very end. "I believe in me," he said, "and in chess and insects. And the stars." My belief in God he regarded as a trivialization of what was more awesome. Alan was in love with infinity. He trundled his two powerful telescopes out to our balcony, eleven floors up in downtown Toronto. I would wake at three o'clock in the morning and hear him coughing out there on one lung. Sometimes I wake now – and listen for that cough.

In downtown Toronto the few starry nights are marred by lights and reflections of lights. Nevertheless, Alan rigged up a timer on his telescope. Once a navigator in the RCAF, for years a professional photographer, he knew how to track a planet, how to sweep the skies, and report, with his old Nikon, far-distant wonders. Our balcony rail is still marked with notches and arrows, our deck, with cabbalistic signs.

Sometimes (not often) he would allow me to peer through the lens. He was impatient with me. "Kee-rist! You can't miss it!" Oh, but I can. The moon and planets go by so fast, so fast. And we own only a little strip of sky. Our balcony faces west. We have to wait for the moon to come round from the south and wheel over the roof of Maple Leaf Gardens. Then we have to wait for it to sort itself out amongst the chimneys and apartment house across a little park. When it reaches Alexander Street, we can skip across Yonge, sight past the Grosvenor Y, past Queen's Park, over the dome on Convocation Hall at the university. Only occasionally can we peer into the Dome of Heaven.

I had thought that to observe the moon all I had to do was find it, fix it in my lens, scan it at my leisure. I can see the moon with my naked eye, of course, but when I look through the lens I have no perspective. I can see only a part, not the whole – and the moon is zipping along. Far away and long ago, when I lived in another galaxy, I used to read to my children: *The moon was a ghostly galleon tossed upon cloudy seas . . .* Even then, I didn't let myself know how fast my universe was sailing away from me.

For just a moment I confront a great golden surface that will not stand still. Like Alan's face, it is full of pits and pocks and imperfections. "Pay attention!" my husband shouts. (Did he really used to shout at me?) Too late. Too soon. Through carelessness, I've let what I *thought* I was observing slip past me. I have lost sight of what I was *just about* to apprehend, understand, truly appreciate.

My lens is empty. I have lost my moon.

CHAPTER 24

The Desert Sighs in the Bed

ALAN DIED JULY 25, 1985. Before he died he said, unexpectedly, "Somehow I keep having this feeling that I should apologize to you, for leaving you alone again. You'll be back where you were when we met." I was astonished by his misperception. "You don't get it," I said. "When I met you, I felt as though I was walking around with a gaping wound. You healed me." I did not mean that I would not carry a scar, a badge for living what had to be lived, but I was whole and healthy. The other thing Alan worried about was the mystery of the whereabouts of Ian. He had hoped that, before he died, I would find out what had happened to my son.

Six weeks after Alan's death, Bette Diver telephoned me. "Sit down," said Bette. "I have astounding news." After thirteen years of silence, Ian had telephoned. She had been at work, but Bob Marisol, the man who was living with her, took the call. He had known me, known Ian; he knew how important the circumstance was. Ian had asked for Bette, or Chris; he gave his name, then hung up! Someone else, a woman, then called; she said she was the director of a halfway house in San Francisco, and that Ian would call back. Bob, bless his heart, did not go to work. He waited. He called Bette, who called me. I called John, to clue him in to what was happening. We all waited. When Ian did phone, I could hardly understand him.

I flew out immediately. Ian's voice was like Robinson Crusoe's, rusty from disuse. He had fainted in the street, weak from hunger and from selling his blood too often under too many names to too many blood banks.

The police knew who he was, but only after a fashion. They did not know his name and he carried no identification. He was the harmless loner who lived in a cave he had chipped for himself in a rotting pillar, under the airport freeway. When the police found him lying in the street, they took him to a hospital. He had suffered a recent blow to his head, either from a fall or from someone striking him. He was being well taken care of: he had even had a CAT scan.

"I kept your son around here longer than I'm supposed to," said the psychiatric social worker. "He's a rare bird." Ian was in the hospital for nine months before they could penetrate his aliases. He gave them a score of names, one of them the right one, some of them puns and anagrams. He mostly went by the name of Jim Rogers. At last, a clever psychiatrist hit on the idea of having someone read the entire list to him every day. *"Ian Bodger is dead!"* he would shout every time that name was called. The force and energy in that response made the psychiatrists think they were on to something. The telephone numbers they pried out of him all began with 914, which they knew meant Westchester County (they didn't know it meant Rockland County, too). No Bodger was listed. Finally he gave them the Divers' number. Because he had so often called the Diver kids, he knew their number better than his own. The social worker told me that, in one more week, Ian would have been sent to a place he referred to as "the big bin," near Sacramento, where thousands of former flower children, now in their thirties and forties, languished unclaimed.

"There was something about your son," he said, "that made me keep saying, 'He's a man of consequence – of consequence to someone. Someone must be looking for him.' For the first few months he didn't speak. He might as well have been dumb. But when we decided to really push him, make him socialize, he finally spoke: 'I may be crazy, but I don't spend my time playing Ping-Pong,' he said. He knew what he was saying was funny, but it was bloody arrogant, too. The arrogance gave me hope. I indulged myself, kept him around longer. Then we discovered the drawings. Hundreds and hundreds of tiny, perfect Napoleonic soldiers, like pattern on wallpaper. And then there was the way he talked, once he started talking. Not just the vocabulary. What he had to say was *textured*, textured with reference. Like I said: a *rara avis*."

Nowadays, when I watch a street person, despised and rejected, digging in the garbage, I think about Ian. What if someone waved a magic wand over this man of sorrows, this filthy vagrant I see here, and wafted him off to a place of unlimited hot water and clean sheets and good food? Ian now lives in a fairy-tale house in a rural village, half a mile away from his father and stepmother. His stepmother was the one who suggested that they buy the cottage and bring Ian to a place near them. When I asked her if she knew what she was getting herself into, she replied, in her New England accent, the accent of Thoreau: "My dear, there are 141 souls in this village, all different. Ian will be just one more different person."

1991. I am visiting Ian. Ian's stepmother is infinitely kind and patient. His father is generous with concern and time and money. *Despite hot water and medical care and all our imprecations, Bearskin does not wash nor comb nor trim. He bites his nails till the quicks are raw. In the Brothers Grimm tale, he did not wipe his tears away; in real life, we have to remind him to wipe his ass.* After days of long silence, I am facing up to the probability that there is nobody there, nobody home. Ian smokes three packs a day; he stares at nothing, through a haze of smoke. I am growing old, I tell myself. I can go through the motions of caring, but, as an act of intelligent self-protection, I must make a decision, to cut the emotional thread, the tie that binds. *I don't know how he knows, but he knows.* At that precise moment, he speaks from his burning bush. "Do you ever feel," he says, "have you ever thought, that most of the time you and I may just be sitting around in a Harold Pinter play?"

One snowy evening, Snow White and Rose Red and their mother sat before the fire while the mother read from a great book. (The book was probably meant to be the Bible, but when I was little, I took it for granted that it was my mother's copy of the Brothers Grimm.) *Suddenly a knock came at the door. When Rose Red opened it, a huge bear shambled in. He lay down on the hearth. All winter he stayed with them. In the spring, when Snow White lifted the latch to let him out, he caught his fur on the haft, and tore a rent in his shaggy coat. Just for a moment – oh, just for a moment! – she thought she saw a gleam of gold shine through.*

Alan did not like to travel, but he liked *me* to travel. He bought me maps and travel books; he helped me check out fares and timetables. The first week I was gone, he said, he would revel in having his dear old apartment to himself. He would spread his work out all over the place, and wonder why he had ever gotten married again! The second week he congratulated himself on getting so much work done, but he began to miss me. By the third week he would be impatient for me to come home. Enough is enough is enough! He was getting angry. Finally, he *yearned* for me.

I loved the going, I loved the coming home. All the time I was away I enjoyed myself the more, knowing that Alan was holding the string to my kite. He made me feel safe. Now that he was gone, I felt the difference keenly. Nobody back home, nobody waiting for me! And yet . . . I planned to explore several offers and commitments I had postponed because of his illness. I had been invited by Rickie Wolf (now Rose Najia) to visit her in Tokyo. She had been classmate during our three-year course at the Gestalt Institute of Toronto, now she was director of the Gestalt Institute of Tokyo. Another classmate, Igor Starak, was teaching at the University of Brisbane. He had invited me to come to Australia, to conduct some workshops, where I would use a folk tale like a shared dream, applying techniques derived from Gestalt and Psychodrama. Robert Wilhelm wanted us to get on with a plan we had to conduct an Arthurian tour in England. But the plan that had excited Alan (and me) the most was the prospect of my trip to Petra, in the Kingdom of Jordan. Ever since the 1930s, when I first read about that place in a book by Richard Halliburton, I had known that one day I would go there – to the "red rose city, half as old as time."

I went to Australia first. Still disoriented by jet lag, from twenty-three hours of travel, I had to force myself to pay attention to the business at hand. I was working with a group of teachers and librarians. I was not even sure which story I was going to tell. Panic! I was not sure if I knew how to tell a story – any story! A red-haired Scots woman (Meg Philp) was in the group; she reminded me of a character from one of the tales collected by Sorche nic Leodha – "The Lass Who Could Not Be Frighted." I opened my mouth. Words came out: *"Once there was a lass who lived on the moor, higher up on the moor than anyone, except Wully, the weaver."* Even as I was laying the scene for "The Lass," another scene flashed into my mind. I saw it clearly: *Once there was a house on the moor. The old Straight Track ran by that house so close, so close that one corner had been hacked off the house and cobbled up again, all askew. That track was a fairy track, and the house had been built too close to it* . . . Oops! Wrong moor! Somehow I had wandered into another story, "My Own Self," from Joseph Jacobs's

More English Fairy Tales. Thank God I had not goofed out loud. My audience was hanging on every word, hanging on my long pause. I stepped back smoothly into the story about the Scots girl, went on from there.

It is always my contention that the more clearly I visualize a story, the more clearly will my listeners see it. My momentary lapse was a purely personal thing; I had fallen down the crack between two worlds. I scrambled back so quickly that I thought no one would ever know about my slide, but I was wrong. An hour later, in the middle of an exercise, a woman, apologetically, described the scene from the *other* story, the one I had suppressed. If I had known the group better, if I had worked with these people over a period of time, if I had built up their trust, if I had not been so weary . . . I should have stopped everything to explore what had happened. I did not have the energy to disrupt a group dynamic that was just beginning to hum and to start it up again. I am afraid that I was almost dismissive in my reaction to her revelation. But what had happened rankled.

A few weeks later, in Japan, I was working with a group of psychiatrists and businessmen. A more unlikely group to attend a session on the use of fairy tales and Gestalt therapy I could not imagine! I worked with an interpreter, which only made the enterprise more bizarre. At the end of the day, on impulse, I said to the group, "I would like to ask your opinion on something that happened to me in Australia." I told how a woman had picked up a scene I had only visualized, never actually described in words. There was a buzz of excitement. Doctors and business moguls turned to each other, engaged in animated conversation. Finally, an elderly psychiatrist, who seemed to have been elected by common consent, rose from his seat and bowed to me: "Today, computer to computer," he said. "Tomorrow, mind to mind."

My mother was gone and Alan was gone. I had talked to my father before I left for Jordan and told him that, if he died while I was away, I might not return for his funeral. He was relieved to know that, he said, and full of admiration for my confidence in his love, and in mine. "I know that you love me, and you have had enough funerals," he assured me. I missed Alan keenly. I thought about *Alan*, rather than his feared and hated cancer, an uninvited house guest who sometimes came between us. My bed seemed dry and vast, with no hope of Alan coming, at three in the morning, to slide between the sheets. (He always came to bed naked; he thought pajamas were immoral.) He did not go to the hospital until the last forty-five minutes of his life. I went from sleeping with a naked man to the prospect of never sleeping with a man again.

And yet . . . I felt a freedom, a secret excitement, like a balloon or a kite cut loose from its string. There are lots of disadvantages in being left alone, but there are also advantages. I intended to take advantage of those advantages. I had no intention of traveling with someone else, male or female, nor of finding another husband. I like traveling alone, being alone, and I am used to it. The separate but equal lives that Alan and I had lived during our marriage had prepared me for the rest of my days – and nights. I like the company and companionship of men, of a man. I like sex, but now I know I am no Aphrodite – and don't want to be. I am comfortable with my autonomy. I can always return to my own secret self, discovered long ago, when I was eleven, content to be solitary, playing in the pine woods, reading and thinking. And yet . . . I wish I had picked up the skill of having occasional, casual sex, without the bother of a relationship. Instead, I learned to name the rigging (of a frigging) three-masted ship.

I had come to Jordan to see the ancient city of Petra, but I lived in a modern apartment house in Amman, the capital city. My landlord there told me to always lock the door behind me or the Bedouins would get in. A Bedouin family camped part of the day in the shadow of the apartment house. They drove their hobbled goat into the tall grass, the children kicking her, beating her, throwing stones at her even while she was letting down milk. Her teats were huge, sore, cobbled with warts. A bell clanked every time she moved. It hung from a chain that looped her neck and right foreleg. Every time she lifted her head she had to lift her right hoof; every time she took a step forward her head was jerked down, almost to the ground.

I had wanted to go to Jordan for a long time, to work on a novel about the Nabataeans. The Nabataeans were pre-Islamic Arabs who held a monopoly on the incense trade. Before I left Canada everyone warned me that, while I was in the Middle East, I should take care to dress modestly. I buttoned my long cotton dress up to the throat; my old-woman arms were covered to the wrists. Palestinian women hid their hair with the traditionally folded shawl; I wore a straw hat. When I walked down the street, my neighbors held up their infants to see the foreign woman go by. They disapproved of me. So did the secretaries at the Canadian and U.S. consulates.

In case of trouble, a sixty-three-year-old woman living alone and unattached would be one more thing to worry about.

Before he died, Alan had worried about my going to the Middle East by myself, but he bought me a copy of Fodor's *Jordan* and a good Bartholomew's map. In Amman, I carried them with me always, glad to know I had his blessing. I had become hooked on the Nabataeans when I read several books by the American-Jewish archaeologist Nelson Glueck, who had discovered a Nabataean temple on a mountain top and excavated the statues there. Quintessential traders, these non-ideological Semites were infinitely adaptable, willing to learn from, borrow from, buy from. When enemies attacked, they folded their tents and stole away. Even when the population of their capital equaled about thirty thousand people, and they had surrounded themselves with temples and palaces, most Nabataeans lived in tents. Several times, when enemies threatened – Jews or Romans or Egyptians – they rode out from their rocky fortresses not to do battle, but to try to persuade their adversary to be reasonable. "It's bad for business," they would say – or something to that effect. "We'll pay you to go away."

Petra, the Nabataean capital, lies 120 miles south of Amman, 40 miles north of Aqaba, the port at the head of the Red Sea. Ruined by earthquakes and the ravages of time, the abandoned city lies in a valley between high sandstone cliffs. It is entered by a tunnel, almost a mile long, made by a stream. The streambed, dry most of the time, serves as road. Thus fortified by nature, Petra was a perfect storage and dispatch center for silk yarn from China, spices from India, ivory tusks from Africa, and, most important, the rare and precious incense from Yemen, in southernmost Arabia. Only the Nabataeans knew how to make the two-month trek to Yemen, and return.

My first day in Amman I went to the folk-art museum, near the amphitheater. When I asked the attendant where I could go to see the Khirbet Tannur sculptures, he did not know what I was talking about and soon trailed off into Arabic. But a young man, hardly more than a boy, stepped out of the crowd to explain, in fair English, that he was an archaeology student and that he just happened to be going up to the Citadel, to the Museum of Antiquities, where the Khirbet Tannur sculptures were housed. He offered to show me the way. I paid for a taxi and, on the trip through the oldest part of the city, we talked a little, chatted. I told him that I lived in Canada, that I had been born in California. My father still lived there.

The boy told me that he knew the custodian well; he would be charmed to be of service. When we arrived, he introduced me to a fat, smiling man, then disappeared. The custodian served me cups and cups of syrupy tea. His English was non-existent; almost an hour went by until finally I made clear to him that I wanted to see the pieces of sculpture that Nelson Glueck had brought down from the temple on Mount Tannur. When I finally extricated myself from the courtesies of the curator, I found myself in a large dusty room with a few old-fashioned glass cabinets set against the wall. On the floor were several cardboard boxes, crumbling away, filled with pieces of sculpture. Two large panels, carved in high relief, leaned against the wall, busts of the goddess Atargatis. I knew them well from the photographs in Glueck's book. Her brow was crowned with a diadem of dolphins; crabs and fruits and stalks of grain were entwined in her hair, draped over shoulders and breasts. Her cockeyed stare entranced me. She was neither Hellenistic nor Egyptian but uniquely Nabataean, a little crude, a little naïve. Adorable.

The Nabataeans fell in love with Atargatis rather late in their history. They must have seen her Greek version, as Aphrodite, at the temple at Ashkelon, on the shores of the Mediterranean, and at her temple at Hierapolis, by the Euphrates. Deep in the desert they worshiped the dolphin goddess and built new temples in her name: on the mountain of Tannur, overlooking the road that runs from the Red Sea to Syria; in the Negev; in the Wadi Ramm and along the Incense Trail; and at Petra, the city carved from living rock. In fishtailed form she promised moisture and fecundity; in dolphin form, she promised safe journey on sea and land and into the life beyond. Womb-shaped, and containing a womb, she was a mystery and a marvel.

And Atargatis loved the Nabataeans. She taught them the secrets of the deep, especially translated for their desert environment. She taught them how to hoard every dewdrop on a dry hillside; how to deflect the runoff by shifting and repositioning stones; how to make terra-cotta pipe; where to bury cisterns in the desert. No matter that they had known how to do many of these things before they ever discovered the dolphin goddess. They attributed to Atargatis all their good fortune, incorporated and integrated all their former deities into her. Dusares, her consort, had still existed and was still worshiped in his own form, a block of unmarked stone, but he paled into insignificance beside flamboyant Atargatis.

Now she sat almost unregarded in this museum. I assumed that she had been sitting there ever since Glueck's American archaeologists had brought her down from her mountain temple, lugged her into this room, and set her on the dusty floor. No one ever got around to putting her into a glass case or up on a pedestal. No one cared about her except as something to hoard. No one worshiped her, no one adored her. I reached out and gave her a little pat. The student had reappeared. He was watching me.

"Don't let me interfere with your plans," I said. "I'm perfectly content to stay here for a little longer, then I'll get a taxi back to the bus stop."

"I'll stay with you," he said.

"No, no. I'm quite capable. I know the way now." He slumped, dejected. I had said something to hurt his feelings.

"Don't you want me for something else?" he asked.

"No," I said, puzzled. "I have my work, and I suppose you have yours. You said you were coming here, too. Do you come often? Are you doing research or do you just like to come and look?"

"I've never been here before," he said.

"Oh, but I thought the curator was a friend of yours. He gave us tea . . ."

"You have offended him. You should pay for the tea."

"Oh, I'm so sorry. Of course I will. Thank you for telling me." (So that's why the old man was so anxious I should stay there, drinking.)

I wandered around the gallery taking notes, trying to remember what I had read. Glueck's book had been too bulky to pack, and the museum offered no labels to explain what I was looking at. My Fodor guide had said there was a book, near the door, but when I had asked the curator, he just smiled. The boy was right; I should have paid him. Now he was nowhere to be seen. I inspected the small exhibit six times over. Finally I gave up. As soon as I made a decisive move towards the door, the curator reappeared. I handed over some money. Too much? Too little?

The boy was waiting for me just outside the door. I started down the hill, hoping I would be able to find a taxi. The boy trotted beside me. "Thank you. You've been very helpful," I said. Patronizing. Cold. "You were very kind to show me the way and I appreciate it, but now I must go." I wondered if I were supposed to tip him, a university student. I wondered if he got a cut on the amount of tea I drank. I wondered, should I take him out to lunch?

"Is that all you want?" asked the boy.

"Yes."

"Then why did you speak to me?"

"You spoke to me first. You said you were going to the museum and would show me the way, remember? You overheard me talking to the guard at the folk museum, to someone else."

"But you said I could show you," said the boy, querulous. "I thought you would take me with you. To Hollywood."

I drew a deep breath, spoke slowly and carefully. "You asked me in the taxi if I had ever been to Hollywood, and I said my father lived near there."

"I thought you would take me," said the boy. We stared at each other, baffled.

"I won't," I said. "Never." His lip trembled. A child betrayed, he turned from me, crossed the road. He walked off rapidly, his narrow shoulders braced under his thin tweed jacket.

I was walking to the grocery store when the car passed me, the driver honking wildly. Just a few yards in front of me he slammed on the brakes, jumped out, looked me straight in the eye, unzipped his trousers, urinated, jumped back in his car, drove off. In the next several weeks, on two occasions, a young man simply stepped in front of me and dropped his trousers. I talked to a young Englishwoman, married to a Jordanian, who kept a shop in town. "Just thank God you don't live in Aqaba," she said. "If you go there, go with a man and make sure that everyone gets the message that he is your husband. From behind every palm tree, from behind every lamp post, they step out in front of you, and flash it."

"But I'm sixty-three years old and it's happening to me right here in Amman," I said. "I seem to have more encounters than you young women."

"Because you're a better bet. The more desperate, the less choosy. The common assumption is that someone your age would not come to Jordan except to shop for a young lover. They drop their trousers to show their wares."

I decided to go down to Petra for a week. In Agatha Christie's day people hired a taxi and drove across the unroaded desert to Thomas Cook's "hotel." Then, the accommodations consisted of camp beds set up in the caves and ruined temples, or in tents in the valley. Prosaically, I rode the bus. The journey was supposed to take three hours, but that was a wild underestimation. We left at six A.M., and reached Petra about noon. I had a reservation at the government hotel, situated outside the city. (Nowadays only Bedouins are allowed to sleep amidst the ruins.) I ate a quick lunch, then set out to explore. No cars go into the city proper, and I had been warned in every guidebook not to hire a horse. They bite, and there is no guarantee against anthrax. The only way to get into the heart of Petra lies through the natural tunnel, carved long ago by a stream sprung from the rock said to be the one that Moses struck. I would have to make this arduous trek every day in order to enter the hidden city.

On the last day, I started early in the morning. I had just picked my way across the pebble-strewn streambed to the raised flagstone platform that is the remnant of a Roman road, when, halfway through the tunnel, I heard voices, and recognized the Europeans. I had seen them in the dining room and in the lounge, heard them talking and laughing over their drinks on the terrace. They spoke several languages, but mostly German. Now they were shrieking and waving at me. They wanted me to get out of the way so they could take a picture. I hauled myself up on the comparatively smooth roadbed, safe at last. Except for this.

"Madame, Missus, Frau," they yelled, trying to wave me aside.

"Wait," I shouted back. "Wait. I'll move on in a few minutes. Then you can take your picture." Or take one of me, I thought. They could label it, "Tourist, Petra." Or "American tourist, Petra." They'd probably guessed as much from my clothes. They were about my age, World War II vintage. Nazis, very likely. How prejudiced I am, I thought. They, probably, just as.

"We want you to move for just a minute," called the taller woman in the group, trying to reason with me. She had hardly any accent. Dressed in green silk, she appeared unexpectedly elegant, cool yet vivid against the sere walls. Where was I supposed to move to? I'd have to jump down from the Roman road, cross the ankle-wrenching streambed, to reach where they were standing on a narrow ledge opposite. I couldn't just stay in the middle. Bedouins and horses galloped through frequently; they would trample me down. Bloody Arabs. Bloody Nazis. My Achilles tendon was killing me. Sciatica threatened. Bloody me!

"Wait," I called again, voice sepulchral in the tunnel. I knew that the Roman road extended only a little farther, then I would have to jump down anyway. But on this, my last day, I had planned to look for the irrigation channel, a broad, shallow shelf that jutted out from the wall. Even before the Romans came, the Nabataeans had hoarded water from the Moses Spring, kept it from seeping away into the dry wadi. (A wadi is a riverbed, usually dry.) At first they had used this open trough, later, terra-cotta pipes with interlocking flanges, to guide water into the city. Yes, there were the pipes, high up on the wall, looking as if they had just been ordered from Beaver Lumber, back home in Toronto.

I glanced over again at the hecklers. Two of the men had expensive Nikons hanging around their necks. I recognized the make. *Alan owned several Nikons. But Alan could take pictures without anyone noticing what he was doing. He would bend down, pretend to polish a speck off the lens, squint through the eyepiece, snap away without any fuss. His pictures were all of people. The last few months he used to take pictures of the people in the waiting room at Princess Margaret Hospital. "Which," he would ask me, "is the one with cancer?" I learned that the anxious-angry-looking spouse was the one who wasn't sick.* Damn these people with their cameras! Aping Alan. Not Alan.

I reached the end of the flagged road and jumped down. I hugged the wall, edging around several bends. A troop of Bedouins galloped by in a swirl of dust and gravel. I opened my eyes again and saw the end of the tunnel, a vaginal slit outlined against bright, sharp light. When I emerged from the tunnel, I took in the famous view, the ornate columned temple facade carved in bas-relief out of striated sandstone. The Arabs sitting on the steps barely reached the height of a column base. Even though the guidebooks sought to warn me, I had not anticipated how immense Petra would be, how overwhelming. Topography and layout were so confusing that only yesterday had I figured out which way was north. On this last day it behove me to make careful choices. What I wanted to see most of all was the temple of Atargatis, and if I wanted to climb the Zibb Attuf I must do so in the early morning.

"Attuf" means merciful, and "Zibb Attuf" means Merciful Phallus, the name of the high holy place where Petra's most ancient sacrificial altar was situated. A ceremonial way had been cut into the rock. Often there were hewn steps, but even so the path was precipitous; it took me several hours to make the ascent. Along the way I paused to gawk at the tombs and temples. Magnificent, ornate, claustrophobic, they too were carved in bas-relief from the cliff face, seemingly bound to the rock by continuums of oozing color: mauve, saffron, silver, peach, rose, chocolate. The architecture was Hellenistic. Not only were doorways and facades culturally incongruous in the Arabic setting, but structurally paradoxical. Delicate detail erupted from unhewn rock beside it. Some of the places, although constructed in the centuries immediately before and after the birth of Christ, looked as though they belonged in the Renaissance, over a thousand years later. Some reminded me of ornate Victorian monstrosities, brownstone mansions, a sandstone building with many towers and turrets on the campus of the University of Toronto. However, they were hardly more than facades, like movie sets. Inside the place was shallow, just enough room for the Nabataean ceremonial meal: thirteen people sitting on a three sided-banquette called a triclinium. I thought of paintings of the Last Supper.

At this hour of the morning the turns and twists of the canyon kept doorways and cornices in shadow. I felt muffled, until I reached the top of the ridge, where the whole expanse of bright blue sky arced over me and the sun shone down with that directness peculiar to desert places. The mountain top was flat but uneven, split across by a jagged crack, narrow enough in some places to jump across. Near me three steps, neatly cut, led up to a low altar. Just as neat, but more sinister, were the efficient-looking drainage hole and channels designed to carry off blood. Goats and rams were the usual sacrifices. Only an *occasional* Isaac, I assured myself. The Edomites used this place to worship before the Nabataeans drove them out, but the altar, steps, and drain were all Nabataean. So were the two stunted obelisks standing a little distance away. I had to remind myself that they had not been *built* here. The Nabataeans had whittled down the whole damned mountain top so the deity's erection could *emerge*. Merciful Phallus indeed!

As noon approached, the sun forced me from the mountain. By the time I had descended to the valley floor, I was thirsty and hungry and ready to use the loo. I sought out the government restaurant, which lies in an elbow of the Wadi Moussa, about halfway through the valley. The place has always been a good business corner. The Romans built a nymphaeum across the street, a sort of tavern, with fountains (probably dry most of the time), and statues of naked nymphs. Nowadays the Jordanian government offers tourists a restaurant and an umbrella-shaded terrace; also, a modern marvel of clean tiles, running water, and flush toilets, a convenience not easy to find in this part of the world.

I chose a table on the terrace and ordered lunch. I sipped my bottled water and worked on my notes. Poppies flared in the dry wadi beyond the wall, and a little blue lizard scuttled by. Those people who, hours ago, had yelled at me in the tunnel, sat themselves down at the table next to me, laughing and talking. Sometimes, for no apparent reason, they switched from German to French to Russian, like the characters in T. S. Eliot's *The Waste Land*. Their tans evoked images of yachts on the Mediterranean, ski chalets in Austria, an amusing little excursion down to Petra in April of the year. Sunlight danced on their coffee spoons.

I tried to figure out their relationships. There was a married couple, the man in his seventies, his colorless wife twenty years younger. The husband wore a blue blazer, white silk shirt, and silk foulard. The two other men, fiftyish, lolled in their chairs, shirts open, exposing hairless, sagging chests. The wife watched passively while her husband flirted with them. The only member of the party who really interested me was the tall woman in green silk. She seemed unattached, detached. I was wearing purple cotton slacks, an unironed pink shirt, a straw hat, and Adidas. I smelled of sweat. The woman in green looked cool, poised. Restless, though. She tapped her fingers, smoked a cigarette, glanced about. Bored. For a moment our eyes met.

The waiter brought my tea and tabouleh. I recognized him as one of the waiters from the hotel. He was tall. His hair, shiny as shoe polish, was neatly parted. He had a black mustache. In his waiter's uniform – black pants, white shirt, red waistcoat – he looked like a painted wooden doll. No, a marionette. He bent assiduously over the Europeans, wrote on his little pad, walked over to the bar, picked up an order, delivered it with mechanical flourish. Smiled. The mustache lifted like a lid, revealed white teeth. Closed lid. Bowed. Withdrew.

After he had left the terrace the tall woman, the one in green, looked at the menu, exclaimed, rushed into the restaurant to talk to the waiter. Through the glass pane I saw him listening, head politely cocked. There was an enameled quality about him. The woman returned to her seat. She seemed relieved but more animated. She asked for another cigarette, joined in on the conversation, laughed throatily. I sat with my finger marking the place in my guidebook, watching her in spite of myself. She was used to being admired, worshiped even. She was still very beautiful: a carefully preserved ruin.

After lunch, I used the loo again, then stopped at the counter to buy bottled water. I returned to my table to leave a tip, repacked my bag. Something in the guidebook caught my eye. I sat down to look at my notes, to check a reference. I unscrewed the top of the water bottle, sipped. Half an hour went by. Damn old age! I had to go to the loo. Again.

I opened the door, started down the short tiled corridor. For a moment I thought I'd made a mistake. The marionette was standing in front of me. I stopped. I stared at him in amazement. He did not see me. I was looking into the mirror. The woman in green was saying, "Do it! Do it!" Her voice was a hoarse, loud whisper. Her blouse was open, her breasts exposed. She took his hand, guided it to her nipple. She sighed hauntingly, as though she were coming home; gave a piteous cry. The man unzipped his fly. She dropped to her knees on the tile floor, glanced into the mirror. Saw me. Froze.

Suddenly she was like a trapped bird, a bird flown through the window, wanting desperately to get out. She beat her wings, darted this way and that. I started to back down the corridor, but she rushed past me, blocked my exit. I rushed into one of the stalls. I peed. She must have decided to come back into the washroom. Through a crack in the door I saw her scrabbling in her purse. "Go! Go!" she said to the waiter. Her voice was a groan of anguish. She was struggling with the buttons of her silk blouse. I waited. I waited. I heard her go out through the door.

After a few moments I went out, too, careful not to look in the direction of the Europeans as I crossed the terrace. I went back to the road that paralleled the wadi. Once it had been a colonnaded street of shops, but now all that was left were rows of broken columns leading to the ruined Temenos Gate. At one time the huge stone piers had been surmounted by an arch; even now the scale was impressive. But I was looking for something else.

I had spent days trying to find out where the Temple of Atargatis was. The guides either did not know of its existence, did not know where it was, or would have nothing to do with a pre-Islamic goddess. Then, just last night, I had found a new guidebook in the hotel shop, Iain Browning's *Petra*. It had an intelligent text that not only made mention of the temple but afforded a sketch and a helpful map. According to Browning, a little bridge had spanned the wadi (the wadi ran parallel to the street), and led to the Atargatis temple porch, which lay some distance beyond. The remains of the bridgehead were supposed to lie this side of the massive gate, but I couldn't sort out which pile of stones was which. The partially excavated temple was supposed to lie across the wadi, but all I could see were earthen hummocks and a stretch of stone rubble, either natural or man-made. In the distance a couple of broken pillars danced in the glare. I was not sure I wanted to venture that far. Hard to get my bearings, hard to think, in the afternoon heat.

Loose stones rattled under my Adidases as I plunged down the bank. I had hoped there were no snakes in Jordan. So far I had not seen any. Vipers, I remembered. Generations of vipers. An asp to her bosom. *And a hand on her breast.* Huge lily bulbs, as large as amaryllis, stuck out of the dried earth. Lilies of the field! I had come to Jordan too late to see them in bloom. Wild hollyhocks abounded though, dirty-white and stunted. *The day Alan died, my friend Anne Kerr volunteered to drive me to the crematorium, the one she had used for her parents. At the top of Church Street, where it curved toward Davenport Road, I had spied a line of salmon-pink hollyhocks as we drove by, flaunting themselves against a chocolate-colored wall.*

I was sweating. My canvas purse bumped between my breasts; its strap chafed my sunburned neck. The oilcloth shopping bag (from Liberty) swung awkwardly in my right hand, unbalanced by the water bottle. I saw an oleander bush; its roots would make a good hiding place. I shoved my purse and the heavy guidebook into the space under the roots. I marked it with a cairn of stones. I once learned most of *The Waste Land* by heart. Now some lines popped into my head:

> *What are the roots that clutch, what branches grow*
> *Out of this stony rubbish? Son of man,*
> *You cannot say, or guess, for you know only*
> *A heap of broken images, where the sun beats,*
> *And the dead tree gives no shelter, the cricket no relief,*
> *And the dry stone no sound of water. . . .*

Half-blinded by sunlight and its reflection, I picked my way through stones and rubble. All of Jordan seemed to be covered with caked sand and scattered boulder pebbles. I looked for chunks and pieces that might have come from ancient buildings. According to Browning, the Atargatis temple was one of the few freestanding buildings to be excavated in Petra. Even so, the dig had been abandoned for lack of money. I was surprised when I came upon a carefully cut pit, about twelve feet in depth. The pillars I had been using as bearings were on the far side, surmounting a parapet. Near me some fallen stones acted almost as steps leading down into the square-cut cavity, which was about the size of our bedroom back home in Toronto. Half the space was in shadow. I descended. I crossed to a corner and sank down, my back to the wall. Sweat poured down my face.

My heart was pounding. I took a swig of water and reveled in the coolness of my sanctuary.

After a while I became aware that I was staring at the wall. Clearly marked layers, earth and gravel and a red-flecked stripe, were repeated at irregular intervals. I reached out and dug delicately at the red. A tiny shard of pottery, no bigger than my fingernail, came away from the wall. It was decorated with the famous black leaf pattern. Nabataean ware! Glueck had said that the Nabataeans used their best dishes ceremonially, smashing them after they had partaken of a sacred meal. I dug out some more fragments. I had not expected the pottery to be so thin, so silky to the touch. It was almost like porcelain. (Once, when I was visiting my parents, I had gone to the Jewish Museum in Los Angeles, where Glueck had sent a few – very few – of his finds. The curator had worn white gloves when she took some pottery pieces out of their acid-free box. She had not offered to let me touch. I had not thought to ask.)

I opened my notebook and began to write. The characters in my novel would have come here to pay homage to their goddess. Caravanners would have come, women as well as men, to give thanks, to ask for safe passage, for good profit. And sailors up from Aqaba. There would have been priests and priestesses, and temple prostitutes to greet and serve the weary traveler. Glueck had suspected that a sacred pool had existed within the temple. There had been one in Ashkelon, on the shores of the Mediterranean, but here, down in the desert, it must have seemed a miracle. Proof that the goddess was *wet*.

For the first time since coming to Jordan I felt that I could breathe. I must have started holding my breath back when the boy at the Museum of Antiquities had asked me to take him to Hollywood. In the apartment house where I was staying in Amman, I listened for any noise that might interrupt the empty silence, then lay awake and listened to the silence. My hotel room at Petra was supposed to be air-conditioned; the air-conditioning didn't work but it made a rattling noise. Only here, in this cool, dry pit, could I relax. I smoothed a place for myself, placed the shopping bag under my head, and tentatively lay down. I wiggled a hollow for my hips. I closed my eyes.

An old familiar tension came into my thighs, my groin, my lower belly. I touched the tips of my sagging breasts. I balled my fist, put it between my legs, rubbed and swayed. Not good enough. I reached for the water bottle, screwed its top as tight as I could, and straddled it, rocked myself against it. So long, so long, it had been so long! The climax was slow in coming, tantalizingly out of reach. Come, come, come!

I heard a clatter, a tapping of heels. Someone was approaching, not from the direction of the Colonnade Street, the Temenos Gate, but from the desolate expanse beyond the temple. A shower of gravel fell down into the pit. I sat up hurriedly, grasped bag and water bottle, stood up with my back against the wall. Two young goats, kids, appeared, poised between the pillars. They gazed at me, capered in the sunlight on their twiggy legs. Small, sharp hooves made a rat-a-tat as they ran along the parapet. I heard voices. Three ragged children, slender and leggy as the goats, came into sight. They stared at me from great brown eyes. The eldest, a girl about twelve, shouted to the goats and waved a stick at them. The youngest child clutched her sister's skirts. The boy chased after the goats. I climbed up the fallen rocks by which I had descended and walked around the parapet to where the children were. The pit, which had seemed so protective, now looked to me like a trap.

The older girl felt deep into the folds of her skirt, brought out two large shards of Nabataean ware, the largest I had seen outside a museum. "How much?" I asked. She may not have known English, but her ancestors had dealt in ivory, apes, and peacocks. I admired her toughness. I tried to play my part well, bargaining hard but being beaten down by her. She asked seven, I offered five, we settled for six. I had lived in Jordan just long enough to know that not to negotiate would have seemed cold-blooded, uncaring, an avoidance of human contact. Besides, if I had simply handed over my money to these urchins, I might not have been able to get rid of them.

"Goodbye," I said. "Farewell." I took out my notebook, my pen. I sat down on a broken pediment and began to write. They edged closer to see what I was doing. I showed them the notebook. "Go. Goodbye. Buzz off." They skipped away, following the goats out into a sunbaked aridity so dazzling that I could hardly mark their disappearance.

I descended again into the pit, returned to my cool corner. I did not lie down, instead I continued to write. "I am here, in the temple of Atargatis," I wrote. "Ashtar. Ishtar. Esther. Star." *I thought of the Catholic church in Astoria, the Catholic church in San Pedro; both were called "Mother Mary,*

Star of the Sea." I thought of the blessing of the fishing fleet, the flowered cross, thrown into Los Angeles harbor. "Those in peril on the sea" like to have it both ways, cover all bets – Mother of God, and goddess.

A shower of little stones. The kids with the kids must have come back again. I looked up and saw the two men before they saw me. They had just stepped up onto the parapet on the far side of the pit, the same place where the children had stood. I rose to my feet silently, scooped up my bag, my notebook, pen. Leave the water bottle, I told myself. I took quick, sure steps up the flight of fallen rock. I was almost to the top before they were aware of me. Now I could see that they were sailors, dressed in traditional middies. They must have come up from Aqaba; they were enlistees in the king's small, snappy navy. Each of them wore a flat white hat encircled by a navy blue ribbon with the word *Jordan* written in both English and Arabic. They were very young, very fit, very surprised to see me. I was on the same level as they were but the pit yawned between us.

One of the men, with practiced agility, leapt down, twelve feet or more, onto the soft sand below. He landed on the balls of his feet, bending his knees so as to regain his balance immediately. Battle trained, I thought. The other sailor started to walk around the rim of the pit. From time to time he stopped to pick a flower. Incongruous as it might seem, he was arranging a bouquet as he progressed towards me. The leaper smiled broadly, ingratiatingly. "English, lady? English, lady? You speak English. I speak English." His shipmate had paused to listen. The leaper looked up at him as though to say, "Let me handle this," then turned to me. "Lady, O English lady, do you want to see?"

The leaper began to unbuckle his belt. "English lady, you will like." He fumbled with his trouser buttons. "Very nice to see." I turned my back on both of them, stepped down from the parapet, and walked determinedly, steadily, back through the chaos of excavation mounds. As I passed the oleander bush I reached down and caught the broad black strap of my canvas purse, slung it over my neck – all in one swooping motion. I abandoned Iain Browning to his fate. Behind me I heard the sailor calling, "You will like. Very nice. Come back and look. Very big to see."

That evening, showered and dressed for dinner, I went into the dining room. As usual, the maitre d' placed me at a table for one in the corner near the kitchen. This was the hard part of the day. Everyone else was in a group or had a friend, a spouse, a lover to talk to. I glanced around the room again, looking for the woman in green, the lily of the field. I was surprised by my sense of loss when I failed to find her.

The marionette had returned from the rest house to help wait on table at dinner. I watched him from across the dining room. He twitched, as though moved by invisible strings. He fetched and carried. He bent assiduously. For a moment I thought of the hobbled goat back in Amman. Then he straightened up and we looked at each other, measured each other. I don't know what he perceived, but what I saw was his hate, his sadness, and his terrible pride.

As is the custom, I ordered bottled water to drink with my dinner. As is the custom, I took the unfinished bottle back to my bedroom with me.

CHAPTER 25

The Well at the World's End

MY TRAVELS ABROAD TOOK place in the first half of 1986. In July and August I stayed with Father, in California. He was surrounded by grocery cartons; they brimmed with the flotsam and jetsam of a lifetime. The task of organizing them was beyond me. I hired a middle-aged graduate student to act as archivist. She helped me organize the clippings, records, letters, and photographs that were overflowing his apartment. An historian, she was interested in writing a Ph.D. thesis on marine oil-pollution, and was therefore glad to find so much material on Father's early contributions to legislation regarding oil spills. An historical society and a museum were also interested in receiving some of the papers. Anne came to visit soon after I left him. She was furious at what she perceived as my meddling. She took all the files away and stored them in a commercial warehouse. She refused to tell me where the papers were. Father died in 1986; Anne would die in 1990 without telling anyone where she had stored his papers.

During that last summer, when I was living with him, Father still attended official ceremonies and professional occasions; he went to the gym at the San Pedro Y almost every day, and he had a busy social life. Sometimes he did not come home at night. He also studied for and passed an examination for his Master Mariner's license, which made him the oldest continually licenced master mariner in the United States, probably in the world. Then, mindful of the difficulty he had had in finding a berth as a merchant marine officer back in the 1920s, he took the Able Seaman's exam as well. Just in case.

At his age (ninety-two), no one was going to give him command of a ship, and no one was going to hire him as a deck hand, so I didn't have to worry. When he passed his California State driving-license exam, part of me was glad, because his life and mine would not have been worth living if he could not have driven his car. On the other hand, I was furious with the Motor Vehicle Bureau, because he was a menace on the road. I almost called to complain. (Even as I write this, a horrid thought occurs! Maybe he *didn't* pass. Maybe he just said that he did, and was driving around without a license. The Master Mariner's certificate was framed and hung on the wall. I never asked to see his driver's license!)

I have two vivid images of Father on that last visit. In one, he is sitting in the living room, overlooking his beloved Los Angeles harbor. He had decided to transfer the good brass buttons from a worn-out blazer to a new blazer. I watched him as he threaded the needle. I, his daughter, made no move to sew on the button for him. Mostly because I am no good at sewing. At the age of ninety-two, he could still thread a needle handily. He demonstrated how he had rubbed the thread across a piece of beeswax to stiffen the end into a sharp point, the better to poke through the needle's eye. He showed me a filthy lump of beeswax, full of bits of lint and dust and god-knows-what. Father said he figured it had been in use for more than a century, maybe almost two. During his first few weeks at sea, the ship's sail-maker, ferreting round the sail locker, had found a worn-down lump and taught a very young and eager seaman the thread trick. (Today, that piece of beeswax languishes in my sewing box.)

The other memory is of the morning when I left. I had hired a car and would return it at the airport, so there was no reason (thank God!) that Father should drive me there. He made my breakfast – not a boiled egg, because of the cholesterol. (Mother had died young, age ninety-one, by eating an egg every day.) We had Shredded Wheat and bananas – for the potassium, he informed me, and to give him energy at the Y. Although he was still in his bathrobe, he insisted on putting my suitcase into the car. When I was in the driver's seat, he leaned in through the window to give me a final kiss goodbye. "Well," he said, "it's been a good visit, all told. We had our fights, but one thing I'll say for you. *You don't sulk.*" Those were the last words I ever had directly from my father. When I watched for him in the rear-view mirror (I knew it was probably for the last time), I saw him standing at the end of the lane, his skinny legs and ankles sticking out from under his bathrobe, feet thrust into worn-out slippers. Wisps of white hair stood straight up on his balding scalp, giving him the surprised look of a little boy.

Father had told me two stories about his childhood. "They aren't exactly memories," he said. "Memory is different. These are things that go beyond. It's like when you open a drawer you've never opened before and find it full of layers of tissue paper. When you pull back the paper, something you lost a long time ago is just lying there, fresh as the day it happened. You are *seeing*, not remembering."

When his father died, ten-year-old Frank, and his younger sister, Agnes, went to live with their grandparents in Des Moines, Iowa. He adored his grandfather, who was a Civil War hero, but he felt out of place in rural Iowa. Besides his grandparents, his grandmother's mother lived with them. "I had forgotten all about her," he explained to me. "There was a fireplace in the kitchen, and she used to sit there in a rocking chair, all day long. She wasn't quite right in the head, and I was afraid of her. Worse, I was ashamed of her. And ashamed of being ashamed. She smoked a pipe! But she didn't smoke tobacco. That wouldn't have been ladylike! My grandma kept a patch of hemp for her out back, next to the corn patch." He paused. "Until last week I never thought about that old woman, not once. Then suddenly she was there, as clear as I see you now. I wish I'd talked to her more. I figure she must have been born about 1812." (As he speaks I am aware of the arc of time. In 1986, age sixty-three, I am talking to my father who, in 1904, when he was ten, spoke to an old woman who, when she was ten, must have lived among people who had fought in the American Revolution.)

The other story was harder to tell. One of the reasons Frank loved living with his grandfather was that the old man was so respected, and so respectable. Not only had Frank's mother run off, but his father was involved in a scandal that had to do with a vague shadow of bankruptcy, or embezzlement – or both. On the day of the story, Frank's grandfather drove himself and his grandson to church in the horse and buggy. On the way home the old man said, "You know what I'm going to do? I'm going to stop in town at that newfangled ice-cream parlor and buy us each an ice-cream cone." When they got into town, good as his word, Colonel Higbee stopped and tied up his horse.

"There were hitching posts along Main Street. Well, wouldn't you know! A couple of old biddies came along from church. They were sitting and waiting in the buggy next to me and I could hear them talking. One of them said – and it was her tone of voice, you know. She said, 'Look at that David Higbee – him supposed to be a pillar of the church and all. Buying ice cream on a Sunday!' It wasn't *what* she said. It was the *way*. The same voice people used when they talked about my mother. I had thought, with my grandpa, that I was safe. No breath of scandal would ever touch him. When my grandpa came out of the store, he looked at me and asked me what was the matter. I'd turned all red, I guess. I was trying hard not to cry. But even though he asked and asked, I couldn't tell him. I couldn't find the words. So I never did tell him. I never told anyone until now. Till this minute." (And suddenly there was my father, ten years old. I put my arms around a little boy, conjured up from long ago, while he wept.)

I took a circuitous route back to Toronto. I went to see Bette Diver, in Nyack, and Ian, now in Maine. When I talked to Father several times by phone, the communication was not satisfactory. He was quite deaf, which was an obstacle, and in the last conversation we had he kept trying to tell me how he had not gained any weight because he had stopped eating entirely. He didn't even *want* to eat, which he thought was an accomplishment. He was elated! Maybe I should have paid more attention. Two days later, when he was at the San Pedro Y, he swam his usual half-mile and was lifting weights with his skinny, muscular little arms, when he gave a sigh, and keeled over. Everyone at the Y knew him. People picked him up and rushed him across the street to the hospital. Thank God, he was dead on arrival! Anne flew out to Los Angeles from Boston; I, from Toronto. Joyce, who was very ill with cancer, barely tottered to the graveside. Besides Father's three daughters, we discovered, there were three other ladies, age sixty-seven, seventy-four, eighty-seven, each contending for place as chief mourner. Father had been sleeping with all three of them.

When Lucy died in 1963, the safe, domestic sphere of the teacup and my perfect sphere of childhood cracked all at once. From that time onwards I believed in the possibility of death.

Mother had died in 1983. Alan died in 1985. Father died in 1986. Joyce would die in 1987, preceded by her daughter, Kate. Joyce's son,

Steven, would die in 1988. Anne's husband, Jim, would die late in 1989. Anne would die in 1990. Evelyn, Bette, and Margo would die in the 1990s.

I returned to my Gestalt practise, and to my storytelling life in Toronto. In 1988, as we had planned earlier, Robert Wilhelm and I went to England, to help lead a tour group. We called the tour "A Winter's Journey to King Arthur's Britain." Robert soon discovered that he did not like being in Britain during the winter; I, on the other hand, reveled in the greenness, the gleam of holly in the hedgerows, the sight of roses by Glastonbury's Chalice Well, on the last day in December. I gloried in the winter landscape, and I liked the fact that there were hardly any other tourists about when we visited Tintagel. Robert generously, and willingly, gave over the trip to me. For the next ten years I continued to lead the tour, first with actor Ed Kiley as partner and assistant, then, after he died, with librarian-storyteller Ken Setterington. As the years passed, I became steeped in the multifarious (and contending) concepts of Arthur, both historical and mythical.

I had hoped to bury Alan's ashes under the new opera house at Bay and Wellesley. I liked the idea of his being part of all that joy and beauty. Moreover, I would be able to see the glass pyramid on the roof of the opera house from the same balcony where we used to watch the moon. I planned to donate money for one of the seats in the opera house, and to have a brass plaque affixed to it. However, the New Democratic Party, unexpectedly winning a majority in the Ontario legislature, scratched the building plans, proclaiming that opera is elitist. (Now that the NDP is out of office, expensive condominiums are being built on the site.) For some eight years the brown packet holding Alan's ashes had languished in my basement storage room.

I went back to Plan One, his idea of being buried under a library. Alan had said he wanted to be buried between University Avenue (where he used to work) and Church Street (where we lived). At first I did not consider the Lillian H. Smith branch, to be constructed near Spadina, then it struck me that nothing as good would be built in downtown Toronto for another half-century. I was willing to nudge the parameters a little. Alan would have to forgive me for going a few blocks farther west.

Excavations had barely begun when winter came. The hole, deep as a quarry, filled up with water. Construction halted. Then, in March 1993,

neighborhood intelligence phoned me that the hole had been pumped out
and concrete was about to be poured. On a bitter cold Sunday morning –
brilliant sun, cruel wind, glacial ice – my friend Ken Setterington and I sur-
veyed the scene. Although he had never met Alan, I chose Ken to be my
accomplice because he would be neither too solemn or not solemn enough.
Besides, he is thirty years younger than I am, adventurous and agile.

We opened the brown paper package and slid the cover off the plastic
box. The stuff inside was white and uniform. It looked like kitty litter. It
looked like the ashes of all the other people I knew, who had died and been
cremated. Maybe it *was* kitty litter! I reached under a chain-link fence and
spilled the first few clinkers. Ken risked life and limb to stretch his body
out over the edge of the precipice, aim toward a wooden form. A cement-
mixer's hose was poised, ready to go on Monday morning. As he poured
the rest of the contents toward the target, a gust of wind caught the ash.
Most of it settled over the planks and ladders and machinery on the site,
some of it whirled skywards, or fell into puddles.

Once the deed was done, I negotiated with the Toronto Public Library
to allow me to present a piece of furniture to the Osborne room in memory
of my husband. I wanted to give one of those revolving bookcases, but they
already had one, and space was limited. I was finally allowed, after months
of committee meetings, to present a Hepplewhite-style lectern, where the
guest book would repose. The committee, of course, was kept ignorant of
my grander plan: to make the airy, playful, much-used library building into
a fitting mausoleum for a man who loved cities, loved books and words,
loved *me*. Affixed to the lectern is a polished brass plaque with the epitaph
that he chose for himself:

Alan Nelson Mercer, 1920-1985.
He could write a good sentence.

I'd like to think of my Etruscan husband as being in Etruscan Heaven,
lying on a couch, knees up, waiting for his Etruscan wife to come home.
No! He'd hate that! Much rather he be whirled away to dwell among the
stars. Or, as dust on a workman's boots, be tramped through the streets of
the city. Or, reduced to an elemental speck, become a component of the
primordial ooze.

For more than a decade, my life wheeled around "A Winter's Journey to Arthur's Britain." The annual tour became a fixture in my life, my "hinge of heaven," like the constellation of the Great Bear, whom Arthur represents on his cosmic level. As the years passed, I not only became steeped in the multifarious (and contending) concepts of Arthur, both historical and mythical, but my private, personal myth became more clothed and manifest. I am beginning to understand how my life infuses and informs the stories I tell, and how, as my experience deepens, my life becomes more mythical. In my private myth, my father's totem is the Great Bear. As such, he could be King Arthur (Arthur means "bear"), but as a child I often confused him with Neptune. Later, when I came to read Celtic myth, I saw him as the sea-god Llyr (Neptune's Welsh-Irish equivalent). There is a connection: Geoffrey of Monmouth, in his "History of the Kings of Britain," lists the god-king Leir in the genealogy of Arthur. In my mythology, Admiral Frank David Higbee, King Llyr-Leir, and King Arthur are all one and the same! If further confirmation is needed, consider: Shakespeare borrowed the name, changed the spelling yet again (to Lear), and wrote a play about a king who sired three contentious daughters.

Our custom was to leave Toronto on the evening of December 26, so as to arrive at Heathrow the following morning. A motor coach would meet us there, and whirl us across England, to the great Neolithic complex of mounds and barrows and stone rings, at Avebury. It was a few years before I contemplated leading a tour, that I had come across *The Silbury Treasure* and *The Avebury Cycle* by Michael Dames. Dames gave me the clues, helped me to understand how the natural landscape of the English downs, and the Neolithic *schema*, spread over several miles, act as metaphor for the cycle of seasons, the cycle of life, the meaning of birth, menstruation, coupling, conception, menopause, death-and-resurrection. The experience of going to Avebury, and of walking the land, has helped me to view my own body as topography – no matter what shape I am in!

At noon, just a few days after the winter solstice, we would be standing on West Kennet Long Barrow, while I declaimed the story of "The Marriage of Sir Gawain" – how, when the Sun God kisses the Winter Hag, he solves the age-old riddle: *What does a woman really want?* Answer: *To be what she would be, when she chooses to be that.* Afterwards, we entered the barrow. Shaped like a woman's pelvis, corbeled with stone, it represents the stony, bony womb of the post-menopausal goddess. Four thousand years ago, it would have been filled with a mash of vegetation, and the severed limbs and bodies of those who had died, to make a kind of sacred mulch.

At the base of the barrow is a large spring, the source of the River Kennet. Until the early twentieth century, the locals pronounced "kennet" without the vowels: kennet = cunt. Across the road is a huge earthen pyramid, Silbury Hill. Over several millennia, the hill was built up, layer on layer: first chalk, then tree branches (interwoven with grass ropes), arranged in the pattern of a spiderweb; then a layer of turfs, always cut in August; then chalk again. The channel is dry now, but there was a time when water had been diverted from the spring in the flank of the barrow, to supply a moat surrounding the hill; the moat outlined the shape of a phallic-necked pregnant goddess, the belly of which was the great earth mound.

Arriving at the same storied places, at the same time, on the same date, year after year, had an accumulative effect on me. "The Winter's Journey" became a pilgrimage, a sort of annual maze-walk, which healed and empowered me. There was a sense of ritual that spilled over to the people who accompanied me, although that had not been my original intent. Years later, participants write to me, or tell me directly, how the experience changed their lives.

When I was thirteen years old, Father spoke glowingly of a book he was reading, *Benjamin Franklin at the Court of Versailles*. I borrowed it, only to find myself wading through eighteenth-century politics, science, and history beyond my comprehension. I read enough, though, to learn that Franklin had been romantically involved with many lovely ladies at Versailles. He could be *bon vivant*, philosopher, or backwoods rustic. He engaged the best tailors in Paris to make his brocade suits *and* he wore a coonskin cap. He enchanted the gaping aristocrats by telling them tall tales from the American frontier.

I was not quite sure what a tall tale was but I read with scholarly interest the observations of the great scientist: "*There is no more noble or magnificent sight,*" Franklin averred, "*than that of the Atlantic whales, as they leap up Niagara Falls on the way to their spawning grounds.*" A child who had not had the advantage of being brought up on the banks of the Columbia, had never heard of the River Wye, might have forgotten that image or been more skeptical. I swallowed the story – hook, line, and sinker. Ever hopeful, I crane my neck whenever I cross the Peace Bridge at

Niagara. *Never once have I so much as caught a glimpse of the Ultimate Salmon making her splendid leap, although, in my personal myth, my mother's totem is the salmon, and she the Fisher, wounded in the groin.*

In the early nineties I received notice of a writers' workshop to be held on Orcas Island, in Puget Sound, near Seattle, Washington. Suddenly I craved the western ocean. Puget Sound is a body of water that is almost as enclosed as the Great Lakes. I wanted the open sea. I made inquiries of Barbara Turner-Vesselago, who was running the workshop. She told me of an Indian reservation on the Olympia Peninsula, at the mouth of a little river. The tribal council there has built well-appointed cabins, which they rent.

I made arrangements to go out to Washington State a week before the workshop. I had a childish illusion that, if only I could get to the great lonely stretches of a northern Pacific beach, I would hear my father's voice again, in the ocean's roar. Through him, I would find the rest of my family. Despite Mother's aversion to the term "gone west," I yearned toward Tir-na n-Og, the land which lies at the world's end – beyond the sunset and under the sea. In Irish mythology it is the Land of Promise, the Land of Everlasting.

Conn, the High King of Ireland, stands at dawn on the ramparts of Tara. He is accompanied by his druids. A horseman emerges from the mist. He per-suades Conn, and his entourage, to go with him to a fertile plain, where there is a golden tree and a house with a golden ridgepole. Inside the house there is a young woman, seated on a crystal throne. She wears a golden crown. The girl is the Sovereignty of the Land. (She is also Lady Ragnell, the Loathly Lady, the hideous bride of Gawain. As we see her now she is beau-tiful – because her sovereignty has been acknowledged). Beside her is a vat of silver, a vessel of gold, and a golden cup. Lugh-Gawain, as Celtic sun god, is there, too. He tells them that he has returned from the Land of the Dead to predict when Conn will die and to name all of Conn's successors. While the girl serves meat and ale to the High King and his druids, Lugh-Gawain disappears, but the vat, the vessel, and the cup remain with Conn.

An almost identical story is told of Conn's grandson, Cormac. It deepens the meaning and enhances the motif. It also carries echoes of the Ojibwa corn-god myth, the Quest for the Holy Grail, the story of Gawain and the Winter Hag, the story of Gawain and the Green Knight, the image of the Green Man, and of the female sheilagh-na-gig.

One May morning, as Cormac waits alone on the ramparts of Tara, a stranger comes riding through the mist. On his shoulder he carries a

branch with three golden apples, which, when shaken, give forth sweet
music, able to free the sick and wounded from pain and to put them to sleep.
"Where have you come from?" asks Cormac.

"From a land where there is only truth," says the warrior. "Where there
is no old age nor decay nor sadness nor envy nor jealousy nor hatred nor
arrogance." The two swear eternal friendship, and the stranger gives the
Healing Branch to Cormac. In exchange he extracts a promise from the
King of Ireland – that, when he returns to Tara, a year hence, three wishes
must be granted him. For a year Cormac and his court enjoy the music and
the healing powers of the Branch, but then the stranger-warrior returns and
demands Cormac's son, his daughter, and his wife. When he takes them
away, Cormac pursues him. A great mist falls. When it is lifted, Cormac
finds himself alone in a vast plain, covered with sheep. The plain is the
Land Under Wave. The sheep are really fishes.

Cormac journeys, and comes to a palace. In the courtyard is the
Wellspring of Inspiration, the Well of the World's End. Sacred salmon swim
in the spring, feeding on hazel nuts that drop from an overhanging Tree-of-
Wisdom. Inside the palace there is a girl and a warrior. The girl cooks and
serves a meal to Cormac, while he tells the warrior his story. The warrior
chants a lullaby and Cormac falls into deep sleep. When he awakes he finds
his family restored to him.

A gold cup is brought to the warrior, who explains its magical proper-
ties, which have to do with truth-telling. The warrior then reveals himself
as the chief god of the sea, Mannanan mac Lir. He has brought Cormac and
his family here to see for themselves that there is a Land of Eternal Promise.
When Cormac awakes next morning he finds himself and his family back at
Tara, standing on real grass and real earth. Clutched in one hand is the
Healing Branch, from which dangle the golden apples. Clutched in the
other is the Cup of Truth.

In these two stories I see my own mythology mirrored. The Cup of
Truth is the depth where lurks my holy Salmon, my unconscious. The
Wellspring of Inspiration is the source, from which I draw in order to write
the story of my life, as truthfully as I can. The hazel nuts and the musical
apples are equivalent to the magic oranges that have appeared and reappeared throughout my life. The wisdom and the healing that they bring are
equivalent to the disenchantment (the Truth) that I seek. Stevie Smith, in
her poem "The Frog Prince" says it better than I:

But always when I think these thoughts
As I sit in my well,
Another thought comes to me and says:
It is part of the spell

To be happy,
To work up contentment;
To make much of being a frog.
To fear disenchantment.

Says, it will be heavenly to be set free,
Cries heavenly the girl who disenchants,
And the royal times heavenly,
And I think they will be.

Come then, royal girl and royal times,
Come quickly.
I can be happy until you come
But I cannot be heavenly.

Only disenchanted people
Can be heavenly.

The motel brochure promised a grocery store at La Push, but warned I
should bring bottled drinking water. I hired a car at the Tacoma-Seattle
airport. At Port Angeles I stopped at a supermarket to lay in my water
supply. I also bought a bag of oranges, but not much else. Part of my illusion was that I would buy salmon from a local fisherman, and cook it
(poached, of course) for a ceremonial meal to which I would invite the
ghosts (the memories) of my family. When I arrived, however, I discovered
that the store at La Push sold mostly canned beans and stale hot dogs.
There was a dock and a small fish-processing warehouse but, because of
ancient treaties, the Indians were not allowed to sell fish directly, to me or
to anyone else.

I have seen the stone carved sheilagh-na-gig under the eaves of the
church at Kilpeck, in Herefordshire. A skeletal hag (the Winter Hag), she
sits, knees wide, in the birthing position. She pulls her labial folds apart to

*display the door to life and death, to heaven and hell. I have seen pictures
of other sheilagh-na-gigs, fecund, with leaves and vines growing out of
their vulvas. They represent what men fear and hate in the power of women.
The priests pushed her out of the church, but the people of the villages stub-
bornly insisted that she continue to live, half-hidden, under the eaves. The
sheilagh-na-gig is Atargatis out of Araby, Kali out of India. She is Demeter,
Morgana, the dark side of Mary. On Hornby Island, off the Pacific coast of
Canada, I have come to know a New World version, carved in the rock,
under a waterfall. In winter the petroglyph is hidden by the falling waters,
but in summer, when there is only a trickle, one can see the outline of a
woman – legs wide apart, knees bent. She is swimming (or is she dancing?)
up the rock face. Not vines, but a salmon, issues from her vulva.*

By day, I walked the beaches or followed paths into the rainforest. At
night I learned to transform the boom and crash of the waves into a lullaby,
chanted by my father's gravelly voice. Every afternoon I hung around the
dock, talking to the fishermen while they cleaned their catch. On the third
day a fisherman took pity on me. He gave me (*gave* me!) a slab of salmon.
I rushed back to my cabin and put the fish in the refrigerator, then I drove
down the road to the rainforest preserve. Breaking the law, I pulled some
wild onions and picked a few fiddleheads. *What my mother had taught me
still prevailed: believe in abundance!* I had barely returned to my cabin
when there was knock on my door. The woman who rented the cabin next
to me (to whom I had not spoken one word) was going back to the city.
Would I like her leftovers? She handed me a box containing a few stalks of
asparagus, a few mushrooms, a heel of sourdough bread, and half a bottle
of wine. The feast would be a holy communion.

That evening I supped with ghosts. I sat at the large round table by the
big window, acutely aware that the empty chairs were filled by imaginary
presences. My view looked straight out at the gray Pacific. Between me and
the beach, enormous logs, heaped like jackstraws, formed a barricade.
Stripped and silvered by the sea, they rubbed their peeled flanks against
each other, creaking and groaning as the tide tugged at their underpinnings.
Sometimes, when the ocean pounced, they screamed. All day long a drizzle
had obscured the horizon. At sunset, sky and sea were pried apart by a
wedge of lemon yellow. A school of whales went by, silhouetted against the
light. They were heading north.

Next morning I, too, headed north, to attend the writers' workshop. After several ferry rides, I arrived on Orcas Island. My friend, Raje Harwood, had come down from Hornby Island to join me, and to attend the course. Even though we roomed together we did not do much talking. Most of the time was spent under a vow of silence. I found a niche in the rocks, where I wrote and wrote and wrote, stared out over the water, and wrote some more. Memories of my family clotted on my pen. When the week was over, Raje and I decided to stay an extra day, to spend more time together.

Raje suggested that we seek out the cove where we had seen a sign, "Canoes for Rent." We decided to paddle over to the next island. The day was soft and sunny, June at its best. Raje has done a lot of canoeing; I am a novice. The distance to the other island was greater than we had thought. We made little headway, and stopped, aghast, when a huge tanker hove into sight from behind a high bluff on Orcas. Father, even in his grave, must have been furious to know he had sired a daughter who could be so lubberly as to enter the shipping lanes. Another ship went by. We pulled back into the lee of the island, stopped paddling, and leaned back in the canoe. Outfall from the wakes lulled us into torpor. After a while I looked over the side. "Raje," I said, *"There's a hole in the ocean."*

"Fish jumped," said Raje. I was rather miffed. I, above all people, know what water looks like when a fish jumps. I lay back. After a while I pointed off to port side. "Hole," I said. "Salmon," Raje mumbled. Dazed by sun and air, we snoozed. After a while I looked over the starboard side. Just below the gunwale I again saw a hole, another one. "Raje," I said, speaking carefully, my voice as calm and clipped as Mother's would have been under the circumstances. "Raje," I said, realization dawning, even as I spoke. *"I do believe, Raje, that there is a hole in the ocean, Raje, and that hole is . . . a . . . blowhole, Raje."* Raje bestirred herself, sat up, peered over the gunwale. I was sitting over the blowhole; Raje was sitting over a great bulging eye. *We were sitting on the nose of a whale.*

We leaned back, speechless, to compute. I was beyond fear. For some reason I bethought myself of my coffee mug, from which I drink every morning. Some friends gave it to me years ago when I happened to be staying with them on St. Patrick's Day. On both sides it carries the sort of Irish sentiment that I usually deplore, yet I love my mug, my Cup of Truth, and guard it fiercely from every visitor and house guest. "May the road rise up to greet you. May the wind be always at your back," says one side of the mug. "May the Lord hold you in the hollow of His hand," says the other.

The blowhole disappeared, the canoe shuddered. The Ultimate Salmon-that-leaps-up-Niagara was diving beneath us! She came up on the other side, a little distance off, and slapped her tail. Slap! Slap! Slap! Here a whale, there a whale. A ring of whales! *Held in the hollow of His hand*, we were surrounded by whales! Perhaps these were the very ones I had seen days ago, outlined against a lemon sky, heading north – to my destiny. I was not afraid. I was exultant. What a way to go! *Teetering on a whale's nose!* After a while, we paddled back to the cove.

I have descended into the Maelstrom, into the Maw and Gullet, and I have been spat out. *Although great harm has come to me no harm has come to me.*

INEVITABLY

Inevitably,
the River meets the Sea.
I hear my father's voice
in the Ocean's throat.
The Columbia flows down
from the Hudson, which flows
down from the waters of the River Wye,
which issues from a crack in my
coffee mug, The Well at the World's End.

I stir my morning with
the Argo's helm, while Tamlyn's
Burd hurls her sword and
my mother's face peers at the
Salmon swimming in circles,
waiting for hazel haws.

Bearskin, with clumsy paws,
fishes in a quiet pool while
whales leap up Niagara, and
Niagara roars up the trunk of
the pin oak in the back yard of
the old house on Ritie Street.

Lucy, with the wisdom
of the Salmon,
floats toward the mill dam on
the Binnorie.
I listen to the silence of the stones,
I sing the song that sings in singing bones,
and everything is
     Story,
          Story,
               Story.

Index